(1

Seventeenth-century England: A Changing Culture

Volume 2: Modern Studies

Edited by W.R. Owens
at the Open University

Ward Lock Educational
in association with
The Open University Press

ISBN 0 7062 4089 8 paperback

First Published 1980
Reprinted 1982

Set in 10 on 11 point Garamond by
Jubal Multiwrite Ltd, London SE13
and printed by Biddles Ltd, Guildford, Surrey
for Ward Lock Educational
47 Marylebone Lane, London W1M 6AX
A Ling Kee Company

CONTENTS

ACKNOWLEDGMENTS

I wish to thank all the members of the A203 Course Team who helped in various ways with the assembly and preparation of this anthology. I am especially grateful to the successive Course Team Chairmen Christopher Hill and Anne Laurence, and to Ann Hughes, editor of the companion volume of Primary Sources, for advice and guidance.

W.R.O.

The Open University and the Publishers would like to thank the following for permission to reproduce copyright material. All possible care has been taken to trace ownership of the selections included and to make full acknowledgment for their use.

Cambridge University Press for 'Economics and Politics in the Seventeenth Century' by Charles Wilson from *The Historical Journal* Vol. 5 (1962) and for 'The Social Effects of Change in Agriculture' by Joan Thirsk and 'The Changing Pattern of Labouring Life' by Alan Everitt from *The Agrarian History of England and Wales 1500–1640* (1969); Chatto and Windus Ltd. for 'Milton's Verse' by F.R. Leavis from *Revaluation: Tradition and Development in English Poetry* (1936); Faber and Faber Ltd. for 'The Metaphysical Poets' by T.S. Eliot from *Selected Essays* (1951); Professor F.J. Fisher for 'Tawney's Century' from *Essays in the Economic and Social History of Tudor and Stuart England in honour of R.H. Tawney* published by the Economic History Society; Dr. K.T. Hoppen for 'The Nature of the Early Royal Society' from *The British Journal for the History of Science* (1976); D.W. Jefferson for 'Milton's Austerity and Moral Disdain' from *The Morality of Art; Essays Presented to G. Wilson Knight* published by Routledge and Kegan Paul (1969); Professor J.R. Jones for 'Britain and Europe in the Seventeenth Century' published by Edward Arnold (1966); Professor Arnold Kettle for 'The Precursors of Defoe: Puritanism and the Rise of the Novel' from *On the Novel: A present for Walter Allen on his sixtieth birthday* published by Dent (1971); Macmillan & Co. Ltd. Basingstoke and London for 'Puritanism, Arminianism and Counter-Revolution' by Nicholas Tyacke from *The Origins of the English Civil War* (1973) and for 'Two Cultures? Court and Country under Charles I' by P.W. Thomas from *The Origins of the English Civil War* (1973); Brian Manning for 'Religion and Politics: The Godly People' and 'The Aristocracy and the Downfall of Charles I' from *Politics, Religion and the English Civil War* published by Edward Arnold (1973); J.S. Morrill for 'The Revolt of the Provinces' from *The Revolt of the Provinces: Conservatives and Radicals in the English Civil War 1630–1650* published by Allen and Unwin (1976); Oxford University Press for 'Milton's Grand Style' by Christopher Ricks (1963) and for 'Consumer Industries and the Political Economists' by Joan Thirsk from *Economic Policy and Projects: The Development of a Consumer Society in Early Modern Britain* (1978); The Past and Present Society, Corpus Christi College, Oxford, England, for the extracts from 'Social Mobility in England 1500–1700' reprinted with the permission of the Society and the author from *Past and Present: a journal of historical studies,* No. 33 (April 1966); K.C. Brown for *Hobbes Studies* published by Basil Blackwell (1965); Professor Christopher Ricks for 'Dryden's Absalom' from *Essays in Criticism* (1961); Routledge and Kegan Paul Ltd. for 'Harrington's Interpretation of his Age' from *History and Society: Essays by R.H. Tawney* (1978) and for 'The Royalists and Sir Robert Filmer' and 'The Leveller Theorists: Lilburne, Overton and Walwyn' by Perez Zagorin from *A History of Political Thought in the English Revolution* (1954); Keith Thomas for 'Providence: the doctrine and its uses' and 'Witchcraft and Society' from *Religion and the Decline of Magic* Weidenfeld and Nicholson (1971).

INTRODUCTION

This anthology brings together a selection of twentieth-century studies of the history, thought and literature of the seventeenth century. In the middle decades of that century England experienced events unique in her history: the judicial execution of the monarch and the establishment of a republic. Although the monarchy was restored in 1660, contemporaries recognized the lasting importance of what had taken place in those tumultuous years. Thomas Hobbes thought that 'If in time, as in place, there were degrees of high and low, I verily believe that the highest of time would be that which passed between the years of 1640 and 1660'. The civil wars were hardly over before historians began the attempt to explain why Englishmen had taken up arms against each other, and the causes and consequences of those revolutionary upheavals have remained matters of intense controversy.

The material collected here spans work from several disciplines because the anthology has been designed for use by Open University students taking an interdisciplinary course on the changing culture of seventeenth-century England. One of the principal aims of the course is to consider how far the political changes of this period related to and were paralleled by changes in other aspects of society, such as the economy, religion, the arts and science. This study of cultural change will focus on the period 1640–1660, with contributions from different disciplines treating the impact of the English Revolution on their particular fields of study. Thus, although some of the articles reprinted here are of an 'interdisciplinary' nature, most are specialist contributions in particular areas of seventeenth-century studies.

The contents have been chosen to serve the purposes of the course, and no attempt has been made to produce a 'representative' selection of recent work on the seventeenth century. In some cases articles have been chosen specifically to suggest a different point of view from that expressed in the course; in others to supplement the course material. For example, since the course was directed by and incorporates the views of Professor Christopher Hill, several articles have been included which present alternative historical interpretations to the one he will be offering, and indeed one of the aims of the course is to introduce students to some of the debates and disagreements between scholars working on the seventeenth century. Articles have been grouped together under broad headings, but this is purely for convenience, and the reader will find that there are suggestive cross-references to be made across the sections.

The seventeenth century was a very different world from ours, and the first group of articles introduces us to certain aspects of the nature of English society then which the twentieth-century student needs especially to bear in mind. Lawrence Stone prefaces an examination of social mobility in the period by showing how the structure of society was founded on a status hierarchy into which the entire population was

1

supposed to fit, building up from the very poorest to the lords of the realm. This 'Great Chain of Being', as it was often called, included not just humanity, but was conceived as stretching from God himself down through descending ranks of angels and the various degrees of men to the very stones of the earth. Since this structure of society was believed to be divinely ordered, those in authority could argue powerfully that each individual should know his place and stay in it. Not only had God created this hierarchical order of being, but his divine providence, as Keith Thomas indicates, was thought to control its most minute workings in the world at large. A general belief in the operation of supernatural powers included an acute awareness of the malign activities of the forces of darkness, and this period is notable for an upsurge of interest in witchcraft, some of the reasons for which are discussed by Keith Thomas.

Of course, neither the shape of society nor its beliefs were static, and one of the chief concerns of both Stone and Thomas is to analyse the ways in which they were changing in this period, and to suggest some of the reasons for these changes. In a wider context, England's position in and relations with the rest of Europe changed fundamentally between the reigns of James I and William III, and J.R. Jones looks in some detail at economic, political and cultural relationships with France, Spain and the Netherlands in particular.

The following section deals with economic practice and theory. In his survey of the English economy in the late sixteenth and early seventeenth centuries, F.J. Fisher discusses some of the impediments to rapid economic growth and the social strains to which this situation gave rise. Joan Thirsk describes the burgeoning development of new manufacturing and agricultural industries supplying the diverse needs of an emerging consumer market. She looks at the attempts of some of the political economists to make sense of what was happening, and analyses their ideas for improving England's trading and commercial position. The most important industry of the time was, not surprisingly, agriculture, and the effects of changes in the nature and methods of agricultural production, and in the lives of farm workers, are examined by Joan Thirsk and Alan Everitt. Finally, in the course of a review of Christopher Hill's *The Century of Revolution 1603–1714*, Charles Wilson enters into the debate over the relationship between economic developments and political change in the period.

The most dramatic political and constitutional changes of the century occurred as a result of a long and bitter civil war, and the next section consists of articles highlighting some of the developments which precipitated the conflict. Brian Manning analyses the causes of the war from two angles; he first recounts the activities of a group of aristocratic opponents of Charles's rule, and the failure of Charles's repeated efforts to defuse or crush their opposition and their influence in Parliament. In his other article he distinguishes between those on the Parliamentarian side, chiefly nobility and gentry, who saw the issues as primarily constitutional and political, and those, over-

2

whelmingly of the 'middling' sort, whose primary concern was religious. Manning argues that these 'Godly people' were more dedicated to the fight, and that their religious radicalism very often combined with or led to a feeling of 'class consciousness' which stiffened them in a rejection of the authority of nobility and gentry of either side. Investigating the roots of the religious controversies which played no small part in the conflict, Nicholas Tyacke argues that initially the revolutionaries were not the Puritans, but the Arminian clergy led by Archbishop Laud and supported by Charles: the Arminians were the religious innovators who aroused the wrath of Puritan upholders of traditional Calvinist beliefs, and it was only in opposing these changes that the initially conservative Puritan party itself became radicalized. J.S. Morrill takes the view that political or religious issues were seldom simply seen in a purely national context, but that local concerns were often of overriding importance when men came to decide whether to take sides for or against the king, or to avoid the conflict altogether.

In the ferment of civil war the censorship broke down, and a flood of books and pamphlets issued as men set about explaining to their fellows what was happening and arguing for or against new political ideas. Some of the most interesting and far-reaching political ideas came from the Levellers, who argued, for example, for the extension of the suffrage to every male householder. Perez Zagorin traces the developing political thought of three of their best-known leaders, and on the opposite side, considers the theories of the most notable Royalist thinker, Sir Robert Filmer. In a famous essay R.H. Tawney elaborates on the ideas of James Harrington, who argued in *The Commonwealth of Oceana* (1656) that political power depended on economic power and that the civil war had come about because the existing political structures had failed to adapt to changing economic realities. Harrington believed that the best, indeed the only possible form of government for England was a Parliamentary Republic. The greatest work of political philosophy of the century was Thomas Hobbes's *Leviathan*, and Keith Thomas, in unravelling the mixture of social assumptions, aristocratic, bourgeois and popular, to which Hobbes subscribed, illuminates some of the paradoxes of his political thought, and places him in the seventeenth-century context.

One of the most significant developments in science in the century was the establishment of the Royal Society in 1660, 'for the promoting of Physico-Mathematicall Experimental Learning'. However in this field, as in others, there was no simple forward progress towards ever more 'modern' thought but, as K. Theodore Hoppen demonstrates here, older assumptions and interests remained just as prevalent as new ideas and methods among the early Fellows. Nor were the concerns and interests of the Society pursued in a vacuum; J.R. Jacob argues that the early members of the Royal Society saw their work as actively promoting particular social, political and religious ideals.

The final group of articles focuses on literature and the arts in a changing culture. No period of English literature is richer than the

3

seventeenth century, and a study of the poetry, prose and drama which was written then affords valuable insights into men and women's thoughts and feelings about what was happening around them. Many writers took an active part in political or religious affairs, and wrote about the great political events of the time. Our own century has witnessed a remarkable revival of interest in the work of a group of seventeenth-century writers known as the 'metaphysical poets', the most celebrated being John Donne, George Herbert and Andrew Marvell. This interest was greatly stimulated by the publication of T.S. Eliot's now famous article on them. The following article by P.W. Thomas shows how deepening political and social divisions were reflected in and paralleled by cultural divisions, as the art and literature which came to be identified with the court of Charles I grew increasingly distasteful to and remote from the interests of a great many of his subjects. The values of the Puritans were most powerfully expressed by the greatest poet of the seventeenth century, John Milton. Milton's poetic achievement was the subject of a considerable debate initiated in the 1930s by T.S. Eliot and F.R. Leavis, and two of the articles reprinted here, by F.R. Leavis and Christopher Ricks, give voice to that debate. D.W. Jefferson discusses Milton's personality as it is presented to us through his poetry. The relationship between the development of Puritanism and the emergence of the English novel is explored by Arnold Kettle, and Christopher Ricks analyses Dryden's presentation of Absalom in his political satire *Absalom and Achitophel*, in the light of the political situation of the 1670s and 1680s.

Only two editorial points require mention here: after some thought it was decided for reasons of space to delete all footnotes. For those interested in following up a particular point, footnotes can be examined in the original source which is cited at the foot of the first page of each article. Secondly, where an extract here breaks into the middle of a chapter or article, a brief headnote has been supplied indicating the general concerns of the foregoing material to serve as a lead in to the extract. All such editorial insertions are indicated by use of square brackets.

W.R.O.

Seventeenth-Century Society:
Structures and Beliefs

1 LAWRENCE STONE

Social Mobility in England 1500–1700

The purpose of this paper is fourfold: firstly to sketch the configuration of a western traditional society at a fairly advanced stage of its development, a model that might be applicable to any European society from the sixteenth to the eighteenth centuries; secondly, to produce the evidence for believing that between 1540 and 1640 English society experienced a seismic upheaval of unprecedented magnitude; thirdly to postulate some reasons both for the development of this upheaval and for its termination; and fourthly to speculate about the political and religious consequences. The paper attempts – perhaps rashly – to take a broad overview of the society as a whole, and therefore ignores the important local variations which undoubtedly existed.

MODELS   I

The first problem is what sort of a visual image we have of this early modern English society. Sociologists tend to describe pre-industrial societies in terms of a stepped pyramid, the lower classes forming the bottom step, and the aristocracy or plutocracy the apex (because of the erosion of the poor and the growth of the middle-class in contemporary western society, it has turned into a stepped lozenge). But one may reasonably doubt whether this model fits a traditional pre-industrial society. Two alternatives present themselves. The first – let us call it the United Nations model – is a tall skyscraper erected on top of a vast low podium. Within the podium, which extends over many acres, live 95% or more of the population, who are free to move along wide corridors and to rise and descend very shallow staircases within this limited level. The skyscraper itself, within which dwell the remaining 5% or less, is composed of a series of floors for status groups based on the ownership of land. Within it is a single infrequent elevator which always goes down with a full load of failures and superfluous younger sons, but often rises half empty. Around the skyscraper itself, however, there wind several ascending ramps, labelled Church, Law, Commerce, and Office. Some people camp out on the ramps, but it is draughty and wet out there, and most of them struggle upwards and then take shelter inside at the highest floor they can comfortably reach.

From *Past and Present*, No. 33 (1966) pp. 16–55. Footnotes have been deleted.

The second – the San Gimignano model – is a series of vertical towers upon a hill. In this model the hill represents the amorphous mass of the poor and the humble, and the towers a series of more or less independent economic and status hierarchies with their own internal elevators: land, church, law, commerce, and government office are the most conspicuous of these towers.

Neither of these models exactly fits the observed facts, but both are an improvement on the conventional stepped pyramid image. It will be argued in this paper that between 1500 and 1700 English society was moving from the United Nations towards the San Gimignano model as the status of business and the professions rose in the eyes of the landed classes.

II

CATEGORIES
The Hierarchy of Status

In the sixteenth century there was a status hierarchy, not the loose competitive status agglomerations to which we are accustomed today. Though there existed a few completely non-integrated groups – artists and stage-players, for example – and four semi-independent occupational hierarchies, the vast mass of the population was fitted into a single hierarchy of status defined by titular rank, and to a certain extent by legal and fiscal privilege. The most fundamental dichotomy within the society was between the gentleman and the non-gentleman, a division that was based essentially upon the distinction between those who did, and those who did not, have to work with their hands. This is a critical division in all societies where human labour is the principal power-unit, apart from the horse and the ox, wind and water. The more extreme conservatives, heralds and others, argued that it took three generations for a family to purge its blood from the taint of inferiority and to become an accepted member of this upper class. In practice such notions seem to have had little effect, but the fact that they could be seriously propounded is evidence that an element of caste theory was to be found in Tudor England.

Within the dual system of gentlemen and non-gentlemen contemporaries recognized a rough sixfold status division:

Group 1 The dependents on charity, whether widows, aged, or unemployed; also the apprentices and living-in servants, domestic, agricultural, or industrial, who composed as much as 15% to 25% of the adult male population.

Group 2 The living-out labourers, both rural and urban, agricultural and industrial.

Group 3 The husbandmen, the lesser yeomen (both tenants and freeholders), and the more substantial yeomen; also the artisans, shopkeepers and small internal traders.

Group 4 The lesser, or parish, gentry.

Group 5 The county élite: squires, knights and baronets.

Group 6 The peers: barons, viscounts, earls, marquises, and dukes.

This sixfold status hierarchy is based on the values of a primitive rural society. At the lower levels of groups 1–3 there already existed two parallel hierarchies for urban and rural society, but they can be roughly matched without too much difficulty. But both contemporaries and ourselves are faced with the more vexing problem of fitting into this scheme four semi-independent occupational hierarchies, whose precise relationship to the basic reference groupings was never fully clarified. These were:

Group A The Merchants. The middling and large-scale exporters of London, Exeter, Bristol, Hull and Newcastle, the wholesalers, the large retailers of the main cities, the customs farmers and government contractors, and the financiers of London. In the sixteenth and early seventeenth centuries they were still regarded in many quarters as distinctly inferior in status to a gentleman. As late as 1669 Edward Chamberlayne stated flatly that 'Tradesmen in all ages and nations have been reputed ignoble', and a generation earlier there had been a brisk pamphlet discussion whether or not a gentleman's son lost his gentle status by becoming an apprentice. Because of this attitude the merchants were a mobile group of transients, very many of whom moved into and out of the group in a single lifetime, and nearly all in two generations; as a contemporary put it at the time, merchants 'do attain to great wealth and riches, which for the most part they employ in purchasing land and little by little they do creep and seek to be gentlemen'. In other words, the most successful tended to merge into groups 4 and 5.

Group B The Lawyers. These ranged all the way from the local attorney and solicitor to grandees like the Master of the Rolls and the Lord Chancellor. Over three-quarters of those trained at the Inns of Court, that is the barristers and above, were of gentry or clergy stock, but we know little about the social origins, economic prospects, or accepted status of the local attorneys.

Group C The Clergy. These ranged in income and position from the curate to the archbishop, and varied in social origin from the copyholder to the squire. Even in a prosperous and socially and intellectually advanced area like Oxfordshire or Worcestershire, between three-quarters and two-thirds of the early seventeenth-century parish clergy were still of non-gentry origin. Though most rectors were comfortably off, and though the overall average real income probably remained much the same, substantial numbers of vicars and curates were existing on an income hardly different from that of unskilled labourers. The higher clergy were ruthlessly plundered under the Tudors, and their social origins were generally inferior to those of the lawyers. For example, of twenty-eight bishops in the 1630s, the fathers of only nine were gentry; eight were clergymen, seven were merchants, one was a yeoman and three were artisans or below. It seems that the highest ranks of the clergy were generally regarded as inferior in status to the highest ranks of the legal profession, despite the presence of the former in the House of Lords. The precise reason for this lowly status is hard to determine. Was it the vigorous and widespread anti-clericalism of the age which both lowered respect for the profession and frightened off prospective entrants of gentry stock? Or the lack of assured tenure during a period of theological upheaval? Or the substantially reduced financial rewards to be expected even from a successful career? We do not know, but it is probable that all three factors interacted one upon the other.

Group D The Administrators. These are the office-holders in the royal household, the major departments of state, and the army and navy, men to whom administration was a professional life commitment. This definition includes all those dealt with by Professor Aylmer in *The King's Servants* except the courtiers at the apex of the system. By the early seventeenth century, these royal servants were predominantly of squirearchy or gentry origin, but with a substantial leavening from yeoman, merchant, and miscellaneous non-gentry stock.

What we have, therefore, is a rural-based status hierarchy running from 1 to 6, the clarity and utility of which is marred by the existence of four occupational hierarchies, A, B, C and D, whose exact positions within this standard system of reference were, and are, uncertain.

Moreover, it is unhappily true that 1, 2 and 3 include well over 90% of the population – perhaps as much as 95% – which means that a great deal of horizontal, and even some vertical, mobility within the vast mass of the population goes unrecognized. In such a society one cannot expect there to be very much upward mobility at the lower levels. Most of the population was living on the land, enjoying a very low income and tied to the soil by the needs of manual labour for food production and distribution. A reasonable guess is that about 95% of the population was still rural in 1500, and about 85% in 1700. Now in a society in which 90% of the population are manual workers on the land, even if every other job and office is filled by one of their sons, still only 11% can expect to change occupations. Under such circumstances it is evident that the chances of upward economic mobility for the great majority of the population must be very small indeed.

The task of the historian of social mobility is complicated by a variety of difficulties. The degree to which a society appears open or closed both to contemporaries and to posterity depends partly on the prevailing myth, and partly on hard facts. For lack of anything better on which to base their judgements, historians tend to see a society much as the contemporaries saw it. Thus if seventeenth-century Englishmen and nineteenth-century Americans thought of their society as exceptionally mobile, then exceptionally mobile they appear in the history books. But there is also the social reality underlying the myth, a reality which cannot be too remote from the image without creating severe psychic tensions. The general contentment of the greater number is probably most strongly determined by the possibility of minor movement up and down at the lowest levels of groups 1, 2 and 3. But the quality of the society as it is seen by the historian is determined by two quite different factors. The first is the proportion of the lower and middling classes who are able to filter through into the élite; that is the number of ambitious youths who can move up from group 3 to group 4, the speed of acceptance of upwardly mobile elements of A, B, C and D by 4 and 5, and the degree to which income, political power, and status are open to talent among 4, 5 and 6. The second factor is the method by which this filtration occurs. Is it 'sponsored mobility' of youths selected for advancement at an early age, an upward movement planned and controlled by the existing élite for its own purpose of functional efficiency and the preservation of status lines? Or is it 'contest mobility', the chance product of prolonged and open competitive struggle?

The Hierarchy of Income

Tax data and other contemporary records suggest that the hierarchy of status corresponded roughly with the pyramid of incomes, and that the same was true within the four anomalous occupational categories of merchant, lawyer, official and clergyman. It should be noted that the spread of income distribution after taxation was enormous by modern standards, perhaps as many as 1,000 families enjoying a net income after tax of £1,000 a year or more, which was a hundred times greater than that of the unskilled labourer.

The Hierarchy of Power

Political power was rather less intimately linked to status than was income, but it was still close. Groups 3–6 and A, B, C and D, nearly all enjoyed the franchise, but in practice contests for seats in Parliament were fairly rare, and political affairs at the local level were run in towns exclusively by A and in the county by 5 and 6, with some support and occasional competition from elements of 4. At the national level, power was exercised by courtiers and officials: that is, a select minority of groups 5 and 6, and the whole of group D.

At Court, a knight from the lower gentry like Sir Walter Raleigh ranked higher in status, wielded more power, and might even enjoy a larger income than a backwoods earl like Bath. But this top Court élite of politicians was too ephemeral in its composition and too amateur in its interests to be regarded as a permanent part of the official class. [. . .]

[In his Section III, which is omitted here, Professor Stone analyses evidence of changing patterns of group and individual mobility which indicates that the period 1560–1640 was an exceptionally mobile one. He opens Section IV by outlining some general features of early modern English society which influenced the extent and nature of social mobility, and then turns to more particular factors which had effect in this period.]

Destabilizing Factors, 1540–1640

There was a whole series of strongly disruptive forces at work on

11

society between 1540 and 1640, but which were not present to anything like the same degree before or after.

(1) *Demographic Growth* Firm statistics are impossible to come by, but the best guess is that between 1500 and 1620 the population of England and Wales nearly doubled, from between 2½ and 3 million to 5 million. This added enormously to the labour force and caused horizontal mobility and urbanization. After 1620, however, there is every sign that, except perhaps in the north-west, plague, land hunger, commercial difficulties, family limitation, and emigration combined to reduce the increase to far more modest proportions.

(2) *Differential Fertility* Between 1500 and 1630 there was almost certainly a differential fertility pattern by which the upper classes produced more children than the poor – the exact opposite of today. Thus an Elizabethan census of some 450 poor families with children in Norwich shows an average of 2.2 children per household, against between 4.25 and 4.7 children per household of well-to-do merchants of Norwich and Exeter. In the countryside the same discrepancy emerges from such data as are available. The causes of this striking difference are not hard to find.

(a) There was a difference in the average age, duration and frequency of marriage. For the eldest sons of peers (and probably also of squires) in the late sixteenth century, the average age of marriage (of those who did marry) was 21, and for all children and grandchildren of peers, including both heirs male and younger sons, it was 25 to 26. For yeomen and below, however, the average age of marriage in the early seventeenth century was 27 to 28. Far more important for fertility is the age of marriage of women, and it is here that the contrast is most marked. Between 1550 and 1625 the daughters of the upper classes married at 20 to 21, whereas daughters of the lower classes had to wait till they were 24 to 25. The reproduction period of the latter was therefore significantly shorter than that of the former, and in the absence of contraception would have resulted in between one and two children fewer per family. The reasons for this pattern of delayed marriage among the lower classes are fairly clear. In the artisan class the seven-year apprenticeship system put a stop to marriage before the age of 25 or thereabouts; in the countryside most young people began as living-in servants for either domestic or agricultural work, while the eldest sons of freeholders or tenant farmers had to wait for the death of their father before they could afford to marry. This pattern determined the female age of marriage, since it seems to have been a convention from top to bottom of seventeenth-century society to marry women only about three years younger than oneself.

Equally important in producing greater upper class fertility was the very high rate of re-marriage at this level of society, so that the interruption of the procreative process by death of husband or wife (which was an extremely frequent occurrence) was reduced to a minimum. There is reason to believe that both marriage and re-marriage was less easy for those in less favourable economic circum-

12

stances, and indeed at Lichfield at the end of the seventeenth century as many as 31% of all women in the fertile age-group between 25 and 44 were either widows or spinsters.

(b) There was a difference in natural fertility: there is clear evidence that lactation impedes fertility, although the precise share of this effect between the physiological prevention of ovulation and a social taboo on sexual intercourse with a suckling woman is at present unknown. Now in the upper classes infants were put on to lower-class wet-nurses at birth, whereas prolonged lactation by the mother for up to two years was normal among the poor.

(c) There was a difference in infant mortality: more upper-class children survived to a marriageable age, since the death rate among upper-class infants was almost certainly lower than among the poor. In one parish of the city of York in the healthy years 1572–85, children under the age of two made up 34% of all burials. The genealogical records of the peerage suggest a considerably lower rate, the expectation of life at birth at that period being abut 35 for boys and 38 for girls. This was presumably because these children lived in the countryside rather than in towns, and were better housed, better clothed and better fed (though they were admittedly exposed to the attentions of feckless wet-nurses and of doctors, who often did more harm than good). Moreover, in the seventeenth century, there grew up institutions whose practical achievement, if not ostensible purpose, was to eliminate the unwanted children of the poor: both foundling hospitals and workhouses were highly effective infanticide agencies. In early eighteenth-century London, the latter were killing off some 88% of their children, and indeed in some parishes it was reported that 'no infant had lived to be apprenticed from their workhouses'.

As a result of all these factors, fertility among the upper classes was very high indeed, and the peers had an effective generation replacement rate of unparalleled magnitude – as high as 1.5 for those born between 1550 and 1600. In other words between about 1580 and 1630 the children of peers were producing 50% more children per generation. The intense competition for jobs and offices in the decades before the Civil War can best be understood in the light of this remarkable demographic phenomenon.

(3) *Price Revolution* Largely, but not entirely, as a result of this demographic growth, prices rose by between 400% and 650% from 1500 to 1640. Food prices (and therefore agricultural profits) soared, wages and other less adaptable revenues lagged behind. Whole social and occupational groups rose or fell as a result.

(4) *Free Land Market* Between 1534 and 1650 the Crown seized all the revenues of the monasteries and the chantries, and substantial portions of those of the bishops. To pay for war, it immediately sold much of it, the rest being disposed of at intervals under financial stress. Including all sales of Crown and Church lands, as much as 25% or 30% of the total landed area of the country, which had previously been locked up in institutional hands, may have been released on to the private market

13

between 1534 and 1660. By the Restoration the process was virtually complete.

This throwing of Crown and Church lands on to the market was accompanied by an equally important development which released a huge mass of private property, which had previously been tied up by legal restrictions against alienation. In the late middle ages the entail was a fairly effective barrier against the free disposition of property by the current owner; in the late seventeenth century the strict settlement served the same purpose. Between 1530 and 1660, however, there were relatively few and weak legal obstacles to the alienation of property. The result of this legal situation and of various economic pressures was the massive transfer of land by purchase and sale, which reached a peak in the 1610s. It should be noted that both factors involved, the seizure and dispersal of Church lands and the freeing of private property from restrictions on alienation, were the result of politico-legal action supported and encouraged by the landed classes themselves.

(5) *Increased Commercial Activity* Foreign trade expanded in sudden bursts, particularly from 1508 to 1551, 1603 to 1620, and 1660 to 1688. More important, but less easy to document, may have been the growth of credit and transport facilities, and the consequent expansion of market activity inside the country. Their development increased both the numbers and the amount and range of mobility of the merchants.

(6) *Increased Litigation* The end of violence, the growth of commercial activity, and the opening of the land market enormously increased the volume of litigation, the main result of which was to transfer wealth from the landed classes to the lawyers.

(7) *The Puritan Ethic* The Puritans took a strongly moralistic –indeed medieval– approach to economic affairs, and the puritan merchant was consequently subject to almost intolerable psychological pressures as he strove both to maximize profits and to conform to ethical doctrines of the just price. On the other hand, insistent puritan indoctrination on self-discipline and the virtue of striving in the calling could hardly avoid producing personalities with strong anal-erotic characteristics and a high achievement motive. Once the children were grown up, their obsession with thrift and hard, rationally planned, work carried them inexorably along towards the corruptions of wealth and upward social mobility.

There is some reason to believe, however, that this ideological factor did not become fully operative until the 1630s, for its best theoretical expression comes from Richard Baxter. Moreover, evidence of close association of religious Dissent with commercial success does not become plentiful until after the Restoration. Even then the association may have been as much an incidental by-product of exclusion from social and political life under the Clarendon Code as a direct consequence of religious ideology.

More important than this possible economic link, are the indirect and accidental consequences of Puritanism. One is the stress the Puritans laid on Bible-reading, and hence the spread of elementary

14

education. Another is the self-confidence and sense of righteousness arising from contract theology and the doctrine of the Elect, which gave men the assurance to aspire high and to challenge their social, economic and political superiors. Furthermore the democratic, or at the very least oligarchic, tendencies of Puritan church organization worked against the hierarchical and authoritarian concept of society and was thus a destabilizing force. 'Purity is Parity' was the slogan of their Anglican enemies, and there was something in the taunt.

Finally one can point to certain chronological correspondences which are, at the very least, suggestive of interconnections. The great age of social mobility precisely coincides with the great age of Puritanism. It is also, perhaps, rather too much of a coincidence that a content analysis of popular literature reveals a high peak of achievement motifs at precisely the same period. This period of widespread challenges to the official system of values contrasts sharply with the post-Restoration development of Divine Right and Passive Obedience notions, and still more with the smug complacency with which Englishmen regarded the existing social and political order after the Glorious Revolution of 1688.

(8) *Educational Expansion* The period 1560 to 1640 saw an unprecedented educational boom, which affected all but the lowest levels of society. This did not only produce quantitatively a remarkably literate society; it also turned out an educated gentry and aristocracy in excess of the capacity of government service to absorb them, and lower-class clergymen in excess of the cures of souls available. If for many the fruits of this educational expansion were bitter, the spread of literacy and the increased opportunities for higher education for the children of yeomen and artisans, must have increased the possibility of upward mobility for intellectual talent. The secularization of the state may have destroyed the opportunity for the occasional child of the moderately humble to shoot up via the church to high political office, but the growth of education and of the professions opened up other and wider avenues to hardly less exalted positions.

After 1640 first the disturbance of the Civil War and then the social reaction of the Restoration put an end to the expansion of secondary and higher education, which went into a decline. After 1660 opportunities for social advancement via the professions must have been proportionately reduced, and confined to those who could still gain access to this narrowed educational ladder.

(9) *Revolutionary Political Action* One would have supposed that the political upheavals of the English Revolution between 1640 and 1660 must have produced far-reaching social changes. Now it is certainly true that revolutionary activity was itself a vehicle for social mobility, in that previously submerged individuals, low-born parsons like Stephen Marshall, backwoods gentry like Oliver Cromwell, frustrated petty bourgeois like John Lilburne, found an opportunity to take the centre of the stage and even to seize power from their social superiors.

But the temporary collapse of the traditional order and the tem-

15

porary inversion of rôles had no lasting effect upon English society. It has been shown conclusively that the old landlords, even the royalists, survived the Interregnum far better than might have been expected. No new class of successful generals, entrepreneurs and parliamentary committee men arose out of the 1650s, if only because Church, Crown, and Royalist lands were nearly all restored to their former owners at the Restoration. Lower down the social scale the schemes of the Levellers for converting copyhold tenure into freehold were defeated, and the tenantry and small freeholders were probably depressed by the burden of war taxation, plunder and billeting, rather than elevated by any new official concern for their welfare. The rising government debt and the expansion of government services enhanced the prestige and increased the fortunes of financiers, contractors and leading officials, but the significance of these factors does not seem to have been very great. Society in 1660 looked much as it had in 1640, and the number of new families who had risen, or old families who had fallen, over the previous twenty years does not seem to have been at all exceptional. In terms of permanent social change (as opposed to a permanent legacy of ideas) the English Revolution was the least successful of all the 'Great Revolutions' in history.

Stabilizing Factors, 1650–1700
During the course of the late seventeenth century, a series of stabilizing factors became operative which severely dampened the process of social mobility, and at the same time eased social tensions.
(1) Of the main destabilizing factors, demographic growth, price revolution, free land market, educational expansion, Puritan ideological enthusiasm, and revolutionary activity had all been substantially reduced by 1660, some of them beginning to decline as early as 1620.
(2) There was a sharp drop in fertility and a sharp rise in mortality among the upper classes, so that cohorts born between 1625 and 1674 were barely reproducing themselves, and those between 1675 and 1749 were actually falling behind. This dramatic change from the pre-Civil War condition of an excess of children to be accommodated in a relatively static job market must enormously have reduced social competition twenty-five years later, that is after 1660.
(3) The natural result of a long period of social mobility, followed by civil war and violent political and social upheaval was a determination in the minds of all classes to put a damper on change, and to reassert traditional control by traditional authorities. Although in some respects it only accelerated trends already visible in Early Stuart society, this post-Restoration conservative reaction was perhaps the most striking practical consequence of the Revolution. The results can be seen most clearly in the field of education, which was now carefully adjusted to the needs of the élite. Between 1570 and 1650 secondary and university education had been running wild, resulting in a free-for-all competitive struggle uncontrolled by the existing élite, which produced a surplus of qualified men for the available élite jobs, and which failed to indoctri-

nate them with élite values and élite behaviour patterns. Hence the lamentations of conservatives like Bacon and Hobbes in the early seventeenth century that education was undermining the basis of established society.

After the Restoration, however, educational opportunities at this higher level were sharply reduced, and English educational patterns settled down to that tradition of 'sponsored mobility' which it has retained ever since. By this system a minority of youths are selected by the élite and their agents at an early age for training in classical studies and aesthetic appreciation, in preparation for admission into this exclusive world. The eighteenth-century grammar schools and universities with their limited scholarship facilities, and the public schools of the nineteenth century, both performed this task of indoctrinating the aspiring few with the ideals and values of the existing élite. A recurrence of the dangerously competitive situation of the early seventeenth century has consequently been avoided ever since.

This adjustment of the education system was only achieved, however, at considerable intellectual cost. It was not only in terms of quantity that English education declined: qualitatively, the Ancients triumphed over the Moderns, and enforced their view of the rôle of classical studies in the curriculum; socially the Royal Society, after a promising beginning as an intellectual group open to talent regardless of rank, degenerated into a club for gentlemanly dilettantes. By 1720 England had lost its scientific pre-eminence, and the Universities had sunk into a torpor which only the pen of Gibbon could adequately describe.

Parallel to this development, rule by a narrow élite was strengthened at all levels of government. Control of the parish fell into the hands of select vestries of 'the better sort'. County administration, for example in Northamptonshire, was confined to a smaller, more stable and more closed-off élite group of families. In the towns the same process had long been at work as control of both guilds and civic government passed into the hands of an ever smaller and less fluid oligarchy. At the Freeman level the same thing was happening, and at York the closing of the ranks seems to have occurred before the end of the sixteenth century. In 1509–18, only 16% of Freemen were sons of Freemen, but the proportion had jumped to 38% by 1594–1603, and to 43% by 1675–99. The same trend is visible at Leicester, and its continuance is indicated by the rise of patrimony and purchase as means of entry into several of the Livery Companies of London in the eighteenth century.

In both the Church and government service, hereditary succession became more marked. In the former this was an inevitable by-product of clerical marriage and growing respect for the dignity of the cloth. In the dioceses of Oxford and Worcester, the proportion of parish clergy who were the sons of clergymen rose from 5% in 1600 to 23% in 1640. In the 1630s, over a quarter of the bishops were sons of clergymen. By 1660 the Anglican Church was well on the way to becoming a markedly hereditary profession.

17

Well before the Civil War there is evidence of considerable nepotism in government service. In the early seventeenth century, patrimony and patronage were the two principal keys to entry into government service, with purchase a bad third. The rôle of patrimony is shown by the fact that the fathers of more than half the officials who were sons of peers or knights, had themselves been in government service. Of the whole body, 18% were second generation in the royal service. Almost half came from the squirearchy and above, and about two thirds from the gentry or above. The critical question is whether or not the situation was getting worse, and this we just do not know. Charles I was certainly reacting against this tendency in the 1630s, but this may be evidence of a new political attitude towards the bureaucracy by the absolute monarch rather than of any actual change in recruitment patterns. All one can say is that an increasing trend towards nepotism and social exclusiveness is what *a priori* one would expect to result from the very high reproduction rate of the landed classes over the previous sixty years.

V

CONSEQUENCES
The Century of Mobility, 1540–1640

Modern societies are learning slowly that widening opportunities and rapid mobility are not necessarily conducive to human contentment. Given the traditional and conservative value system of the age, the great increase in mobility of all kinds in the hundred years from 1540 to 1640 probably created discontent rather than satisfaction, due primarily to the wide discrepancies which developed between the three sectors of wealth, status and power.

(1) *Social Discontent* This was felt by both the upwardly and the downwardly mobile. One economically rising group, the merchants, felt themselves denied social prestige, and resented the affront. Other economically advancing groups, the successful lawyers and the greater squires, felt themselves excluded from power by the Court, and also resented the affront. Of the declining groups, the wage-earners were in a state of abject misery which found intermittent relief in rioting and mob-violence. The clergy lamented their loss of income and status relative to those of the laity, and under Laud they allied themselves with the Crown in a vain attempt to recover both. An economically static group, the humble parish gentry, resented their stagnation and were consumed with envy at the conspicuous success of merchants, courtiers and squires. Those nearest London felt the resentment most keenly, since they were most aware of the discrepancy in opportunities. Though the gentry of the home counties were better off economically than those of the north and west they were more bitter since they knew what they were missing. Hence the loyalty to Church and King of the poor backwoodsmen of the west and north in the Civil War, and the rallying to the Independent cause of a section of the small gentry of the home counties.

(2) *Religious Discontent* How Puritanism affected mobility has already been discussed, but we must now examine how mobility affected Puritanism. After all, the two rose and fell together in extraordinary unison, and a reciprocal feed-back system of causation is by no means theoretically impossible. Professor Walzer has suggested that rigid self-discipline at the service of an ideology is one possible response to a condition of anxiety induced by the overthrow of stable social relationships and agreed political, ethical and religious ideals; cheerful opportunism, quietistic withdrawal, and fierce nostalgia for a lost world are others. It is not difficult to understand the predicament of the late sixteenth- and early seventeenth-century Englishmen as the ancient props of their universe fell away. Competing religious ideologies shattered the unquestioning and habit-forming faith of the past; the failure of the Anglican Church to put its house in order left it open to every enterprising undergraduate to draw up an alternative scheme for ecclesiastical organization; constitutional conflicts between Commons and Crown disturbed conventional notions of the rôle of the state and posed the insoluble question of sovereignty; the collapse of the quasifeudal ties of hereditary dependence left men free to seek clientage where they could find it; the decline of the craft guilds freed labour from both rules and companionship; the bonds of kinship were loosened under pressure from new religious and political associations, and from new ideals of love and freedom within the nuclear family. The upsetting of the hierarchy of status as a result of rapid social mobility was thus just one of many factors which generated unease, anxiety, anomie.

At present, it is hardly possible to identify Puritanism as the ideology of groups clearly moving in any particular direction. Many were undoubtedly members of upwardly mobile groups seeking security, companionship and assured status in the emerging society of the seventeenth century. There were newly risen Henrician peers and officials like the Dudleys, Cecils, Norths; rich squires at last freed from dependence on aristocratic power, like Knightley, Barrington and Hampden; new academics and preaching ministers like Laurence Chaderton and Anthony Gilby; new merchants, shopkeepers, and artisans in the flourishing towns. Others were members of the static small gentry class bewildered by the transformation around them and seeking some support, like Oliver Cromwell. Both revolutionary Puritanism and the reactionary 'Church and King' conservatism of Laud, Strafford and the backwoods royalists are alternate responses to identical pressures of social change. On the other hand, many of the key figures in the movement, like their Huguenot counterparts in France, seem to belong to rich, ancient, self-confident families, who should have been immune from such fears. The thesis is an attractive one, but there are still many loose ends to be tidied up.

The Decades of Revolution, 1640–1660
I have argued at length elsewhere that it was the temporary decline in

19

status and income of the nobles relative to the gentry which allowed the house of commons to take the centre of the political stage; and that it was this decline in prestige, together with a similar decline of the higher clergy and the ineptitude of the remedies adopted by the Stuarts, which allowed the gentry in the Commons successfully to challenge the establishment in Church and State in 1640. Furthermore it was their vision of an increasingly corrupt, wealthy, wasteful and wicked Establishment which galvanized the squirearchy into action. Finally, it was the rise in education and in numbers of the urban petty bourgeois, especially of London, which made possible the development of the Leveller Party and of Leveller ideas in the late 1640s. If these hypotheses are correct, the shifts in wealth and prestige among the various status and occupational groups, and the 'contest mobility' created by the expansion of education during the previous hundred years, played no small part in generating the tensions that led to political breakdown in 1640, to Civil War in 1642, and to the emergence of radicalism in 1647.

Post-Restoration Stability, 1660–1700

One of the obvious conclusions of this paper is that much more, and more sociologically and statistically sophisticated, research is needed before we will be in a position to confirm or refute some of the most basic assumptions that are commonly made about the character of early modern English society. Contemporaries asserted, and posterity has followed them in believing, that by European standards England was an exceptionally mobile society in the sixteenth, seventeenth and eighteenth centuries, and that this was perhaps the main reason why England was the first European nation to industrialize and why it was successful in avoiding bloody revolution in the process. Now there is no doubt that primogeniture and the confining of a title to the eldest son ensured a steady flow of downwardly mobile younger sons, and so made English society at all times different from that of Europe. But recent work on France has revealed a hitherto unsuspected degree of upward mobility in the apparently caste-structured society of the *ancien régime*. It was Turgot who remarked that 'il n'est aucun homme riche qui sur le champ ne devienne noble; en sorte que le corps de nobles comprend tout le corps des riches'. It may well be that it was only in the century 1540–1640, when land was changing hands at a speed which was quite unprecedented between 1200 and 1900, that there was any unusual mobility in the upper ranks of English society as a whole. Could it be that English society closed ranks a century earlier than France, in the late seventeenth instead of the late eighteenth century, and that the reputation enjoyed by pre-industrial England as an unusually mobile society is largely an illusion based on false assumptions and a dearth of statistical evidence?

If high mobility was only a temporary phenomenon, however, it effected certain structural changes which had profound and lasting results, and which undoubtedly made England rather different from

France in the age of Voltaire. The first was the increase in numbers of the squirearchy and gentry, which had far-reaching political and social consequences. Politically, it meant a massive numerical extension of the political nation and so provided the basis for the eighteenth-century constitutional system, which was operated in rough conformity to the interests and aspirations of this broad-based class.

Socially, it meant that for the first time in history the majority of the population were living directly under the eye of a member of the ruling élite. If we may generalize from Buckinghamshire and Rutlandshire, in 1522 only about one village in ten had a resident squire; by 1680 the proportion in the whole country had risen to over two thirds. The potentialities for social and political control were thus greatly increased over what they had been two hundred years before.

The second structural change was the rise of the commercial and professional classes in numbers and wealth, and their consequent acquisition both of a share in political decision-making and of social recognition. The massive increase in numbers had the important social function of absorbing the younger sons pushed out of the landed classes by the primogeniture system. The merchants had little formal power but their economic interests closely interlocked with those of the landed classes, thanks to the dependence of the price of land on the price of wool, in turn dependent on the cloth export trade. The maintenance of this trade was also of vital concern to the government, since a slump not only created a threat to social stability in the clothing areas due to unemployment, but also reduced government revenue from the customs. Furthermore, the growing rôle of the leading London merchants as government creditors and contractors, culminating in the foundation of the Bank of England, gave them considerable behind-the-scenes influence. As a result, foreign, military, and economic policies were increasingly conducted with an eye to the interests, and with the advice, of this merchant élite.

Along with their admission to the political nation went a rise in their social status. There was a slow but steady shift of attitudes on the part of the landed classes, a growing recognition that the previously anomalous occupational categories formed a series of semi-independent and parallel status hierarchies – the 'San Gimignano model'. By the late seventeenth century merchants, lawyers, clergymen and officials were held in much less contempt than they had been a century earlier. The hypothesis (which has yet to be proved) that many of these middle-class occupational groups were of gentry origin would make it that much easier for the landed classes to treat them with respect. It was perhaps this which gave foreigners the illusion that England was a more mobile society than their own.

Three consequences followed from this rise in status. Firstly, there was much more intermarriage between the landed classes and the appropriate economic strata of these occupational groups. Thus of the 105 armigerous gentry of Warwickshire recognized by the Heralds in 1682, two-thirds had mercantile connections (mostly with London) built into their pedigrees somewhere, though only a handful may have owed their economic prosperity primarily to this source. Secondly, the gentry lost their earlier reluctance to put their sons into trade. By the middle third of the seventeenth century nearly half the Freemen of the Drapers' Company of Shrewsbury and nearly a fifth of the London Stationers' Company apprentices were coming from gentry stock. Thirdly, the business or professional man could acquire the title of 'Gent.', and on occasion even 'Esquire', without having to buy an estate and cut himself off from his economic roots. As early as 1635, there were nearly 1,200 persons resident in London who described themselves as gentlemen, the great majority of whom were engaged in trade or in some professional occupation. In one Hundred of Warwickshire, in the late seventeenth century, a third of the 'gentlemen' of the area were now resident in the town of Warwick, and most of them were probably earning their living there. The substantial shrinkage of land offered for sale on the market thus coincided with a distinct, if less pronounced, shrinkage of demand. An estate was still essential for entry into the restricted élite who wielded political and administrative power at both county and national levels, but it was no longer necessary to be recognized as the social equal of a minor landed gentleman. If 1540–1640 saw the rise of the gentry, 1600–1700 saw the rise of the 'pseudo-gentry'.

A striking example of this development is Henry Bell. He was born in 1647, his father being an Alderman of King's Lynn, a mercer by trade, and twice mayor of the town. Henry was educated at the local grammar-school and at Cambridge, then spent his life as a merchant and civic dignitary of Lynn, following in his father's footsteps as alderman and twice mayor of the town. But despite this impeccably bourgeois family and career, Bell had gone on the Grand Tour, and was a virtuoso whose great passion in life seems to have been the arts. He wrote a treatise on the invention of painting before the Flood, he was one of the half-dozen Englishmen with a good professional knowledge of Italian architecture, and he practised as an architect on the side. On the other hand his clientele was as urban as himself, being the corporation of Northampton, who enlisted his services in the rebuilding of the town after a disastrous fire, and the authorities and dignitaries of his home town of Lynn. Here in the flesh is the true *bourgeois gentilhomme*, the self-assured townsman and tradesman with the education, the values and the interests of the cultivated aristocrat. He is a peculiarly English phenomenon, impossible before the late seventeenth century, whose like was unknown to Molière.

Further evidence of this trend rather further down the social scale may be seen in the blurring of that previously crucial division between gentlemen and others by the emergence of a new titular group, sandwiched in between, and comprising parts of, the lesser gentry on the one hand and the upper yeomanry and shopkeepers on the other. These were the people, the numbers of whom were steadily increasing as the seventeenth century wore on, whose names in official lists, etc.

were prefixed by the word 'Mr'. By 1700 the topmost elements of Group 3 and the lowest elements of Group 4 were beginning to form another status group of their own.

These two structural changes caused by the mobility of the previous hundred years were accompanied in the late seventeenth century by that deliberate restriction of mobility channels which has already been described. At the upper levels there was the narrowing of the avenues of mobility, partly by legal changes devised to preserve existing fortunes and property, and to restrict to established families access to positions of wealth and power; partly by biological changes which caused the striking reduction of the reproduction rate of the upper classes between 1630 and 1740; and partly by economic changes which shut off the disturbing forces of demographic growth and price inflation. At the lower level there was the attempted restriction of horizontal mobility by the pass-law system introduced by the Act of Settlement of 1662; the reduction of educational opportunities to a pattern of carefully sponsored mobility for a selected few; the reduction of the last remaining democratic elements in parish, guild and urban government; and the perversion of the national electoral process by the extravagant use of corruption. These developments prepared the way for the political and social stability of the century following the Glorious Revolution of 1688, during which England was governed by a broad-based but relatively closed oligarchy, part landed, part monied, under the leadership of a still narrower élite of extremely wealthy and influential noble landowners.

2 KEITH THOMAS

Providence: The Doctrine and its Uses

[One of the beliefs most widely held in the seventeenth century was that nothing in the world happened by chance or accident, but was expressly ordained by the 'providence' of God. In his chapter on 'Providence', a section of which we reprint here, Keith Thomas discusses the significance of belief in this doctrine on the lives of people then. In an existence fraught by the perils of disease, injury, or natural disaster against which they were largely defenceless, men could find in a belief that life was ordered to some higher end a degree of consolation and an explanation for the seemingly inexplicable. They searched diligently to determine what were God's purposes in events, and were greatly exercised by such phenomena as comets, great storms, or eclipses, regarding these as divine warnings of punishment to fall. Much of the historical writing of the period was devoted to tracing out the providential plan of God in history.

This attitude was not necessarily an 'unscientific' one, even though it may appear so today; the search for correlations between events was a reasonable line of enquiry which was often pursued with careful attention to detail, and increasing information about the natural causes of physical phenomena did not immediately conflict with the doctrine of providential control. Keith Thomas points out that it sprang 'not from ignorance about the workings of nature, but from the ancient belief that there was an intimate relationship between man's moral behaviour and the apparent caprices of his environment'. Throughout the century many Puritans especially recorded in faithful detail the particular 'providences' which had affected them, and printed collections of instances of God's providences and judgments became immensely popular. In the passage which follows, Keith Thomas indicates some of the uses to which the doctrine was put, and suggests reasons why belief in it was declining in the latter years of the century.]

Most anecdotes about God's judgments were intended to reinforce some existing moral code. To the Puritan there was no more powerful argument for sabbath observance than the case-histories of the disasters which had overtaken individual sabbath-breakers. An immediate didactic purpose was served by these tales of men drowned while bathing in sermon-time or of towns burned down after shops had been allowed to stay open on Sunday. The same was true of the carefully preserved

From Keith Thomas, *Religion and the Decline of Magic* (Weidenfeld and Nicolson, 1971), pp. 104–112. Footnotes have been deleted.

stories relating to the fate of such notorious perjurers as Elizabeth Earwacker of Meonstoke, who 'fell dead on appealing to God in confirmation of a lie', or the vengeance which had overtaken those who had the temerity to persecute God's people. Political attitudes could also be reinforced in this way. In the sixteenth century official histories specialised in retailing the disasters which infallibly overtook rebels and disobedient children. During the Civil War the Royalists were no less ready than the Parliamentarians to see God's judgment behind the defeats of their enemies; and the misfortunes of republicans and sequestrators were retailed in the same way as had been those of sabbath-breakers and blasphemers.

As a means of influencing opinion, however, such stories were of limited value. No doubt the occasional godly youth owed his conversion to the sudden fate which overtook some notorious reprobate with whom he had previously associated. But the seed could only grow in favourable soil and an accident was unlikely to be recognised as a 'judgment' at all unless the appropriate moral attitude was already held by the eye-witness. For what was an obvious providence to one man might be only a case of bad luck to another. On 26 October 1623 nearly a hundred persons were killed or injured when the floor collapsed under the weight of a Roman Catholic congregation at Blackfriars, London, assembled to hear a Jesuit preacher. For Protestants this was a manifest judgment, but the Papists stressed the accidental nature of the tragedy and drew attention to the rotten state of the floorboards. The great Fire of London was hailed by clergy of all denominations as a punishment for the sins of the inhabitants. But the sins they had in mind varied according to sectarian taste; the Dutch regarded the Fire as a divine judgment upon the country with whom they were at war, while a Spanish account noted that a Catholic chapel in the Strand had been miraculously spared: sure evidence that God's intention was to rebuke the Protestants for their heresy. The decline of old landed families appeared to some High Churchmen as a judgment for their sacrilegious appropriation of monastic lands, but to the Dissenter Oliver Heywood it was a punishment for their idleness and self-indulgent style of life; the fact of social mobility impressed everyone, but it was interpreted in different ways.

It was, therefore, the observer's point of view which determined whether, and by whom, an event was held as a judgment or a deliverance. Contemporary Royalists were unlikely to be impressed by the tales of Parliamentary soldiers whose lives were saved by the pocket Bibles which preserved them from a passing bullet. Neither were Catholics much worried by such stories as that of Elizabeth Middleton, who in 1679 wished a judgment upon herself if there was any truth in the talk of a Popish Plot, only to be mysteriously deprived of her sight two days later. 'Everyone that seems to prevail over another', observed Gerrard Winstanley, 'says God gave him the victory.' When Oliver Cromwell saw the defeat of his naval expedition to Hispaniola as a divine judgment against him he was displaying a magnanimity which was unusual in such circumstances. Normally men saw only those judgments and providences which appeared to reinforce their own prejudices.

But the very subjectivity of the belief gave it its power. By unconsciously selecting only those episodes which were capable of a favourable interpretation a man could powerfully fortify his conviction that the Lord was on his side. So long as some casuists taught that every lucky chance was to be seen as a God-given opportunity which it was a man's duty to exploit to the full, the doctrine of providences became a morale-booster of some consequence: when the Dissenter Colonel Blood attempted to steal the Crown Jewels in 1671, he carried with him a book containing the record of sixty notable deliverances from situations of great danger. The tendency of the Puritans to see the hand of God behind their individual choices was peculiarly irritating to their opponents, although the habit was sometimes so guileless as to be inoffensive: when the godly John Bruen was attending a religious exercise, his eye was caught by an unusually attractive young woman. The immediate thought arose in his mind: 'Lo! this may be the woman that the Lord hath intended for my wife.' And so she turned out to be, though neither Bruen nor his biographer saw any irony in regarding his courtship as the solemn pursuit of the Lord's purposes. Less self-indulgent was John Winthrop, who, finding that he was a bad shot, took this to be an indication of the sinfulness of wildfowl shooting (which he very much liked).

But sometimes the doctrine took more savage forms. In 1658 John Beverley, minister of Rothwell, Northamptonshire, complacently recorded the death of the child of one of his parishioners, 'by God's stroke; for . . . a little before he had scornfully objected to me that I had no children, nor never would, when I reproved him for no better educating his'. Only too often the belief in providence degenerated into a crude justification of any successful policy. Preachers warned their flocks against making providence 'a warrant of our actions', insisting that although God might sometimes make the meaning of his judgments clear they were normally unsearchable. The relish with which the Puritans recorded any monstrous births or comparable misfortunes which befell their opponents led one Anglican clergyman to wish that those who preached so much about judgments might have their tongues clipped, since God was after all the God of mercy. No one laid more weight upon 'extraordinary dispensations' than did Oliver Cromwell; as a member of one of his Parliaments remarked, the doctrine of Providence and Necessity was a two-edged sword; a thief might lay as good a title to every purse he took upon the highway.

Such a link between virtue and success is taken for granted in many primitive societies. Modern, post-Kantian moralists assume that duty and inclination are likely to conflict. But the older assumption, common, for example, among the Greeks, is that virtue and material prosperity are closely connected. In a primitive society the first reaction to a misfortune is to identify its moral origin by taking stock of the previous conduct of the individuals involved.

In Tudor and Stuart England the same assumptions were widely held, by scientists as well as by theologians. They were reflected, for example, in the microcosm theory, whereby physical disorders in the heavens were believed to presage or reflect moral and social disorders upon earth. They also permeated the science of embryology. Moralists had always taught that incest, adultery and other forms of sexual immorality were punished by ill-health and monstrous births; this belief was taken over by doctors and midwives, who as late as the eighteenth century held that deformed children might well result from indecent sexual relations – on the faintly rationalised ground that the state of mind of the copulating parties helped to give the embryo its distinctive shape.

Behind such ideas lay the universal reluctance to recognise that the rewards and punishments of this world did not always go to those who deserved them. The doctrine of providences was a conscientious attempt to impose order on the apparent randomness of the human fortunes by proving that, in the long run, virtue was rewarded and vice did not go unpunished. In place of unacceptable moral chaos was erected the edifice of God's omnipotent sovereignty. But as a fully explanatory system the device was only moderately persuasive. Despite the attempts of the covenant theologians to bind God to keep his promises, it was impossible for even the most optimistic exponent of the doctrine of providence to maintain that virtue was *always* rewarded; instead he was forced to concede that it was only the justice of the next world which would fully compensate for the apparent capriciousness of this one. All he could do was to argue that there were many instances in which the link between morality and material success was too close to be ignored.

But by the later seventeenth century even this proposition seemed unconvincing. It had never been clear by what mechanism God's rewards and punishments in this world had been distributed. Miracles as such had been relegated by most Protestants to the days of the early Church. Under the influence of the mechanical philosophy even the Biblical miracles began to evaporate. In his pamphlet, *Miracles no violations of the Laws of Nature* (1683), an anonymous author, probably the deist Charles Blount, drew on the writings of Hobbes and Spinoza to support the view that there never had been a miracle which went against the laws of nature. The botanist Nehemiah Grew denied that the Biblical miracles had supernatural causes and the astronomer Halley argued that even the Flood could be explained scientifically. In the eighteenth century such writers as Thomas Woolston, Conyers Middleton and David Hume were to press these arguments home to their logical conclusion. Portents and prodigies were similarly rejected by scientists who specialised in devising the most ingenious 'natural' causes for bizarre events. For Bishop Sprat it was quite sufficient that God governed by natural causes and effects: Christianity did not require the acceptance of vulgar prodigies.

27

Meanwhile, stricter standards of proof were employed to challenge the doctrine of immediate providences. New emphasis was laid on the original Calvinist principle that God's secrets were inscrutable. 'We cannot tell what is a judgment of God', declared John Selden, ' 'tis presumption to take upon us to know'. The eighteenth-century physician, Richard Mead, similarly refuted the view that sickness might come direct from God by pointing out that the supreme lawgiver could hardly achieve his object this way, 'unless a sure rule was given whereby his vengeance might be distinguished from common events, in as much as the innocent may be equal sharers in such calamities with the guilty'.

In historical writing it became increasingly unfashionable after the mid-seventeenth century to explain events in terms of God's providence. The Earl of Clarendon did not deny that God's finger could be perceived in the Great Rebellion; but he nevertheless chose to concentrate on the 'natural causes' which had brought it about. Most men reacted against enthusiasts who readily identified the judgments of God in daily life; and even the Dissenting sects came to lay less emphasis upon providences than they had once done. No religious group had given more publicity to such 'judgments' than the Society of Friends, but when the Quaker Thomas Ellwood brought out his edition of George Fox's Journal in 1692–4 he tactfully omitted some of the 'judgments' on persecutors which it had originally contained. In 1701 the Quakers put a stop to their practice of requiring every Friends' Meeting to make an annual return of the judgments which had come upon persecutors during the previous twelve months.

Fashionable infidelity worked in the same direction. At Christ Church, Oxford, in 1666, there had been 'wits' who publicly disputed 'whether there be any such a thing as the providence of God'. In 1682 John Oldham wrote:

There are, who disavow all Providence
And think the world is only steered by chance;
Make God at best an idle looker-on,
A lazy monarch lolling on his throne.

Without reverting to Epicurean scepticism of this kind the Anglican clergy were nevertheless changing their views on the way in which divine providence could be expected to work. If temporal felicity infallibly attended all good actions, remarked John Wilkins in his *Principles and Duties of Natural Religion* (published posthumously in 1678), virtue would lose its merit. The world for most eighteenth-century clergymen was to be a place of probation, not of retribution. This did not mean that virtue could no longer be expected to pay. On the contrary, there was a close correlation between the vices castigated by moralists and the imprudent habits which precipitated the downfall of the economically unwary. Drinking, wenching, idleness; all brought a speedy retribution. The sanctification of the economic virtues during the years after the Restoration made honesty literally the best policy. It also reduced the old need for supernatural intervention to justify the righteous and punish the sinner. Ungodly conduct would bring its own punishment. 'When persons are very sinful and profane', wrote Oliver Heywood, 'God leads them into such ways... as... may form and hasten their own ruin.' Even when vice was not brought to book, there still remained the horrors of a disturbed conscience. The less they spoke of divine judgments the more did Protestant moralists elaborate upon the pangs of a troubled mind.

Of course the belief in God's immediate providences did not wither away altogether. 'The vicissitudes of the seventeenth century enhanced rather than weakened the providential view of politics', says a recent writer. Many intelligent contemporaries found it impossible to believe that catastrophic events like the Great Plague of 1665 had only natural causes. In the later seventeenth century it was still necessary for the Marquis of Halifax to warn against 'that common error of applying God's judgments upon particular occasions'. In the 1680s and 1690s many clergymen waged a last-ditch defence of the doctrine of special providences against the new mechanical philosophy.

In fact the belief in God's immediate providence proved remarkably tenacious. Eighteenth-century epidemics, fires and earthquakes continued to be hailed as acts of God. Methodists and Evangelicals saw 'providences' and 'deliverances' as frequently as their Puritan predecessors. Victorian clergymen could regard venereal disease as a punishment for fornication, and recognise in the cattle plague a retribution for the ill-treatment of farm labourers. The ninety-first psalm continued to be cited to prove that the godly would not be touched by epidemics, and smallpox inoculation was seen by some as a 'doubting of providence'. In many respects nineteenth-century Evangelicals and sectarians had as literal a faith in the doctrine of divine providence as any to be found in the age of Cromwell or Baxter. Here, as with so many other beliefs, the distinction between its status in earlier and later times seems to be only one of degree. But there is a difference none the less. In the sixteenth and early seventeenth centuries we are confronted by a coherent theory to which most educated members of the community subscribed. In the nineteenth we meet only the survival of earlier assumptions, no longer fully compatible with the scientific principles of the day, and no longer accepted by many of the clergy themselves.

But even in the sixteenth and seventeenth centuries there had been limits to the doctrine's influence. The post-Reformation emphasis on God's sovereignty had itself been something of an innovation, designed to supersede the notion of a capricious Fortune, Fate or Chance, inherited from classical times, and still enjoying a good deal of literary esteem during the Middle Ages. It is possible that the notion of a random distribution of worldly rewards and punishments enjoyed greater currency before the Reformation than it did for some time afterwards. In ordinary life medieval people were fully acquainted with the idea of chance, and felt no need to ascribe every event to the workings of divine providence. There was undoubtedly greater credulity extended to tales of miraculous prodigies: most seventeenth-century Englishmen, for example, would have had little time for the fourteenth-century story that the corn crop in Norfolk had been destroyed by a plague of flies bearing the words *Ira* on one wing and *Dei* on the other. But when confronted by routine misfortunes our medieval ancestors did not necessarily invoke a supernatural explanation. 'Death by misadventure' was a common verdict at inquests, both in the Middle Ages and thereafter; and the concept of 'chance' as a lucky accident was also current by the thirteenth century. There were plenty of proverbs about good and bad luck in circulation by Tudor times. In his *Institutes* (1536) Calvin remarked that the opinion 'almost universally prevailing in our own day' was that all things happened fortuitously. 'The true doctrine of Providence has not only been obscured, but almost buried.'

> If one falls among robbers, or ravenous beasts; if a sudden gust of wind at sea causes shipwreck; if one is struck down by the fall of a house or a tree; if another, when wandering through desert paths, meets with deliverance; or, after being tossed by the waves, arrives in port, and makes some wondrous hairbreadth escape from death – all these occurrences, prosperous as well as adverse, carnal sense will attribute to fortune.

The theologians of the post-Reformation period were thus imposing the doctrine of God's omnipotence upon a populace long accustomed to a variety of other types of explanation. They had been able to explain misfortune in terms of the working of good and evil spirits; or they could see it as the result of the neglect of sundry omens and observances relating to good or bad luck; or they could regard it as random and capricious. The doctrine of providence was meant to override these other theories. It also drew a more direct connection between misfortune and guilt by suggesting that there was an element of punishment for past offences in many of God's judgments.

The appeal of an explanatory theory based on guilt may have been assisted by new methods of child-rearing, based on the small, nuclear family, and designed to instil a strong sense of personal responsibility in the growing child. Certainly there is some reason for thinking that in other societies different types of adult reaction to misfortune are linked with the different ways in which children are brought up. But too little is known at present about child-training in Tudor and Stuart England for it to be worth speculating along these lines. Instead it may be pointed out that the doctrine of providence was always less likely to appeal to those at the bottom end of the social scale than the rival doctrine of luck. For the believer in luck can account for misfortune without jeopardising his self-esteem. The concept of luck explains any apparent discrepancy between merit and reward and thus helps to reconcile men to the environment in which they live. 'The best seed ground for superstition,' wrote Gilbert Murray, 'is a society in which the fortunes of men seem to bear practically no relation to their merits and efforts.' The worship of the goddess Fortune began in the classical world, where the social system gave little opportunity for hard work to reap its own reward. In modern times the gambling complex – seeing life in terms of 'the lucky break' – remains the philosophy of the unsuccessful.

The belief that men usually got their just deserts inevitably made its greatest appeal to those with the opportunity to better themselves. The merchant, the shopkeeper and the aspiring artisan might all hope to see their virtue gain its own reward. Indeed the paradox was that those who did most to proclaim God's sovereignty were also those most active in helping themselves. They combined a faith in providence with an active reliance upon self-help, though the alliance was sometimes subject to strain. Even in Tudor England the *Homilies* complained that men were often reluctant to admit that all their successes came from God: they might allow this to be true of spiritual goods, but as for 'such good things which we call goods of fortune, as riches, authority, promotion and honour, some men ... think that they ... come of our industry and diligence, of our labour and travail rather than supernaturally'. This was the attitude which the fashionable clergyman Robert South, preaching in 1685, could safely challenge, stressing that it was chance not merit which did most to determine human fortunes; and that chance was controlled by God.

But lower down the social scale the problem was different, for there was no risk that the poor would overrate the potentialities of self-help. In the seventeenth century most economic writers were happy to teach that the poor had only themselves to blame; it was their idleness and improvidence which had landed them where they were. This was a comfortable doctrine for the well-to-do, but it can hardly have appealed to that sizable proportion of the population which never had any hope of dragging itself above subsistence level. The clergy therefore endeavoured to console these unfortunates with the doctrine of divine providence, stressing that there was a purpose behind everything, even if an unknown one. It was a gloomy philosophy, teaching men how to suffer, and stressing the impenetrability of God's will. At its most optimistic it promised that those who bore patiently with the evils of this world would have a chance of being rewarded in the next. But, as a contemporary remarked, 'the poor man lies under a great temptation to doubt of God's providence and care'. It is not surprising that many should have turned away to non-religious modes of thought which offered a more direct prospect of relief and a more immediate explanation of why it was that some men prospered while others literally perished by the wayside.

3 KEITH THOMAS

Witchcraft and Society

[The belief in witches is a very ancient one, but active, legal prosecution of witches in England only arose in the second half of the sixteenth and first three-quarters of the seventeenth century. In answering the question why this should have been so, Keith Thomas approaches the problem from several standpoints. Seeking an intellectual explanation, he points to the intensity of belief in the devil and evil spirits inculcated by contemporary religious teachers, which led to frequent occurrences of what was seen as possession by the devil. Because of Protestantism's disapproval of the Roman Catholic rites for exorcism which had traditionally kept these things under control there was a move towards legal remedies against witchcraft. The psychology of those involved in witchcraft was various, but there was undoubtedly an element of desire for some form of retaliation by weak, nonconforming members of society who felt that they were being illtreated. Finally, Keith Thomas comes to analyse the circumstances in which accusations of witchcraft were made. He argues that a belief in witchcraft could often take the place of belief in God's judgment when some individual, personal misfortune happened. The attraction of witch-belief was that it offered some prospect of redress for the victim, either by the use of magical counter-remedies, or by identifying and accusing the witch to blame. In the extract which follows, Keith Thomas examines the relationship between the accuser and the witch, before finally suggesting a social explanation as to why witchcraft accusations became such a feature of life in the seventeenth century.]

[. . .] Is it possible to generalise about the sort of grudge which the witch was believed to bear towards her victim? Or was every conceivable type of animosity involved? The answer can only be extracted from those cases where the depositions or pamphlet accounts are sufficiently detailed, and is therefore impossible to represent statistically. But close examination of those cases where the circumstances can be adequately reconstructed reveals that the charge was normally only levied when the accuser felt, not merely that the witch bore a grudge against him, but that the grudge was a *justifiable* one. The witch, in other words, was not thought to be acting out of mere vindictiveness; she was avenging a definite injury. It was not just that victim and witch

From Keith Thomas, *Religion and the Decline of Magic* (Weidenfeld and Nicolson, 1971), pp. 552–567. Footnotes have been deleted.

had quarelled. The important point is that, paradoxically, it tended to be the witch who was morally in the right and the victim who was in the wrong. This result corresponds with what many anthropologists have found elsewhere.

There was a wide variety of ways in which the witch might have been caused to take justifiable offence. Sometimes the victim had refused to pay her some legitimate debt which she had called to collect. Thus, in Hertfordshire in 1659, when Frances Rustat was 'strangely handled with great pain, racking and torment', she 'did often say . . . that if she died of that distemper . . . Goody Free was the cause of her death', adding significantly that she had never been well after buying eggs from the old woman and denying her payment on the excuse that she had no small change. Similarly, when the London cunning woman Joan Peterson had cured Christopher Wilson in 1652, he refused to pay her the fee he had agreed, whereupon she prophesied correctly that he would get ten times worse; and in Yorkshire in 1632 when Mary Atkinson refused to pay Margaret Awcock the money she owed her, the child she was nursing duly fell ill. More direct assaults were also followed by evil consequences. When John Orkton struck Mary Smith's son at King's Lynn in 1616, he found himself growing 'distempered in stomach', and his fingers and toes began to rot. When a servant snatched a pair of gloves from the pocket of Mother Nokes's daughter in Essex, around 1579, he suddenly lost the use of his limbs and was bedridden for eight days. When William Beard of the same county was taken ill in 1651, it was remembered that he had previously cut the tail off Margaret Burgis's cat. After pursuing Margaret Simons's dog with a drawn knife, the fourteen-year-old son of the Elizabethan vicar of Brenchley fell sick, until a white witch was found to cure him. Unprovoked aggression against old women and their dependants was thus thought likely to invite magical retaliation, and many of the extant witch cases follow this same pattern, in which unreasonably injurious behaviour towards the witch is followed by a speedy vengeance.

But the most common situation of all was that in which the victim (or, if he were an infant, the victim's parents) had been guilty of a breach of charity or neighbourliness, by turning away an old woman who had come to the door to beg or borrow some food or drink, or the loan of some household utensil. Thomas Ady described the house-holder's likely reaction when some misfortune followed on the heels of such an encounter:

> Presently he cryeth out of some poor innocent neighbour that he or she hath bewitched him. For, saith he, such an old man or woman came lately to my door and desired some relief, and I denied it, and, God forgive me, my heart did rise against her . . . and presently my child, my wife, myself, my horse, my cow, my sheep, my sow, my hog, my dog, my cat, or somewhat, was thus and thus handled in such a strange manner, as I dare swear she is a witch, or else how should these things be?

The overwhelming majority of fully documented witch cases fall into this simple pattern. The witch is sent away empty-handed, perhaps mumbling a malediction; and in due course something goes wrong with the household, for which she is immediately held responsible. The requests made by the witch varied, but they conformed to the same general pattern. Usually they were for food or drink – butter, cheese, yeast, milk or beer. Sometimes, she would ask to borrow money or a piece of equipment. In all cases denial was quickly followed by retribution, and the punishment often fitted the crime. When Robert Wayts refused Mother Palmer a pot of his beer in Suffolk around 1637, his servants could no longer make beer which would keep fresh. After Mary Ellins, daughter of an Evesham gardener, had thrown stones at Catherine Huxley in 1652, she began to void stones and continued doing so until the witch was executed. At Castle Cary around 1530 Isabel Turner denied Christian Shirston a quart of ale, whereupon 'a stand of ale of twelve gallons began to boil as fast as a crock on the fire'. Joan Vicars would give her no milk, and thereafter her cow yielded nothing but blood and water. Henry Russe also refused her milk, only to find himself unable to make cheese until Michaelmas.

A typical case was that of Margery Stanton of Wimbish, who was tried for witchcraft at Chelmsford in 1579. During the hearing it emerged that her first victim, Thomas Prat, had scratched her face with a needle, and had been subsequently racked with aches and pains; later he snatched a handful of grain from her and gave it to his chickens, most of whom promptly expired. Richard Saunder's wife had refused her yeast, whereupon her child was 'taken vehemently sick, in a marvellous strange manner'. Robert Petie's wife had her turned away from his house, and her child fell ill. William Torner denied her requests, and his child was taken with a fit. Robert Cornell's wife refused her milk, and was taken sick with a great swelling. John Hopwood denied her a leathern thong, and his gelding suddenly died. John Cornell denied her requests, whereupon his cows yielded blood instead of milk. The vicar's wife turned her away, and her little son became sick. Finally, Robert Lathbury refused her request, only to incur the loss of twenty hogs.

These depressing peregrinations from door to door, which were the background to the prosecution of Margery Stanton, are typical of a host of similar cases. They are not to be confused with vagrant begging, but illustrate the breakdown of the tradition of mutual help upon which many English village communities had been based. The loan of equipment, or the giving of food or drink, were neighbourly activities, in the common interest. Lending and borrowing had long been standard features of community life: 'The love of thy neighbour shall stand thee in stead', Thomas Tusser told the Tudor farmer. 'No man of ability is long free from poor coming to his door', thought Ady in 1655. Margery Stanton's requests were typical enough; what was distinctive about them was that they were consistently refused. The fact that she should be accused of witchcraft, by the very people who had failed to fulfil their accepted social obligations to her, illustrates the essential conflict between neighbourliness and individualism which generated the tensions from which the accusations of witchcraft were most likely to arise. Margery's neighbours were denying her the charity and help which was traditionally required. When shutting the door in her face, however, they were only too well aware of having departed from the accepted ethical code. They knew that they had put their selfish interests before their social duty. When some minor accident subsequently overtook them or their children or animals, it was their own guilty conscience which indicated to them where they should look for the cause of their misfortune.

Refusal of alms was the most characteristic way in which the witch's supposed victims had failed in their obligations towards her; many of the accused persons, as Scot pointed out, were women in the habit of going 'from house to house, and from door to door for a pot full of milk, yeast, drink, pottage, or some such relief, without which they could hardly live'. But there were other possible sources of conflict. Witch cases could arise after disputes over gleaning, common land, rights of way, or trespass. Witches were accused of retaliation against such local tyrants as the village constable who pressed their sons to be soldiers, or the overseer of the poor who put their children into compulsory service. Joan Pechey, tried at Chelmsford in 1582, had fallen out with the poor relief collector who doled her out what she considered to be inferior bread.

The conflict between neighbourliness and a growing sense of private property is clearly seen in the case of Margaret Harkett, a sixty-year-old widow of Stanmore, Middlesex, who was executed at Tyburn in 1585. She had picked a basketful of peas in a neighbour's field without permission. Asked to return them, she flung them down in anger; since when, no peas would grow in the field. Later, William Goodwin's servants denied her yeast, whereupon his brewing-stand dried up. She was struck by a bailiff who had caught her taking wood from his master's ground; the bailiff went mad. A neighbour refused her a horse; all his horses died. Another paid her less for a pair of shoes than she asked; later she died. A gentleman told his servants to refuse her buttermilk; after which they were unable to make butter or cheese.

Another cause of offence was a failure to invite the witch to some common celebration. In the village community a man had a social duty to invite his neighbours to participate in his christenings, funerals, sheep-shearings or harvest homes. Guests attended such occasions as of right, and it was a positive slight to refuse an invitation to anyone who was eligible. When Anne Kerke of Broken Wharf, London, was offered no share of the traditional doles for the poor at the funeral in 1599 of Anne Naylor (for whose mysterious death she was supposed to have been responsible) she was sorely 'vexed that she had none, being a parishioner', and accordingly directed her magical practices against a member of the family. In 1570 an Essex witness deposed against one Malter's wife, that he, 'having a sheep-shearing, about this time, and not inviting her thereto, being his neighbour, she, as he supposed, bewitched two of his sheep; for immediately after they were taken with sickness'. When Jane Milburne pointedly failed to ask Dorothy Strangers to her wedding supper at Newcastle in 1663, the justly aggrieved Dorothy declared she would make her repent it; Jane was subsequently plagued by several mysterious cats, whom she knew at once to be Dorothy in supernatural disguise. The classic malevolence of the wicked fairy sprang from the failure of the Sleeping Beauty's parents to invite her to the christening.

Witchcraft could also be a justified response to other kinds of uncalled-for behaviour. When Jane Slade, one of Sir Richard Napier's patients, found herself stricken by a mysterious disease in 1634, her first reaction was to suspect Joan Bruce's son, a former suitor, whom she had jilted in favour of another. It is a reasonable guess that she felt herself to have behaved badly towards him. Other typical victims of witchcraft included the gaoler's man who chained old Mother Samuel of Warboys to a bedpost, the Earl of Rutland, who dismissed Margaret Flower from her post in Belvoir Castle, the drunkard in Royston alehouse who persistently abused Mother Stokes, and all those persons who had offensively taunted old women with being witches, only to find themselves struck down as a result. In such cases remorse was an indispensable ingredient, if not in bringing about the misfortune, then at least in providing the victim with an explanation for its occurrence. Even in the accusations stirred up by Matthew Hopkins, the same factors were present; the witches may have been formally accused of devil-worship, but the witnesses against them tended to be victims who had treated them ungenerously in one way or another.

Two essential features thus made up the background to most of the allegations of witchcraft levied in sixteenth- and seventeenth-century England. The first was the occurrence of a personal misfortune for which no natural explanation was immediately forthcoming. The second was an awareness on the victim's part of having given offence to a neighbour, usually by having failed to discharge some hitherto customary social obligation. As often as not, the link between the misfortune incurred and the obligation neglected was furnished by the frank expression of malignity on the part of the suspected witch. Thus when Thomas Harrison and his wife of Ellel, Lancashire, turned the old widow, Jennet Wilkinson, out of her house around 1620, she came and cursed them bitterly, saying, 'Hearest thou, hearest thou (clapping her hands together), . . . this shall be forty pounds loss to thee', and in due course some of their animals were taken sick and died. Of course such threats were sometimes uttered when the witch was technically more in the wrong than her victims, as for example, when she would not pay her debts, or her rent; when she asked for credit; or when she was caught trespassing or stealing. But always there was the clear innuendo that, if only the victim had been kindlier, more charitable, less disposed to stand on his property rights, more understanding of the plight of the weak, the quarrel would not have occurred.

In many cases, moreover, it was not necessary for the suspected witch to have given evidence of her malevolence. The victim's guilty conscience could alone be sufficient to provoke an accusation, since when a misfortune occurred his first reaction was to ask what he had done to deserve it. When William Hoppgood's young pigs behaved peculiarly in 1589, he recalled how, on the previous day, Widow Wells had come to his door on two occasions, 'there sitting, asking nothing; at length having not anything given unto her [one may note his assumption that something should have been], she departed from thence'. On the basis of this coincidence he warned her that, 'if he took any hurt by her afterwards, he would have her burned for a witch'. It is clear enough from Hoppgood's account of this incident that the source of the witchcraft was his own troubled conscience. A similar case was that of Elizabeth Jackson, convicted of bewitching Mary Glover in 1602. The old woman had passed by the door, where the girl was eating a new wheaten loaf. She 'looked earnestly upon Mary, but, speaking nothing, passed by; and yet instantly returned, and with the like look and silence departed. At which doing the bread she was chewing fell out of Mary Glover's mouth, and herself fell backwards off the stool where she sat, into a grievous fit'. The Harrison couple who turned Jennet Wilkinson out of her house had been cursed by the widow, but it was their own hard conduct which explained why the wife was unable to rest at night, because of her conviction that 'the said Jennet was at the bed's side disquieting her'.

A similar instance of how the relatively secure might be haunted by their ill-treatment of the poor is furnished by Dinah Wiffin's statement, made at Bedford in 1680, that she

> several times, upon the sight of John Wright in the street and at her door a-begging, fell a-trembling at the sight of him; and, being forbidden by her husband to give him anything, she did forbear, and hath not given him anything above twice or thrice since about a fortnight after Michaelmas last; and she saith that within three or four months last past she hath in her dreams several times seen the representation of (or imagined she hath seen) the said John Wright stand by her bed-side, and sometimes when she hath been awake. Once she dreamed he was laying his hand upon her throat to choke her; another time she thought he was going to lie on her; . . . and on . . . Friday last was fortnight, about one o'clock at noon, the said John Wright came to her door a-begging, at which time this deponent was very well, and told him there was nothing for him, upon which he went away, and presently [i.e. immediately] . . . this deponent fell a-trembling and so fell into a very violent fit.

Her fits indeed were so persistent that John Wright found himself in Bedford Gaol on suspicion of witchcraft, though there was no evidence of any malevolence on his part at all. Before a misfortune could be plausibly attributed to witchcraft, therefore, it had to be seen as the outcome of a certain type of social situation. This was why it was very unusual for large-scale disasters, like famine, plague or fire, to be blamed on a witch. For in a witch-case the suspect was usually a person who had been involved in a relationship of real or presumed hostility towards the victim. But the victim of an epidemic or a flood was not an individual or a family, but a whole community. To be plausibly suspected of bringing about such a disaster, it would be necessary to stand in a relationship of hostility, not to this or that individual, but to the community as a whole. The guilty party could only be someone whom everybody was conscious of having ill-treated. An old woman might conceivably be the enemy of a small community, as some of the arson cases show. But she was hardly a suitable adversary for a city or a whole nation. Any scapegoat had to be found elsewhere: sometimes in a fifth-column of Frenchmen, Catholics, or similar national enemies, but usually in the sins of the people, and their misconduct towards, not an individual beggar, but God himself. Those seeking to establish a link between guilt and misfortune had, therefore, to regard such large-scale disasters as acts of God, rather than as the *maleficia* of witches. [...]

Witch-beliefs are therefore of interest to the social historian for the light they throw upon the weak points in the social structure of the time. Essentially the witch and her victim were two persons who ought to have been friendly towards each other, but were not. They existed in a state of concealed hostility for which society provided no legitimate outlet. They could not take each other to law; neither could they have recourse to open violence. In Africa accusations of witchcraft frequently spring from conflicts within the family, for example, between the co-wives of a polygamous husband. But in England the witch and her accuser were very seldom related. The tensions which such accusations usually reflected arose from the position of the poor and dependent members of the community. The charges of witchcraft were a means of expressing deep-felt animosities in acceptable guise. Before a witchcraft accusation could be plausibly made, the suspect had to be in a socially or economically inferior position to her supposed victim. Only then could she be presumed to be likely to have had recourse to magical methods of retaliation, for, had she been the stronger party, more direct methods of revenge would have been at her disposal. This is why there are hardly any cases in which the witch was socially more elevated than the victim; and why witches tended to be poor. It may be that it was easier to pin an accusation on a poor man because he was less able to defend himself. But the essential reason was that the poor man was the one most likely to find himself in the social situation from which witchcraft accusations sprang.

The great bulk of witchcraft accusations thus reflected an unresolved conflict between the neighbourly conduct required by the ethical code of the old village community, and the increasingly individualistic forms of behaviour which accompanied the economic changes of the sixteenth and seventeenth centuries. Of course, there has never been a time when there was no conflict between the needs of the individual and the demands of charity. It would certainly be wrong to think that there were no such difficulties and conflicts in the medieval village. But such tensions as there were then had to find some other outlet, for, as we have seen, it was only the Reformation which, by taking away the protective ritual of Catholicism, made witchcraft appear a serious danger to ordinary people.

Moreover, there is some reason to think that during the Tudor and Stuart period these village conflicts grew particularly acute. The old manorial system had done much to cater for widows and elderly persons by a built-in system of poor relief. The widow enjoyed the right of freebench, that is, of succession to a portion of her late husband's holding, ranging from a quarter to the whole, according to local manorial custom. Should she be incapable of cultivating it herself, she could surrender it to a younger member of the family in return for a guarantee of maintenance. This was a more generous arrangement than the ordinary common law rules for succession to a rent-paying land, by which the widow's dower was limited to a third. There were also various local customary privileges of the poor, varying from the right of three days of gleaning before the stubble was given over to pasture (conceded at some point before the eighteenth century, but taken away in a legal judgment of 1787), to permission to sleep in the church if they had no other accommodation.

The decline of the manorial system has not yet been charted by modern historians, and the working of the laws of inheritance also awaits fuller study. But it seems clear that this period saw the decay of many of these traditional arrangements. Population pressure eroded many of the old customary tenancies, and led to the taking in of the commons and the rise of competitive rents. The shift from copyhold to freehold and rack-renting was disadvantageous to the widow. So were the enclosures and engrossing which broke up many of the old co-operative village communities. This deterioration in the position of the dependent and elderly helps to explain why witches were primarily women, and probably old ones, many of them widowed. 'They are usually such as are destitute of friends, bowed down with years, laden with infirmities', said a contemporary. Their names appear among the witchcraft indictments, just as they do among the recipients of parochial relief. For they were the persons most dependent upon neighbourly support.

At the same time as the position of the poorer members of the community was being exacerbated, the old tradition of mutual charity and help was being eroded by such new economic developments as land hunger, the rise in prices, the development of agricultural specialisation and the growth of towns and commercial values. These trends were accompanied by the disappearance of some of the old mechanisms for resolving village conflicts which had been provided by the manorial courts and by the religious gilds. Many contemporaries believed that theirs was a time of disintegration, by contrast with the vanished harmony of the Middle Ages. Robert Burton, for example, attributed the unprecedented volume of litigation to the decay of the old social bonds: 'no charity, love, friendship, fear of God, alliance, affinity, consanguinity, Christianity, can contain them'.

Much more historical research will be needed before we can see comments of this kind in their proper perspective, and distinguish genuine social analysis from a fuzzy nostalgia for some imaginary merry England. But there was one innovation of the sixteenth century which did undoubtedly sap the old tradition of mutual charity, and that was the national Poor Law, created by a series of Tudor statutes which set up overseers of the poor, charged with levying a rate and making provision for the dependent members of the parish. Nothing did more to make the moral duties of the householder ambiguous. On the one hand the State forbade indiscriminate begging; on the other it continued to uphold the responsibility of the inhabitants of each parish for their own poor, even allowing begging within the parish, if permitted by the overseers. The clergy from the pulpit continued to insist on the moral duty of charity, although many local authorities now forbade house-holders to give alms at the door. In Tudor times the national system was only invoked at times of special emergency, and the loan of food and equipment to neighbours continued in many places to be essential for the routine maintenance of the elderly and infirm. It was probably as important a means of poor relief as the public levies of the poor rate, or the great private benefactions; not for nothing did John Hales describe godly charity as the sinews which held the Commonwealth together.

This uneasy conjunction of public and private charity exacerbated the uncertainty with which contemporaries viewed the poor. They hated them as a burden to the community and a threat to public order. But they also recognised that it was their Christian duty to give them charity when no public relief was forthcoming. The conflict between resentment and a sense of obligation produced the ambivalence which made it possible for men to turn begging women brusquely from the door, and yet suffer torments of conscience after having done so. This ensuing guilt was fertile ground for witchcraft accusations; any sub-sequent misfortunes could be seen as retaliation on the part of the witch, and class hatred constituted a major stimulus to her prosecution. The tensions which produced witchcraft prosecution at the popular level – and it should be emphasised that these conflicts were not between the very rich and the very poor, but between fairly poor and very poor – were the tensions of a society which no longer held a clear view as to how or by whom its dependent members should be maintained.

In these circumstances, witch-beliefs helped to uphold the tra-ditional obligations of charity and neighbourliness at a time when other social and economic forces were conspiring to weaken them. The fear of retaliation by witchcraft was a powerful deterrent against breaking the old moral code, for to display a lack of generosity to one's neighbours was the quickest way of getting hurt. Witches, it was rightly said, could not harm those folk who were liberal to the poor, and the most Christian preservative against witchcraft was to be charitable.

When overtaken by a disaster, thought Thomas Ady, we should not ask ourselves, ' "What old man or woman was last at my door, that I may hang him or her for a witch?" . . . We should rather say, "Because I did not relieve such a poor body that was lately at my door, but gave him harsh and bitter words, therefore God hath laid this affliction upon me." ' This fitted in well with the clergy's teaching that men who helped the poor would prosper themselves, and that covetousness did not pay.

Conversely, an old woman's reputation for witchcraft might be her last line of defence, ensuring that she was decently treated by her fellow-villagers. An essayist wrote of *A Witch* (1615) that 'a very noble-man's request may be denied more safely than her petitions for buttermilk and small beer'. He was echoing Reginald Scot, who had noticed how 'these miserable wretches are so odious unto all their neighbours, and so feared as few dare offend them, or deny them any thing they ask'. One of the characters in George Gifford's *Dialogue concerning Witches* (1593) observes of a suspect: 'I have been as careful to please her as ever as I was to please mine own mother, and to give her ever anon one thing or other.' We give them charity 'that they may not hurt us,' said Thomas Cooper.

The records confirm the evidence of the pamphleteers on this point. 'I am loathe to displease my neighbour Alldridge,' said an Elizabethan husbandman in 1580, 'for I can never displease him, but I have one mischance or another amongst my cattle.' In Devonshire in 1565 Edward Goodridge advised a neighbour not to pursue a lawsuit against the suspected witch Alse Martyn, 'because he knew what harm she could do'. In the great Lancashire witch-trial of 1612 it was revealed that Jennet Device had been taught a charm by her mother 'to get drink'; that no one could escape the fury of Elizabeth Southernes ('Old Demdike'), if he gave her family 'any occasion of offence, or denied them any thing they stood need of'; and that John Device had been so afraid of being bewitched by the aged crone, Anne Chattox, that he had covenanted to pay her a yearly dole of meal, on condition that she hurt neither him nor his goods; on his death-bed he was convinced that he had been bewitched because the latest instalment had been left unpaid. In Jacobean Yorkshire Elizabeth Fletcher, 'a woman notoriously famed for a witch, . . . had so powerful hand over the wealthiest neighbours about her, that none of them refused to do anything she required; yea, unbesought they provided her with fire and meat from their own tables.' In Flintshire during the Protectorate, Anne Ellis lived by begging and knitting stockings, for which people were prepared to over-pay her, out of fear of her witchcraft. In Hampshire in 1575 Thomas Gooter knew that old Mother Hunt was a witch, because, he said, 'I can no sooner shake a pig of hers or pound her cattle but presently either I or my master have a shrewd turn'. So long as the belief in witchcraft survived, it had a semi-protective character for those who were thought to possess this magical power. As the Chartist, William Lovett, recalled from his Cornish childhood, a reputed witch was treated with respect in the village. 'Anything that Aunt Tammy took a fancy to, few who feared her dared to refuse.'

Witch-beliefs thus discharged a function in early modern England similar to that which they perform in many primitive societies today. They reinforced accepted moral standards by postulating that a breach in the norms of neighbourly behaviour would be followed by repercussions in the natural order. They were a check on the expression of vicious feelings by both the likely witch and her prospective victim. As Professor Evans-Pritchard has written of the Azande, 'their belief in witchcraft is a valuable corrective to uncharitable impulses, because a show of spleen or meanness or hostility may bring serious consequences in its train'. Witch-beliefs, like the belief in divine providence, were a manifestation of the same assumption that the likely cause of material misfortune was to be found in some breach of moral behaviour.

From this point of view witch-beliefs may be fairly described as 'conservative social forces', upholding the norms of village life. But they could also have a more radical function. For, although most contemporaries warned men to be charitable, so as to avoid supernatural retaliation, there were others who stressed that it was dangerous to give anything to a suspected witch, and advised that she be ostracised by the community. A witch who was known to be such could be subject to violence and harsh treatment. Jane Wenham was described in 1712 as 'a poor woman that has lived for sixteen years under the character of a witch, and by this means . . . become so odious to all her neighbours as to be deny'd in all probability the common necessaries of life . . . The more firmly her neighbours believed her to be a witch, . . . the worse they would use her'.

These two different ways of treating a witch were not really inconsistent, for it was only the person suspected of witchcraft who was to be turned away; and such a suspicion was unlikely to arise so long as men were neighbourly and charitable. Witch-beliefs, in other words, upheld the conventions of charity and neighbourliness, but once these conventions had broken down they justified the breach and made it possible for the uncharitable to divert attention from their own guilt by focusing attention on that of the witch. Meanwhile, she would be deterred from knocking at any more unfriendly doors, for fear of swelling the ranks of her accusers. In England, as in Africa, the belief in witches could thus help to dissolve 'relations which have become redundant'. [. . .]

The European Context

4 J.R. JONES

Britain and Europe
in the Seventeenth Century

Although the seventeenth century has probably received more attention than any other period in British history, it can be said that a great many historians who have studied the period and written about it have shown a marked insularity in their approach to its developments and problems. The main thesis of this study is to emphasize the close interdependence of Britain and Europe in the seventeenth century, to show that events at home cannot be fully understood unless they are related to developments and forces abroad. Indeed in cultural and intellectual, as well as political and economic, matters, the effect on Britain of foreign influences is for most of this period greater than that of Britain on Europe; one of the main questions to be considered is why this relation was later reversed.

Writing in the 1960s, when the relationship between Britain and Western Europe has been, and is likely to become again, a matter of acute and general controversy, it would be easy to read back into the past our own partisan views and current preoccupations. This temptation must be resisted; we have before us the example of the classic Whig historians. For Hallam and Macaulay, and for Trevelyan and Churchill later, the period contained the decisive conflict between the cause of constitutional and religious liberty, which prevailed only in Britain, and the reactionary systems of absolutism, which generally triumphed throughout Europe. Their insular confidence, and their trust in the inevitable victory of the 'progressive' cause, coloured their view of the past. They condemned Stuart conduct of foreign affairs as severely as their domestic policy, drew an unfavourable comparison of a cowardly James I with the glorious Elizabeth, and regarded the profligate Charles II and his bigoted brother James as the puppets of Louis XIV. The Cromwellian interlude, if tyrannical at home, was depicted as glorious abroad, but only William III received unreserved praise for both his home and his foreign policies. Only after 1688 were events abroad seen to have had a positive connection with developments at home; until then, apart from the sinister intervention of foreign powers – Spain in the reigns of James I and Charles I, France from 1660 to 1688 – events in Britain were presented as if they had

From J.R. Jones, *Britain and Europe in the Seventeenth Century*, (Edward Arnold, 1966), pp. 1–2, 12–25, 38–41, 67–68, 105–107.

taken place in a separate hemisphere.

William III, the hero of the Whigs, has been less favourably treated by more modern historians, including those who use Marxist analyses. For Marxists the 'Glorious Revolution' of 1688 was merely the final stage in the bourgeois capture of power, a postscript to, or consolidation of, the far more significant English Revolution of the 1640s and 1650s. Unlike the Whigs, they are concerned to relate developments in Britain to those in Europe. The English Revolution is interpreted as part of a 'general crisis' caused by the transition from feudal to bourgeois economic, social and ultimately political systems; it is compared with the mid-century movements and revolutions in France, Naples, Catalonia and even the Ukraine, but, surprisingly, far less attention has been paid to the political and social comparison with the Netherlands.[. . .]

During the seventeenth century English commerce expanded into new trades and new areas, so that the country was bound to become more widely involved in European affairs even before it became involved in the actual diplomatic system as a principal. Trade protection required a naval presence in the Mediterranean from the 1650s, and we were also impelled to intervene in crises over the Sound in order to secure access to the Baltic. Of all connections the closest were with Spain, France and the Dutch; we were constantly involved with all three as allies or as enemies in the political as well as in the commercial and colonial fields. The main emphasis must, however, be placed on relations with France and the United Provinces. Spain was at first the great power in Europe. Her ambassadors intervened in English politics. However, culturally and ideologically her influence was slight, except on recusants. In France and the United Provinces, on the other hand, Englishmen could see societies, cultures, ideologies, institutions and economies all sufficiently alike our own to be comparable, and yet vitally different both from ours and from each other's. All educated Englishmen were attracted and repelled by various aspects of French and Dutch life; writers constantly advocated their conscious rejection or their emulation and imitation.

The final point to be made in introduction is to explain why the main emphasis must be placed on the latter part of the period. Until the decisive year, 1667, the choice between France and the United Provinces was implicit; thereafter it was explicit and unavoidable – although the final decision was not to be made until 1688. In the perspective of relations with Europe the Revolution of the seventeenth century is that of 1688, not the 'English Revolution' of the mid-century. Only after 1688 did Britain become a European power of any consequence, but it must be emphasized that this was not an easy or an automatic process. The real revolution, it might be said, came in the painful and difficult process of readjustment which had to be made in every aspect of life during the wars against France. The wars against Spain and the Dutch may be described as trade wars; the wars against Louis XIV were for nothing less than national survival.

BRITAIN AND EUROPE 1603–42

Popular historians have usually described the years 1603–42 as an inglorious period in comparison with the Elizabethan Age. Of course it must be said that James I was far less capable, yet much more ambitious, than Elizabeth, that his policies ended in humiliating and muddled failures, and that the last years of his reign were a time of prolonged economic depression. However, there are two qualifications to be made. First, too much emphasis should not be placed on diplomatic and political events; some branches of trade expanded, laying a basis for future economic developments of great importance, and there was a considerable growth of cultural and intellectual connections with Europe. Secondly, the basis of much seventeenth-century criticism of Stuart foreign policies, on which the Whig historians relied, was negative and unrealistic. It is a mark of the prejudiced and stubborn insularity of a majority of the popular and parliamentary critics that their case varied so little through the century, and that they should have learnt so little from experience. They enshrined Elizabeth in an entirely unhistorical myth of glory, and they took no account of the changes which were continually modifying Britain's relationships with Europe. They persisted in calling for a 'Protestant' foreign policy, in regarding all Catholic powers as hostile. The critics demanded exclusively maritime and colonial war, denouncing continental alliances and campaigns as unnecessary. Such an attitude may have been appropriate in the eighteenth-century wars against France, but historians have tended to overestimate the importance in the seventeenth century both of extra-European trade and of colonies as a cause of wars, and as strategic objectives in the conduct of wars.

However unsuccessful in their results, James's policies were at least an attempt at adjustment to the changes which were transforming Europe. He wisely concluded peace with Spain in 1604. The last stages of the war had not been very profitable; privateering (except apparently in the Mediterranean) had ceased to pay well, and the enemy had learnt to hit back through the dreaded Dunkirkers. The financial burden was increasing because of rapidly mounting prices and costs. National security had been assured by the defeat of Tyrone in Ireland. The peace itself conceded nothing that was vital: Spain did not obtain a total renunciation of trade with the Indies, but only of those parts it effectively occupied, the Catholics did not receive legal rights in religion, the cautionary towns in the Netherlands continued to be held by English garrisons. The peace brought material advantages. Royal finances gained temporary relief. Most valuable was the opening to traders of the Spanish possessions in Europe. Merchants were hampered by seizures of ships for trading with the Turks, and by protracted law cases over customs and smuggling, but it was trade in and with the Mediterranean which expanded fastest and most profitably during the first decades of the century. Solid gains from legal trade were more attractive than the lure of enormous, if hypothetical, profits to be made from the conquests in the New World which Raleigh advocated.

47

Spanish merino wool was needed for the 'new draperies' which captured Mediterranean markets and offset the decline of the older types of textiles. A favourable balance of trade with Spain produced a regular inflow of bullion. The Spanish Netherlands offered a valuable market to which the Merchant Adventurers considered returning. Thus economic ties underlaid the *rapprochement* with Spain – as in the time of Henry VIII.

✗ This fact was not appreciated by parliamentary critics, who belonged mainly to the landed classes. They believed that James's correct place was at the head of the European Protestant interest, united to defy all Catholic sovereigns. For the critics, advantages in trade did not outweigh their fears of Spanish power and ambition. They believed that Spain had both the military capability and the considered intention to strive for 'universal monarchy', and that its plans were being actively promoted by a 'Spanish party' at court – a charge which has been echoed by historians but is at present being subjected to critical examination. There is no doubt that the Howard group at court, headed by Northampton, accepted Spanish pensions and consisted largely of crypto-Catholics, but this does not mean that they were traitors or acted as mere instruments of Spanish policy. They were as convinced by the advantages of peace as much as by Spanish money when they resisted pressure for an aggressively 'Protestant' foreign policy. The Howards used Spain for purposes of their own, and in any case they never completely dominated James. For instance they could not prevent him encouraging Venice to defy Spanish pressure in 1619. The return that Spain got for its money was a group at court and in the Council which acted as a counterweight to the 'Protestant' and pro-French interests, the latter consisting largely of Scottish nobles.

Obsessed as they were with Spanish power and ambition, most Englishmen virtually ignored France – as had been possible during the religious wars of the previous century – and did not realize that under Henri IV she had re-emerged as a great power whose interests and policies might clash with ours. They would not admit that lack of resources compelled Britain, if she was to follow an active European policy, to choose between a French and a Spanish orientation. Instead English opinion was concentrated almost entirely on the Huguenots, who were still regarded as the outer bulwark of our own defences, comparable in importance to the Dutch, and as being entitled in return to call on the King of England for protection. Surprisingly, and in contrast to his suspicion of the Dutch as rebels, James was ready to accept this role. He sent emissaries to Huguenot assemblies, and repeatedly claimed the right to mediate on their behalf with Louis XIII. All this was unrealistic, because of the abrupt decline in Huguenot political strength. Some of their aristocratic adherents, like Rohan and Bouillon, would use Britain (or Spain) for factious purposes of their own, but the bourgeois appreciated the danger of appealing to a weak England for protection against their own sovereign.

The prevalent English attitude towards the Dutch was unrealistic and obsolescent for the opposite reasons. Englishmen saw them as our natural friends, almost dependants, tied by 'the bond of love on our part towards those we have preserved from bondage and the like bond of their thankfulness towards us'. After 1604 many followed events in the Netherlands with anxiety, wondering if the Dutch could stand alone. Only the comparatively few who were directly affected expressed sustained resentment at the outrageous Dutch attacks on our ships and traders in the Arctic and the East Indies. The nation as a whole was slow to realize that in both the military and economic fields the United Provinces were fast becoming a major power. Except in the Mediterranean it was the Dutch, not the English, who achieved an ascendancy in trade, and it was all the more frustrating that often the English pioneered new trades, like the Russian and the Greenland whale fisheries, only to be forcefully supplanted by the Dutch. Eventually hostility towards them was to build up, but during James's reign his own distaste for the Dutch, because it was based on his detestation of rebellion, was not shared by many of his subjects. They interpreted it as further evidence of his subservience to Spain, the 'Spanish party' and to Gondomar, the Spanish ambassador.

James's apparent infatuation with Spain, and the alleged ascendency gained over him by Gondomar, were deeply resented by contemporaries and have been denounced by most historians. The assumptions which underlaid his persistent attempts to achieve an *entente* with Spain need therefore to be emphasized. First, Spain was the major European power so that without her co-operation general peace could not be obtained. Secondly, James cannot be blamed for believing in the early years of his reign that the long period of religious wars was coming to an end, and that consequently a permanent equilibrium could be established between Catholics and Protestants. James saw himself as a mediator and pacificator, in his more fanciful moments bringing together all confessions into one common faith; but at least he was trying to escape from the sterile position of regarding all Catholic states as axiomatic enemies. He had reconciled England and Scotland, and he later mediated successfully between Sweden and Denmark, Sweden and Russia, Venice and Savoy and Venice and Spain. But in trying to act as a universal mediator he went far beyond what was practicable. Lack of resources weakened his occasional threats, inconsistency affected his reputation, and James and his servants simply lacked the skill, experience and knowledge of European affairs to be able materially to influence the course of events.

James intended that the marriage of his daughter Elizabeth to Frederick, Elector Palatine, in 1613, should be deliberately balanced by a Spanish marriage for Charles. James had not realized that Frederick's minister, Christian of Anhalt, had intended the Palatine marriage and a treaty which James signed with the Evangelical Union, of which Frederick was head, to commit England to a militantly Protestant policy in Germany. Similarly James seems to have had no insight into Spanish motives behind the protracted marriage negotiations. At first the Spaniards intended them primarily to block French approaches. Only when Gondomar arrived as ambassador in 1614 did the negotiations become serious. His ultimate aim was the conversion of Britain to Catholicism, to be achieved through either James or Charles embracing the faith; and this, in an age of *cuius regio eius religio*, was not so foolish as Victorian historians thought, with their belief in Britain's destiny as a Protestant country. Moreover, conversion of the sovereign, together with the marriage, would bring Britain permanently within the Spanish orbit. In the short term, the negotiations in themselves would ensure that a series of treaties which James had signed with Savoy, Denmark, the Dutch and some German princes would not become, as a few councillors hoped they would, an anti-Habsburg *bloc*.

The outbreak of the Thirty Years War, after Frederick had disregarded James's advice and usurped the Bohemian throne, multiplied his problems. At first, when they were weak, the Habsburgs accepted James's offers of mediation, only to disregard them after their victory at the White Mountain in 1620. English public opinion was apathetic at first, having little knowledge of, or interest in, the problems of Central Europe. A voluntary loan failed miserably, few volunteers came forward. But the attack on Frederick's own territories, by a Spanish army acting nominally under Imperial orders, created a crisis. A small English army under Vere tried to resist the Spaniards, the Dutch appealed for support. The reaction of the House of Commons was largely irrelevant. Members preferred to demand repression of recusants at home and a purely maritime war against Spain, to voting money for intervention on the Continent. Their vehement language, and in particular their attacks on the Spanish marriage negotiations were resented by James as encroachments on his prerogative. He chose to persist with the negotiations as the only way of obtaining the restoration of the Palatinate and stopping the spread of the war.

In fact, although promises of restoration were made, Spain was not in a position to fulfil them, because of the involvement of Imperial and Bavarian interests. Nevertheless, continuation of the marriage negotiations served a purpose from the Spanish point of view, by neutralizing Britain, even if, as the Spanish Council recognized in November 1622, they must ultimately fail. James characteristically and obstinately refused to admit this. From the start he was faced with demands from Spain that the Infanta should have the right to exercise her religion publicly, that her children should be educated as Catholics and that the penal laws should be repealed. These difficulties could hardly have been overcome, especially the last since it would require a parliamentary statute; but James never tried seriously to resolve them. He could not confess that the whole project had been futile from the beginning, and that there was no peaceful means of regaining the Palatinate. Towards the end, in 1622–24, he made one concession after another, as did Charles and Buckingham during their stay in Madrid. Even after their return, in October 1623, when they belatedly turned against the

50

marriage and demanded war, James still tried to continue negotiations.

During the years 1622–28 Buckingham ruled Britain. The methods which he used in government, and in consolidating his position by the control of patronage, still need detailed investigation, but his whole career of self-aggrandizement and misrule illustrates the importance of purely personal considerations under the Stuart system of government. Personal favour, originating in a homosexual relationship with James, brought him supreme power. Apart from an attempt at reform and reconstruction of the navy he seems to have made no positive use of it. Beyond some experience of the French court, and a share of the essential political gift of using men cleverer than himself, Buckingham had no qualifications to conduct foreign affairs. He failed to overcome any of the difficulties which he encountered – diplomatic, parliamentary, administrative and military. His ambitious plans in 1624–25 for a grand alliance against Spain ignored European realities. Each power tried to exploit Britain for its own purposes. Sweden wanted more money than could be provided. Savoy hoped to use an English fleet against Genoa. The mercenary general Mansfeld saw in James a new source of income. Perhaps the most abject failure in all British military history resulted from the attempt to recover the Palatinate by providing him with an army. Several thousand wretches were illegally pressed, shipped abroad in colliers and died on board while the powers quarrelled over their employment. The Dutch wanted them for their own operations. France was more devious, aiming to involve Britain in a permanent conflict against Spain without committing herself – as might have happened if Mansfeld's men had been allowed to land at Calais. The marriage negotiations with France confirmed this fact; Louis XIII would not consider a full alliance between equals. He demanded ships from Britain to suppress Huguenot privateers, concessions for the recusants in the British Isles and full exercise of her religion for Henrietta Maria, but he offered only a dowry in return, and deliberately vague promises over the Palatinate.

The offensive against Spain in 1625 took the form of a naval expedition like that of 1596. The fleet, with soldiers embarked, was to capture shipping, seize and perhaps hold an Atlantic port (Lisbon, Cadiz or San Lucar), intercept the treasure fleet and attack the Spanish Indies. Even one of these tasks proved to be too difficult. The long delays in mounting the expedition revealed the limitations of English resources and the inadequacies of Buckingham's administration of the navy. Money was desperately short. Arms proved defective, the recruits needed more training and equipment than they could be given. Without the experienced officers, quartermasters and engineers who were seconded from the Dutch service the force could not even have started. There was not a single capable naval commander, the military officers quarrelled violently and soldiers and seamen died in over-crowded, insanitary ships. Troops were landed near Cadiz, but all opportunities were missed through lethargy or cowardice – only the allied Dutch contingent even tried to fight. After a few days the force had to be evacuated without achieving anything. The rest of the war, apart from Sir Kenelm Digby's spectacular raid on Spanish and neutral shipping in the Mediterranean, was occupied with ineffective attempts to protect merchant shipping from the constant attacks of the Dunkirkers. Losses appear to have been serious – over 300 ships – but their effect on the economy still needs evaluation.

Buckingham's provocation of a simultaneous war against France in 1627 can only be described as lunatic. After the negotiations for a Spanish marriage broke down he plunged into the treaty for a French match without realizing its one-sided nature. Subsequently the concessions made to the Catholics were repudiated in order to placate Parliament, the promise of ships for use against the Huguenots had to be broken when the seamen refused to serve. Richelieu made repeated and genuine attempts to avoid a break, but Buckingham deliberately aggravated the disputes, hoping that a war in defence of the Huguenots would be popular. In fact, only the aristocratic faction of Rohan and Soubise, who were already in rebellion, invited English intervention. When Buckingham sailed to the relief of La Rochelle the city had not broken with Louis XIII and had not asked for help. The citizens hesitated before taking the decisive step of making an agreement with him. So far from getting any material assistance, they actually supplied Buckingham's army during his campaign on the near-by Ile de Ré. The French drove this army off the island and repulsed two feeble relief expeditions in 1628, failures which were mainly due to defective preparations and supply. Maladministration, and an economic depression which was itself caused partly by the wars, prevented the government from mobilizing enough resources to mount a successful operation, still less a major campaign. These revelations of weakness contrasted with the power of the United Provinces, who for five years virtually sustained the anti-Habsburg cause. The parliamentary opposition was confirmed in its reluctance to support any but purely naval wars – the one success of the French war was Pennington's sweep of shipping in the Channel, and the sale of these prizes to finance the expeditions of La Rochelle was taken as proof that wars could be fought without heavy taxation. The officers who were seconded from the Dutch service reacted differently. Wimbledon blamed the failures on a decline of martial spirit among the upper classes and inexperience of war. Secondly, for the same reasons that he and other officers supported the Orangists in Dutch politics, he believed that the needs of security required a stronger executive. The King should be able to impose taxes whenever he judged them to be necessary for defence – an argument which was being used throughout Europe to justify royal absolutism.

During the years 1629–40 Charles could not afford an active foreign policy. He ended the French war in 1629, the Spanish in 1630, and for the rest of these years he and most of his ministers (including Wentworth and Laud) were absorbed by the problems of domestic, and especially financial, administration. Foreign affairs were left largely to

Portland and Cottington who, as Lord Treasurer and Chancellor of the Exchequer, knew that financial stringency limited any possible action. They were often labelled pro-Spanish at the time, and other ministers as pro-French, but neither France nor Spain was greatly interested in Britain. She was neither valued as an ally nor feared as an enemy. Both countries engaged in desultory negotiations for an alliance, but they were satisfied if Britain was neutralized.

Nevertheless it would be wrong to describe the years of Personal Government as unimportant. They saw the beginning of policies and trends which, although restricted during this period and temporarily checked by the civil wars, were to come to fruition after the Restoration. Neutrality was seen to benefit trade. Reconstruction of the navy was undertaken in an attempt to assert sovereignty over the narrow seas. Finally, a wider outlook among a section of the upper classes gave Charles's court a cosmopolitan and cultured character including, fatally, a tolerant attitude towards Catholicism.

Economic recovery from the depression of 1630 was uneven. Some trades, notably the old draperies with their markets in Central and Eastern Europe disrupted by war and intensive Dutch competition, remained depressed. Significantly reinforcing the arguments of the so-called 'Spanish party', who stood for non-involvement in European wars rather than for intervention on the Habsburg side, the trades which flourished most were those connected with Spain. Merchants exploited Britain's neutral position so as to gain some advantages in relation to the Dutch. Only in the Mediterranean, where English ships were employed between Spanish-controlled ports, did they have an edge over the Dutch in the carrying trade. Military and commercial cargoes were shipped into Flemish ports in defiance of the Dutch blockade. Dover became an entrepôt for goods interchanged between Spain and Scandinavia and the Baltic – the very type of trade on which the prosperity of Amsterdam had been built. Imports from the East Indies were re-exported to Mediterranean countries. Bullion was shipped from Spain, coined at the Mint and then transported to the Spanish Netherlands, the King being paid a commission. Warships were used to convoy, and sometimes convey, contraband. Spanish troops were landed at Plymouth, taken overland to Dover and embarked for the short crossing to Dunkirk. Dunkirk privateers were allowed to shelter and refit in English and Scottish ports.

These activities in favour of Spain inevitably caused a steady deterioration in relations with the United Provinces. It is true that commercial rivalry with the Dutch, and their failure to give reparation for damages suffered in the East Indies, led many commercial interests to support royal policies, but opinion generally still sympathized with the Dutch as fellow-Protestants. Charles I's policies were personal rather than national, they were the work of a restricted group of courtiers, acting largely in their own interests, and those of groups of business and financial associates. This is a subject which requires more investigation, but the outlines seem to be clear. For instance, the East

India Company had suffered most from the Dutch, and welcomed royal pressure on them, but its members were unnecessarily antagonized by royal approval of the establishment of a rival company by Courten. The Soap monopoly and the Fisheries' company actually impeded those who were already struggling in the face of Dutch competition. Similarly the construction of a formidable fleet did not bring direct benefits to the merchant community who helped to finance it through ship-money. The ostensible purposes of this fleet were to protect shipping from corsairs and privateers, and to enforce grandiose claims to the sovereignty of the 'British' seas. In practice it was used primarily as a means of raising revenue, like so many other aspects of the Personal Government. The fleet did not prove particularly effective in protecting commerce, instead it was employed in the attempt to exact money from Dutch fishing vessels in the North Sea. In 1639, when a Spanish fleet took refuge in the Downs, the sheltered anchorage within the Goodwins, Pennington was ordered to protect it with the English fleet, while Charles demanded £150,000 from Spain as the price of protection, and help towards the restoration of the Palatinate from France as the price of betrayal. Eventually Pennington was a virtually helpless spectator when Tromp attacked in what were, by any definition, British waters. Nevertheless the fleet was a potential challenge to Dutch power and prosperity; it would give teeth to English policy, whereas Charles's remarkably inconsistent intrigues during the 1630s possessed no practical importance. In 1631 and 1635 he actually agreed to a joint attack on the United Provinces, and their partition, in an alliance with Spain which was never ratified. This was hardly reconcilable with his clandestine negotiations in 1632 and 1633, behind Spain's back, for the establishment of a protectorate over the Spanish Netherlands, still less with negotiations in 1637 for an anti-Spanish alliance with the French and the Dutch.

Charles's friendship with Spain was popularly associated with the increased influence of Catholicism which was so obvious at court. By this time the special relationship between Spain and Catholicism was diminishing in intimacy, and Spanish cultural influences on thought, art and literature were far less than those of France, Italy and even the Spanish Netherlands. Sympathy towards Catholicism was a facet of the cosmopolitan, cultured and tolerant atmosphere of court circles; it was personal, based often on an artistic sympathy for its forms of worship, a product of extensive foreign travel or residence abroad. But this fashionable lack of prejudice against Catholicism could not help having political implications. The Queen was hated as the conscious instrument of the Pope and of Louis XIII in a campaign for the conversion of Britain. Henrietta Maria did in fact look on herself as a missionary, and in demonstrating her sympathies caused Charles worry and unpopularity. But, in contrast to the later situation under Charles II and James II, Catholicism and absolutism were not in reality indissolubly linked. The 'Spanish party' consisted largely of death-bed Catholics who would not take personal risks for their religion. The Queen acted provocatively, but her practical importance was limited. Her connections were with the dissident elements in France – her brother Gaston, her exiled mother and Mme de Chevreuse – so that as long as Richelieu lived she could not expect official French support. She was, moreover, a woman of limited intelligence, with incompetent and disreputable advisers, Holland, Jermyn, and Walter Montague. The greatest damage she did to her husband was by persuading him to receive papal agents accredited to her court. Nothing inflamed public opinion more, nothing could have been more futile. Con and Rossetti were cultured, amiable men, but they soon found that Charles had no intention of changing his faith, that the Pope refused to make concessions (over the Palatinate and the oath of allegiance) and that a reunion of churches, occasionally talked of, was a chimera. It is hard to see what, apart from some money collected from Catholics, Charles had to gain from these negotiations, but it is obvious that they contributed substantially to the storm which was to sweep both him and his Court away. Nevertheless in this, as in many other matters, the civil wars were to be only an interruption. The same factors which produced the atmosphere of Charles I's court were to reproduce, in the Restoration court of Charles II, a stronger centre of Catholic and absolutist ambitions. [...]

THE BRITISH AND THE DUTCH

Elizabeth, in her *Declaration* of 1585, referred to the Dutch as our 'most ancient and familiar neighbours'. The events of the following twenty years strengthened and extended the relationship. Apart from ideological considerations based on the shared experience of war against Catholic Spain, Britain's links with the United Provinces continued to be closer than with any other country. Trade provided the chief connection. The Merchant Adventurers exported large quantities of cloth, which constituted over 80 per cent of exports in the first decades of the century, to their staple at Middelburg for finishing and distribution. English, Scottish and Irish ports were always full of Dutch 'flutes', the recently developed class of ship which operated as universal short-haul carriers. During the season thousands of Dutch fishermen came ashore at east coast ports, particularly Yarmouth. Travel, on business rather than for pleasure, was on a large scale. Englishmen and Scots served in the garrisons of the cautionary towns or in the Dutch army. Sizeable English and Scottish communities existed in the big Dutch cities, and a large Dutch population lived in London. The ease with which emigrants crossed the North Sea in both directions, settled and were assimilated into the local population, is evidence of the similarity of the life, customs and composition of the English, lowland Scots and Dutch. The Pilgrim Fathers' fear that they, only one among many groups of religious refugees, would soon lose their national identity, prompted them to leave Leiden for America. In the previous generation, when thousands of merchants and artisans had left Flanders to escape Spanish re-conquest, religious persecution and punitive taxation, most had left for the Dutch cities, but a considerable minority had settled in London and East Anglia. That they made a distinctive, as well as demographic, contribution to English life is certain, but this is a field which merits further investigation.

Despite language difficulties cultural connections were strong and continuous. Dutch universities, recently established and so free from scholastic and Catholic traditions, attracted students, particularly of medicine and theology. Some Dutch scholars, including Arminian refugees after 1618, worked in England. Translated works of Puritan divines like William Perkins formed a large part of the reading of the pious Dutch middle-class. Books of all kinds poured into England from the Amsterdam presses. Some were theologically or politically subversive but the steadiest demand was probably for navigational and technical books. English readers gained most of their knowledge of European affairs from the Dutch news-sheets. Dutch artists of the second rank, such as Honthorst and Mytens, worked in England. Art collection was the main motive for gentlemen to travel to the Netherlands. In contrast, when sons of the Dutch ruling oligarchy, the Regents, travelled, they did so for a characteristically more practical purpose, to form an understanding of the world as a preparation for their part in public affairs. Unlike most Europeans they gave England as much attention as France; De Witt, for example, visited England only six years before he became Grand Pensionary.

The course of domestic politics in each country was followed with close attention in the other. Englishmen uncritically hero-worshipped Maurice of Nassau as a true son of William the Silent. They generally accepted Oldenbarneveldt's condemnation as a traitor and this seems to have stimulated popular fears of similar treachery in English court circles. The condemnation of Arminianism by the synod of Dort (1619) was used as ammunition for attacks on the English high-church party. English divines were uneasy participants at this synod; a more influential and forthright part was played by the English ambassador, Sir Dudley Carleton, who had a place in the States-General, *ex officio*. It would be valuable to know more about both him and his equivalent in London, Sir Noel Caron, who was a key figure in Anglo-Dutch affairs until his death in 1624.

The aspects of Dutch life which English observers chose to emphasize are revealing. They admired the practical and effective provisions for charity, town architecture and planning, the cleanliness of houses and streets, the banks and exchanges, the busy wharves, the rivers and harbours full of shipping. Unexpectedly they praised the Dutch countryside, neat and orderly, intensively farmed, bisected by canals, much of it expensively but profitably reclaimed. They envied the industry of the workpeople, the frugality of all classes, the universal devotion to business. Now these are commercial virtues and the pattern of life depicted was urban. Not all Englishmen sympathized; caste-conscious aristocrats despised the Regents as tradesmen and social upstarts, writhing in fury at the claim of the States-General to be addressed as 'Hogen Mogen' (High Mightinesses). Religious toleration, praised by Temple and Shaftesbury because it encouraged merchants, artisans and Jews to settle in Holland, displeased the clergy. Those who hated London were even more suspicious of its links with Amsterdam.

It is a dangerous simplification to over-emphasize the resemblances between Britain and the United Provinces. The basis for comparison was much narrower; it was between London, the Home counties and East Anglia on the one hand, and Holland and Zeeland on the other. London, the one great concentration of population, was to Britain what Amsterdam was to Europe, the great centre of trade and shipping, the chief market for food and consumer goods, the centre of finance. London alone had a tradition of municipal independence comparable to the Dutch cities; in London, as in Amsterdam, the choice and control of magistrates and militia officers was a crucial political issue through the century. In both cases there was a duality in politics, relations between London and Westminster (meaning both Parliament and the Court at Whitehall) were as intricate and important as those between Amsterdam and the Orange court at The Hague. Just as Amsterdam interests financed and so controlled the shipping of other ports like Hoorn and Enkhuizen, so London was pre-eminent in foreign trade. The surrounding countryside served the capital cities, while the larger towns – Haarlem and Leiden, Norwich and Colchester – contained the cloth industries, much of which had emigrated to both areas from Flanders.

In emphasizing these important resemblances two provisos must be made. London was not England. While Holland was economically independent from the other provinces and the major political force in the United Provinces, London could never depend upon influencing either court or Parliament. Trade was only a segment of a predominantly agricultural economy, and the fact that Britain had potentially greater resources than the United Provinces did not necessarily give London any advantage. Secondly, and more immediately relevantly, London was less successful even though it was the base for most of the new and expanding trades. Its merchants, captains and seamen invested money, ships, lives, courage and endurance in the dangerous and difficult trades to India and the East Indies, the Persian Gulf, Guiana and the Caribbean, North America and West Africa, on a far larger scale and with far greater eventual results than the grossly overestimated ventures of the Elizabethans. In all these new trades, as in those long established, Englishmen found themselves in direct competition, and all too often in physical conflict, with Dutch rivals, and in almost every case they had to acknowledge Dutch superiority.

This conflict of economic interests with the Dutch was a relatively sudden development, and had far-reaching repercussions. The Dutch were capturing new markets and invading old ones, which meant that those classes and sections who most closely resembled the Dutch were also those most directly and adversely affected. The clash of material interests cut across religious and political sympathies. [...]

BRITAIN AND FRANCE

To the British upper classes in the seventeenth century France was the best known, most accessible and most frequently visited European country. For them, connections and resemblances with France were closer than those with the United Provinces. Like Britain, France was a predominantly agricultural country, dominated socially, economically and, at first, politically by the landowning class. Most gentlemen who travelled in France regarded themselves, and were accepted, as equals to the French aristocracy, and found a pattern of life congenial to their taste –particularly as they usually travelled when young and impressionable. The returned traveller who insists that they order things better in France was a familiar figure long before Sterne's time, and never have French influences and fashions been more potent than in the years after 1660. The French language was the most widely known among educated people. It was in common use by the cosmopolitan society at court. French literature enjoyed considerable popularity; the Restoration stage was largely supplied with adaptations of French successes. Poets and writers tended to employ French words and phrases. Charles II's court, which always contained many French visitors and exiles was dressed *à la mode*, listened to French music, watched French ballets and was served by French cooks, domestics, whores and physicians. Whitehall was in effect a satellite of Louis XIV's court and reflected its life and style. For every rather patronizing French visitor there were many more impressed British visitors to the Louvre or Versailles. Cadets of Scottish and Irish noble families followed a tradition of entering the French service, in which they became almost indistinguishable from their French counterparts from the poorer provinces.

This leads to an important conclusion. Whereas those commercial and bourgeois sections and interests who most closely resembled the Dutch were their direct rivals and competitors, there was no such direct or general conflict of interests between the upper classes and France. Many who lived in exile during the interregnum returned with a permanent admiration for French ways of life, culture and government. Moreover, until the 1660s there were also mutually advantageous and long-established economic connections. Cloth and lead were exported in large quantities, wine and silk formed the main imports, and English merchants and shipowners came second to the Dutch in handling France's overseas trade. The main ports contained prosperous English communities.

In addition to these close personal, cultural and commercial connections, political relations during the first part of the century were relatively friendly, although they were interrupted by the unnecessary war of 1627–29, the unofficial war of 1649–53 and the war of 1666–67 into which Louis entered reluctantly and half-heartedly only because of his diplomatic engagements to the Dutch. The old traditional enmity of the Hundred Years War and Henry VIII's reign had been forgotten, and there were no serious or chronic causes of conflict. The Restoration of a francophile King and court consolidated existing ties of friendship.

But this *entente* was not to last. Spread over twenty years from the mid-1660s there occurred a significant and general change in opinion, attitudes and policies. The whole British relationship to France was transformed, so that by 1688 all but a small minority were to regard French political, diplomatic, religious, commercial, naval and military policies as intrinsically dangerous or detestable, and as constituting an intolerable threat to vital British interests. [...]

CONCLUSION

In surveying the period as a whole there is a clear contrast between Britain's comparative isolation and unimportance in European affairs at the beginning of the seventeenth century, and her full involvement as a major influence after 1688. This is as true in intellectual as in political matters. Intellectual influences are, by their nature, difficult to trace and substantiate. In individual cases it is possible to estimate the importance of travel or education abroad in a man's intellectual development (for instance, Hobbes's periods of residence in France and Inigo Jones's Italian travels), and of meetings and correspondence between scholars and academies or societies. But it would be accurate to say that, in general, European intellectual developments during the first part of the century did not significantly affect the main currents of English life, and that English influences on Europe (apart from the United Provinces) were negligible. It is significant that the only groups interested in, and connected with, developments in Europe were those minorities who were dissatisfied with the established order in Britain. For most of those who can be described as 'Puritans' the Calvinist churches of Europe provided the model which they hoped to establish in England. During James I's reign they were directly inspired by Dutch divines, universities and controversies, and encouraged in their opposition to royal and episcopal policies by the decrees of the synod of Dort. In intellectual as in economic matters Scotland was virtually a colony of Holland. But the partly formed Calvinist international, to which English Puritans and Scottish Presbyterians belonged, together with German, Czech, Swiss, Magyar, French and Dutch churches, did not survive the 1620s. It was shattered in the early disastrous phases of the Thirty Years War, and by the submission of the Huguenots (when Louis XIII insisted on the elimination of foreign pastors), so that by the time that English Puritanism temporarily triumphed during the abortive English Revolution it retained few European connections of any importance, and was dependent on its own intellectual resources, supplemented by those of Scotland and New England – a very different position from that of the Reformers a century before.

The connections which bound militant Catholicism with Europe were more durable. Isolated and often under pressure at home, English Catholics regarded themselves as part of the community of Christendom and as following the tradition of the past, from which their fellow-countrymen had been severed by the arbitrary decisions of Henry VIII and Elizabeth. Before 1640 it was the religious doctrines, rituals and claims to universality of Catholicism that attracted converts, but after 1660 it was the political rather than the religious aspects of Catholicism which attracted those court circles which admired and wished to imitate the France of Louis XIV. The prestige of French culture, imbued as so much of it was with Catholic principles and beliefs, and the power and glory of the French monarchy reinforced the purely religious appeal of Catholicism to the upper classes. The defeat of Catholicism, inextricably connected as it was in the minds of contemporaries with absolutism and Louis XIV, is the main theme of English history in the late seventeenth century, while the events of 1686–90 renewed and strengthened the links between Catholicism and the Irish national spirit.

The end of isolation was a very gradual process. The most important factor before 1688 was the diversification, as well as expansion, of overseas trade, in both exports and imports. Instead of trade being confined largely to a few traditional staple products, and following routes and patterns going back to medieval times, the new trades which were developed – the European being at first far more important than the oriental and colonial – assumed greater economic importance. A study of the relations of Britain with each European country that was open to maritime trade would show how closer economic ties inevitably produced political connections years before Britain became fully and permanently involved in the European diplomatic system. For example, Britain had to become a Mediterranean power and began to intervene in Portuguese politics during Charles II's reign. In addition, foreign travel on an expanded scale widened the outlook of the educated, and there appears to have been a more extensive knowledge of foreign languages, particularly French. But it must be stressed that, apart from this economic impact, England made little impression on Europe before 1688. There was almost universal ignorance of the English language, so that English literature was hardly known to exist. The political instability and continual violence of British affairs bewildered or horrified all Europeans except the Dutch, so that to them the issues at stake were unintelligible. Again only the Dutch had any realization of actual or potential English power. It was only after 1688 that Britain became fully and irrevocably involved in European affairs, so that even if, as the Whig historians claimed, the Revolution involved no essential break in constitutional continuity, it must be emphasized that it entirely transformed Britain's relationship with Europe. [. . .]

ECONOMIC PRACTICE AND THEORY

5 F.J. Fisher

Tawney's Century

[. . .] The reasons why the twentieth century should be interested in the economic history of the sixteenth and seventeenth are no doubt various, but one is suggested by Sir Theodore Gregory's shrewd description of that part of the world which it is now fashionable to call underdeveloped:

> There may be a fringe of plantation-cultivation and some large-scale industrial and mining enterprise, but there is also a mass of peasant cultivators . . . and an indigenous industry organised not on the basis of power-driven machinery but on the basis of the human hand. Finance is provided by the 'money-lender' not by a commercial bank; life flows in a traditional pattern. Birth rates are high and so is mortality, production *per capita* is low and the struggle for existence is hard . . . It is a familiar pattern and the danger is of over-simplification. There is the temptation to suppose that because the technical way of life in many parts of the world is traditional, therefore the populations who live that life are simple, unsophistica-ted souls, unaffected by the economic calculus, unaware of the pull of the more or less, the greater or the smaller gain. Nothing could well be more mistaken. I venture to think . . . that it is not in those parts of the world . . . that self interest and the profit motive are tempered by considerations of the public good.

Those words might well constitute a description of the England of which Tawney is the great expositor, for the late sixteenth and early sevententh centuries constitute perhaps the last period in English history in which economic appetites were remarkably vigorous but in which economic expansion was still slow.

Of the vigour of economic appetites under the later Tudors and early Stuarts there can be little doubt. Both contemporary comment and contemporary behaviour testify to it, and Weber's attempt to identify a capitalist ethic distinct from the simple desire for economic gain appears increasingly unconvincing as more about individual capitalists becomes known. The slowness of economic growth must, in the absence of statistics, be more open to question. Clearly, it was not an age of stagnation. The growth of population was undoubtedly accompanied by some expansion of the national income. As a result of the developments in foreign trade and of the growth of London there

From *Essays in the Economic and Social History of Tudor and Stuart Engand in Honour of R.H. Tawney*, ed. F.J. Fisher (Cambridge University Press, 1961), pp. 2–14. Footnotes have been deleted.

was a widening of the range as well as an increase in the volume of the goods and services available for consumption. Yet the steep and prolonged rise in agricultural prices may reasonably be interpreted to mean that agricultural production was slow to expand. For what they are worth, the Customs figures suggest that for much of the period exports were sluggish. The persistence of high interest rates may well mean that the rate of capital accumulation was slow. The lag of wages behind prices, the contemporary concern about pauperism, and the mounting fear of over-population all suggest that the growing labour force was absorbed into employment only with difficulty; and it is perhaps significant that the second quarter of the seventeenth century, when the upward swing of agricultural prices began to flatten out and real wage rates began to rise, was also a time when disease and emigration were probably combining to check the rate of population growth. With respect to such an economy, the task of the historian is less that of demonstrating the expansive force of economic ambition than that of examining the impediments which contained it, less that of proclaiming its success than that of recording the strains and stresses to which it gave rise.

In primary production, the obstacles to expansion lay mainly in the field of supply and arose largely from the limitations of contemporary techniques. In fishing, it is true, men seem to have found it easier to catch herrings than to sell them; but elsewhere the difficulty lay in raising output rather than in disposing of it. The story of mining was one of a growing struggle with the problems of drainage and ventilation as deposits near the surface became exhausted. That of agriculture was largely one of the increasing difficulties with which men wrested an adequate supply of commodities from the soil. At first sight, that difficulty may seem surprising since the labour force was growing and land was, by modern standards, still plentiful. But much of that land was infertile; much was waterlogged; many areas were still thinly peopled; yields were generally low; and the demands upon the soil were many. For in the sixteenth and seventeenth centuries, as in the Middle Ages, men looked to the land not only for their food but also for their drink, for their fuel, and for such basic industrial materials as timber, wool, hides, skins and tallow. It was called upon to provide, not only the horses which maintained the internal system of transport, but also the fodder by which those horses were themselves maintained. And much land was still required to satisfy the appetite of the king and upper classes for the chase. Under such circumstances economic and demographic expansion tended to place upon the land a strain that, in later ages and under different circumstances, they were to place upon the balance of payments. In the course of time, the combined pressure of these competing uses was to be relieved in a variety of ways. For both political and economic reasons the hunting rights of the king and his subjects were to be curtailed. The pressure of the demand for fuel was to be eased by the substitution of coal for wood, by the concentration of the major fuel-using industries in those regions where fuel was most abundant, and by the importation of iron smelted abroad. The pressure of the demand for timber was to be eased by the greater use of brick in building and by the growth of substantial imports from Scandinavia and the Baltic. Improvements in water transport were to bring with them economies in horse power. English pastures were to be supplemented by those of Ireland, Wales and Scotland, which sent increasing quantities of wool and livestock into the English market. And as the pressure of these competing claims was eased, the efficiency of land use was to be raised by the introduction of turnips and the artificial grasses to raise the fertility of the lighter soils and to improve the country's grasslands. But those developments belonged to the seventeenth century rather than to the sixteenth, and to the later years of that century rather than to the earlier. It was not until the later years of Charles II that the flow of produce from the land was to become so great as to inflict upon men the horrors of plenty. Bacon looked back on the reign of Elizabeth as a critical period during which England had become dangerously dependent on foreign grain, and both the course of prices and the literary evidence suggest that, despite land reclamation and the increased use of lime, marl and leys, the pressure upon the land continued to mount at least until the reign of Charles I.

Given these competing demands upon land, it was inevitable that the question of land use should become a major issue. Should men be allowed to change the use of their land – and in particular to convert arable to pasture – as considerations of profit prompted them? Should the forest rights of the king and the hunting grounds of his greater subjects, compatible though they were with both rough grazing and the production of wood and timber, be swept away to permit an extension of arable and improved pasture? Above all, should rights of common grazing – a relatively inefficient form of land use – be preserved in the interests of social stability or be suppressed in the interests of productivity? In large measure, no doubt, those questions were resolved by the forces of the market. Men converted their land from arable to pasture, or from pasture to arable, as prices dictated. More than one landowner converted his chase or his park into farms. Enclosure – i.e. the suppression of common grazing rights – by agreement was a feature of the age. But as the pressure upon land mounted, the question of its use became increasingly a political one. Despite growing criticism in the Commons and the ranks of the landlords, the Crown clung to the Tudor policy of forbidding the conversion of arable to pasture save where that conversion ministered to the improvement of arable farming itself. The Crown clung to its forest rights, partly for reasons of prestige and partly, perhaps, because the surrender value of those rights tended to increase with time. Although enclosure by agreement was legal, the difficulties of obtaining agreement were sometimes such as to produce demands that agreement should be dispensed with. As one Jacobean, probably an M.P., argued, 'the difficultys attending inclosures lye only in the preposterous wills of perverse men who may, and will not, understand reason nor entertain a benefit offered them; and it is therefore not fit that matters of publick good should rest on the consultation and determination as such as afore resolve wilfully to withstand it, not knowing truly what they oppose.' But the political climate was not yet favourable to enclosure by compulsion.

In secondary production, by contrast, the obstacles to expansion seem to have lain in the field of demand rather than in that of supply. Technical difficulties, it is true, existed. As in mining and agriculture, men's impotence in the face of wind and weather tended to make employment irregular. Changes in their relative scarcities raised the problems of substituting coal for wood as an industrial fuel and long wool for short in the manufacture of textiles. In some industries English methods were poor by comparison with those of the Continent, and skilled immigrants were required to repair the deficiency. But these problems were either solved or remained comparatively unimportant in the century before the Civil War. Both the course of prices and the literary evidence suggest that, although secondary producers may have found it difficult actually to reduce their costs, they did not find it difficult to increase their output at current prices. In most industries, the main factor of production was labour and labour was both plentiful and cheap. It was easy enough to set more men and women on work; the problem, as many a poor law officer found, was to dispose of their output. The situation was, in short, one that is often found in countries in which the agricultural sector is large but agricultural productivity is low. High food prices meant that the industrial worker had little to spare for the purchase of manufactured goods, but the low output which made those prices high also limited the purchasing power of many agriculturalists. The labourer and cottager, irregularly employed and miserably paid, were poor customers. The small husbandmen, most of whose petty surpluses might be swallowed up in rent, were little better. Prosperity was largely confined to the landlords and more substantial farmers, and although their purchases of manufactured goods were no doubt considerable they were hardly enough to ensure a high level of industrial output. Much of their wealth went on personal services; much on building; much on luxuries and imports. Industrial activity was, moreover, further discouraged by the fact that the bulk of the population lived scattered in small communities with the result that much production was for local markets too small to encourage any high degree of specialisation. One of the most striking features that emerges from the probate inventories of the time is the extent to which the more prosperous artisans tended to diversify their interests instead of ploughing back their profits into their basic activity.

The effects of that situation on thought and policy are obvious enough. On the one hand, there was a series of attempts to check the production of industrial goods – or at least to restrict the number of industrial workers. The commercial crisis of 1551 was followed by a series of measures designed to prevent any repetition of the mushrooming of textile production that had characterised the preceding boom. Although it is possible that the Statute of Artificers was primarily designed to ensure an adequate supply of cheap agricultural labour – in a letter to Sir Thomas Smith, Cecil described it as 'a very good law agreed upon for indifferent allowance of servants' wages in husbandry' – in its final form it placed serious restrictions on the flow of labour into industry. And although there is no evidence that the government, either central or local, took positive steps to enforce those restrictions, Mrs Gay Davies has shown that common informers were sufficiently active to make them of some significance. Moreover, in the late sixteenth and early seventeenth centuries, many of the corporate towns reconstructed their gild systems and tightened up their bye-laws in an effort to ensure full employment for their citizens by suppressing the enterprise of those who did not share their freedom. On the other hand, men increasingly looked to the manipulation of foreign trade to solve the problems of industry. The curtailment of manufactured imports would create and stimulate the production of native substitutes for them; new markets overseas could make good the deficiencies of the market at home. Unfortunately, the circumstances of the time tended to favour the growth of imports rather than that of exports.

From the later middle ages until the eighteenth century, England's major export consisted of woollen textiles; no other English product – and certainly no other English manufacture – was in great demand abroad. In the late fifteenth and early sixteenth centuries England had enjoyed important competitive advantages in the production of the heavier fabrics suitable for the climate of north, central and eastern Europe and exports of those fabrics had risen substantially, with the consequence that more labour had found employment in the textile industry and that more land had been put down to grass. By the middle of the sixteenth century, however, that rise was virtually over. During the next hundred years such exports, for a complex variety of reasons admirably discussed by Dr. Supple, were to fluctuate around a trend that rose scarcely at all and by the reign of Charles I was undoubtedly falling. By that reign, it is true, the trade in heavy woollens was being significantly and increasingly supplemented by a trade in the lighter and cheaper fabrics known as the new draperies. But under the early Stuarts those draperies were still very new, and for most of the century before the Civil War English industry can have received but little direct stimulus from expanding exports. Admittedly, that century was a time of great mercantile activity and saw the creation of great mercantile fortunes. But the aim and effect of much of that activity was less to increase the volume of English trade than to transfer that trade to English hands. Under the later Tudors, tariff changes and the cancellation of the privileges of the Hansards gave native merchants a predominant position in the shipment of goods from England. Under the early Stuarts, and to some extent even before, those goods were increasingly being shipped, not to some cross-channel entrepot, but to more distant regions whither they had previously been taken by Continental middlemen, and imports were more frequently being obtained in or near their countries of origin. By the reign of Charles I, moreover, a re-export trade in Asiatic and colonial produce was beginning to appear and Englishmen were carrying goods between foreign ports without ever bringing them to England itself. Thus commercial expansion took the form, not only of a slowly increasing export of native commodities, but also of a rapidly increasing export of commercial and shipping services. This export of services enriched the merchants, added to the national income, and led to a growth of imports. But its effects on industry were essentially indirect and ambivalent. Greater imports of raw materials such as wool, silk and cotton no doubt gave some stimulus to English manufactures: but greater imports of consumer goods must have had a contrary effect.

Modern experience suggests that economies in which the competition between alternative uses for land is keen and in which industry is sluggish are likely to see the development of two phenomena. There is likely to be a vigorous struggle for the occupancy and ownership of land; and ambitious young men are likely to seek in the professions the wealth that is not abundantly available in the business world. Tudor and Stuart England was characterised by both. 'Do not', wrote Winstanley, 'all strive to enjoy the Land? The Gentry strive for Land, the Clergy strive for Land, the Common people strive for Land; and Buying and selling is an Art whereby people endeavour to cheat one another of the Land.' At the bottom of the social ladder there was a growing competition for agricultural holdings, a competition that was reflected in a steep rise of rents and entry fines. In the middle of the sixteenth century it had been usual to attribute that rise to the avarice of landlords, but by that century's end the more percipient observers saw that it had its roots in the struggle of tenant against tenant. Even from remote Pembrokeshire it was reported that whereas 'in tymes past . . . fewe sought leases for most commonly the Landlord rather made suite for a good tenante to take his lande then the tenant to the Landlord . . . and as for fynes yt was not a thinge knowne among them a hundred yeares past . . . nowe the poore tenants that lyved well in that golden world ys taughte to singe unto his Lord a newe songe . . . the world eys so altered with ye poore tenants that he standeth so in bodylie feare of his greedy neighbour, that ii or iii yeares eare his lease end he must bowe to his Lord for a newe Lease and must pinche yt out many yeares before to heape money together.' Nor was that struggle surprising. It was the result, partly of the growth in population, but partly of the state of agricultural technique. A man's ability to profit from the rise in agricultural prices obviously depended on his having a worthwhile surplus for sale; and since the limited range of knowledge at his disposal made it difficult to obtain that surplus by more intensive cultivation there was an obvious temptation to seek it by enlarging his farm. In practice, no doubt, the tendency thus to create larger farms was kept in check. But it was often kept in check by competing offers from desperate smallholders driven to offer rents greater than their agricultural output really justified.

Further up the social scale, there was a parallel competition for estates. 'For what purpose', wrote Sir Richard Weston, 'do soldiers, scholars, lawyers, merchants and men of all occupations and trades toil and labour with great affection but to get money, and with that money when they have gotten it but to purchase land?' Such men competed to purchase, not only manors, but also freeholds, copyholds and even long leaseholds. For, as an investment, land offered the attraction of relative safety combined with the prospect of a rising income. And, as a consumer-good, an estate, with the amenities and status that accompanied it, was among the most seductive that the age could offer.

The history of the professions in the sixteenth and seventeenth centuries has yet to be written, but at least its main outlines are becoming clear. As C.S. Lewis has pointed out, those centuries saw education move up the social scale. Grammar schools multiplied and the more successful among them significantly changed their social complexion. The universities not only expanded but were gradually converted into congeries of boarding schools for the sons of gentlemen. Increasingly, the Inns of Court served as finishing schools for men who had no intention of devoting themselves to the law. That growing demand for education may, in part, have reflected a growing demand for culture. But contemporary comment leaves no room for doubt but that education was looked upon mainly as an avenue leading, through the professions, to influence and affluence. For that reason, some were to argue that it should be denied to the sons of the lower orders and Bacon was to warn of the dangers of educating more persons than the market could absorb.

Both the vigorous demand for land and the enthusiasm for a professional career may legitimately be held to reflect the relative unattractiveness of the alternative employments for capital and skill. In that sense, they appear as results of the slowness of economic growth. Yet in economic affairs cause and effect are not always clearly distinct, and the diversion of so many resources into those two channels may also be seen as one reason why that growth was, in fact, so slow. With respect to the demand for land the case is clear enough. The purchase of an estate did not necessarily mean any increase in the amount of real capital invested in agriculture; a rising rent roll might well represent the results of inflation and hard bargaining rather than of any growth in real output; the briskness of the land market was partly the result of a process whereby the savings of the professional and mercantile classes were used to finance the expenditure on consumption of those from whom they bought. It is difficult to believe that, in an age when capital accumulation was slow and the rate of interest was high, such was, from the point of view of the community, the most beneficial use to which savings could be put. Those contemporaries who attributed the growing commercial supremacy of the Dutch partly to the fact that, whereas English mercantile fortunes were often transmuted into land, the fortunes of the Dutch were retained in trade, did so with some justice.

With respect to the professions, the case is perhaps more tenuous. Professional services are an integral part of the national income; their growth in volume and quality no doubt made England richer; it would be ludicrous to dismiss the works of Shakespeare as products of the mis-allocation of economic resources. Yet two points may, perhaps, be made. The first is that, if contemporaries are to be believed, there was not always a close relationship between rewards obtained and the services rendered, and some men achieved wealth without adding much to the public welfare. The second is that, whatever was to be the case in later periods, in Tudor and Stuart England success in the professions depended on qualities very similar to those required for success in business. On the acquisitiveness and business capacity of lawyers it is needless to comment, for they were long to remain a feature of English life. According to at least one contemporary, medical men showed similar qualities; and the fact that Barbon, Petty and Hugh Chamberlayne, three of the biggest speculators of the later seventeenth century, were all doctors certainly suggests some affinity between medicine and money-making. As the Church became poorer, financial success within it came often to depend upon the discreet purchase of benefices, the operation of those benefices by means of dependent wage labour supplied by an ecclesiastical proletariat, and the astute exploitation of any real estate that such benefices carried with them. Many public offices, it is clear, were treated less as contractual obligations than as a species of property that could be bought, leased and mortgaged and that yielded its fruits in the form of fees and perquisites which it was the incumbents' responsibility to maximise. Even University teaching, sometimes regarded as the last resort of the unworldly, showed some of the same characteristics. 'I am credibly informed', wrote Burleigh, 'that thorowe the great stipendes of tutors and the little paines they doe take in the instructinge and well governinge of their puples, not onely the poorer sorte are not able to maintaine their children at the universitie; and the ritcher be so corrupte with libertie and remissness so that the tutor is more afrayed to displease his puple thorowe the desire of great gaine, the which he haithe by his tutorage, then the puple is of his tutor.' The professions, it would seem, were absorbing talents that the business world might well have used.

The vigorous demand for land and the scramble for professional employment are, it has been suggested, found in many underdeveloped economies. But in Tudor and Stuart England they were encouraged, not only by the nature of the economy, but also by the contemporary system of public finance. As John Aylmer pointed out to his fellow-countrymen, that system was essentially one of light taxation.

Now compare them (i.e. the Germans) with thee: and thou shalt see howe happye thou arte. They eate hearbes: and thou Beefe and

Mutton. Thei rotes: and thou butter, chese and egges. Thei drinck commonly water: and thou good ale and beare. Thei go from the market with a sallet: and thou with good fleshe fill thy wallet. They lightlye never see anye sea fish: and thou has they belly full of it. They paye till theire bones rattle in their skin: and thou layest up for thy sonne and heir. Thou are twise or thrise in thy lifetime called uppon to healpe thy Countrye with a subsidie or contribution: and they daily pay and never cease. Thou livest like a Lorde, and they like dogges . . . Oh if thou knewest thou Englishe man in what welth thou livest and in how plentifull a Countrye: Thou wouldst vii times of the day fall flat on thy face before God, and geve him thanks, that thou wart born an English man, and not a french pezant, nor an Italyan, nor Almane.

The attractions of light taxation are never difficult to perceive. But when it is accompanied by heavy government expenditure such attractions are apt to be delusive, since the alternative methods of financing that expenditure may well prove more burdensome. Such, it may be argued, was the position that obtained by the end of the sixteenth century. By that time the Crown was relying to a significant extent on the sale of privileges, which tended to restrict economic activity; on the creation and sale of offices, which drew more labour and enterprise into the performance of unnecessary professional duties; and upon land sales that tended to absorb the country's savings. There can be little doubt that one reason for the attractiveness of land as an investment was that royal sales kept its price lower than it would otherwise have been. It may well be significant that, as the sale of royal lands declined, the rate of interest tended to fall and men turned more of their attention to land drainage, land reclamation, and colonisation.

If it be granted that, in the century before the Civil War, circumstances raised the questions of land use, land ownership, land occupancy, foreign trade, public office and public finance to the status of major issues, it is easy enough to see why the century may aptly be described as Tawney's. For each of these questions has been illuminated both by his own writings and by the work of those whom he has taught. Nor is that all. History is concerned, not only with men's behaviour, but also with their beliefs; and men's changing beliefs with respect to individual ambition, business enterprise, and economic innovation provide economic history with one of its most important themes. After the Restoration, those forces were to be increasingly sanctified by both theory and experience. But before that happy event neither theory nor experience offered them much support. The view that the golden age lay in the past, that men were living in a senile universe, that all change was the equivalent of biological decay was repeatedly advanced in the later sixteenth century and was expounded at length by Goodman in the reign of James I. Nor do Hakewill's attacks on that argument seem to have had much immediate effect. And Goodman found no difficulty in supporting his pessimism with appeals to contemporary economic experience. For at a time of rising food prices, low wages and growing pauperism it was easier to demonstrate that many men were becoming rich by methods which made others poor than to show that there was any increase in total wealth. Under such circumstance, the economic appetites inevitably became objects of suspicion and controversy, and the most perceptive accounts of contemporary attitudes to them are still contained in the famous introduction to Wilson's *Discourse on Usury* and in *Religion and the Rise of Capitalism*. In the history of social thought, as well as in the history of economic practice, Tawney has made the late sixteenth and early seventeenth centuries his own.

6 JOAN THIRSK

Consumer Industries and the Political Economists

[Dr. Thirsk's concern in her book is to trace the emergence of new industrial and agricultural occupations in the later sixteenth and seventeenth centuries, and to show how these gave rise to new theories of political economy. The contemporary word for these new enterprises was 'projects'. A 'project' was a practical scheme for exploiting natural, material resources which was capable of being set in motion by ingenuity and industry. The blossoming of such projects led to the manufacture of an extensive range of wares which were produced first for consumption at home and later for export. A few examples would include stocking knitting, button and pin making, and flax and hemp growing for the making of thread, linen and canvas. The significance of such new industries was twofold: they provided employment, and they heralded the development of a widely based consumer society. In the extracts which follow, Dr. Thirsk discusses the distribution of some of these products, and outlines how contemporary political economists slowly grasped the significance of these new developments on the English industrial scene.]

[. . .] How, it must be asked, did the wide selection of consumer goods that were being produced in England after 1570 find their way so surely to all their potential customers? This question directs our attention at the organization of the home market. Local market towns were the immediately obvious selling places for new wares. Sometimes they had a long-standing reputation in the district for selling similar goods, though they were now being produced by a new technical process or to satisfy a new demand. Sometimes the new industries or agricultural occupations, like woad growing, were located in areas where other associated activities indicated that the potential demand was strong. Thus when traditional wares, of new design, were put up for sale, customers were ready to hand. Thereafter the reputation of a good market was carried as quickly as the wind far and wide. Among the upper ranks of society, among gentry, yeomen, and merchants with an eye for good business, an almost encyclopedic body of knowledge existed by the late sixteenth century about where the best markets

From Joan Thirsk, *Economic Policy and Projects: The Development of a Consumer Society in Early Modern England* (Clarendon Press, 1978), pp. 118–148. Footnotes have been deleted.

were to be found for different types of goods, and gentlemen or their servants, not to mention merchants, travelled long distances in search of their special needs.

After 1600 when English colonists settled on the other side of the Atlantic and learned new ways of farming and new foods to eat, they nevertheless looked to particular places in England to supply them with humdrum household tools and wares that had been familiar equipment at home. When cargoes were loaded at Bristol for voyages to Virginia between 1619 and 1633, the weeding and holing hoes and felling axes were procured from the Forest of Dean; Benedict Webb, based in Gloucestershire, supplied the broadcloths; some of the stockings were woven linen stockings from Ireland, while the others, knitted of wool, and shipped from Bristol, surely came from the Midland counties, perhaps even from Tewkesbury and Winchcombe, whence the passengers themselves were recruited. When Richard Ligon wrote in 1657 advice to shopkeepers setting up business in Barbados, they were told that nails of all sorts, together with hooks, hinges, and iron cramps should be bought at Birmingham and in Staffordshire for they were much cheaper there than in London. Gloves of thin leather, supple and washable, that would not shrink – presumably for work purposes – could be bought at easy rates at Yeovil, Ilminster, and Ilchester, in Somerset. Shoes and boots should be bought at Northampton.

The speed with which the new-style consumer goods penetrated the length and breadth of the kingdom should also be noticed, for markets quickly expanded by this means. At a time when courtiers relied on London for the latest haberdashery and fashion clothing, almost as much variety was being offered to the purchaser shopping in far distant counties. [. . .]

Shops in English provincial towns became increasingly numerous in the seventeenth century, but they were not the only sellers of consumer goods, turned out in country workshops. Rural craftsmen had other loyal allies in pedlars and chapmen. Walking the length and breadth of the kingdom, selling their wares from door to door, they enlarged the market for country crafts to an unprecedented extent. [. . .]

Among what classes of customers did the consumer industries achieve their main successes? It has become a convention to treat the mass market for consumer goods as a product of the Industrial Revolution, insignificant before the later eighteenth century. It is then argued that demand built up first, and was met first, among the middle class, and gradually filtered down to the working class. But the seventeenth-century evidence for the production of such articles as knitted stockings, knitted caps, cheap earthenware, nails, tobacco pipes, lace, and ribbon proves the existence at a much earlier date of a mass market for consumer goods. And if we lengthen our perspective to accommodate it, we have to admit at once that the mass market did not always obediently follow the one-way traffic system that economic historians have prescribed for it. Reality was much more complex.

The stocking knitting industry, for example, was launched by the rich man's fashion for silk stockings, imported from Spain. But as soon as Italian fashions in knitted worsted stockings came in, they stimulated an occupation that already existed among poor people. Under Continental influences the knitting industry then improved its techniques to reach standards that, at their best, satisfied the middle and upper classes, but still catered for the labouring class. Then English stockings began to go overseas. They first appeared in vessels going to Ireland in the later 1570s from Chester. [...]

English soldiers and civil servants spread the fashion to the native Irish, and a century later the Irish were such large customers for English knitted stockings that loud cries of dismay were raised in England when the Irish Cattle Act killed the trade dead. Demand in this case had spread from English soldiers and government officials (the middle and labouring classes in England) to the Irish peasantry (or those who were their social equivalents).

When demand for English stockings built up on the Continent of Europe, revealing itself conspicuously in the port-books by the 1590s, the quantity involved, the wide range of qualities of woollen stockings, *and* the diversity of markets suggest that purchasers were again found among the middle *and* lower classes. [: ...] Few countries in Europe were ignorant of what English knitted stockings looked like. Clearly, they were not rich men's wares, but the clothing of the common people. The market was lodged mainly at the lower end of the social scale. [...]

If space permitted, the success of projects, first in English, and then in European markets, could be demonstrated in the history of many other wares: felt hats, Caster hats, Monmouth caps, buttons, copper thread, tobacco pipes, girdles, gloves, glass, and earthenware. It must suffice to consider the growing overseas market for wares that *have* received attention. About 1679 a list was compiled of goods exported from London in the year Michaelmas 1662 to Michaelmas 1663. It claimed to be an account of English manufactures, and to exclude re-exported goods. Being confined to London, it is only a rough-and-ready indicator of the way the new industries were competing overseas, but it is better than nothing.

English alum now went (in order of value) to Holland, Germany, France, Spain, Portugal, the American Plantations, East Indies, Scotland, and Ireland. Aqua vitae went to the Plantations, Russia, the East Indies, Africa, and Portugal. Strong waters went to Africa, Spain, Germany, Portugal, France, Scotland, and Italy. Copperas went to Holland, Germany, France, and Spain. Leather gloves went in large quantities to Germany, Holland, and Sweden, and in lesser quantities to five other European countries as well as to the Plantations, Scotland, and Ireland. Gold and silver lace went to Portugal in quantity, less to Italy and Spain, to the Plantations, and to Scotland. English wrought silk went to Spain, Portugal (4,105 lb) the Plantations (3,427 lb), France (2,346 lb), Holland, Italy, Scotland, Germany, Ireland, Flanders, Africa, and Denmark (amounts ranging from 200 to 2,000 lb). English thrown silk went to Germany, Portugal, and Scotland (over 1,000 lb apiece), and in small quantities to Denmark and the Plantations. Every single country in this list invites us to investigate the manufacturing centres in England of these commodities, and the quality of the wares that yielded them such a market overseas. Gold and silver lace was being sold in Italy, whence the manufacture had first infiltrated into England. Wrought silk was being sold in Spain, whence the first silk stockings had come to England. Alum was sent to Spain, whence it had been imported in the sixteenth century. How had quality and price been upturned in the interval?

Differentiation plainly deserves attention as a positive force in expanding consumption. It is a subject that is generally ignored in studies of long-term economic development, even though it may contain the most valuable clue to the vitality or decay of particular regions in England, each having its own peculiar mixture of industrial specialities, employing large populations. [. . .]

In a discerning book in 1958 on *The Cultural Foundations of Industrial Civilization*, Professor Nef made the distinction between the industries of the Continent, especially Holland and France, which concentrated on artistic wares in the sixteenth and seventeenth centuries, and Great Britain (and Sweden) which produced a flood of cheap wares. For England we begin to measure the full truth of this generalization. English industries selling overseas for the most part succeeded best with cheap consumer wares. There were some exceptions, of course: some English knives achieved a high reputation abroad, but the craftsmanship in that case seems to have been of London not of the rural areas. The truth touched some writers with melancholy. One wrote in 1662 sadly reporting how the Dutch commanded the quality market for cloth in France, Poland, the East Indies, Scotland, Ireland, and even England itself, leaving England to 'become the poor man's clothier'. Seen by those who wanted England to have the prestige of making the best of everything, it was, indeed, a sad business. But seen from the point of view of the large rural populations at home, more fully employed in the seventeenth century than at any earlier time, it was a matter for congratulation not lamentation. It was the political economists who first recognized in the success of the new consumer industries a changed situation that they could contemplate with satisfaction, not with dismay. [. . .]

At the beginning of the seventeenth century their basic article of faith was summed up in the title of Thomas Mun's famous essay, written in the early 1620s, on 'England's Treasure by Foreign Trade'. England's treasure *was* her foreign trade, or, as the sub-title expressed it, 'the balance of our foreign trade is the rule of our treasure'. The writer's attention was riveted on England's overseas trade, and especially on the cloth industry as the main export. This had to pay, and more than pay, the cost of imports, if England's wealth was to be increased.

'The ordinary means therefore to increase our wealth and treasure is by foreign trade, wherein we must ever observe this rule: to sell more to strangers yearly than we consume of theirs in value.' To obtain this surplus, two alternative or complementary courses were open: Englishmen must reduce their consumption of foreign goods, or sell more of their native products overseas. It was anathema to Mun to observe in the frequent changes of fashion in food and clothing –many of them imported from France, Italy, and Spain – the signs of a developing home market in consumer goods. He would have had laws curbing such excesses. As for his second objective, to promote the sale of English goods overseas, he agreed that every effort had to be made to suit our wares to the foreigners' taste and purse. He did not seem to see the irrationality of his double standard.

Common sense prevented Mun from judging *all* manufactures by their contribution to foreign trade. The luxury needs of the English nobility and gentry created work for the poor, he conceded, and this was beneficial to the commonwealth. But better by far to engage in activities that enriched the whole kingdom, including the King. This was achieved only by exports. These secured a favourable balance of trade, gave a living to labourers, manufacturers, and merchants, *and* brought in customs revenue to the Crown. As McCulloch graphically phrased it, when reviewing the theory in 1856, the balance of trade was thus erected into a 'gilded image of clay and mud' standing for more than a century as 'an object of slavish adoration'.

The tricky arithmetic necessary then, as now, to arrive at a final account of the overseas trade balance need not concern us. Built upon shaky foundations, a seemingly firm figure was somehow arrived at. In 1612–14 it seemed that England had a favourable balance of trade. In 1616 it was pronounced unfavourable, and it was still deemed so in 1622–3, when a serious economic crisis provoked a long and deep inquiry into its causes. This was wholly concerned with the terms of overseas trade and the exchange rate. The solution to the depression seemed to lie in exporting ever more competitively, ever more cheaply.

In fact the influence of this way of thinking was an obstacle to industrial advance along the lines now being charted by projectors. The campaign waged at this time to improve the quality of English cloth (the main export) insisted on uniform lengths and widths. It was contrary to the wishes of the English consumer who rejoiced in the variety of price and quality that was available; for him, the more variety, the better. But since it was the merchant who held the balance of trade in his hand, and was responsible for tilting it one way or the other, the merchant's word carried most weight. He wanted uniformity and this therefore became government policy. Fortunately, it proved impossible to put this policy effectively into practice. Variety rather than uniformity continued to sustain the domestic market. It was even encouraged by foreign demand. According to William Temple, writing in 1668, foreigners found cheap English manufactures as useful as did their English customers. The Dutch made a good bargain out of selling their own fine-quality cloth to France and buying the coarse cloth of England for their own wear. They sent their best butter abroad, and bought for their own use the cheap butter made in Ireland and in northern England. In this casual remark from a contemporary, we solve the mystery of why northern English butter became an export from Northumberland and Durham in the second half of the seventeenth century. Its quality is the vital clue that explains its success as a new export. It was cheap, and Holland's own butter was now in the luxury class, too expensive for ordinary Dutchmen to put on their own tables.

Thus, while Thomas Mun and Edward Misselden concentrated their attention in the early 1620s on the problems of overseas trade, the world around them was being shaped in a new image. Industrial and agricultural producers were toppling the gilded image of clay and mud from its pedestal by producing goods, many of them cheap and cheerful, for the home market; if they attracted purchasers from abroad so much the better but that was incidental. We may remind ourselves by a few random illustrations of the projects that were well under way or were being initiated in these same years in villages scattered all over the kingdom. Already in 1608 men confidently claimed that English manufacturers had triumphed over foreign competitors in the making of fustians, cards, silk laces, ribbons, points, silk garters, girdles, bewpers, bolsters, and knives. In 1620 John Stratford, who had once traded as a merchant buying undressed flax from Holland, started to grow flax at Winchcombe in Gloucestershire. The same John Stratford had launched the earlier venture of tobacco growing in 1619, that had been brought to an end by government edict. But as a *peasant activity*, tobacco growing forged ahead in the 1620s and was destined to enjoy a long, though illicit career in twenty-two counties, likewise supplying the home market. In Somerset flax growing was being assiduously promoted in 1625 by various local gentry who invited Christopher Cockerell of Elham in Kent to go to Glastonbury to improve local skills in growing flax and dressing it for the spinner. Cockerell remained in the Somerset Levels for more than thirteen years, demonstrating his way with flax as an *agricultural* crop in newly drained fen, and *industrially* as an employer of poor spinners. Even while he promoted this project, stocking knitting and the spinning of wool for the knitters were already keeping many others occupied in Glastonbury. In these same years, Anthony Cope of Hanwell was growing woad in Spalding, Lincolnshire, and despite the gloomy tales that some men circulated in the 1580s about the inferior quality of English woad, it nevertheless built up a solid reputation as a profitable crop in the course of the seventeenth century. Men came to terms with its cultivation and recognized that it could not be grown on half-acres and small quillets of land. It had to be a well-organized enterprise, backed by men with enough capital to own a woad mill and keep it busy, but when these requirements were met, as Walter Blith affirmed, it made a fortune for many a Midland landowner in the mid-seventeenth century, and gave plenty of work to labourers. In Northamptonshire it remained a favourite crop well into the eighteenth century. 'Of all the Midland counties', wrote John Morton in the *Natural History of Northamptonshire* in 1712, 'this I am pretty sure is, or has been, woaded most'. Among yet more successes in this period, trials with rapeseed oil for cloth making were brought to fruition by Benedict Webb in Gloucestershire shortly before 1620. In 1625 he grew 550 acres of rape in the Forest of Dean, while others in the East Anglian fens grew hundreds of acres more. From a Scotsman travelling south to congratulate George I on his accession to the English throne in 1714, we catch a glimpse of the quiet diffusion of this innovation. At Easingwold in Yorkshire James Hart reported seeing fields of 20 to 30 acres, all sown with rapeseed, destined to be crushed for oil to serve the clothiers. The crop yielded a very satisfactory profit to the farmer of £10 an acre, and even served overseas as well as domestic demand. Some was shipped from London, but the trade had greater proportionate importance in lesser places: a petition to the House of Commons in 1719 described the shipping of a thousand tons annually from the little port of Wisbech.

These are but a few of the industrial and agricultural occupations that transformed the pattern of employment in the seventeenth century. They serve as a reminder that important initiatives were being taken in the 1620s, at the very moment when Mun and Misselden tendered their advice in quite other terms in an effort to ameliorate the trade depression. Political economists did not then appreciate the role of consumer industries and of the expansive home market, and it was not for another twenty years, not until the Civil War, that fresh experience drove home the lesson. The Civil War was indeed a landmark in developing a new economic policy out of the history of projects, simply because it gave influential writers and politicians a deeper knowledge of the variety of local economies than they could ever have acquired in peacetime.

Men moved around the country more than was their wont. Some were men of influence on the Parliamentary side, serving on Parliamentary committees as sequestration commissioners, militia commissioners, surveyors, and so on. They carried with them on their journeys political and social ideals and a practical concern for economic progress. The urgency of measures to revive the economy was impressed upon them by the severe depression, which began in 1646, deepened in 1649 with the execution of the King, and plumbed the depths between 1649 and 1651. The new republic had to revive confidence and infuse fresh economic energy by a programme that made the new Commonwealth more than just a new name. Pamphlets enumerating the great economic possibilities that lay ahead clearly reflected the lessons which their authors had learned in their perambulations of the kingdom. Their first concern was to mitigate poverty and unemployment that had been grievously aggravated by the war. They placed their strongest hopes, not unnaturally, on agricultural improvement, especially on the improvement of wastes, forests, and parks which might be made into smallholdings for cottagers and farms for husbandmen. The confiscation of Crown, Church, and royalist lands made this an immediately attainable goal. The second theme in their campaign was the economic value of vegetables, fruit, and industrial crops. These demanded intensive labour but yielded a large profit. Their third recommendation was for industrial work to employ the poor, and in pamphlets on this subject an appreciation of the role of rural industries was clearly discernible. It was clearest of all in Henry Robinson's wide programme of economic reforms, which gave prominence to the value of the home market. Even though it was still regarded as the handmaid of overseas trade, it was deemed indispensable in that role, for what else was overseas trade but 'exportation of the overplus of all such commodities as the inland trade hath produced more than are sufficient for service of the nation'.?

Henry Robinson was groping his way only slowly towards an understanding of the economic potential of rural industries. In 1641 he had written a brief essay suggesting that improved river navigation would assist inland trade, a matter on which England, he thought, was backward compared with Germany and Italy. In a new survey in 1649 Robinson wrestled with a related problem – the difficulties created by the existence of scattered populations, all having to be supplied with the raw materials of manufacture. The straggling sprawl of hamlets and villages greatly increased the costs of transport and put up the prices of manufactured goods. These passed back and forth too many times between the markets and the craftsmen who specialized in different operations. He proposed to tidy up the time-wasting pattern of dispersed settlement by grouping tenements into villages and establishing cities near rivers. The solution was unrealistic, and we can imagine what his critics said to him in private. His scheme finally appeared in a much more acceptable guise in his third essay, written in 1652, urging that all rivers be made navigable, and canals be built to towns lacking rivers. This was a suggestion that bore a rich harvest. Rural industries continued in the same locations, but the improvement of navigable rivers became one of the most impressive achievements of the second half of the seventeenth century.

In some ways it is surprising that the theoretical insights of men like Henry Robinson, whose ideas, we may reasonably assume, were discussed with his contemporaries before they appeared in print, and reflected more than one man's individual and eccentric opinions, did not result in another outburst of projects initiated by a fresh generation of projectors with strong Parliamentarian sympathies. It would not have been unreasonable to expect more projects, similar in purpose to those of the period 1540–1630, started this time by Commonwealthmen as courageous and public-spirited as those of the Elizabethan age. In fact, the evidence points rather to projects of a more personal kind at a more experimental stage. The experiments of John Beale with ciders that would sell in wider markets, the experiments of Sir Richard Weston with clover on the sandy heaths of his own estate in Surrey, the trials of flax growing by Parson Giles Moore of Horsted Keynes in Sussex, the collecting and publicizing of new varieties of vegetables and trees, were all intended to improve employment prospects in the long run. Men, in the Hartlib circle especially, were planning economic growth in many different directions, confidently predicting that each scheme would greatly increase employment for the poor. But the schemes were in their initial stages, and consisted in individual experiments in the private houses, gardens, and fields of gentlemen and parsons.

One is driven to the conclusion that men were now more cautious, partly because the economic and political climate was different, and the future still uncertain, but also because, for other reasons, men were less sure of themselves. They were not now copying foreign models, of whose success they could be confident. They were venturing upon newer and less well charted paths.

At a lower level of society, however, the industries launched earlier were forging ahead under their own momentum. Poor men, and the not so poor, were pursuing their own solutions without assistance from above. The history of tobacco growing is the superb, and unusually well documented, illustration of a new enterprise that had cost its pioneer hundreds, even thousands, of pounds in 1619. But two years were enough to set it going among humbler men. It became an occupation that employed hundreds of poor by the 1640s and 1650s.

The full strength of the many novel industrial undercurrents in the economy was fully recognized at last in the 1670s when a new depression deepened and pamphleteers took up their pens again in an effort to alleviate 'the fall of rents and the decay of trade'. Much the most discerning writer of the new generation was Carew Reynel, a Hampshire country gentleman, educated at Oxford and the Inns of Court, who made his only appearance on the political stage when he took part in Penruddock's Rising in 1655, and was charitably pardoned on account of his extreme youth. His later years were spent in economic studies that were presented in his book, *The True English Interest*, published in 1674. Who would have expected that this man, seemingly with the conventional upbringing of an English landed gentleman, would so eloquently urge the expansion of domestic industries, even shaking himself free from the most deep-rooted prejudices against forbidden occupations such as tobacco growing? He had listened to government propaganda over several decades proclaiming that tobacco growing injured the health of Englishmen. Yet he boldly dedicated a chapter of his book to this topic, advocating tobacco as a crop that improved the rent of land extremely, 'as well as employing great numbers of people . . . Land otherwise worth 10s. an acre was worth £3 p.a. under tobacco (and hence was highly satisfactory to the landlord), while the tenant could make a profit of £30 and £40 an acre, all charges paid . . . All the objections that are against it cannot vie with the advantages that it produces', he asserted, in defiance of all received doctrine. Even the argument that English tobacco was inferior to foreign was summarily dispátched. 'If people will take it as they do, and it will go off, what matter is it? . . . Others say 'tis *better* than any foreign tobacco, especially for English bodies.' In fact, it was a common practice to mix English tobacco with foreign, and when this was done, it passed for foreign tobacco, commanding the higher price.

Carew Reynel was clearly an original mind, and offered a remarkably penetrating commentary on the English economy and the way forward. To encourage England's wealth and prosperity, he held it necessary to encourage home trade rather than foreign. His message was now much clearer and more positive than Henry Robinson's had been. 'Trade is to be advanced every way at home and abroad, but especially the home as being of more consequence than the foreign . . . Foreign trade is a secondary help, home trade is our primary advantage.' To encourage home trade, river transport must be improved; even now two new engines were being offered as a method of cutting rivers at an easy rate. Turning to agriculture and measures to employ the population on the land, he favoured small farms rather than large: 'the smaller estates the land is divided into, the better for the nation; the more people are maintained, and the land better husbanded'. Here was another original and unfamiliar argument reflecting accurate observations on the success of intensive cultivation – of vegetables, and industrial crops like dyes, hemp, and flax, as well as tobacco. Reynel came from Hampshire, be it noted, the first home of woad growing in its new phase, launched under the projectors' stimulus in the sixteenth century. As for industrial occupations, he handed out warm praise for rural industries that employed a large labour force – lace making in Manchester, band-string making at Blandford, Dorset, knives at Sheffield, fustians in Lancashire, sail making in Ipswich ('the best sails that ever were made', he claimed), liquorice at Worksop, hops at Farnham, saffron at Saffron Walden, tobacco at Winchcombe, stuffs, silks, satins, and velvets at Norwich, Canterbury, Colchester, Spitalfields, and in the London suburbs, thread making at Maidstone (where they sold a thousand pounds' worth a week), and serges at Exeter. What were these but sixteenth-century projects – new industries, and old ones that had been transformed by new techniques into a virtually new occupation? Only saffron at Saffron Walden looks like a survival from a medieval past, though, for all we yet know, the method of cultivating saffron may well have been improved by Dutch expertise, renowned in Holland, in the later sixteenth century. Reynel associated all these new occupations with towns, for towns were the collecting centres and markets, but much of the labour force, as we have seen, was mixed, partly of the town, and partly of the countryside, where a duality of occupation still held sway. [. . .]

As Carew Reynel stressed in 1673 past achievements and the future potential of many new industries, he went out of his way to proclaim the benefits of diversity. 'It is an advantage to have variety of manufactures', he argued. The more numerous they were the better. Unconsciously, he echoed the words of Lord Burghley whose interest

82

in projects in the Elizabethan period had had the same end in view. Studying the new industrial pattern, contemporaries grasped another truth that found its way with increasing frequency into economic treatises: occupations which passed work through many hands benefited the nation more than those which involved one process only and passed directly from producer to consumer. In the sixteenth century men had held the opposite view. They had favoured as much direct contact as possible between producer and consumer, and in rural areas where markets were distant, and pedlars and chapmen found a niche for themselves as middlemen, they legislated strenuously to eliminate these parasites. The success of the new industries taught another philosophy which was eloquently expressed by John Corbet, chaplain to the Gloucester garrison in 1647. It was appropriate that he should write in this vein of a county where many different rural industries were flourishing in a pastoral setting: wool cloth making, silk weaving, pin and nail making, wiredrawing, card making, edge tool making, mining, wood trencher making, bottle making, and cider making, not to mention tobacco and woad growing. He viewed with sympathy and approval the rural society of Gloucestershire, unencumbered by lords, and composed rather of yeomen, farmers, and petty freeholders, and 'such as use manufactures that enrich the country and pass through the hands of a multitude'. Defoe writing in 1725 preached the same argument when applied to commerce. Describing with pride the organization of the corn trade and the hierarchy of dealers in corn from corn factors and mealmen, to maltsters and carriers, he declared it to be a wholesome rule of commerce 'that trade ought to pass through as many hands as it can'. The many labour-intensive consumer industries of the seventeenth century surely passed this test with flying colours.

As the employment of labour now ranked high as a criterion for judging the merits of new industries and agricultural occupations, a quiet revolution occurred in attitudes towards arable and pastoral husbandry. It had been axiomatic in the sixteenth century that tillage should hold first place in farming. Cereals were the staff of life and ploughmen formed the backbone of the nation. But seventeenth-century experience taught that pastoral products like cattle hides, sheepskins, wool, and timber in the long run created more employment than cereals since they provided raw materials that then passed through the hands of a multitude on their way to becoming ready-made goods.

This novel argument in favour of pastoral as against arable farming first occurred in Sir Richard Weston's writings in the 1640s, and reflected his experience in France, Holland, and Flanders where he noted that the pastoral regions were the most populous. Dairy farms of 100 acres, he claimed, employed many more hands than 100 acres of corn; sheep-keeping gave more work than corn growing, if you included the spinning and weaving of wool, and the manufacture of sheepskins. The argument subsequently became a commonplace. It was advanced by Samuel Fortrey in *England's Interest and Improvement* in 1663. It was restated by John Houghton in 1692, and rephrased by

Charles Davenant in 1699, when he claimed that pasture farming was more in the national interest than corn growing. Thus the ploughman was dethroned. It had been an article of faith with Mr. Secretary Cecil in 1601 that 'whosoever doth not maintain the plough destroys this kingdom'. The new rural economy of pastoral England with its combination of farming and industry taught another point of view.

To sum up, the new consumer industries and the success of industrial occupations combined with farming in rural areas introduced new propositions that displaced some long-established tenets of the old political economy. These were, firstly, that the home trade was as advantageous to the nation as foreign trade, if not more so, 'the people of Great Britain being the best customers to the manufacturers and traders of Great Britain', as David Macpherson roundly put it in 1760. Secondly, the more variety of these manufactures, the better; thirdly, the most beneficial manufacturing industries were those that passed through the hands of a multitude; fourthly, pasture farming benefited the nation more than corn growing. The old theories of how to increase the wealth of a nation were accommodating themselves to the new facts. The way was being paved for Adam Smith who would fundamentally and heroically revise the whole theory. [. . .]

7 JOAN THIRSK

Social Effects of Change in Agriculture

[The following passage forms the conclusion to a detailed survey of the farming regions of England in the sixteenth and seventeenth centuries. Dr. Thirsk has earlier pointed out that in terms of agriculture England may be divided between the highland north and west, where the land was mountainous, the soil poor, and the climate wet, and the lowland south and east, where the soil was rich and the climate dry. Highland England practised pasture farming, rearing and grazing livestock, and the farmers tended to live on and work their own land largely free from outside interference. Lowland England practised mixed farming, growing crops as well as fattening stock, and then tended to cultivate the land in common, and in some areas accepted a high degree of regulation from the lord of the manor. There were, of course, local variations, but there were also observable contrasts between some of the highland communities which were rather isolated from the wider commercial world, and areas of the south and east which were beginning to get involved in large-scale commercial dealings in food.]

The contrast between the communities of mixed and pasture-farming is the main general conclusion to be drawn from this examination of farming regions, and it needs no further emphasis by way of conclusion. Its significance, however, calls for further comment.

It is clear that within these two broad categories, some subdivision of the pasture-farming communities is necessary to distinguish between the open pastoral and the forest communities, for the latter, particularly those inhabiting royal forests, who had been subject until recently to forest law, possessed unique features. They had rewarding land awaiting colonization; they alone among all the regions of the kingdom offered the greatest opportunities to the land-hungry. And in the more densely populated lowlands, these were the only regions in a position to absorb immigrants.

By examining farming communities at a period when men were unusually zealous to improve their conditions, we are in an except-

From *The Agrarian History of England and Wales IV, 1500–1640*, ed. Joan Thirsk (Cambridge University Press, 1969), pp. 109–112. Footnotes have been deleted.

ionally good position for observing changes under way. It becomes apparent, then, that all three types of community, whether they inhabited forest, open pasture, or mixed farming country, were liable to change their nature. A forest economy could easily give way to a pastoral when once restrictions were lifted on the felling of trees. This in its turn did not necessarily remain a permanent state of affairs. Periodic ploughing of the pasture, as it was practised in the west Midland counties and elsewhere, prepared the land for more permanent cultivation, and in the course of generations such improvements could result in the enlargement of the arable until ploughland and pasture were more evenly balanced and a system of mixed farming evolved.

Indeed, the fact that such changes were in progress has occasionally made it difficult in this narrative to define the frontier between the three types of farming, to differentiate between the forest regions with their spacious commons and lavish timber rights, and the more open pastoral regions with their abundant commons and shrinking woodland, to differentiate between the more fertile pastoral lowlands with a disposition steadily to increase their arable, and the fielden areas which still had pastures awaiting conversion to cornland. In some places, such as the Severn valley, for example, which possessed lush meadows for feeding cattle as well as fertile fields and orchards, only local investigation in detail could establish with certainty in which category this region belongs.

Not all regions, of course, were capable of passing through these three phases of development; some were prevented by physical limitations, some were not impelled to do so owing to the absence of population pressure. But certain districts in the west Midland counties and the south and central lowlands of Lancashire afford excellent examples at this period of communities in process of transforming their land from forest to open pasture, and from open pasture to mixed arable and pasture, while the counties of the east Midlands show that this was not necessarily the end of the process. Economic circumstances could persuade communities to embark on yet another revolution, and turn their land back from mixed to pasture-farming. In counties like Northamptonshire and Leicestershire this change began in the sixteenth century. In other districts it was postponed until the later nineteenth century.

In what circumstances, and at what period, then, did these changes generate tension and cause the worst conflict? This is a question which has hardly been asked as yet. But it is clearly a valid one if we accept the proposition that certain kinds of farming specialization were associated with certain kinds of social organization. Signs of strain would be almost inevitable as the economy of the community underwent fundamental alteration and its long-standing institutions no longer fitted the new framework. Possibly this explains the large populations and onerous poverty of parts of Herefordshire, where specialization in corn-growing was at odds with some of the social institutions appropriate to pasture-farming. The outcry against enclosure in the east Mid-

86

lands, similarly, must be considered in the light of the fact that its corn-growing economy – so completely in harmony with its highly manorial-ized society – could not but be disturbed by the change to pasture-farming.

That contemporaries were aware of the distinction between the two types of community and the two kinds of farming is a conclusion difficult to avoid. 'Woodland' and 'champion' were the terms commonly used to contrast them, 'the woodland' describing the forest or pastoral country, the 'champion' describing the countryside of mixed farming in common fields. Suffolk was deemed a county 'of two several conditions of soil, the one champion, which yields for the most part sheep and some corn, the other enclosed pasture grounds employed most to grazing and dairy'. Norfolk's two regions, and the Arden and Felden regions of Warwickshire were contrasted in similar terms.

Contemporary comment, however, was not confined to contrasting the physical appearance and the farming of the two kinds of country. The contrasting temperament of the peoples inhabiting each also seems to have been familiar to sixteenth-century writers. As Norden explained it: 'the people bred amongst woods are naturally more stubborn and uncivil than in the champion countries'. John Aubrey described the woodlanders as 'the mean people [who] live lawless, nobody to govern them, they care for nobody, having no dependence on anybody'. Lord Burghley also alluded to the phenomenon when he declared that the clothworkers, most of whom, after all, were inhabi-tants of pastoral and woodland country, were 'of worse condition to be quietly governed than the husbandmen'.

This independence of spirit was displayed in the revolts against disafforestation under Charles I in Wiltshire and Gloucestershire, for example, and also in the battles waged by the fenlanders, another pastoral community, when they fought the drainage of their commons. In the light of this evidence it is also worth considering what support these people contributed to other disturbances in the realm which were not connected with enclosure – the Pilgrimage of Grace, for example, which recruited followers from the valleys of Cumberland and West-morland, and Ket's rebellion, which started in the wood-pasture region of Norfolk. And some attention needs to be given to two comments on the religious inclinations of people living in the forests. Of the forests of Wiltshire, John Aubrey remarked, 'It is a sour, woodsere country, and inclines people to contemplation. So that, the Bible, and ease, for it is all now upon dairy grassing and clothing, set there with a-running and reforming.' The Weald of Kent was described as 'that dark country, which is the receptacle of all schism and rebellion'. Was it generally true that pastoral regions were also the most fertile seedbeds for Puritanism and dissent?

8 ALAN EVERITT

The Changing Pattern of Labouring Life

[At the beginning of the seventeenth century about one-quarter or one-third of the population of the countryside were farm labourers, a proportion which increased significantly in the course of the century. In the following passage Professor Everitt considers how their lives and attitudes were affected by political, social and economic changes in this period.]

During the seventeenth century the unity of peasant labouring society, and the protection afforded to the labourer by the customary order of society, were beginning to break down. That unity had no doubt never been complete, and its basis was not finally destroyed till the eighteenth or nineteenth century. But it was probably in the latter half of our own period, with the growth of population, the decline in real wages, and the progress of commercial farming, that some of the most distinctive changes in labouring society took their rise. By the time the Civil War broke out, the labouring community was manifestly split by a twofold cleavage within its own ranks.

In part this cleavage was an economic one. As the labouring population increased, the pressure on land became continually more acute, an ever-growing army of landless labourers came into being, and the distinction between rich and poor labourers became more pronounced. A minority of farmworkers, still possessed of sizeable holdings or valuable common rights, were enabled to profit by the new commercial openings of the age and work their way up into the ranks of the husbandmen; while the middle and lower ranks of cottagers were slowly losing their landed rights and sinking to the level of mere wage-workers. The former were able to add new rooms to their cottages, invest an increasing proportion of their income in domestic comforts, purchase a few pieces of good joined furniture, and leave a modest competence to their sons and widows. The latter inhabited flimsy cots and hovels, fed 'very hardly with oaten bread, sour whey, and goats' milk,' lived very close to the poverty line, and in time of dearth sank far beneath it.

The cleavage in labouring society was not only economic, however. It also consisted in a growing distinction between the working com-

From *The Agrarian History of England and Wales IV 1500–1640,* ed. Joan Thirsk (Cambridge University Press, 1967), pp. 462–465. Footnotes have been deleted.

munities in forest and in fielden areas. In the nucleated villages characteristic of the latter, forms of society were often deeply rooted, social classes were relatively stable and distinct, manorial customs fairly rigid, political habits comparatively orderly, and the labourer's outlook deeply imbued with the prevalent preconceptions of church and manor-house. In these fielden areas labourers often tended to remain rooted in the same district from one generation to the next: working on the same farm, specializing in the same crafts, passing on the same customary skills to their children, and more or less freely accepting their dependence on squire and parson. Few of them were really well-off, their holdings were usually small, and their common rights often negligible; but the very poor were less numerous than in remote woodland settlements, and manorial charity was probably more abundant.

In the isolated hamlets characteristic of forest settlements, by contrast, the roots of society were often relatively shallow, the population was largely composed of a single social class, the customs of the manor were sometimes vague or difficult to enforce, the instincts of the poor were anything but law-abiding, and the authority of church and manor-house seemed remote. In these areas, labouring society frequently consisted, on one hand, of a core of indigenous peasants with sizeable holdings and a relatively high standard of living; and, on the other, of an ever-growing number of very poor squatters and wanderers, often evicted from lately closed fielden villages, 'given to little or no kind of labour . . . dwelling far from any church or chapel, and . . . as ignorant of God or of any civil course of life as the very savages amongst the infidels . . .' In consequence of their semi-vagrant origins, many forest labourers were less rooted in their own community than their fielden cousins; more willing to migrate at certain seasons in search of employment elsewhere; more independent and eager to take up the cudgels in their own defence; and more prone to pick up new ways and new ideas. It was primarily in heath and forest areas, visited as they were by travelling badgers and tinkers, that the vagrant religion of the Independents found a footing in rural communities; it was principally thence, there is reason to think, that the godly (or not so godly) troops of the Parliamentarian armies were recruited during the Civil War. It was also in heaths and forests that the millenarian leaders of the Interregnum, the Methodist preachers of the eighteenth century, and later messianic sects like that of John Nichols Tom in East Kent, found many of their most devoted adherents.

Essentially the difference between fielden and forest societies was that of a relatively static and a relatively mobile way of life. Of the latent jealousy between them, the last embers continued to smoulder on until the closing years of the nineteenth century. In Oxfordshire, at the end of Queen Victoria's reign, the hamlet people of 'Lark Rise', though then bereft of all their common rights, still maintained an attitude of independence and mild animosity towards the parent village of 'Fordlow', with its parish church, its Tory parson, and its decrepit little manor-house; while the labourers of the village itself, still sunning themselves in the fading rays of parish gentility, retorted by calling the hamlet children, 'That gypsy lot from Lark Rise'.

Hand in hand with the break-up in the unity of labouring society itself went a decline in the protection afforded to the labourer by the customary social order. There was of course no sudden or universal change in that order; traditional ideas of social duty still lingered on for generations after the end of the period. But in some districts, at least, a definite decline in the sense of responsibility to dependants and a widening psychological gulf between gentry and peasantry was coming into evidence. In newly enclosed parishes, and in the eastern counties with their relatively advanced economy and acute land-hunger, these developments seem to have been particularly pronounced. In Norfolk some poor people apparently felt 'that the gentlemen had all the farms and cattle in the country in their hands, and poor men could have no living...' In Suffolk a sharp linguistic division between gentry and peasantry was already emerging, and the 'honest country toiling villager' would 'many times let slip some strange different-sounding terms, no ways intelligible to any of civil education...' In Essex the abominable Lord Rich actually wished 'none else to be put to school, but only gentlemen's children,' since the poor were fitted for nothing but to be unlettered ploughmen and artificers: a sentiment which Archbishop Cranmer, to his credit, indignantly repudiated.

With the Civil War these social cleavages were suddenly deepened. The reins of traditional authority were inevitably relaxed, the bonds of society weakened, and the gentry driven into harsh repressive measures to restore order. The strict enforcement of military discipline, more-over, and the herding together of social classes in cramped quarters with the king or with Fairfax, unavoidably accentuated those status symbols by which rich and poor were distinguished. With rival armies plundering the countryside, and with thousands of estates under sequestration, many labourers could not tell to whom their rents, and their loyalty, were due. With many squires taking up arms for Charles I or Parliament, and leaving their home locality for years on end, the direct interest of many landlords in farming ceased, and absenteeism became, first a military necessity, then a social habit. As a consequence, an attitude of supercilious contempt for social inferiors developed, amongst both cavaliers and puritans, which must have filled old-fashioned squires like Sir George Sondes with shame and dismay. In a word, the Civil War and the Interregnum dealt a death-blow to the age-old conception of society as a hierarchy of interdependent orders, and went far to replace it by the notion of society as a series of independent and necessarily antagonistic classes.

From the Civil War onwards, the preconceptions of labouring society thus became increasingly alienated from those of the country at large. In all the cant of contemporary demagogues about 'the people', Hodge was the one individual whose aspirations were never considered: it was scarcely proper that he should have any. Even the well-meant lucubrations of his few champions, like William Walwyn, displayed no real understanding of his problems: the wish of that London silk-merchant 'that there was neither pale, hedge, nor ditch in the whole nation' must have struck village labourers, of all people, as strangely absurd. But for another two centuries Hodge's feelings necessarily remained unspoken and unknown; for his was a way of life whose secret springs became more and more unintelligible to polite society. Yet nowadays, in the mid-twentieth century, as we watch the autumnal sunshine cast lengthening shadows across the meadows of a Pennine valley, or the deserted cattle-pastures of a Wealden farm, it is but just to remember how much we still owe to the labours of the Tudor and Stuart farmworker. For the fact that 'things are not so ill with you and me as they might have been, is half owing to the number who lived faithfully a hidden life, and rest in unvisited tombs'.

9 CHARLES WILSON

Economics and Politics
in the Seventeenth Century

[The following article is reprinted here for two reasons: for its intrinsic interest, and because it is a substantial, critical review of one of the set books on the course for which this anthology was created, Christopher Hill's *The Century of Revolution 1603–1714*. It should be noted that in the latest edition of *The Century of Revolution*, Professor Hill has taken several of Professor Wilson's criticisms on points of detail into account. Also, where page references to the original are given these have been followed with the new page references in square brackets.]

[. . .]Mr Christopher Hill is one of the most stimulating of the seventeenth-century historians. His recent books – *Puritanism and Revolution* (1958) and *The Economic Problems of the Church* (1956) – combine a Marxist approach with an insight and sympathy that come from years of dedicated inquiry. Like his latest book, *The Century of Revolution*, they make it plain that the Civil War lies at the centre of his interests. Brisk, clear and readable, the latest study is likely to be widely read. One can imagine that many a student, bewildered by the complexities of older works, will turn with relief to an account that provides attractively neat explanations of the upheavals of the seventeenth century. For 'explanation' is Mr Hill's declared purpose, and he has never concealed his opinion that there is a kind of history that conspicuously fails to give the 'explanation' at which he aims. Of Miss Wedgwood's history of the Civil War he wrote that it was 'a narrative, not an explanation. It tells us all about the war except what they fought each other for – Miss Wedgwood's refusal to analyse makes it impossible to see below the surface of mere events.' By contrast, Mr Hill's method is to explain – as current jargon has it – 'in depth'; to see politics and social movements as the reflexion of larger economic movements of change, and economics as in turn controlled by the distribution of political power. 'Narrative' history is accordingly reduced to four rather casual pages of 'what happened'. Yet from the final analysis the Civil War and its effects emerge as central. This formed 'the turning-point in the evolution of capitalism', eliminating the 'one barrier' to the entrepreneur and a *laissez-faire* economy. Here was a victory for the 'propertied classes', followed in 1660 by a compromise between Cavaliers and Roundheads 'directed against the lower classes'. 1688 saw

From *The Historical Journal*, V (1962), pp. 80–92. Footnotes have been deleted.

a second turning-point as the 'industrialists' defeated the monopolistic ends of the great commercial capitalists of the trading corporations. At both points political revolution deriving from fundamentally economic causes broke up the established order. Plainly Parliamentary victory in the first Civil War is crucial to Mr Hill's reading of seventeenth-century history.

In his *Puritanism and Revolution* Mr Hill took Messrs Brunton and Pennington to task for contenting themselves with an analysis of loyalties in the Long Parliament that did nothing to explain why the Civil War was fought, why large numbers of men were roused 'to heroic activity and sacrifice' about 'issues of principle' (pp. 20, 23). 'The Civil War', he then sensibly remarked, 'did after all take place . . .' (ibid. p. 24). But is there not another question? If the Civil War was so decisive economically, politically, socially, is it of no importance to establish how it was waged? Why and how did the Parliamentary forces manage to win, and the Royalists to lose, the Civil War? In the *Century of Revolution* the decisive phase of the Civil War itself – from 1642 to 1647 – is dismissed in two pages. What of any 'explanation' of the Civil War itself? 'If we want to understand the Civil War,' Mr Hill writes, 'a glance at the maps on p. 122 [p. 103] is far more important than the most elaborate analysis of members of Parliament.' The two small sketch-maps purport to show the geographical nature of what Mr Hill calls 'support' for the Parliament and the King on 1 May 1643 and the end of 1645 respectively. 'Support' for Parliament came, he says, from 'the economically advanced south and east of England', support for the King from the economically backward ones of the north and west. To this he adds one or two more suggestions: that the local 'industrial areas' (as he calls them) were for Parliament, the 'agricultural' ones for the King. Thus in Yorkshire it was Bradford which 'forced a reluctant Fairfax' to lead them into action. Since Lord Fairfax does not appear in Mr Hill's index, this presumably refers to Tom Fairfax. That few of the later leaders on either side were itching to precipitate war is a commonplace that needs no further proof. But no source is quoted to substantiate this implication that the Rider of the White Horse, whose zeal, courage and military prowess are beyond doubt, needed to be prodded into action by eager capitalists. It was, in fact, the other way round. Fairfax had to strain every nerve to rouse support in an area where most of the cards were stacked against Parliament. But the picture takes shape. 'The ports were all for Parliament.' Were they? London, of course. Hull also, but more, it would seem because of Hotham's hatred of Strafford than because of the loyalties of the citizens, which were evenly divided. At Bristol Parliamentary sympathies were uppermost but there was strong support for the King, and Bristol served the Royal cause well from its capture by Rupert early in the war to its surrender in September 1645. So did Falmouth and Chester. Exeter, with its small but useful port of Topsham was a Royalist centre. Newcastle was the funnel through which the northern Cavaliers got valuable foreign help, which Mr Hill says they were denied. The defection of the Fleet was not the social revolt of professional 'tarpaulins': naval loyalty had been badly strained by Charles's unpopular pro-Spanish policy. The genuine popularity of Warwick and sheer confusion did the rest. That the loss of London, Hull and the Fleet was a grievous blow to Charles is true, but these events do not of themselves explain his failure. Even less is it to be explained in terms of the other military factor to which Mr Hill attaches great importance: the performance of the London trained bands who were 'the most reliable Parliamentary troops in the early stages of the war'; which in turn presumably reflects his belief that Calvinism turned out 'the most effective fighters' (p. 168) [p. 145]. Twice he credits them with 'checking the royalist advance at Turnham Green and preserving the army at Newbury'. It is no doubt attractive to think of these middle and working class regiments as playing a decisive part in the war. But did they? The battle of Turnham Green was never fought. It was not valour but numbers that frightened the impressionable Charles, who promptly retired to Hounslow. The account of their valorous stand at Newbury rests mainly on Serjeant Foster's patriotic apology for his regiment in that battle. It is not altogether easy to reconcile with his earlier confessions that it was a complaining and mutinous collection that marched west – even more mutinous, it has been expertly said, than Hopton's Irish. In November 1643 the Westminster regiment refused orders and when directed to attack deserted with loud cries of Home! Home! It seems more than likely that at Newbury the trained bands were preserved by the efficient deployment of the Parliamentary artillery. Even Foster's account breathes gratified relief at being preserved by the Almighty, rather than pride in superior skill or valour. Perhaps a just verdict is Colonel Burne's conclusion that the prowess of the London trained bands 'seems to have been somewhat exaggerated'.

The picture that emerges from Mr Hill's account is simple but unsatisfying: an England divided geographically between an advanced economic region attached to advanced political causes, producing a valorous, eager volunteer army, against a retarded region led by reluctant semi-feudal commanders. This, as far as I can judge from Mr Hill's further three pages of 'explanation' is his version of the royal defeat. Well over half a century ago, Trevelyan wrote of the Civil War that it was 'on the whole a war of North and West against South and East'. But he added a saving clause:

> . . . the North never felt that it was engaged in a death struggle with the South, nor were West and East roused to battle by conscious intention to subdue one another. In every shire there were two parties, of which the weaker only waited opportunity to join hands with an invading force from the other side of England. For in motive it was a war not of class or of districts, but of ideas. Hence there was a nobler speculative enthusiasm among the chiefs and their followers, but less readiness to fight among the masses of the population, than

in other contests that have torn great nations.

This still seems to me to tell us more than Mr Hill's maps: and nothing in it is contradicted by more recent research.

Nevertheless, the valour of tradesmen or mechanics apart, the theory that victory was assured to the Roundheads by superior material resources is not to be dismissed lightly. It has been accepted quite lately by the authors of what is far the best analysis of the tactics of the Civil War yet written: *The Great Civil War*, by Col Burne and Col Young. On the face of it, their argument corresponds closely to Mr Hill's. But a little analysis reveals a major fallacy in the belief that the outcome of the war was determined, *ab initio*, by what are called 'resources'. This is to ignore a vital period during which the whole issue of victory or defeat was in the balance. In their conclusion, the authors of this excellent book descry four strands of war (as they call them): leaders, the led, morale and resources. 'The Led', they describe as being 'fairly similar', 'all of the same blood', with a leaning towards Cavalier superiority. Under the heading of 'morale', they see the Cavaliers with an initial superiority which was slowly lost to the Parliament. But Parliament they explain, enjoyed a great preponderance in resources, and 'this fourth strand had greater effect than the other three strands combined', so that by late 1644 it made the issue of the war 'as nearly a foregone conclusion as anything in the realm of war can be'. The late date is worth noting. So too is their conclusion about leadership, for from this issues their conclusion about resources. In the matter of leadership, they see 'a glaring contrast throughout the greater part of the war. Whereas on the Royalist side, there was *unity of command, under one supreme and unquestioned head* [my italics], on the side of Parliament the war was conducted by a committee, consisting mainly of civilians who naturally were ignorant of military strategy... Furthermore, the Royalist commander was the sovereign, respected and implicitly obeyed.' As a commander, Charles is credited with keeping 'steadily before his eyes the primary principle of war that the essential target is the enemy's main field army...' together with a 'resolution and determination – Charles never abandoned hope; his optimism was unquenchable, and often unjustifiable – it was also encouraged by Lord Digby who even after Rowton Heath was writing letters full of confidence and hope'. [. . .]

That the Roundhead conduct of affairs was a fumbling business it is not necessary to question. This certainly contributed to Charles's early successes. The Cavaliers won (as Messrs Burne and Young point out) seven out of the sixteen main battles of the war all in the earlier stages. After Edgehill, Charles sat down before Banbury in that state of continuous indecision that was his natural posture, refusing Rupert's offer to push on to London. Arrived at Turnham Green, his 'prudence' (not the valour of the London trained bands) again supervened and he lost one of the biggest chances of the war by being dilatory and indecisive. The decision to besiege Gloucester instead of marching on London was another example of the same fatal indecision mixed with obstinacy. At the first Battle of Newbury, Charles's decision to withdraw instead of inflicting a final defeat on Essex probably determined the course of the war. As Messrs Burne and Young themselves put it, 'Had he [Charles] decided to bluff it out next day, it is now by no means certain that Essex would have continued with the fight'. But at Newbury as at Turnham Green it was apparent that the capacity of bluff was no part of Charles's make-up as a commander. At Cheriton the caution of the indifferent Ruthven, his chief of staff, was allowed to overtop the zeal of Hopton, one of his best commanders, and again disaster followed. Even so, in the summer and the autumn of 1643, the advantages had nearly all still rested with the King. There were risings for the King in Kent and Shropshire. At King's Lynn the Royalists held out for a month. Lynn could have proved the centre from which the eastern Association might have been overrun if Newcastle had not been too obsessed with the disastrous siege of Hull. Charles's army was well quartered, when the enemy were in want and without shelter. His forces lay between them and London. Only the fatal decision to ignore Rupert's advice to wait brought disaster. On the field of battle, Charles's claims to ability seem negligible, unless we allow his gallantry at Lostwithiel when it was probably too late to retrieve victory.

That Charles possessed courage is beyond doubt: optimism too. But in a commander-in-chief these are not the only necessities. The combination of general optimism with tactical caution was fatal. Worse than anything he did or failed to do in the field of battle were Charles's faults as strategic organizer, which reduced to a shambles any chance that the Royalist cause might be led and decided (as Col Burne thinks it was) by 'a single and unchallenged supreme commander'. On the contrary, the story of the Royalist strategy is an unbroken series of decisions taken only to be countermanded, commands created only to be invalidated, intrigues that went unchecked until it was too late, dissensions fostered by weakness and delay. It was this 'fatal facility and weakness' [as Warburton called it] 'so often and so pertinaciously misconstrued into perfidy and crime' that wrecked the Royalist hopes in the first two years of the war. Even when he was roused to some energetic action Charles invariably compromised it by half measures that nullified the effects of his decision.

This personal defect in Charles was all the more disastrous because there was not until late in 1644 any acknowledged commander-in-chief. Theoretically, strategy was determined by a Council of War, with Ruthven as a kind of military chief of staff. In practice, there was perpetual chaos and dissension. Of the generals in the field – and indeed off it too – Rupert was unquestionably the greatest. Time after time, Rupert's strategic judgement proved correct. Time after time his plans were rejected, or worse still, accepted only to be changed when his back was turned. After Edgehill Rupert would have pressed on to London: would have pursued Essex after Newbury. He was not allowed to do so.

The Oxford campaign in the spring of 1644 was wrecked because no sooner had he gone north to relieve Newcastle than his plan for reinforcing the west midland garrison was abandoned, and Abingdon was lost. Marston Moor was the direct result of Charles's disastrous letter commanding and conjuring Rupert to relieve York. Rupert, well aware of likely recriminations, carried the letter with him till his dying day. The decision to attack at Naseby was the work of Digby and Ashburnham, those 'two hopeful and inexperienced civilians', as Miss Wedgwood has called them, who saw yet another chance to thwart Rupert, left as always to make the best of a strategy he deplored. On the field, at the crisis of the battle it was Charles's failure to throw in his cavalry reserves that lost the day. And with Naseby the contest was virtually over. Throughout all these sordid and miserable episodes, Rupert had the consistent support of the best men amongst the Royalists – the gallant Hopton, Will Legge, Nicholas, the Duke of Richmond. But he faced the opposition of a group round the King and Queen, whose talents for intrigue were strictly professional, even if as soldiers they were amateurs: Digby, gay, optimistic, irresponsible, the worst of Charles's advisers, who 'promised all things and succeeded in none', Wilmot, Percy, Ashburnham. Then there was the Queen, the arch intriguer and Rupert's worst enemy. No one has ever calculated what was lost by the diversion of resources to escort her on her absurd perambulations about the Kingdom. Her arrival at Oxford put an end to any hope of either peace or victory.

It may be argued in defence of Charles that his position was hopeless from the start because of the semi-independence of his semi-feudal local commanders like Newcastle, whose troops consisted to a large extent of his local tenantry and supporters: that Rupert was a foreigner, without lands or followers, too young to be made commander-in-chief. This will not hold water. In the end, when it was too late, Charles did appoint Rupert commander-in-chief. If it could be done in 1644 it could have been done earlier and there is plenty of evidence to show that with Charles's firm backing Rupert could have easily made his authority unquestioned. But this did not happen. The Royalist command was, through all the crucial stages when Parliament's own affairs were in a catastrophic muddle, divided and distracted, the very reverse of that unified command described by Messrs Burne and Young. To quote Warburton again, it was '... the disuniting of the army to conciliate private and petty interests ... the want of one far-reaching, resolute and commanding mind to rouse, concentrate and direct the vast energies and powerful elements combined in the Royal Army, that was truly wanting'. [...]

The theory that the unequal distribution of resources and support doomed the Cavaliers to inevitable failure must be rejected. Economic resources do not, by themselves, win wars. Mr Hill's maps and analysis of 'support' explain nothing in the early decisive phases of the war. It was the failure in leadership, the dissensions and intrigues in the high command, that prevented the King from exploiting the considerable tactical victories he won, and dispersed and dissipated his resources. Only this gave the Parliamentary command time to organize itself. While the bold and brilliant Fairfax held off the enemy with one hand, Cromwell was busy organizing and training the Army, though it is important to remember that he was never an Army Commander in the first Civil War, and that he may have been amongst those generals who (in the famous phrase) 'took to their heels' at Marston Moor. But slowly the superior *potential* available to the Parliament was made actual. In the interval while that was being done, Charles lost the war: and – to avoid any misunderstanding of the purpose of this review – let it be added, a very good thing too.

The theory that 1660 represented a 'compromise' of the victorious class with their defeated 'class' adversary, directed against the lower classes (p. 308) [p. 264] derives from the theory that the Civil War was in origin a class struggle. Closely related to this is the theory that resources ineluctably determined the victory. Neither the parent theory nor its offspring stands up to examination. One error has merely generated another. The Marxist theory that the Civil War represented the bourgeois revolution, with parties following closely economic and social lines, has been set out succinctly by Mr Dobb. Mr Hill's account follows the orthodoxy but with variations forced upon it by historical facts. The dominant economic classes, finding their path obstructed by government, broke the absolute monarchy by a bourgeois revolution. This cleared the way for a reunion of the parties divided in the Civil War; a two class society emerged, with a *laissez-faire* economy and a new system of government in which the propertied classes determined policy by pulling all the strings. But Mr Hill knows too much history to propound, or expect others to accept, the 'class' interpretation in its primitive form. The explanatory process, therefore, is not so much devoted to explaining 'what happened' as to explaining why Mr Hill's chosen instrument of explanation – class interest and solidarity, provoking class hatreds and the class struggle – breaks down at all the crucial points: why the ruling class was divided in the 1640's, still divided in 1660, why the lower orders cheered on the Seven Bishops at the Revolution. The necessity for much of this 'explanation' derives from the assumption, which Mr Hill seems to take for granted, that class solidarity based on economic interest is the natural state of affairs in seventeenth-century England. In reality the world of seventeenth-century politics was one of the multiple factions, based on personal, family and local sympathies and antipathies. These tended to polarize round a two-*party* organization, an entirely different matter from a two-*class* organization. We need only look at the social structure of a small part of the gentry (as Professor Trevor Roper has done) or at the gang structure of the City merchants (as Mr Price and Mr Letwin have done) to see that the notion of class homogeneity is a myth. In rejecting political narrative in favour of history 'in depth' Mr Hill has merely substituted one type of historical oversimplification for another.

In the process, history has been chopped into pieces not only by topics but by periods. Where older historians used to divide by reigns, Mr Hill divides by 'revolutions'. The attempt to correlate political, economic and social history means that dates like 1640, 1660, 1688, acquire, or have to be assigned, economic and social as well as political significance. The weakness of this is that vital underlying economic trends are obscured, vital continuities of policy suppressed, to suit a pre-determined chronology of socio-political development. Thus the crisis of the 1620's is interpreted in terms of the shortcomings of Stuart government, which was a part, but only a part, of the story. The organic and fundamental economic problems faced by government – the changing structure of England's foreign trade, the collapse of the Old Draperies, the increase of population within a still rigid economy – are mentioned. Their crucial importance is obscured in an account which concentrates upon James's picturesque and corrupt bargain with Cockayne and the tycoons. This, as Dr Supple has recently shown, is only an incident in the economic fluctuations of the age, whose complexity would have taxed the resources of any government, however businesslike. Nevertheless, early Stuart government was not without some claim to pioneer work on economic policy. The Commission on Trade of 1622 was a watershed both in thought and policy. The prohibition of wool export, which aimed to keep prices low for the local manufactures, dates effectively from this period. It formed, as even its later opponents recognized, one of the two principal pillars of the regulated economy they later called the mercantile system. Nobody who has examined the petitions from trade and industry that streamed into the Privy Council and its *ad hoc* committees in these years, or the measures taken to deal with them, can suppose that government was any less 'responsive to the interests of trade' than its successors in office whom Mr Hill credits with more commercial ideas. That it was less wise or successful is a different matter.

By Cromwell's time (we are told) things had changed. Cromwell's foreign policy 'was dominated by economic considerations'. Why then did he wind up the successful Dutch War in 1654 and resist business pressure to start it again? Mr Hill's attempt to represent the treaty of 1654 as a victory for 'trade' is unconvincing. Cromwell forced the Dutch, he says, to pay tribute for fishing in English waters – 'a matter no previous English Government had been able to secure'. But Cromwell did nothing of the kind. On the contrary, Cromwell deliberately dropped the claim in the interests of a reasonable settlement with a potential Protestant ally. The Dutch got a peace on far better terms than they might have expected after a disastrous war. As Clarendon points out, the merchant warmongers always believed that Cromwell could have 'totally subdued' the Dutch in 1654 if he had not deliberately chosen to subordinate economic to political and religious aims.

The continuity of policy and ideas on foreign trade, maintained by successive governments faced with similar problems of national responsibility, has been clearly brought out in another study which Mr Hill quotes with approval: Dr Hinton's *The Eastland Trade and the*

Commonwealth in the Seventeenth Century (1959). But Dr Hinton's main conclusion does not at all bear out Mr Hill's contention that the nature of government 'response' to traders' demands altered. On the contrary, it concludes that the relationship between successive governments and the Eastland Company were based on 'ancient and conventional ideas about the common weal which the subjects abundantly shared and *which easily transcended the interests of particular groups'* [my italics].

The idea of policy evolving by revolutionary jerks as successive governments responded to the demands of dominant economic classes seems to lie at the heart of Mr Hill's historical 'explanation'. But to deny to government any autonomous, or at any rate arbitrating, role in policy leaves many major problems unsolved and insoluble. How and why was a House of Commons, where trade was represented by only some 10 per cent of the membership, persuaded repeatedly to pass, maintain and strengthen laws to keep down wool prices, and to maintain the land tax as by far the largest single source of income? If fiscal policy was merely a wangle by men of property, why was land taxed so heavily? If Parliament was merely a struggle decided by the weight of money-bags, how were the great trading companies eased out of their monopolies? Because, Mr Hill argues, they were opposed by the rising power of the 'industrialists'. But where was the 'industrialist' – the title itself is anachronistic – who could outbid great merchants and financiers like Child, Heathcote and Janssen? And if the effect of the Navigation Acts was to divert capital from investment in industry generally and retard industrial development (p. 213) [p. 183] (a doubtful proposition to say the least of it) how had 'industrialists' suddenly become so influential? Petitioning the Privy Council was the traditional method of bringing pressure – not least from manufacturers – on government. Consideration of only one party to such transactions – industry – does nothing to explain the increased efficacy of that pressure, especially when, according to Mr Hill's argument, the industrial interest was being neglected or starved of capital.

The improvement in economic conditions later in the century owed much to improved economic conditions generally after the Peace of Westphalia. In the altered conditions, England, with an increasingly diversified economy and a strong navy, was able to enlarge her share of trade. More coherent policies helped, as Mr Hill recognizes. But the alteration of policy was not simply due to the more effective lobbying power of new economic groups, exercised through Parliament. Unless there had been a different, wider and more experienced assessment of the nation's economic needs by government and informed (not necessarily self-interested) opinion, the lobbying might well have produced mere chaos. Along with the changes in the economic and political context went a change in the relationship of the executive and its immediate advisers. In James's time, the Privy Council had often shown itself wiser but weaker than its master. Few things were more important and few have been less investigated than the influence of a succession of Crown servants of high intelligence after the Restoration

– Downing, Pepys, Blathwayte, Newton, Locke, Davenant and many others. Such men were able to draw on a wealth of economic debate that was the outcome of successive economic crises, and to bring the immense inherited power and patronage of the executive to bear on economic expansion. Theirs was not merely a response to the irresistible or obvious demands of dominant economic groups. Parliamentary sovereignty should not be confused with effective government. Lobbies rarely got everything they wanted. The Navigation Acts satisfied none of those who petitioned for action completely. Often the function of government was to resist pressure groups as much as to satisfy them. Downing defeated the bankers, whom he hated as the King's enemies. Charles, in person and through the ministers, urged war for years against the East India Directors, Child and Papillon especially, as Whigs displeasing to his person (not Tories as Mr Hill supposes). The enlarged Council of Trade, with its fringe of merchant advisers, disintegrated in 1670 because Charles came to the conclusion that its merchant members were 'a pack of knaves' incapable of giving him the disinterested advice on policy he needed.

Politics and government did not operate simply as a function of bloc interests, nor can economic development be explained in terms of political arrangements that altered radically within short periods. Mr Hill recognizes that social mobility frequently brought with it an identity of interest between land and trade. But it also needs to be recognized that the merchant 'community' had no community sense. The great tycoons were always split into warring cliques, as the East India, Turkey and Atlantic traders were. On few issues did any economic class present a united front, so that, except when the Government behaved with crass stupidity and aroused inter-class opposition, it could rely on its traditional prestige and immense powers of patronage to get its way. Generally, governments acted from a variety of motives that varied from a genuine concern for the national welfare to a natural desire for convenience and a quiet life. Administrative convenience was as powerful a determinant of tax policy as class interest. Excise appealed to every politician from Pym to Walpole because it was easy to collect and because there was an obvious limit to the Customs revenue, more than because it suited bourgeois interests. Against that consideration, even the concerted opposition of that powerful gang of 'industrialists' (almost the only ones to qualify plausibly for the title) – the London brewers – was impotent. To tie the revolutions of 1640–60 and of 1688 to changes in the power of economic interests is to attribute a homogeneity to them which they did not possess. The one kind of opinion no seventeenth-century government could safely ignore was religious, and many of Mr Hill's pages bear unacknowledged witness to the fact.

Mr Hill wisely enjoins his readers not to force later categories of analysis on his century of revolution. But in spite of refinements and concessions, the essentially Victorian structure repeatedly shows through his own synthesis. He remains as enchanted by the explanatory power of Marxist economics as Mr Betjeman by St Saviours, Aberdeen Park. Thus the political influence of 'property' is invariably discussed in terms that remind one of more recent Marxist assessments of the political influence of industrial capital, whereas it was in fact the vestigial remains of the medieval equating of political power with land. The key quotations that justify Mr Hill's pin-pointing of the Civil War's central economic importance come from Mr Lipson's text-book, a synthetic compendium in many respects outdated by recent research. Figures of wages and prices come from Thorold Rogers's history of 1887. Recent research that threatens to disturb the neat pattern of historical evolution dictated by the older orthodoxy gets short shrift. Thus, much is made of the importance of the transfer of land during the interregnum from the Royalists to the new property seekers. This is followed, somewhat contradictorily, by the admission that after all the bulk of the Royalist landlords stayed put. Mr Hill does not mention Miss Thirsk's important article which shows that for the most part, the *status quo ante* was restored before 1660. Professor Jordan's study of charity as mainly a function of the social responsibility of merchants, gets a brief acknowledgement (pp. 26 and 103) [pp. 20 and 88]. But it should not be forgotten that a whole generation of historians who persisted in regarding the seventeenth-century merchants as a hard-fisted, socially irresponsible class who subordinated social welfare to ideas of economic nationalism have been put totally out of countenance by Professor Jordan's discoveries. One might have expected that the simple political deductions implied by diagrams 2 and 3 (based on Thorold Rogers's figures) would have been accompanied by some reference to Professor Jordan's total scepticism about their value as a source of information about social standards. There is none. In any case, Professor Jordan is quickly forgotten. By the later years of the century, the poor have been abandoned, and the only hope is held to be in trade unionism (p. 154) [p. 131]. But who in 1700 were still founding schools, apprenticeships, preaching high wages? Was it not still merchants like Child, Firmin, Cary, Nelson, Mackworth? The most detailed analysis of Professor Jordan's statistics comes in appendix C and its purpose is significantly different. Between 1601 and 1640, Mr Hill notes, the total of charitable benefactions was over £1 million. By 1660 it fell to £387,000. But for Mr Hill the interest lies in 'the significant decline (in the second period) in the relative contributions of the nobility . . . and the equally significant rise of the contributions of yeomen'. Significant? The proportionate decline of noble contributions was 2.43 per cent: the rise in yeomen contributions 1.25 per cent. Are we intended to infer that these risible fractions confirm the old thesis of a declining aristocracy and of a rising yeomanry? Why not go on to infer that the increase in the gentry's offerings by 0.77 per cent supports the theory that the gentry were in the ascendant? The treatment is nevertheless revealing. New discovery has to be trimmed, new wine put back into the old Marxist bottle. But these manipulations are not limited to modern work. The essence of late seventeenth-century economic thought is summarized on p. 272 [p. 233] thus: 'the poor were unproductive, the rich alone productive'. This is, of course, a caricature of a generation which first formulated the concept of labour as a factor in production. No topic occupied thinkers of the age so much as the problem of training the potential labour force represented by the poor. The insouciant handling of detailed economic problems such as this makes it difficult to take seriously the analysis (on the same page) of the alleged disequilibrium between trade and luxury and what is called 'industry'. Subsidized shipping, overseas trade, aristocratic building and luxury court expenditure (we are told) absorbed capital which might otherwise have been 'invested' in industry. But were not shipbuilding, housebuilding, with their ancillary industries, and all the industries which worked for the upper and middle class market, to say nothing of industries like sugar boiling, tobacco cutting, and a score of industries that depended on the import trade for raw materials, 'industry'? Has Mr Hill read *The Fable of the Bees*?

So back to the fundamental problem: the relationship between economic interests and policies, economic classes, political action and political and economic results. The Civil War remains crucial. The problem, Mr Hill says, is to decide how Charles I 'got a party at all', to explain why his supporters in and out of the House of Commons increased after May 1641. The formation of a royal party was due, he suggests, to 'shifts of opinion among the propertied classes'. But why 'propertied'? Was it not that when it came to the sticking-point, men of all classes were drawn back into allegiance to the monarchy – often in spite of the person and qualities of the King himself? Neither the formation of the Royal party, nor the course of the war to 1644, nor the settlement of 1660 or 1688 can be satisfactorily explained in terms of socio-economic movements that give at most only a peripheral importance to non-economic factors, including personal loyalties and antipathies and beliefs that a later generation may (if it likes) regard as irrational or superstitious. Anglicanism emerges as a function of the interest of patrons, tithe impropriators and avaricious bishops, all with their hands deep in the till. Lancelot Andrewes comes on stage only to feature in a rather good anecdote about James I and taxation. *Paradise Lost*, by a tortuous process, becomes a reflexion of the new (?) attitude to marriage as a function of money and property. Mr Hill ends his book by commending to us the actions of the men of the seventeenth century. Yet one looks in vain for a single case where a man of action in that century is credited with a human virtue or a human capacity of decisive historic importance. Even Cromwell's claim to applause rests on his love of the arts and his openmindedness in allowing himself to be painted warts and all. No doubt the older historians were too little conscious of the social context within which the historic individual acted. Here he is too often reduced to a mere reflexion of social forces. The result is not to explain greatness but to explain it away. Significantly the one paragraph of unstinted admiration for an individual is devoted to Harrington for fathering the idea that history could provide 'laws relating to the behaviour of human beings in the mass'. Few identified members of what Mr Hill usually calls 'the propertied classes' emerge with any credit. The non-propertied naturally do better. They have the advantage that they are collective, anonymous, unidentified. They only stand and wait. Perhaps they are lucky.

The charge that the older narrative history failed to answer the questions that a present-day student wants answered is not entirely unfounded. But at its best the narrative method was rooted in a sound instinct – the sense of the essential wholeness of history, the close texture of causation in which historic event and individual, however much themselves the product of larger causes, in turn influenced the new phase of history they initiated; the perception that the anatomist has to begin by killing his subject.

The felt need for a new historical synthesis transcending the conventionally circumscribed task of the narrative historian derives from several sources. The specialized inquiries of non-political historians in recent times have revealed a world of interests, tensions and conflicts often unknown to older generations of historians. At certain points these appear to have important affinities with contemporary political action. Sociological method suggests that such affinities can be multiplied as explanations of political behaviour. From Marx is derived an interpretative theory that offers a consistent and dogmatic explanation of those affinities in terms of material group interests. Thus is generated the ambition to provide not merely partial explanations of self-evidently related groups of actions, phenomena or institutions but a total explanation of every aspect of history through a synthesis of the disparate analyses of the historical specialists. Yet the synthesis remains mechanical, not dynamic. For the Marxist cannot opt out of his self-created dilemma. His own 'explanation' is ineluctably the product of its own age. Its value as an historical tool is essentially in relation to the long-term trends of economic and social development. Applied to the short-term, it positively invites contortions while the attempt to sophisticate the Marxist analysis merely produces contradiction and confusion.

We end with precisely that imposition of later categories of analysis on the material of earlier times which Mr Hill rightly deplores. The evidence adduced to correlate political behaviour, religious belief, group interests and economic development is obviously inadequate for scientific proof. This poverty of immediately relevant evidence forces the historian saddled with an *a priori* theory to adapt whatever evidence he can. Each category of evidence – economic, political, philosophic – tends to be treated not for its inherent importance but for its convenience in explaining the other categories. Ponderous and far-reaching generalizations about the attitudes of whole classes of men have to rest on the slenderest foundations: second-hand expressions of opinion, casual allusions, literary evidence, or pseudo-statistical evidence which has been shown to be of limited validity. Class hatreds, for example, are the 'essential background to late seventeenth-century politics'. They lie 'at the back of gentry political thinking'. But this 'deep hostility', Mr Hill adds, is 'usually unspoken' – 'rarely openly discussed'. This reticence (odd in a century which was rarely mealy-mouthed or inhibited) is apparently broken by four pronouncements (two of them anonymous) during a period of more than a quarter of a century after the Restoration. This appears to be the only warrant for a generalization crucial to Mr Hill's argument. It does not self-evidently support the claim that history 'in depth' represents a scientific advance over the methods of earlier historians. [. . .]

Mr Hill is right to stress the historians liability 'to explain'. But the liability is not unlimited. It is bounded by the evidence available, by the rules of evidence, by a strictly finite human capacity to explain. Anyone who has tried to write contemporary history knows how convincingly the documentary evidence and rational deduction combine in a natural process of expansion, until the apparently inescapable solution presents itself. But he knows also how often the living testimony, itself checked and cross-checked, explodes this balloon of imperfect logic. For earlier periods, the historian can only remind himself continually of the limited and defective nature of most of his evidence. Otherwise he may end, like Buckle, with history that is no longer a seamless garment but a ready-made suit.

TOWARDS CIVIL WAR

10 BRIAN MANNING

The Aristocracy and the Downfall of Charles I

Charles I increased rather than reduced the cost of the court, and the burden of paying for this expensive establishment fell more heavily on the lesser gentry and the richer peasants and the tradesmen than on the aristocracy and the greater gentry. Nevertheless, the latter had grievances of their own against the Personal Government of Charles I: '... All the rich families of England, of noblemen and gentlemen, were exceedingly incensed' by the intensification of the exactions of the Court of Wards under the administration of Lord Cottington, which made them 'even indevoted to the Crown, looking upon what the law had intended for their protection and preservation to be now applied to their destruction...' But, above all, the fines for encroachments on the royal forests 'brought more prejudice upon the court, and more discontent upon the King, from the most considerable part of the nobility and gentry in England, than any one action that had its rise from the King's will and pleasure...' However, it was rather the style of government in the 1630s than specific grievances that offended an aristocracy which had become hypersensitive to slights and threats to its rights and privileges and social superiority. 'There were very few persons of quality who had not suffered or been perplexed by the weight or fear' of the 'censures and judgements' of the Court of Star Chamber. Worse than that, 'persons of honour and great quality ... were every day cited into the High Commission Court, upon the fame of their incontinence, or other scandal in their lives, and were there prosecuted to their shame and punishment... (which they called an insolent triumph upon their degree and quality, and levelling them with the common people)...'

The king's two chief ministers in the 1630s did nothing to conciliate the aristocracy in court or country. Wentworth (who was made Earl of Strafford in 1640) combined 'too elate and arrogant' a nature with too rapid a rise to power, which 'made him more transported with disdain of other men, and more condemning the forms of business' than was tactful. He 'too much neglected' the opinions of other ministers and he engaged 'too often, and against too many' great men; even Laud warned him to be careful of 'being over-full of personal prosecutions against men of quality'. His 'sour and haughty temper' led him to expect 'to have more observance paid to him, than he was willing to pay

From *Politics, Religion and the English Civil War*, ed. Brian Manning (Edward Arnold, 1973), pp. 37–47, 54–57, 79–80. Footnotes have been deleted.

to others, though they were of his own quality; and then he was not like to conciliate the good will of men of the lesser station'. He was 'a man of too high and severe a deportment, and too great a contemner of ceremony, to have many friends at Court . . .' 'It was a great infirmity in him, that he seemed to overlook so many, as he did; since everywhere, much more in court, the numerous or lesser sort of attendants can obstruct, create jealousies, spread ill reports, and do harm: for as 'tis impossible, that any power or deportment should satisfy all persons: so there a little friendliness and openness of carriage begets hope, and lessens envy.'

Laud 'was a man . . . of too warm blood and too positive a nature towards asserting what he believed a truth, to be a good courtier; and his education fitted him as little for it, as his nature; which having been most in the university . . . gave him wrong than right measure of a Court.' He had 'usually about him an uncourtly quickness, if not sharpness, and did not sufficiently value what men said or thought of him . . .' 'He could not debate anything without some commotion when the argument was not of moment nor bear contradiction in debate, even in the Council where all men are equally free, with that patience and temper that was necessary . . .' While he insisted on being treated with respect himself, and kept a 'state and distance . . . with men' that 'he thought . . . not more than was suitable to the place and degree he held in the church and state', he would not treat others with their due respect. He 'did court persons too little' and was unceremoniously short with 'those persons, who thought their quality, though not their business, required a patient and respectful entertainment'. Edward Hyde tried to give him a friendly warning of the danger of speaking sharply and ungraciously to 'persons of the best condition': 'that this kind of behaviour of his was the discourse of all companies of persons of quality'. He advised him 'that he would more reserve his passion towards all persons, how faulty soever; and that he would treat persons of honour and quality, and interest in their county, with more courtesy, and condescension . . .' An arrogance that might be more excusable in a gentleman like Wentworth was less excusable in a plebeian like Laud: 'a man of mean birth, bred up in a college,' Viscount Saye called him; 'a fellow of mean extraction and arrogant pride,' wrote Mrs Hutchinson.

Laud tried to uphold the authority and defend the wealth of the church by encouraging the clergy to be less subservient to the nobility and gentry. This was seen by the Long Parliament as incitement 'of ministers to despise the temporal magistracy, the nobles and gentry of the land'. When the Earl of Portland died in 1635 and the Lord Treasurership became vacant—which 'is the greatest office of benefit in the kingdom, and the chief in precedence next the archbishop and the Great Seal'—'the eyes of all men were at gaze who should have this great office; and the greatest of the nobility who were in the chiefest employments looked upon it as the prize of one of them, such offices commonly making way for more removes and preferments.' But Laud secured the appointment of Juxon, the Bishop of London, 'a man so unknown that his name was scarce heard of in the kingdom, who had been within two years before but a private chaplain to the king and the president of a poor college in Oxford.' Laud rejoiced at this coup, thinking he had secured the church: 'And now if the church will not hold up themselves under God, I can do no more'; but it 'inflamed more men than were angry before . . .' who now looked on the church 'as the gulf ready to swallow all the great offices' that rightfully belonged to the nobility.

The peers were obsessed with the need to preserve respect for their order. The Earl of Arundel affected the antique dress of the time when the nobles 'had been most venerable'. 'He was a great master of order and ceremony, and knew and kept greater distance towards his sovereign than any person I ever observed,' wrote his secretary, 'and expected no less from his inferiors . . .' 'He was a person of great and universal civility, but yet with that restriction as that it forbade any to be bold or saucy with him . . . He was not popular at all, nor cared for it, as loving better by a just hand than flattery to let the common people to know their distance and due observance.' The Earl of Northumberland 'was the proudest man alive' and 'was in all his deportment a very great man, and that which looked like formality was a punctuality in preserving his dignity from the invasion and intrusion of bold men, which no man of that age so well preserved himself from.' The Earl of Clare 'was of a most courteous and affable disposition, yet preserved exactly the grandeur and distance of his quality.' The Earl of Southampton 'had a great spirit, and exacted the respect that was due to his quality . . .' The Earl of Essex, though unlike the Earl of Arundel he 'too immoderately and importunately' affected popularity, yet he 'set as great a price upon nobility as any man living did . . .'; and 'no man valued himself more upon his title' than the puritan Lord Saye. Sir John Suckling 'did not much care for a lord's converse', Davenant recalled after the Restoration, 'for they were in those days damnably proud and arrogant . . .' The Earl of Arundel regarded his function as Earl Marshal as being to support 'ancient nobility and gentry, and to interpose on their behalfs' and to keep the common people in their proper place. A waterman pressing a citizen of London for a fare, showed his badge, which was a swan, the crest of an earl whose servant he was; and the citizen, thinking the fare excessive, said 'Begone with thy Goose', and was fined and imprisoned by the Earl Marshal's court for insulting the crest of an earl. A tailor, trying to get a gentleman to pay his bill and being called a 'base fellow' for his pains, answered 'that he was as good a man as the other', but was forced by the Marshal's court to pay damages to the gentleman for the insult. Hyde thought that the Marshal's court was one of the greatest grievances of the people in 1640.

The unpopularity of the war with Scotland in 1640 gave the aristocracy the opportunity to assert itself in more popular ways. On 31 August 1640 Secretary of State Windebank wrote from London to the king, who was with his army in Yorkshire, to report 'the resort hither to this town of some lords, and other persons of quality, who have been observed not to be very well contented with the time: namely, the Earls of Essex, Warwick and Bedford, the Lords Saye, Russell and Brooke, Pym and Hampden. These have had their meetings . . .' and Windebank heard that they intended 'to join in a petition to your Majesty' and he feared some dangerous practice or intelligence with the 'rebels of Scotland'. The privy council sent the Earl of Arundel to try to persuade the Earl of Bedford to return to the country; but they were more worried about the Earl of Essex and they advised the king to write 'with your own hand' a 'most obliging' letter to Essex, calling him to York and offering to employ him in the army. Windebank stressed that this advice 'is of extraordinary consequence to your Majesty's present affairs; and therefore I most humbly beseech your Majesty to take it to heart . . . If this lord were taken off, the knot would be much weakened, if not dissolved. And besides that it will be of great importance to sever him from that ill-affected company; he is a popular man, and it will give extraordinary satisfaction to all sorts of people to see him in employ-ment again.' So important did the privy council think this advice that they asked Henry Percy, the courtier brother of the Earl of Northum-berland, to persuade the queen to support it. Percy reported back to Windebank: 'I thought time very important in this matter, therefore I waited on her Majesty this night, and according to their instructions represented those reasons to her that might conduce most to make her a party in this design, which she apprehended so rightly that she instantly wrote as one much concerned and gave them many thanks for preparing this which she believes will prove much for his Majesty's service.' The factions of the Earl of Bedford and the Earl of Warwick were the core of the aristocratic opposition to the king in the country; but Essex, as the privy council recognized, was more formidable. As the son of Queen Elizabeth's fallen favourite, the great Earl of Essex who was executed as a traitor in 1601, he was heir both to a following and to a popular legend of heroism, royal injustice and martyrdom. He was both the champion of the rights of the nobility and the champion of the rights of the people. He was both 'the darling of the swordmen' and 'the most popular man of the kingdom'. He was connected with the discontented country magnates – his ally the Earl of Southampton, his cousin the Earl of Warwick – and with the discontented court lords – his cousins the Earl of Northumberland, the Earl of Holland, the Earl of Newport. He was the link between Country opposition and Court opposition, and between aristocratic opposition and popular op-position; he stood between the Court and the Country and held the balance between them. But the king feared and disliked him; he was unmoved by the pleas of his wife and his councillors and replied that he had already asked Essex to come to him, and would write again, but he would not employ him.

On 28 August the country lords drew up a petition to the king, which was signed by the Earls of Essex, Hertford, Bedford, Warwick, Exeter and Rutland, and by the Lords Saye, Brooke, Mandeville, Mulgrave,

Bolingbroke and Howard of Escrick. They complained of innovations in religion, the increase of popery, shipmoney, monopolies, the long intermission of parliaments and the precipitate dissolution of the Short Parliament. They demanded the summoning of a parliament to remove these grievances, to punish the authors of them, and to make peace with the Scots. Lord Mandeville and Lord Howard took the petition to the king at York; the Earl of Bedford and the Earl of Hertford went to the privy council in London and asked 'the Lords to join with them in it'. Every day more nobles were arriving in London to give their support to the petition. The privy councillors considered advising the king to appoint 'some of the country nobility' to the privy council, 'if it be but to engage them'. But the situation was becoming too urgent and the movement among the nobility too widespread to be dealt with in this manner. So when the council met on 2 September the Earl of Manchester, the Lord Privy Seal, put forward a proposal to advise the king to summon a Great Council of all the peers. The Earl of Berkshire objected that such an assembly would do no more than demand a parliament. Lord Newburgh and Sir Thomas Roe thought that the only solution to the crisis was to call a parliament, but that if it were thought that an immediate assembling of the peers would have some good effects, then they should advise the king to summon a parliament and in the meantime to hold a Great Council of the peers. The Earl of Dorset objected that it would take just as long to assemble the peers as to call a parliament. Manchester replied that he was 'wholly averse from advising a parliament, and wholly for calling the peers, the council of the kingdom, consiliarii nati; Edward III called his great council upon a like occasion; they raised great sums of money without a parliament, and assisted the king. The kingdom will follow the peers.' Lord Cottington was also against advising the king to summon a parliament, and he supported Manchester's proposal, but on the grounds that if the peers declared for a parliament, it would be more acceptable to the king as the request of the whole of the nobility than as the advice merely of the privy council. Dorset objected that the privy councillors might do better to earn for themselves popular approval by advising the king to call a parliament. Laud could give no lead: he agreed with Manchester's proposal but recognized that such a Great Council could not be an alternative to a parliament and would be bound to lead in the end to the summoning of a parliament, and he concluded that they should 'put to the king, that we are at the wall, and that we are in the dark, and have no grounds for a counsel'. But Sir Thomas Jermyn supported Manchester's proposal on the grounds that it would be a means to redress the grievances of the discontented lords and to engage them against the Scots; and the Earl of Arundel declared that a Great Council was 'the only way, the best and the shortest way'. The privy council voted by a majority to advise the king to summon a Great Council of the peers.

Windebank forwarded this advice to the king with a covering letter which is an interesting revelation of how the councillors saw their

113

constitutional position: they were only advisers to the king, but the language of Windebank's letter does not conceal that they were giving the king an ultimatum. 'Your Majesty will please to understand that the proposition I have sent from the Lords is only a mere humble advice of theirs . . .; it is the best they could think upon for the present; that it is no way binding, but that, if your Majesty dislike it, or shall in your wisdom advise or command some other way, they will in all humility submit to it, and lay it aside; that the ground and motive of it hath been the uniting of your Majesty and your subjects together, the want whereof the Lords conceive is the source of all the present troubles; and they are confident, if your Majesty and your people had been well together, the rebels durst not have thus insolently affronted your Majesty and the nation; that in probability the Lords being made sensible of your Majesty's and their own danger, and participants of your counsels, will be won to lay aside all private animosities and discontentments, and unanimously join to save the monarchy, and to repel the common enemy by a present assistance; that the lords, thus gained, will in all likelihood train with them their friends and adherents and many of the people; besides the satisfaction that is conceived the people will receive by this calling of the lords to your counsels; that it is likely these lords, when they shall be called, and shall meet . . . will fall upon grievances, and the present calling of a parliament, which also are the pretences of the rebels. And the question is, whether your Majesty will not rather give the glory of redress of grievances, and of a parliament, to your own lords, or rather to yourself by their common advice, than to the rebels, if your power and force be inferior to theirs; that in outward appearance, considering the constitution of the city and the generality of the kingdom, without some such sweetening of the lords and people as this, it is to be doubted, if your Majesty should receive a blow . . . monies and forces will be raised very coldly and slowly; and without a voluntary assistance of both these, the kingdom must be in danger; for to force supplies of either in this conjuncture is not held practicable . . .' Thus the privy councillors saw the gravity of the crisis to lie in the discontent of the peers; they pointed out the dependence of the Crown upon the peers; and they spoke to the king as the representative of the peers. They told the king that he was beaten: the prospect of defeat at the hands of the Scots combined with mounting popular discontent at home meant that the king must reconcile the peers and follow their advice in dealing with his discontented subjects in Scotland and England.

The advice of the privy council reached the king just as he was considering what reply to make to the petition of the Twelve Peers for a parliament, and he seized upon the alternative and summoned a Great Council of the Peers to meet at York on 24 September. On 7 September the privy council in London met the Earl of Bedford and the Earl of Hertford and informed them of the king's decision. The two earls approved of a Great Council, providing that it was not intended as an alternative to a parliament nor as a means of raising money without a parliament; but Windebank reported that 'the Earl of Bedford seemed not to like it so well as the Earl of Hertford; and I have heard since, he hath let fall discourses against it . . .' There was activity at court: Sir John Suckling and Henry Jermyn were urging the queen to advise her husband to summon a parliament; and when the Earl of Essex and the Earl of Hertford came to see her they were able to persuade her to support the demand for a parliament. The action of the Twelve Peers had released a popular agitation. On 10 September three hundred citizens of London met and drew up a petition for a parliament, and obtained 10,000 signatures, including those of four aldermen; and the efforts of the privy council to get the Lord Mayor and aldermen to suppress or condemn this petition were unsuccessful. It became obvious to the whole of the aristocracy, as it had been before to Bedford and his friends, that the lords themselves would be endangered by the popular discontent if concessions to the peers were not accompanied by concessions to the people as well. The Earl of Arundel changed his mind and Laud gave in: at the meeting of the privy council on 16 September Arundel moved that they advise the king to summon a parliament, he was seconded by Laud, and the rest of the councillors agreed. When the peers assembled in the Great Council at York on 24 September the king announced that parliament would meet on 3 November.

With the meeting of the Long Parliament, and the fall of Strafford and Laud, the great aristocrats began to grasp at the power which had fallen from the hands of those two great ministers. The court magnates like Arundel, the Earl Marshal, and Northumberland, the Lord Admiral of the Navy and General of the Army, who held great offices but were critical of the government in the 1630s, seem to have expected this power to come to them. Arundel began to play a more dominant role in the government; and Northumberland discussed with his sisters, the Countess of Carlisle and the Countess of Leicester, whether the Earl of Leicester should be Lord Deputy of Ireland or Lord Treasurer of England. They do not seem at first to have expected to share their power with the country magnates, who had not held offices in the 1630s. When rumours were heard, early in December 1640, that the Earl of Bedford would be Lord Treasurer, the Countess of Carlisle thought it could be 'neither true or possible without such a change as I dare not think of. They have disposed and changed all the officers of this kingdom. The king makes himself merry at it, though I believe there is not much cause for that . . .' But by the middle of January 1641 the story had become general, not only that Bedford would be Lord Treasurer, but that John Pym, Bedford's closest political adviser, would be Chancellor of the Exchequer; the Earl of Bristol would be Lord Privy Seal and his eldest son, Lord Digby (Bedford's son-in-law) would be Secretary of State, and the Earl of Essex Lord Deputy of Ireland. By 14 January the Countess of Carlisle was persuaded that 'we shall have great change of officers, and contrary to what I thought that Bedford will be treasurer . . .' This pointed to a serious effort to come to terms with the parliamentary opposition. Sir John Temple wrote to the Earl of Leicester:' . . . I understand the king is brought into a dislike of those counsels that he hath formerly followed, and therefore resolves to steer another course . . . And I do believe some ways are laid upon the bringing in of those men to make up an entire union between the king and his people, and so to moderate their demands as well as the height of that power which hath been lately used in the royal government.' This was connected with the two main aims of the king – to save the life of Strafford, who had been charged with treason by the House of Commons, and to preserve episcopal government of the church: on both these issues there were good prospects that the House of Lords would support the king, provided that he would take new ministers that they could trust and make some concessions to the complaints of lords and commoners against the bishops. Temple understood that 'His Majesty is well enough inclined to lessen' the power of the bishops, 'and take away the abuses introduced into the church by them', and 'to have them moulded into the ancient primitive way, and to see them reduced into the same state wherein they continued many hundred years after Christ . . . These preparatives make us now hope for a happy success of this parliament . . .' [. . .]

The intrigues of the aristocratic factions for places seemed to be on the verge of success in the first months of 1641. The first instalment of new appointments began on 20 January, when Lyttleton was promoted Lord Keeper, Bankes became Chief Justice of the Common Pleas and Heath was made a judge. Sir Edward Herbert succeeded Bankes as Attorney-General, and the king originally intended to fill Herbert's place as Solicitor-General with Gardiner, the Recorder of London, and to make Oliver St John Recorder of London, but at the last moment he substituted the name of Oliver St John for that of Herbert as Solicitor-General. This was politically significant because St John was the Earl of Bedford's legal adviser and close adherent; and the king's change of mind indicated that pressure had been applied. On 19 February the Earls of Bedford, Essex, Hertford and Bristol, Viscount Saye, and Lords Savile and Mandeville (and a few days later the Earl of Warwick) were appointed privy councillors. They were 'all persons at that time very gracious to the people, or the Scots . . . and had been all in some umbrage at court, and most of them in visible disfavour. . . .' All but two of them had been signatories of the Petition of the Twelve Peers for a parliament in 1640. Sir John Temple's information was that [the Marquis of] Hamilton had joined with [Henry] Jermyn to secure the promotion of these eight peers. At the beginning of April Temple still thought that Jermyn's influence was dominant, and that not only was the queen guided by him but also 'a strange interest hath he gotten now in the king'. It may have been through Jermyn that the queen had 'secret interviews with Bedford and Pym' and offered to secure their appointments as Lord Treasurer and Chancellor of the Exchequer. In April Nathaniel Tomkyns told Sir John Lambe that Pym 'has been with the king twice of late'. In this negotiation the king had three aims: first, to obtain from parliament an adequate revenue for the crown in place of the extra-parliamentary taxes of the 1630s which had been condemned by parliament; second, to preserve episcopacy; and third, 'to save the life of the Earl of Strafford'. On the first point Bedford and Pym seem to have satisfied the king of their good intentions. Pym drew up a memorandum of 'the king's revenue and expenditure' for Bedford's information, and, according to Clarendon, he and Bedford 'engaged to procure the king's revenue to be liberally provided for and honourably increased and settled', and they laid plans for 'many good expedients by which they intended to raise the revenue of the crown'. On the second point they 'would have been willing to have satisfied the king, the rather because they had no reason to think the two Houses, or indeed either of them, could have been induced to have pursued the contrary'. On the third point they also reached agreement with the king, on the basis that Strafford would be made incapable of any public employment and banished or imprisoned for life. But the negotiations were weakening their position in parliament, where the country gentry were suspicious that if the 'great men' got places they would do little to reduce the cost of the court, and would become 'desirous more to pacify the irate prince, and to comply with his desire in keeping up bishops and other things' than to proceed with 'the thorough reformation of Church and State'. They did not feel strong enough to proceed without the support of the Earl of Essex, who vetoed the whole scheme by insisting on nothing less than the death penalty for Strafford, telling Clarendon, who was employed by Bedford in an effort to change his mind: 'Stone-dead hath no fellow.' The king resolved that he would not appoint the opposition leaders to the vital political offices until they had proved that they would and could do him service in parliament by voting him new revenues, preserving the bishops, and saving Strafford's life. Clarendon thought that this would have been 'very reasonable at another time' but was 'very unseasonable' in this crisis; for by advocating the king's views before they were responsible for his policies they would risk undermining their base of power in parliament before they had secured a new base of power in the court, and 'it could not be expected they would desert that side by the power of which they were sure to make themselves considerable without an unquestionable mark of interest in the other, by which they were to keep up their power and reputation.' And the opposition leaders in parliament resolved that they could not do any service for the king in parliament in relation to his revenue, the bishops, and Strafford, until they were appointed to the chief offices in the government and so assured that the king had really abandoned past policies and past advisers, and really meant to reform church and state. [. . .]

[In the passage omitted, Dr Manning describes in detail the king's attempts to deal with the growing opposition to his rule in Parliament.]

Belatedly and half-heartedly Charles had reacted to the crisis of 1640 by adopting a policy of coming to terms with the opposition in parliament by appointing its leaders to the chief places in the government and making concessions to their demands for reforms in church and state. This policy had been abandoned because the king would not agree to the death of Strafford. The king had toyed with the idea of using the army against the parliament, but when this proved impossible he had tried to win over his opponents by appointing them to lucrative or prestigious offices. Still forced to concede demand after demand of the parliament, he had resolved to make no more concessions and to build up a party of his own in parliament to support his stand, by means of a new policy of appointing to offices peers and MPs who had demonstrated concrete support for his views and of dismissing from office peers and MPs who opposed his views. While the king did manage to win over to his side some who had opposed him earlier, he also drove into complete identification with the opposition those court lords and office-holders who did not share his views. The king had shown clearly that he did not rely on the advice of his ministers and privy councillors, but on the advice of his personal friends and court favourites. This caused the final breach between the opposition and the king. He had ignored the party that was appearing for him in parliament and resorted to a coup that failed. Only the threat of civil war and social disorder led a large part of the nobility to rediscover an identification between their interests and those of the crown, and so gave Charles a party with which to fight to recover his power.

11 J.S. MORRILL

The Revolt of the Provinces

[In the section of the book from which the following extracts are taken, Dr Morrill is concerned with what was happening in the shires and boroughs of England and Wales in the years leading up to 1642. In general, his argument is that although the gentry who ran local government shared many assumptions about the nature of the crisis, their responses to it were largely conditioned by local concerns. When faced with national political issues, they considered them in relation to possible effects on their local community. Thus national political and constitutional questions took on local colours and were debated within a local rather than a national context. As part of his argument Dr Morrill examines provincial reactions to the imposition of ship-money in 1634–35.]

[...] Let us examine provincial reaction to one of the most controversial of all the government's expedients in the 1630s, ship money. Based on precedents as recent as 1594 and 1626, this was not a tax but a rate levied by the King, by virtue of his emergency powers, to safeguard the narrow seas. Opposition to it mounted, but only when it became apparent that the rate was to become an annual one, and the King's discretionary power to proclaim a permanent state of emergency was questioned in the courts by John Hampden. But it was not until the summer of 1639 that opposition became effective. Between 1634 and the autumn of 1638, 90 per cent of the assessments were paid, an extraordinary achievement by seventeenth-century standards, and a far higher percentage than was later achieved by the parliamentary subsidies and poll tax of 1640-1.

Provincial opposition mounted from 1636 onwards. Yet the crisis seems to have come not when the judgement in Hampden's case became known, but when the King compounded his folly by demanding coat and conduct money for the army he intended to use against Scotland. Professor Barnes believes that the judgements of the two judges who found for Hampden on constitutional grounds were widely circulated, but their views seem to have made less impact than we might have expected. The case aroused intense interest, and the court was packed to hear the cut and thrust of legal argument. Yet the King's right to levy the rate was rarely questioned in the provinces. Ship money was hated for its costliness and its disruptive effects on the social and political calm of the communities, but remarkably few references

From J.S. Morrill, *The Revolt of the Provinces: Conservatives and Radicals in the English Civil War 1630–1650* (Allen and Unwin, 1976), pp. 24–31, 42–47. Footnotes have been deleted.

to Hampden's case can be found in the records. Many, reasonably enough, delayed making payment in the hope of a favourable opinion for Hampden which would absolve them from paying. Yet once the King had won, the great majority did pay. The efficiency of the tax in the year of the Hampden case (October 1637–September 1638) was still over 90 per cent. Thus in Yorkshire, where a sheriff had earlier reported that the Hampden case 'did much retard the service in respect of the greate expectation men had thereof', almost eleven of the twelve thousand pounds assessed were eventually collected. Sir Francis Thornagh, Sheriff of Nottinghamshire, was the only one to report that the outcome had actually stiffened resistance.

One reason for the fiscal success of ship money in the early years was the studiedly moderate policy adopted by a government which, for once, was determined not to create martyrs. Refusal to pay led to the unpleasantness of distraint, but not to arrests or imprisonment. Lord Say and Sele, who made a great fuss about refusing to pay, was left to bluster, while payment was exacted by distraining and selling his cows on an outlying farm. As the sheriff of Merioneth reported, 'I believe it is his Majesty's pleasure that his subjects shall be mildly dealt with, which makes me presume to levy the mize [assessments] more leisurely of the poorer sort, but I shall have the money to pay in such time as shall be acceptable'. Even Hampden was left undisturbed after his counsel had charged the King with constitutional impropriety. The King could afford to be magnanimous; he was winning.

The pattern of opposition is curious; many of the men who were later to become prominent in the opposition within the Long Parliament were diligent ship money sheriffs (these included Sir Simonds d'Ewes in Suffolk and Sir John Gell in Derbyshire), while many future royalists appear amongst its most trenchant opponents (these included Sir Marmaduke Langdale in Yorkshire, Sir Thomas Aston in Cheshire, and Sir Francis Seymour in Wiltshire). There is a further point; in many places such opposition as existed in 1634-8 came not from the county leadership but from the yeomanry and tenant farmers. In Lancashire, only three gentlemen can be found who were actively opposed to ship money, and popular resistance was confined to the backward and largely recusant Lonsdale and Amounderness hundreds. The heavily puritan area around Manchester paid up apparently without trouble. Only one Yorkshire gentleman appeared in opposition before 1638, a recusant who claimed he was being made to pay twice. Sir Francis Astley, Sheriff of Norfolk, listing defaulters in May 1638, could name no one more prominent than four head constables, two attorneys and a clergyman. In 1636, a report from Dorset claimed that 'the greatest part of the arrears falls among the poorer sort'; East Anglia generally paid above the national average until the end of 1638; and as late as 1640, the escheator of Worcester wrote that the gentry were not to blame for the remissness of the county.

Some reports do mention gentry leadership, but they were a minority until 1639. Hampden, then, represented the articulate, official opposition position, but it is not clear that the provinces as a whole were behind them on the issue. A great county leader like Warwick could instigate a tax strike as early as 1636, but he backed down when the King threatened to break his local power by dismissing his nominees from local posts, and the county paid up throughout 1637-8. What produced the collapse of co-operation in 1639-40 was not a growing awareness of the great constitutional issues raised by Hampden's lawyers, but a growing fear of the consequences of ship money for the economic and social stability of each county community.

As Professor Barnes has pointed out, the earliest complaints about ship money were made not on constitutional but on administrative grounds; the instructions of the Privy Council were contradictory and confusing. Sheriffs were instructed to proceed on the basis that ship money should be assessed like any other county rate (such as those for poor relief or for the repair of highways and bridges). But because of the scale of the ship money rate (equivalent to more than two parliamentary subsidies) and because it was recognized that many local rating lists were out of date, sheriffs were given discretionary powers to make adjustments. This allowed endless disputes to develop within each county with the possibility of an appeal over the sheriff's head to the Privy Council. Delays, disputes and violence were the natural outcome and almost all the opposition in the years 1635-8 can be said to have arisen from this confusion. One prevalent source of dispute was the distribution between boroughs and county; another was that between different hundreds. The system required the sheriff to divide the total for his shire between the hundreds and then, assisted by the head constables, to subdivide these sums amongst the parishes and townships. He was then required to assess individuals within each village by calling on the help of 'the most substantial' inhabitants, and he would frequently find himself being offered contradictory advice by different groups within a village. Indeed it is surprising that the consequent administrative chaos did not lead to even greater trouble. Many of the problems were intractable. A sheriff of Lincolnshire inquired whether newly drained fens were to be assessed according to traditional rates or new ones; the assessments in Huntingdonshire in 1637 were delayed by disputes about which local rates were to be employed (some townships paid their tithes and ecclesiastical rates, including poor rates, to one parish, other 'leys' to another). The sheriff defended his delay, pointing out that he had 'to take special care lest he should break their ancient customs, which would much disturb the business'.

Many of these disputes reawakened dormant but profound juris-dictional conflicts. The city of Chester, for example, had long wanted to destroy the independence of the enclave of Gloverstone within its walls but excluded from its charter. The enclave was a haven for unlicensed, unincorporated tradesmen and retailers. The city used the ship money writs as an excuse to reopen the whole question. Similarly, the city sought to treat all dean and chapter revenues as liable to assessment towards the city's rate, and also to assess the county gentry on their business interests within the city. The Privy Council, by deciding against the city on the first two counts and against the county on the third, succeeded in alienating everybody.

Many prominent opponents of the Crown were only concerned with such issues. Robert Phelipps, a leading member of the parliamentary opposition in the 1620s, and William Strode were only interested in protecting their own hundreds from over-assessment, and Phelipps's son expressed an open willingness to pay so long as customary procedures were followed. Sheriffs had a vested interest in exaggerating rather than minimising the extent of opposition, yet they all agreed that rating disputes were the real, not just the feigned, ground of opposition. The sheriff of Shropshire in 1637 wrote that only 'the inequality of assessments has caused delay'. A sheriff of Somerset expected no opposition once he had completed his adjustment of the assessments, and others concurred.

Ship money opposition was first evident amongst the middling sort because this was the first heavy burden paid by them to the central government for decades. Except for the now defunct fifteenths and tenths, the burdens of taxation had come increasingly to fall on a smaller percentage of the freeholders. The subsidy rolls now included about 10 per cent of all householders, far fewer than those assessed for local rates, such as those for the poor or for bridge repairs. It may be true that the burden of the subsidies fell heaviest on the poorer of those included, but a majority of freeholders escaped altogether. Ship money was the first rate or tax ever paid by a majority of freeholders for a use outside the shire. In Essex, for example, where only 3,200 names occur in the 1640 subsidy roll, 14,500 families were assessed for ship money. Elsewhere the rating books for the poor, for landscot or other local rates unquestionably brought thousands of families into a national rating system for the first time.

Such opposition as was dignified by legal arguments was concerned more with questioning the sheriffs' powers and authority to enforce payment than with the legality of the rate itself. The Privy Council had characteristically decided to issue ship money writs to the sheriffs rather than to the justices in the hope that a single man would be more easily browbeaten than a bench. But the sheriffs' powers to modify rates and to sell distrained goods were far from clear, and there was a growing feeling that the Council's instructions required sheriffs to exceed their legal powers. In 1640 for example, Sheriff Warcopp of Oxfordshire reported that 'no constable will assist distraint, as they will be sued by those claiming the sheriffs' warrant not sufficient to bear them out'. Pleas by the sheriffs to the justices for help were rebuffed with the claim that they had no power to intervene; elsewhere justices supported men whose goods had been distrained and who claimed that such distraints were illegal. The position of sheriffs once they had left office was particularly difficult. Wherever magistrates can be found intervening, their actions appear to reflect a sincere desire to uphold custom and law and order. There is little evidence that they were concerned to use ship money as a cover for deeper political designs. There is also a great difference between this concern with local traditions and local stability, and the preoccupation with fundamental laws and with the belief that ship money constituted an instrument of absolutism which some historians have discerned in their actions. Ship money created feuds between town and country, hundred and hundred, village and village; it angered and embittered the poorer members of the community; it required the sheriffs to strain their powers; above all it exemplified the government's insensitivity towards localist sentiment and belief. No wonder that by 1639-40 the gentry were united in their determination to halt the progress of a régime bent on novel, socially disruptive policies. The constitutional propriety of ship money was not the main reason for the opposition to it. What had changed between 1634 and 1639 was not the gentry's opinion of Charles's constitutional arguments but the breakdown of peace, quiet and order in the local communities. The gentry were less concerned with the theoretical implications of Charles's use of his prerogative than with the unacceptable consequences of his actions. Even if Charles's *constitutional* position had been impeccably orthodox and uncontroversial, he would still have been faced by a tax strike in 1640.

The growing unrest finally found expression in outbreaks of popular violence and in the non-cooperation of county governors during the summer of 1639. The turning-point came not with the judgement in Hampden's case but with Charles's fresh demands for men and money for his war to enforce obedience and the new Prayer Book on the Scots. Sheriffs, now faced with the responsibility of helping to raise and equip (by coat and conduct money) men for the war, could no longer put pressure on their subordinates to gather ship money. 'I could not possibly effect it now, having been employed . . . in impressing soldiers out of the trained bands for his Majesty's service in the Northern parts,' wrote the sheriff of Northamptonshire. The sheriff of Worcester even released constables whom he had imprisoned for opposing him over ship money: 'in respect of this great service concerning the soldiers I thought fit to set them at liberty, that there might be no neglect in the execution of that service'. The mayor and sheriffs of Bristol sought to 'excuse their neglect in omitting to give an account of the ship money by the time spent in collecting the late coat and conduct money and exercising the soldiers'. In Denbighshire the sheriff was powerless to prevent the constables using the money they had collected as ship money to cover coat and conduct money assessments. The Bishops' wars brought fresh local grievances: the use of the carefully stored arms of the county militia, and of the militia itself, was resented not only because of the drain on resources, but because the gentry (already anxious about rumours of invasions from Ireland or the Continent) found the prospect of being left without local defence intolerable. Many regiments raised for the campaign mutinied, and riots by troops were reported from over twenty counties, the soldiers destroying altar rails and stained glass windows in the churches, symbols of the new Laudian idolatry, or joining the enclosure rioters to pull down hedges. The winter of 1639-40 was a bleak time as local government ground to a halt and the economic depression, particularly in the clothing areas, led to a fresh wave of rioting. Yet throughout 1640 Charles intensified the crisis; a new writ for ship money, the largest yet (after a lowering of his demands in 1639); fresh levies for a second war against the Scots; fresh initiatives from Laud with his canons of convocation, still prescribing purgatives rather than ointment for the fevered Church. It may be that if coat and conduct money had not brought about its collapse, a more formidable opposition to ship money would have developed in any case as its permanence became recognised. Professor Barnes has argued that in Somerset opposition was developing constitutional overtones by 1638-9, and a parallel might be drawn with the gradual shift from administrative to principled opposition to patentees in Elizabethan Norfolk. But I must say that there is little evidence that this shift had in fact already occurred. This is surprising, but not more so than the fact that so little fuss had been made of the extension of ship money to the inland counties. Indeed complaints about this appear to have diminished with time. Initially, it was used as a subsidiary ground of complaint (especially by the towns), but little is heard of it after 1637. Small wonder that both elections in 1640 were so fiercely contested and witnessed the rout of the Courtiers. But it is equally clear that even opposition magnates had difficulty in securing the election of clients 'foreign' to the seats. As Professor Gruenfelder says: 'national issues played an important role . . . these issues added to the growing spirit of localism a desire to elect men of reputation and connection within the county or borough'. Of course the elections of 1640 were about ship money, religious innovations and other royal policies. But this does not mean that the elections were about the opposition leaders' constitutional case against those policies. They were against the *effects* of royal policy on the local community. Each county reacted differently according to the particular local burden of particular policies. Dr Slack, correcting Gruenfelder's thesis in a study of the Salisbury elections of 1640, shows how concern with national political issues arose out of local controversies.

The petitions which the communities sent up with their members (local factions frequently sinking their differences for this, if not for the elections themselves) were a curious blend of national and local issues. [. . .] [In many counties, local factions contended to portray themselves as the men best able to demand a restoration of good government. The electorate listened gratefully to those pushed forward by great men who seemed to speak knowledgeably and authoritatively about the grounds of misrule. The voters put their trust in men whose religious, even political, radicalism did not emerge until later; either it was hardly mentioned or the electors were deafened by the talk of an end to the past innovations. Only later did the implications emerge. In Cheshire, for example, the conservative gentry backed Sir William Brereton, a puritan with 'official' Country connections through the Massachusetts Bay Company and known to be popular with the freeholders. They had no doubt that he was really 'their' man. They cheered the early measures of the Long Parliament but grew alarmed when Brereton took up the cause of presbyterianism and the ideal of the godly commonwealth. By the middle of 1641 his erstwhile backers had turned against him. One of them said that he 'loved Sir Wm Brereton well, but yet... loved decency, order and good discipline better'. Brereton represents the articulate minority swept in by the spring tide of fear and confusion of 1640. When the panic receded, they were left far more prominently placed in the political landscape than would have seemed possible in terms of their actual numbers and representativeness at other times. By mid-1641 the Long Parliament had ceased to represent the views of the English provinces.

In 1640 Charles I had no party. He was faced by a national tax strike and a parliament containing men who sought power for themselves as the prelude to a radical shift of policy. He was also faced by massive desertions from the Court, both by men who shared the principles of the opposition groups, and by those prepared to ally with the opposition in order to dump Strafford and advance themselves. What is remarkable about the outbreak of the civil war is not why the Crown was confronted by an organised opposition: it is how the Crown gained a party of its own. [...]

At times of crisis men look to known patterns of political and social behaviour. Passivity is the simplest way out, the line of least resistance. To obey an order is less of a political act than to reject it. Anyone who claims to stand for the protection of traditional values and the maintenance of order will be widely supported. In this context, localism meant not an indifference to the great issues agitating Church and State, but a preoccupation with the way these issues could be harmonised with the restoration of normality. The pre-existent power groupings within each county buckled under the pressures and tensions of national events, but each county retained a distinctive pattern.

In Leicestershire, two implacably opposed gentry factions – both traditionally puritan – had long struggled for local dominance. Both the leading families, the Greys and the Hastings, had connections with the Court and with the leading members of the opposition. The original cause of their feud had long been forgotten. When civil war broke out, both groups tried to prevent the involvement of Leicestershire. Only haltingly was the county forced into the war. Then the line-up followed the traditional one; the families who had always been attached to the Hastings's interests declared for the King, those who had always supported the Greys declared for Parliament. Yet the county remained largely apart from the war, with very little military activity until 1645; the royalists dominated the north and west, Parliament the south and east.

A similar situation prevailed in Wiltshire. The two ancient factions were headed by the Marquis of Hertford and the Earl of Pembroke, and the rivalry of their families had been worked out for generations in struggles to control the Lieutenancy and the commissions of the peace. In 1640 Pembroke was a Courtier; despite his distinguished lineage the Earl was a profligate who had run through the family fortune and was only semi-literate. His religious views were confused, combining a vindictive puritan hatred of catholicism and support for a preaching ministry, with a staunch liking for the Prayer Book (he was later to oppose the Presbyterian Directory of Public Worship). In 1640, Hertford was in self-imposed exile from the Court. By inclination and family ties (for example to Essex) he was one of the inner circle of Country leaders (and his brother, Francis Seymour, had been a leading opponent of ship money). He was one of the hard-line peers who demanded in a petition of August 1640 that Charles call Parliament to redress the ills of the nation. In the elections of 1640 Pembroke used his influence on behalf of Court candidates, but his position was an ambivalent one for he was bitterly opposed to other Courtier groups, being a long-standing supporter of the pro-French party, along with the Earls of Northumberland and Holland. He thus allied himself with the opposition over the attainder of Strafford in the hope of strengthening his position. The plan misfired, and he was shortly afterwards dismissed from his office as Lord Chamberlain. This was disastrous for a man dependent on the profits of office to remain financially afloat. He was forced into an ever-closer liaison with the opposition as the only way back to office. Almost simultaneously Hertford (who had used his electoral influence for the opposition) was brought into the government as part of Charles's policy of conciliation. He became a Privy Councillor and, a month after Pembroke's disgrace, governor to the Prince of Wales. By the spring of 1642 the change of roles was complete. Hertford voted against the Militia Ordinance and set out to join the King, while Pembroke voted for the Ordinance and became a leading figure on parliamentary committees. But as late as June an upset to the new alignment seemed possible. Hertford reappeared at Westminster and asked that charges of delinquency against him be dropped; immediately Pembroke entered into correspondence with Hyde and tried to rebuild his bridges with the King; but both sets of negotiations broke down, and Hertford returned to York. Shortly afterwards he was appointed Charles's Lieutenant General in the West, while Pembroke was granted a similar commission by Parliament. Both were largely motivated by personal rivalry and self-interest, although a measure of wider concern is evident in Hertford. However, both soon got cold feet, fearful that they were becoming over-committed. The rivalry of their families over the years had never before taken on such a winner-take-all air. Although both set their commissioners to work to call out the militia, their concern with the outcome is shown by the petition drawn up by their representatives three weeks after the battle of Edgehill, in which they called for a cessation of hostilities. Eight future royalist leaders and nine future parliamentarians were amongst the twenty-five signatories. Subsequently they went separate ways,

Hertford remaining an active royalist (though prone to costly disagreements with rival commanders), Pembroke retreating as governor to the Isle of Wight where he could, if necessary, bargain himself out of trouble. Only when the war was won did he once again appear prominently at London, swimming with the strongest currents (he was one of the few peers to take his seat in the Rump when the House of Lords was abolished in 1649). Yet the local gentry continued to support whichever of the two great families they had been traditionally allied with. Neither group wanted a civil war, but throughout the period and notwithstanding the political gyrations of the leaders, membership of the two great Wiltshire interests remained stable. The ancient Seymour (Hertford) and Herbert (Pembroke) rivalry remained the unchangeable basis of local politics.

In Cheshire, a rather different pattern prevailed. The élite there had been divided for some years over issues of local precedence. Faced by the political crisis of 1640–1 and by the emergence of a radical puritan group amongst the lesser gentry and freeholders, one of these groups gradually moved into an alliance with the Court, prompted largely by their determination to protect a modified episcopacy. The other group attempted to remain neutral, using its influence to keep the peace. In the autumn of 1642 this group petitioned for a national settlement and tried to raise a third force to keep both sides out of the county. After the failure of this scheme, the group divided, its leaders working for a pacification from within the ranks of the royalist and parliamentarian parties.

Where there were no traditional and deeply felt divisions within a county, the élite might act together throughout. Thus in Buckinghamshire, despite the clear preference of men below the highest ranks for keeping out of the conflict, almost all the leading families cooperated closely with John Hampden. In Shropshire, opposition to the solidly Royalist front presented by the justices was soon suppressed, and here commitment to the King did mean more than the use of his name and commission for essentially local peace-keeping aims.

The situation in many other counties was more deeply confused. In Devon the royalists were the first to appear but the commissioners of array were deeply distrusted. In July many leading gentry had sent petitions to both King and Parliament seeking a peaceful settlement, and the execution of royalist commissions in August led to further demonstrations, for 'the Arraymen... are look'd upon as the first instigators of a breach of the peace'. Although a great many of the gentry were later to appear for the King, the overwhelming feeling in the autumn of 1642 was a desire to procrastinate. The majority opposed the commission of array as they were shortly to oppose the militia commission: it was the same spirit which led them to oppose ship money and court and conduct money. Similarly in Kent, men who were later, in 1643 and 1648 (in response to parliamentary attempts to destroy local autonomy), to fight in the name of the King, stayed at home in 1642. At Westminster in later 1642 any action was a positive one; to stay was to identify with the parliament, to leave was seen as a declaration of royalism. In the shires, a dogged stay-at-home policy could still be construed as loyalty to both sides.

Just as pre-existent alignments played distinctive roles in determining allegiance in many counties (Somerset and Lancashire affording two more clearcut examples), so every town reacted in its own way. The city of Chester, torn by disputes over local trading rights, recently compounded by religious differences, split along the lines laid down in these essentially local divisions; so did Newcastle, despite the fact that the warring factions had made common cause in the crisis of 1640–1. In Ludlow a long-standing local dispute only took on national dimensions in the course of 1641–2, in Lincoln there had long been an anglican and a puritan dimension to a broader local conflict which bequeathed the royalist and parliamentarian factions to the days of the civil war. But in the main urban centres the initial response was a desire for conciliation and non-commitment. The Chester corporation drew up a neutrality petition; the Bristol common councillors appointed a committee of Ten which spent two months trying to draw up a petition in favour of reconciliation which could be addressed severally to King and Parliament; Dr Manning has drawn attention to neutralist sentiment in Hull, Salisbury and the Cornish boroughs. Sandwich reflects the passivity of the smaller towns, publishing propaganda letters from both sides until late in 1642 (for example the council posted up copies of the Militia Ordinance but did not command its execution). Tewkesbury submitted passively to both sides in turn.

The lesson is the same as that for the counties. Side-taking for the great majority was largely arbitrary. Men delayed declaring themselves until forced to do so by the appearance of activist groups on one or both sides. Polarisation then usually followed the lines of purely local groupings and although many families were divided, and many friends parted, the prior sub-political divisions within each shire or borough were reflected in the line-up of forces by early 1643. It was not always obvious which group would support each side: it was frequently determined by the attitude of the leaders or simply by the accident of events. Since indecision sprang from a loyalty to both sides, an express command from one of them would often lead to reluctant acquiescence in that command and only thus to commitment; in the case of Chester, for example, it was probably the arrival of royalist commands and commanders which swung the corporation away from neutralism into acquiescent royalism; the arrival of Sir George Booth or Sir Richard Wilbraham at that juncture could easily have swung the city into acquiescent parliamentarianism.

All this emphasis on neutralism and pacifism begs the question: Why did civil war break out? Who were the activists and how did they break down the pacifism of the majority?

Although the final breakdown between King and Parliament concerned control of the militia, the provincial significance of this issue should not be overrated. Few petitions from the provinces referred to it, or to the constitutional amendments called for by Pym in the Nineteen Propositions, or to the general question of trust. All petitions, royalist and parliamentarian, assumed that the political and constitutional differences were negotiable. The concept of mixed monarchy was universally acclaimed in the counties. What emerges quite clearly from a study of the activists in the summer of 1642 (those who pushed themselves forward) is that, for them, religion was the crucial issue. Quite simply, in most counties the active royalists are the defenders of episcopacy who saw in puritanism a fundamental challenge to all society and order, and the parliamentarians are those determined to introduce a godly reformation which might, for a few of them, leave room for bishops, but in most cases did not. What the puritan activists did agree on, however, was the need to go beyond a restoration of traditional pre-Laudian erastian anglicanism to create a new, militant evangelical Church. It may well be that amongst the peerage and ancient gentry, the tug of honour, indoctrination into the values of a patriarchal society, a reflex obedience to the anointed King, were finally decisive in committing them to fighting with their monarch, but the great majority of royalists in 1642 are more likely to have agreed with Thomas Holles, the ex-puritan ('truly I love religion as well as any man, but I do not understand the religion of rebellion') than with the Earl of Cumberland ('the same loyal blood of my ancestors runs still in my veins which they were never sparing of when their sovereign commanded them to fight'). [. . .]

12 NICHOLAS TYACKE

Puritanism, Arminianism and Counter Revolution

I

Historians of the English Civil War all agree that Puritanism had a role to play in its origins. Beyond this however agreement ceases. For some, particularly the Marxists, Puritanism was the ideology of the newly emergent middle classes or *bourgeoisie*, as they are sometimes called. Puritan ideas, it is argued, complemented and encouraged the capitalist activities of 'progressive' gentry, merchants and artisans alike. On the assumption, again made by those most under the influence of Marxism, that the English Civil War was a 'bourgeois revolution' the Puritans are naturally to be found fighting against King Charles and his old-world followers. An alternative and widely held interpretation sees Puritanism as a religious fifth column within the Church of England, and one whose numbers dramatically increased during the first decades of the seventeenth century; by the early 1640s, with the collapse of the central government and its repressive system of church courts, the Puritans were thus able to take over at least in the religious sphere. These two schools of thought, the Marxist and the fifth-columnist, are best represented by the writings respectively of Dr Christopher Hill and Professor William Haller.

In the following essay however a different view will be put forward, to the effect that religion became an issue in the Civil War crisis due primarily to the rise to power of Arminianism in the 1620s. The essence of Arminianism was a belief in God's universal grace and the freewill of all men to obtain salvation. Therefore Arminians rejected the teaching of Calvinism that the world was divided into elect and reprobate whom God had arbitrarily predestinated, the one to Heaven and the other to Hell. It is difficult for us to grasp how great a revolution this involved for a Society as steeped in Calvinist theology as was England before the Civil War. But whether or not we agree with the arguments of Christopher Hill, it is clear that the Puritan ideas to which he ascribes so much importance for the development of modern, capitalist society are in the main predestinarian ones. Similarly with Haller's thesis concerning the growth of Puritanism, the message preached with such

From *The Origins of the English Civil War*, ed. Conrad Russell (Macmillan, 1973), pp. 119–143. Footnotes have been deleted.

success from Puritan pulpits was rooted in the Calvinist theology of grace.

At the beginning of the seventeenth century, a majority of the clergy from the Archbishop of Canterbury downwards were Calvinists in doctrine, and the same was probably true of the more educated laity. So Puritanism in this Calvinist sense was not then seen as a political threat. Only when predestinarian teaching came to be outlawed by the leaders of the established church, as was the case under Archbishop William Laud, would its exponents find themselves in opposition to the government. Any doubts that the Church of England was doctrinally Calvinist, before Laud took control, can be resolved by reading the extant doctoral theses in divinity maintained at Oxford University from the 1580s to the 1620s. There, year after year predestinarian teaching was formally endorsed, and its opposite denied. The following are a representative selection of such theses, translated from the original Latin and listed in chronological order: 'No one who is elect can perish' (1582); 'God of his own volition will repudiate some people' (1596); 'According to the eternal predestination of God some are ordained to life and others to death' (1597); 'Man's spiritual will is not itself capable of achieving true good' (1602); 'The saints cannot fall from grace' (1608); 'Is grace sufficient for salvation granted to all men? No.' (1612); 'Does man's will only play a passive role in his initial conversion? Yes' (1618); 'Is faith and the righteousness of faith the exclusive property of the elect? Yes' (1619); and 'Has original sin utterly extinguished free will in Adam and his posterity? Yes' (1622). The licensed publications of the English press tell the same Calvinist story, albeit in a more popular vein, as do many religious preambles to wills where the testator confidently affirms belief in his divine election. A good example of this type of Calvinist will is that made by Lord Treasurer Dorset, who died in 1608; George Abbot, future Archbishop of Canterbury, was so impressed by Dorset's claim to be an elect saint that he quoted the will verbatim when preaching his funeral sermon in Westminster Abbey. Calvinism at the time was clearly establishment orthodoxy, and contemporaries would have found any suggestion that Calvinists were Puritans completely incomprehensible.

Puritanism around the year 1600, and for more than two decades subsequently, was thought of in terms either of a refusal to conform with the religious rites and ceremonies of the English Church, or as a presbyterian rejection of church government by bishops. At that date conformists and nonconformists, episcopalians and presbyterians all had in common Calvinist predestinarian ideas. Here however we come to the crux of the matter, for Calvinism also helped to reconcile the differences between them. Thus the late Elizabethan Archbishop of Canterbury, John Whitgift, who was a Calvinist in doctrine, regarded Puritan nonconformity in a different light from that of the Arminian Archbishop Laud. This did not stop Whitgift as Archbishop from attacking nonconformists, especially with Queen Elizabeth hard on his heels, but it did impose important limits on the extent of his persecution. Before the advent of Laud, nonconformists and even presbyterians were never regarded as being totally beyond the pale; they were seen instead as aberrant brethren deserving of some indulgence. Symbolic of the pre-Laudian state of affairs is that in the 1560s Whitgift had been a nonconformist and Thomas Cartwright, the later presbyterian, a candidate for an Irish archbishopric and, despite a long history of public controversy between them, they ended up on good terms in the 1590s. Calvinist doctrine provided a common and ameliorating bond that was only to be destroyed by the rise of Arminianism. As a result of this destruction, during the 1620s, Puritanism came to be redefined in terms which included the very Calvinism that previously had linked nonconformists to the leaders of the established church, and the nonconformist element in the former Calvinist partnership was driven into an unprecedented radicalism. The Arminians and their patron King Charles were undoubtedly the religious revolutionaries in the first instance. Opposed to them were the Calvinists, initially conservative and counter-revolutionary, of whom the typical lay representative was John Pym. [. . .]

[Dr Tyacke in the passage omitted here goes on to present evidence supporting his argument that in the late sixteenth and early seventeenth centuries a shared adherence to Calvinist predestinarian theology formed a bond between Puritan nonconformists and the ecclesiastical authorities which limited the extent of persecution. In addition to this common doctrinal belief, another factor making for toleration of Puritan nonconformists in the early seventeenth century was an intensified fear of Catholicism, which represented a common enemy. That Calvinist theology was not adhered to by Puritans alone but was common to almost the entire English Church was impressively demonstrated in 1618, when King James sent an official delegation of English churchmen to the international Synod of Dort where Arminianism was condemned and Calvinism affirmed.]

Hindsight is often the curse of the historian, and none more so in attempting to reconstruct the religious history of the pre-Civil War era. The battle lines of 1640-2 were not drawn by the early 1620s in this any more than other spheres. The parliaments of 1621 and 1624 were remarkable for a dearth of religious grievances. 'Godly reformation' was limited to allegations of corrupt practices by certain ecclesiastical officials, and requests that the recusancy laws be more strictly enforced. Among the clergy an appeal from Bermuda in 1617 by the presbyterian Lewis Hughes, to avoid persecution by emigration, fell on deaf ears. Moreover in 1621 Hughes's own form of catechism concerning 'public exercises of religion', as well as a tract on strict sabbath observance, were licensed for publication by one of Archbishop Abbot's chaplains. When therefore the Spanish marriage negotiations finally collapsed in

1624 it was natural for the favourite Buckingham to cultivate closer relations with John Preston, at that date 'leader of the Puritan party', to quote Christopher Hill. Two years before, Buckingham had secured for Preston the mastership of Emmanuel College, Cambridge, and now held out promises of further preferment. Preston was a Calvinist conformist and the Cambridge protégé of John Davenant, who had been a delegate to the Synod of Dort and was now bishop of Salisbury. Far from being an untypical eccentric, Davenant was in the mainstream of Calvinist episcopalianism, and that Preston also found favour was of a piece with Jacobean religious developments. Indeed Preston might well have ended up adorning the episcopal bench. This was the context in which John Pym, during the parliament of 1621, rejected 'that odious and factious name of Puritans' which a fellow member had tried to fasten on the promoters of a bill for the better observance of Sunday. Pym thought that the speech was especially reprehensible in that it tended to 'divide us amongst ourselves . . . or at least would make the world believe we were divided'. As it turned out however Preston died in the ecclesiastical wilderness in 1628, and a doctrinal revolution took place within the established church which shattered the Jacobean dispensation. The two events were intimately connected, for during the 1620s the Calvinist heritage was overthrown and with it the prerequisite of English Protestant unity. The result was a polarisation of extremes unknown since the Reformation, and one which rendered earlier compromises unworkable. It is this triumph of Arminianism, and its divisive consequences, which we must now consider.

II

England in the early seventeenth century was doctrinally a part of Calvinist Europe, and it is within this ambience that the teachings of the Dutch theologian Arminius at Leyden have to be seen. During the first decade of the century, Arminius elaborated a critique of doctrinal Calvinism so systematic as to give his name to an international movement, namely Arminianism. He was concerned to refute the teachings on divine grace associated with the followers of Calvin, but he spoke as a member of the fully reformed and presbyterian Dutch Church, whereas his doctrinal equivalents in England were part of a different ecclesiastical tradition. There the most notable survivor of the English Reformation, apart from episcopacy, was the Prayer Book which, as its critics were pleased to point out, was an adapted version of the old Catholic mass book. Consequently Arminianism in England emerged with an additional, sacramental dimension to that in the United Provinces. Arminius was read with approval by anti-Calvinists in England but adapted to the local situation. English Arminians came to balance their rejection of the arbitrary grace of predestination with a new found source of grace freely available in the sacraments, which Calvinists had belittled. Hence the preoccupation under Archbishop Laud with altars and private confession before receiving communion, as well as a belief in the absolute necessity of baptism.

By the 1620s the Church of England had been Calvinist in doctrine for approximately sixty years. There had however always been a minority of dissidents, who led a more-or-less clandestine existence; in so far as these had a collective designation in the Elizabethan period they were known as 'Lutherans', after the second-generation followers of Luther who had rejected Calvinist predestinarian teaching. Not until Bancroft did the English 'Lutherans' find a champion holding high office and not even he was strong enough to swim against the Calvinist tide. But after Bancroft's death in 1610 other lesser figures emerged to lead what it now becomes proper to call the Arminian party within the Church of England. The most powerful member of this early Arminian leadership was Bishop Richard Neile, although it also included Bishops Andrewes, Buckeridge and Overall; Laud was still a relatively obscure figure, dependent on Neile's patronage. They were not allowed to air their Arminian views in print, but managed to register them in a variety of covert ways. For example, in 1617, Neile, on his translation to the bishopric of Durham, had the communion table transformed into an altar at the east end of the cathedral and supported Laud in a like action the same year at Gloucester, where the latter was dean. A few years later Overall and Andrewes can be found advocating the novel practice of private confession before receiving the communion. As Laud was to say, during the 1630s, 'the altar is the greatest place of God's residence upon earth, greater than the pulpit; for there 'tis *Hoc est corpus meum*, This is my body; but in the other it is at most but *Hoc est verbum meum*, This is my word.' Such a view involved the replacement of preaching as the normal vehicle of saving grace, and one restricted in its application to the elect saints, by sacraments which conferred grace indiscriminately; baptism of all infants, without qualification, began the process of salvation, and this was to be followed by the regular receiving of communion as a result of which all partakers, provided they confessed past sins, were renewed in grace. This flank attack on predestinarian Calvinism has misled historians into thinking that the Dutch and English Arminian movements were unconnected. In fact both Arminian parties considered themselves to be engaged in a mutual duel with Calvinism; as early as 1605 the views of Arminius were being cited with approval by anti-Calvinists in Cambridge, and the Dutch Arminians can be found from 1613 until the eve of the Synod of Dort appealing for help to Arminian bishops like Andrewes and Overall. But the latter were powerless to intervene in the United Provinces, engaged as they were in their own English struggle for survival.

If the situation was ever to alter in favour of the English Arminians, their best hope lay in trying to capture the mind of the King or at least that of the royal favourite. This was the course on which they embarked, during the aftermath of the Synod of Dort. Neile was the chief intermediary between the Arminians and King James, while Laud came to play an equivalent role in Buckingham's entourage. Apart from direct theological argument in favour of Arminianism, one powerful lever was to suggest that Calvinist conformists were Puritans at heart and as such politically subversive, or again that predestinarian Calvinism lent itself to so much popular misunderstanding that its widespread propagation inevitably led to religious conflict. By 1624 arguments of this kind seem to have affected adversely James's attitude towards Calvinism. Fear of approaching death may also have helped sap his confidence in deterministic teaching, for should doubt as to whether one was an elect saint ever become unbearable, there was always the Arminian possibility of denying that the predestinarian scheme was true. As regards Buckingham, opportunism was the most effective argument for his listening sympathetically to the Arminians. In 1624 he was identified with war against Spain, and was temporarily the hero of the parliamentary and ultra-Protestant camp. Buckingham was well aware however that the situation could rapidly change and a need arise for new allies. His willingness to support the Arminian Laud, while at the same time patronising the 'Puritan' Preston, was part of a double insurance policy for the future.

It was in this more hopeful atmosphere that the Arminian party decided on a test case. This took the form of publishing a book in 1624, by the Arminian Richard Montagu, which while ostensibly answering Roman Catholic criticisms of the Church of England also rejected predestinarian Calvinism, on the ground that this was no part of the teaching enshrined in the Thirty-Nine Articles. The interpretation of these articles was and still is debatable, but not only were Bishop Neile and his chaplains able to get Montagu's book, the *New Gag*, past the censor; they also managed to prevent its subsequent suppression. In terms of previous Arminian experience in England this was a dramatic breakthrough. Outraged Calvinist clergy appealed to Parliament; John Pym took up their cause in the House of Commons, and Archbishop Abbot made representations to King James. The only result was a royal request that Richard Montagu clarify his views by writing a second book. Yet it soon became clear that the final arbiter of England's theological fate would be the heir to the throne, Prince Charles. Prior to his accession some observers considered Charles to be inclined towards Puritanism, but those closer to him, among them the Arminian Mathew Wren, claimed the reverse was true and that on this score his reign would contrast with James's. Wren's prediction was to prove abundantly true, for King Charles became the architect of an Arminian revolution which had at most been dimly foreshadowed in the last year of his father's reign. As the House of Commons was to complain in 1629: 'some prelates, near the King, having gòtten the chief adminis-tration of ecclesiastical affairs under his Majesty, have discountenanced and hindered the preferment of those that are orthodox [i.e. Calvinist], and favoured such as are contrary.'

The suddenness of James's death in March 1625 seems to have taken most people by surprise. Buckingham survived as royal favourite, but it was now Charles who increasingly made the religious pace. The new King had never apparently been a Calvinist; certainly a decisive bias in favour of Arminianism became clear during the first few months of his reign. Calvinist bishops were excluded from the royal counsels, and in July 1625 the Arminian Richard Montagu was placed under Charles's personal protection. In February of the following year Buckingham, clearly acting with the approval of Charles, chaired a debate at York House on the subject of Montagu's writings, in the course of which he made plain his Arminian sympathies. The Arminian Bishop Buckeridge was pitted against the Calvinist Bishop Morton, and during their exchanges the question arose as to how predestinarian doctrine could be reconciled with Prayer Book teaching on the sacraments of baptism and communion. 'What,' exclaimed Morton, 'will you have the grace of God tied to sacraments?' Buckeridge's seconder, Dean White of Carlisle, replied that all baptised infants were 'made the sons of God by adoption', and Buckingham told Morton that he 'disparaged his own ministry, and did . . . debase the sacrament'. White further argued that the Synod of Dort, by limiting Christ's redemption to the elect, had overthrown the sacrament of communion; he asked how on such predestinarian assumptions could ministers 'say to all communicants whatsoever, "The Body of our Lord which was given for thee", as we are bound to say? Let the opinion of the Dortists be admitted, and the tenth person in the Church shall not have been redeemed.' This clash of interpretation underlines the sacramental emphasis of the English Arminian rejection of Calvinism, whereby the Prayer Book was thrown into the scales against the Calvinist interpretation of the Thirty-Nine Articles which had been so prevalent in Elizabethan and Jacobean times.

The York House conference was however far from being a mere wrangle among theologians. It had been called at the request of Viscount Saye and the Earl of Warwick, who were two of the government's most prominent critics and subsequently leaders of the Parliamentary party in the Civil War. Moreover Bishop Morton's seconder at the conference was the 'Puritan' John Preston, and their ability to collaborate in this fashion exemplified the sixty-year-old shared Calvinist assumptions which were now at risk. Immediately after the conference, the Arminian John Cosin was reporting that the King 'swears his perpetual patronage of our cause', and the rebuff that Calvinism received at York House was the signal for the House of Commons to begin impeachment proceedings against Buckingham for alleged gross mismanagement of the government. The fiction was maintained by the opposition that Buckingham's policies were distinct from those of the Crown, but this became increasingly unconvincing especially as regards religion. In June 1626 Buckingham was foisted on Cambridge University as chancellor, and all predestinarian teaching was forthwith forbidden. This was backed up by a royal proclamation which effectively outlawed Calvinism on a national basis. The London and Cambridge printing presses rapidly succumbed. At Oxford University however under the chancellorship of the Calvinist third Earl of Pembroke predestinarian views were preached and printed for another two years. But even Oxford yielded when in late 1628 Charles reissued the Thirty-Nine Articles with a prefatory declaration which insisted on their 'literal and grammatical' sense and commanded 'that all further curious search be laid aside, and these disputes shut up in God's promises, as they be generally set forth to us in holy scriptures'. As Prideaux the Oxford Regius Professor of divinity put it, 'we are concluded under an anathema to stand to the Synod of Dort against the Arminians'.

Reaction in Parliament to this Arminianisation of the Church of England became increasingly strident, and the situation was made worse by the readiness of the Arminians to brand their Calvinist opponents as Puritans. We know from Laud's diary that in 1626 he had been promised the succession to Canterbury, and from this date he comes into prominence as the chief religious spokesman of the government. His sermon at the opening of Charles's second parliament in February 1626 was remarkable for its aggressive tone. He conjured up the vision of a presbyterian conspiracy, aiming at the overthrow of church and state. 'They, whoever they be, that would overthrow *sedes ecclesia*, the seats of ecclesiastical government, will not spare (if ever they get power) to have a pluck at the throne of David. And there is not a man that is for parity, all fellows in the Church, but he is not for monarchy in the State.' The reply of Pym and numerous other Calvinist members of the House of Commons was that on the contrary they were the true orthodox loyalists and that the new Arminian religion was both heterodox and the means of introducing Roman Catholicism into England. Some went further and claimed that the denouement would be the murder of the king at the hands of Jesuit-inspired plotters. They took particular exception to Richard Montagu's use of the term Puritan – a use shared by Laud who in 1624 had written on the subject of 'doctrinal Puritanism'. A Commons committee reported in 1625 that Montagu 'saith there are Puritans in heart' and that 'bishops may be Puritans'; since Montagu also defined predestinarian Calvinists as Puritans, the committee were quite correct to conclude that 'by his opinion we may be all Puritans'. More generally the Commons appealed to recent history in justification of their Calvinist exposition of English religion.

Arminianism was of course only one among a number of reasons for the breakdown of relations between Charles and his parliaments in the late 1620s, but some idea of its relative importance is conveyed by the last parliament before the Personal Rule, that of 1628-9. The first session was largely taken up with the Petition of Right, in an attempt to prevent any future resort by the crown to forced loans, but the second session saw Arminianism as an issue taking precedence over other questions; charges of heterodoxy were levelled at Neile and Laud, who had both been made Privy Councillors in early 1627, and it was claimed the path of ecclesiastical preferment was blocked to all but men of their persuasion. The debate on Arminianism was opened on 26 January 1629 by Francis Rous. The issue he said was 'right of religion . . . and

137

this right, in the name of this nation, I this day claim, and desire that there may be a deep and serious consideration of the violation of it'. The violations, he thought, reduced to two, consisting of both a growth of Catholicism and Arminianism, the latter being 'an error that maketh the grace of God lackey it after the will of man, that maketh the sheep to keep the shepherd, that maketh mortal seed of an immortal God'. Moreover he claimed that the two phenomena were biologically connected, 'for an Arminian is the spawn of a Papist', and it was now high time for the Commons to covenant together in defence of true religion. Arminianism and the more mundane subject of tunnage and poundage were the main items of the session until it was forcibly terminated on 2 March. Rous and all the other contributors to the debate on religion, with one Arminian exception, spoke as Calvinist episcopalians. The rise of Arminianism was seen as a function of clerical pretentiousness, but was not yet considered to discredit the episcopal order as such. Indeed Sir John Eliot, speaking of Richard Montagu who had been consecrated a bishop in August 1628, said 'I reverence the order, I honour not the man'. But this reverence was subject to the continued existence of other bishops 'that openly show their hearts to the Truth'.

John Pym was not given to the rhetoric of Eliot and Rous, but he more than any other MP inspired the Commons' case against Arminianism. From 1624 to 1629 he can be found chairing committees, delivering reports, and preparing impeachment charges on the Arminian question. Like many of his fellow MPs, Pym had imbibed Calvinism both in the home and at university. For them cynical calculations of the kind made by Buckingham were not a primary motive, nor in most cases did their religious stance disguise materialistic hopes of stripping the church of its remaining wealth. Nevertheless speeches on the floor of the House of Commons were not made *in vacuo*, and it is therefore particularly interesting to penetrate where possible behind the public image. While this cannot on present material be done for Pym, considerable evidence has survived for Oliver St John who was to inherit the leadership of the Long Parliament on Pym's death in 1643. St John, who was about fourteen years younger than Pym, had been a pupil of Preston at Cambridge, and there still exists a religious commonplace book which he kept during the 1620s and early 1630s. This allows for a reconstruction of his beliefs before the Civil War experience intervened, and an illuminating portrait emerges. He appears quite prepared to accept the order of episcopacy and has no objection to ceremonial conformity, in both cases quoting with approval the views of Bishop Davenant. Especially noticeable however is his dominating concern with predestinarian theology, Calvinist views being listed at length and their opposites labelled as 'heterodox'. Although he seems to agree with William Prynne's hostile views on the subject of bowing at the name of Jesus, so did Archbishop Abbot. The only other signs of Puritanism are some doubts about whether clergymen might hold civil office, and strong disapproval of men growing their hair long or any similar marks of what St John calls 'effeminacy'.

All the indications are that Pym's brand of Puritanism was much the same as that of St John. This is supported by a mass of material relating to the fourth earl of Bedford, who was both St John's employer and Pym's close associate. The evidence, again consisting of commonplace books, has only recently become available to historians and investigation is not yet complete. Like St John, Bedford appears to be a firm Calvinist and much exercised about the predestinarian controversy. At the same time he does not think of himself as a Puritan, whom at one point he dismisses as a person who 'will eat his red herring on Christmas day, and his roast beef on Good Friday'. He sees Arminianism leading logically to Catholicism, writing of the former as 'the little thief put into the window of the church to unlock the door', and cites Bishop Williams against the altar-wise position of the communion table. Unfortunately such entries cannot be dated as accurately as those from St John, and the *terminus ad quem* is Bedford's death from smallpox in 1641. Thus it is not clear from how long before the Long Parliament dates his dislike of lordly bishops. He writes, or quotes from some anonymous authority, that 'lordship [was] forbidden to the apostles, Matth. 20.25, therefore dars't thou assume it?' But he also notes that when the Hussites thrust out bishops there was left 'neither bishop nor earl'. His general social conservatism and concern to preserve the aristocratic order are revealed in a number of passages, as for instance when considering the rise of favourites or quoting Viscount Saye on the ambitions of plebeians. Bedford perhaps carried the greatest weight among the leaders of the opposition to Charles I. His religious views seem to have been fairly typical of the opposition leadership as a whole, although Saye, his son Nathaniel Fiennes, and Lord Brooke all held more radical beliefs. Their families, who tended to intermarry, sometimes had formidable Calvinist matriarchs in the background like Elizabeth Clinton, countess of Lincoln. It was she who campaigned against the upper class practice of putting children out to wet nurses on the ground, among others, that the infant might be 'one of God's very elect . . . to whom to be a nursing mother, is a queen's honour'. Her son, the fourth earl of Lincoln, was also a pupil of the 'Puritan' Preston at Cambridge, and married a daughter of Viscount Saye. He distinguished himself by raising troops to fight for the recovery of the Palatinate, and in 1626 refused to contribute to the forced loan. Not very surprisingly he ended by siding against the King in the Civil War. Another Calvinist bluestocking, this time from the upper gentry, was Lady Mary Vere, wife of the hero of the siege of Mannheim and instrumental in securing the archbishopric of Armagh for James Ussher in 1624. Ussher was a close friend of some of the leading Puritan nonconformists, and his scheme for limited episcopacy put forward in the first months of the Long Parliament looked briefly like proving an acceptable compromise. With the subsequent destruction of the hierarchy he was appointed, at the instigation of St John, lecturer at

Lincoln's Inn. Indeed the 'godly bishop' long remained a legitimate Puritan aspiration.

Among the clergy in the late 1620s, as with the laity, the hallmark of opposition to the Arminian policy of the government was still Calvinist episcopalianism. Puritan nonconformity although subsumed within this Calvinist episcopalianism was not the question at issue. As for presbyterianism, it was a negligible element in the situation, being confined to a handful of survivors from Elizabethan days. Nevertheless, it has been argued by Christopher Hill that English Puritanism in the first decades of the seventeenth century was taking on a new and looser institutional form, along the lines of congregationalism *within* episcopacy. In so far as this was the case, it still implies a compatibility of religious approach prior to the Arminian 1630s. The continued failure however of Calvinist episcopalianism to withstand the pressures of Arminianism was bound in the longer term to result in its being discredited as a viable church system. Charles's decision in 1629 to rule without parliament brought that time nearer, for it meant there was now no court of Calvinist appeal left. In 1630 died the third earl of Pembroke, who had been the most influential Calvinist among the king's privy councillors. He was moreover succeeded as chancellor of Oxford by Laud, who since 1628 had been controlling the London printing press as Bishop of London. The York primacy had been filled with a succession of Arminians since the Calvinist Matthew's death in 1628, and from 1632 was occupied by Neile. At Canterbury the Calvinist Abbot, in disgrace ever since refusing to license a sermon in support of forced loans in 1627, lingered on until 1633 when he was succeeded by Laud. By this process the court increasingly isolated itself from Calvinist opinion in the country. Arminian doctrines were now freely published while Calvinism languished in silence. An instance of the lengths to which propaganda went is supplied by the 1633 edition of the standard Latin–English Dictionary, compiled by Francis Holyoke. Published at Oxford and dedicated to Laud, this new edition contained for the first time the word *Praedestinatiani*, who were defined as 'a kind of heretics that held fatal predestination of every particular matter person or action, and that all things came to passe, and fell out necessarily; especially touching the salvation and damnation of particular men'. While Calvinists would regard this as misrepresenting their views, the definition was clearly aimed at them. This is confirmed by its citation in a book of 1635 by the Arminian Edmund Reeve, called *The Communion Catechisme Expounded*. Dedicating the work to Bishop Wright of Coventry and Lichfield, he claimed Bishops Overall and Buckeridge as his mentors. The exposition, which grew from the needs of his congregation at Hayes in Middlesex, contains an explicit refutation of predestinarian Calvinism and is a typical product of the decade.

Theory went hand in hand with practice. In November 1633, three months after Laud became Archbishop of Canterbury, King Charles by act of Privy Council established the precedent that all parochial churches should follow the by then general cathedral practice of placing communion tables altar-wise at the east end of chancels. We have already had cause to comment on the sacramental undermining by English Arminians of the Calvinist theology of grace, and on the basis of this Privy Council ruling Arminianism during the 1630s was made manifest throughout every parish in England, the sacrament of the alter becoming henceforth a propitiation for the sins of all partakers. These were the years too which saw an unprecedented onslaught on the lecturing movement, the *cause célèbre* being the dissolution of the Feoffees for Impropriations in 1633. The Feoffees were a trust, administered by a group of clergy, lawyers and merchants, and set up in an attempt to improve the level of clerical incomes. Laud, supported by Charles, claimed that a plot was involved to destroy episcopal jurisdiction. This sinister interpretation was not however shared by bishops like Morton, who in 1630 can be found recommending an impoverished curate to the charity of the Feoffees. Morton was, as we'have seen, a Calvinist, and did not agree with Laud's dictum that the altar took precedence over the pulpit. The attitude of the hierarchy to lecturers was in fact largely a matter of theological perspective. From a Calvinist standpoint preaching, whether by a beneficed incumbent or a lecturer, was the chief means of salvation. Only an episcopate dominated by Arminians could contemplate with equanimity, and indeed pleasure, a diminution in the number of sermons preached. Similarly Arminian bishops had little compunction in silencing nonconforming lecturers, whereas their Calvinist predecessors had so far as possible avoided this extreme.

This change in attitude was not confined to the treatment of lecturers, but extended to nonconformity in general, and not only did the breaking of the Calvinist theological bond lead to the stricter enforcement of conformity: nonconformity itself acquired a much wider definition. Nonconformist offences now included expounding the Thirty-Nine Articles in a Calvinist sense or any form of predestinarian preaching, objecting to the new ceremonies associated with the transformation of communion tables into altars, and refusal to implement the Declaration of Sports which was reissued by Charles in 1633. The surviving Calvinist bishops found themselves in an alien world, and were distrusted by their colleagues; the Arminian Laud went so far as to put a spy on the tail of the Calvinist Morton. We have already noted that the English Arminians redefined Puritanism so as to include doctrinal Calvinism and this elicited from Bishop Davenant of Salisbury the anguished complaint: 'Why that should now be esteemed Puritan doctrine, which those held who have done our Church the greatest service in beating down Puritanism, or why men should be restrained from teaching that doctrine hereafter, which hitherto has been generally and publicly maintained, (wiser men perhaps may) but I cannot understand.' When however in 1633 the Calvinist Davenant, who was also a sabbatarian, had to discipline the recorder of Salisbury, Henry Sherfield, for destroying an allegedly idolatrous window in a church, doubts were expressed by his cathedral dean as to whether he would take a sufficiently firm line. Hardly surprisingly the 1630s as a whole saw a great increase in the number of prosecutions for Puritanism, an indirect measure of this being the large scale emigration to New England. In addition to creating widespread resentment of the episcopal hierarchy, these persecuting activities generated a Puritan militancy which in the early 1640s was to erupt in the shape of presbyterianism and congregationalism.

Arminian clerics also revealed themselves as very hostile to lay intervention in church matters. This was partly because parliament had proved so antagonistic, and they were in any case completely dependent on royal protection, but there was also a novel sacerdotal element in their teaching whereby the priestly replaced the preaching function. Evidence exists to suggest that one of the factors involved here was a desire to compensate for a sense of social inferiority. Certainly the Calvinist bishops had better blood relations with the gentry and aldermanic classes than did their Arminian successors, and there was some substance to Lord Brooke's derogatory remarks in 1641 about low-born prelates. At the same time the reassertion of sacramental grace lent itself to the view that clerics were almost a caste apart, but because of their magical not their preaching roles. Indeed many English Arminians consciously regarded themselves as engaged in a counter-reforming movement dedicated to undoing the Protestant damage of the Reformation.

While English Arminianism did not automatically result in the theoretical advancement of royal absolutism in the secular sphere, the injunction 'render unto Caesar' might seem a fitting counterpart to the idea of a holy priesthood with consecrated property rights. The Calvinist opposition however conveniently forgot that during the debates on the Petition of Right the Arminian Bishop Harsnett had spoken out in defence of the subject's liberties, and instead they remembered the stance of Archbishop Abbot, in condemning the arguments of Sibthorpe and Mainwaring for unparliamentary taxation. Indeed as early as the 1590s Abbott had taught that 'God is better pleased, when good things shall be commanded, first by the highest in place, and then after it shall be added, by the Lords spiritual and temporal, and by the assent of the commons. And Princes which are gracious do never grieve at this, and wise men do love that style, when all is not appropriated to one, but there is a kind of parting.' Yet a decade or so earlier Archbishop Sandys, a man of similar theological colour to Abbot, had preached that taxation was a tribute due to the King and not a gift freely given. Thus there was an element of accident in the Arminian and royalist partnership. But in practice the religious policy of King Charles meant that during the Personal Rule absolutism and Arminianism became closely identified in the popular mind.

On the future Parliamentarian side there did however exist a positive link with Calvinism, concerning the right of political resistance. Calvinists held no monopoly of such views, but among Protestants they had developed the most explicit body of teaching on the subject. In

England by far the most important vehicle of their thought was the Genevan annotated version of the Bible, which among other things had a predestinarian catechism bound up with it. Not always entirely consistent and stopping considerably short of an outright doctrine of tyrannicide, the Genevan commentators were prepared to admit the legitimacy of resistance to magistrates in certain circumstances, especially when the issue was religion. Their medium was Biblical history, notably that contained in the Old Testament, and the use they made of it led King James to insist that the new Authorised translation of the Bible should contain no marginalia at all, apart from variant readings and cross-references. Illustrative of the political tendency of the Genevan annotations is that Ecclesiastes, viii. 3. had been glossed as 'withdraw not thy self lightly from the obedience of thy prince', and the famous opening verse of Romans xiii, 'Let every soul be subject unto the higher powers . . .' was described as relating to a 'private man', thus in principle leaving inferior magistrates free to act against erring superiors.

Despite the existence of an official rival from 1611 onwards, the Genevan Bible long retained its popularity, being printed latterly in the Low Countries with the fictitious date 1599 on its title page. In origin the Genevan version was the work of a group of Marian exiles. They had included Goodman and Knox, who were both authors of works advocating the right of armed defence, particularly against heretical and persecuting rulers. Although the product of a specific exilic situation, ideas of this type survived the turn of the century, by which date however they were usually confined to discussions about continental Protestantism. Thus in 1603 Robert Abbot, brother of the future Archbishop, dedicated a book to King James which contained a defence of both Dutch and French Protestant rebels. At the same time there existed a competing body of passive-resistance theory, against which the only regular antidote was the Genevan Bible. With the subsequent rise of English Arminianism, Calvinist ideas of resistance took on new domestic relevance; as early as 1632 a Puritan lecturer, Nathaniel Barnard, dared to make the connection in a sermon. After the actual outbreak of hostilities, one of those to be found defending the Parliamentary cause on religious grounds was Stephen Marshall, who has been described as 'the most famous political parson of the Revolution'. Eschewing legal arguments, Marshall cited Biblical precedent and, among more recent authorities Bishop Abbot.

Perhaps even without a rebellion in Scotland the finances of the Personal Rule would have foundered on their own inadequacies, and a parliament have had to be summoned. What however until recently has largely gone unnoticed, is the part played in the Scottish disturbances by Arminianism. The Scots at this time are usually thought of as intransigent presbyterians for whom Charles's attempt to impose an English-style prayer book was simply an excuse to throw off the whole episcopalian system. But it has been pointed out that many of the members of the Glasgow Assembly, which in 1638 abolished bishops, had never known a fully presbyterian church. Moreover someone like Robert Baillie, who is traditionally thought of as a presbyterian diehard, was even at that date not prepared to deny that a form of episcopacy had scriptural warrant. Arminianism however appears to have been the deciding factor. The Glasgow Assembly explicitly modelled itself on the Synod of Dort and listened to a series of harangues on the Arminian question. What really seems to have rankled was not so much the office of bishop but that the hierarchy were mostly Arminians. Again and again this charge features in the indictments, and heterodox teaching on predestination clearly is meant. The dual association with unpopular royalist policies in the secular field and with Arminianism in the religious meant that episcopacy went down even faster in Scotland than it was to in England where the system was more indigenous.

The Short Parliament of 1640, called to subsidise the suppression of the Scottish rebellion, did not last long enough for the religious question fully to come out in the open, although 'innovations in matters of religion' were high on Pym's list of grievances. The fact that after the dissolution of parliament the convocation of clergy continued in session and proceeded to enact a series of canons which included a strong statement of royal absolutism, all fostered a mounting hostility to the episcopate. Nor was the example of Scotland lost on the English opposition, and increasingly too a presbyterian model in religion became the price of Scottish support. When the Long Parliament assembled later in the year more radical pressures were brought to bear by the London populace, and the Root and Branch Petition of December, which called for the abolition of bishops, in part represented such interests. Even here however it was the woeful results of episcopacy, with Arminianism taking a prominent place, that were stressed rather than the essential unlawfulness of the order. Moreover, Calvinists like Archbishop Ussher and Bishop Morton meeting in committee during March 1641 with Puritan ministers such as Marshall and Calamy looked like agreeing on a common reformist platform. But the basic Arminian intransigence of King Charles, combined with the sheer speed of events, made religious compromises of this kind unworkable. Conciliation was overtaken by the drift to war.

As an old man looking back on the Civil War at the end of the century, Philip fourth Lord Wharton, who had fought against the king, claimed that 'a hundred to one of the Calvinists... joined the parliamentarians'. The process which had brought this alleged situation about was highly complex, and even Wharton would not have seriously maintained that all they were fighting about was Calvinism. At the same time the propaganda put out by Parliamentary army officers in the early stages of the war does suggest a high degree of religious motivation. This declaration of sentiments took the visual form of battle standards flown by the captains of each cavalry troop, who incidentally all claimed to be gentlemen. While Magna Carta and a blood-stained head, probably Strafford's, were occasionally chosen as symbols, the dominating motif was the Bible with accompanying slogans such as 'Verbum Dei', 'Sacra Scriptura' and 'Jehova Nisi'. Also depicted were bishops tumbling from their thrones with the caption 'Antichrist Must Down', a lethal rain of arrows labelled 'Contra Impios' and cloud-wreathed anchors illustrating the assertion 'Only in Heaven'. Comparable propaganda on the Royalist side was of a much more secular kind, displaying the insignia of monarchy or satirising the 'roundhead' opposition. One popular emblem was a pack of hounds all barking 'Pym'. Revealingly, Charles described his opponents as consisting mainly of 'Brownists, Anabaptists and Atheists'. Such was the gulf of misunderstanding that had opened up between the Arminian king and his Calvinist subjects.

In terms of English Protestant history the charge in 1640 that King Charles and Archbishop Laud were religious innovators is irrefutable. The reaction provoked however by the Arminian revolution was of such violence that it could be transformed with relative ease into a call for 'root and branch' remedies, and presbyterianism emerge as the cure of Arminian disease. Thus what had begun as a counter-revolution itself became radicalised.

13 BRIAN MANNING

Religion and Politics: The Godly People

I

Richard Baxter, the puritan divine, observed that constitutional and religious grievances had become intertwined by 1640, because 'the King had at once imposed the Shipmoney on the Commonwealth, *and* permitted the Bishops to impose upon the Church their displeasing Articles, and bowing towards the Altar, and the Book for dancing on the Lord's day, and the liturgy on Scotland, etc. and to suspend or silence abundance of ministers...' Nevertheless, Baxter made a distinction between the constitutional and the religious opposition to Charles I, and he believed that there were 'two sorts of men' in the Long Parliament: the 'one party made no great matter of these alterations in the Church; but they said, that if Parliaments were once down, and our propriety [i.e. property] gone, and arbitrary government set up, and law subjected to the Prince's will, we were then all slaves, and this they made a thing intolerable; for the remedying of which, they said, every true Englishman could think no price too dear: these the people called Good Commonwealth's Men. The other sort were the more religious men, who were also sensible of all these things, but were much more sensible of the interest of religion, and these most inveighed against the innovations in the Church, the bowing to Altars, the Book for Sports on Sundays, the casting out of ministers, the troubling of the people by the High Commission Court, the pilloring and cutting off men's ears, (Mr Burton's, Mr Prynne's, and Dr Bastwick's) for speaking against the Bishops, the putting down lectures, and afternoon sermons and expositions on the Lord's Day, with such other things, which they thought of greater weight than shipmoney. But because these latter agreed with the former in the vindication of the people's propriety and liberties, the former did the easilier concur with them against the proceedings of the Bishops and High Commission Court.'

In Baxter's view this distinction between the 'Good Commonwealth's Men' and 'the more religious men' corresponded to a social division: the nobility and gentry were more concerned about the constitution, the middle rank of the people about religion. The nobility and gentry who 'adhered to the Parliament' in the civil war did so, in Baxter's opinion, chiefly out of concern for 'the Publick Safety

---

From *Politics, Religion and the English Civil War*, ed. Brian Manning (Edward Arnold, 1973), pp. 83–123. Footnotes have been deleted.

and Liberty', that is, for political rather than for religious reasons. They agreed, no doubt, with the reasons given by the Earl of Northumberland in May-June 1642 for supporting parliament: '... we believe that those persons who are most powerful with the King do endeavour to bring Parliaments to such a condition that they shall only be made instruments to execute the commands of the King, who were established for his greatest and most supreme council'; '... let us but have our laws, liberties and privileges secured unto us. ....' Sir John Hotham was one of those who adhered to parliament for political rather than religious reasons. He 'was as well affected to the government of the Church of England ... as any man that had concurred with them ...', but he 'was a man that loved liberty, which was an occasion to make him join at first with the Puritan party ...', though '... in more than concerned the civil liberty he did not approve their ways'. '... He was manly for the defence of the liberty of the subject and privilege of Parliament, but was not at all for their new opinions in Church government.' In this he reflected the views of many of the gentry in his own county who supported parliament in the civil war, for exactly half of the parliamentarian gentry in Yorkshire were not puritans. And in the House of Lords there were thirty-one peers who supported parliament at the outbreak of the civil war, but about half of them showed no signs of puritanism. Thomas May observed that the nobility and gentry thought it much clearer that the king had violated the laws and liberties of the kingdom than that he had favoured popery, and even puritan gentry thought that there was more justification for parliament to go to war in 1642 for 'defence of the just English liberties' than for defence of 'the true protestant religion': John Hutchinson, a Nottinghamshire gentleman and puritan, was 'convinced in conscience of the righteousness of the parliament's cause in point of civil right; and though he was satisfied of the endeavours to reduce [i.e. bring back] popery and subvert the true protestant religion ... yet he did not think that so clear a ground for the war as the defence of the just English liberties. ....' The immediate issue over which the civil war broke out – the Militia Ordinance – was not a religious issue. Oliver Cromwell recalled that '... religion was not the thing at the first contested for, but God brought it to that issue at last, and gave it unto us by way of redundancy, and at last it proved to be that which was most dear to us', implying that he himself had at the beginning seen the issue as political, and this no doubt reflected the fact that he was a gentleman as well as a puritan. For the leaders of the parliamentarian party, puritan or not, 'the thing at the first contested for' was the limitation of the king's power; but those that were not puritans tended to desert the party when religion came to obtain 'the most eminent place in the parliament's cause', while those that were puritans, like Hutchinson and Cromwell, remained loyal.

Non-puritan gentlemen supported parliament for political reasons alone, but puritan gentlemen did so for both political and religious reasons. Sir Simonds D'Ewes, a wealthy Suffolk squire, was as con-

147

cerned as any nobleman or gentleman with constitutional questions, and with the defence of 'the liberty of the subjects of England'; but when in June 1642, like the Earl of Northumberland, he had to make a choice between king and parliament, he referred, unlike the Earl of Northumberland, to religion rather than to politics. His younger brother had joined the king at York and had written to Sir Simonds on 17 June: 'I was in good hopes to have seen you here before the arrival of these will come to your hands: but I should think this or any other pains well awarded, if I could be the happy inducement to bring you hither. I daily understand how you stand affected, and what your opinions are, and out of that sincere affection I bear you, I heartily wish you fortunate in their continuance.' On 21 June Sir Simonds sat down to compose the most important letter of his life, for it was to announce his decision to remain with the two Houses of Parliament rather than to join the king: 'I would be willing to redeem the reunion of his Majesty and the two Houses with my dearest blood; that so religion might be established in that power and purity amongst us, and preaching so settled in those places where atheism, profaneness, and ignorance now reigns, as that all men might know their duty to God and the King. . . .' Although Sir Simonds was an expert 'in the municipal laws and ancient records of this state', and was well qualified to make up his mind about the legal and constitutional issues in 1642, it was not in the end on these grounds that he justified his stand, but on religious grounds. And his religious reasons were more positive than dislike of 'innovations in the Church', or fear of a return to popery, for they were based on a desire for 'reformation' and the rule of godliness in England. Similarly, although Hutchinson studied 'the things then in dispute, and read all the public papers that came forth between the king and parliament, besides many other private treatises, both concerning the present and foregoing times', and became convinced of 'the righteousness of the parliament's cause in point of civil right', this was not sufficient to persuade him to take up arms for parliament, and he was not drawn into the fighting until he found 'a clear call from the Lord' – in other words, a religious justification. D'Ewes and Hutchinson put religion first, but whether gentlemen put religion or politics first in 1642, they were all aware that there were both religious and political issues, and that these, though interrelated and interdependent, could be distinguished from each other.

D'Ewes and Hutchinson felt able to understand and competent to decide the legal and constitutional questions, but others of the gentry, and most people of the middle and lower ranks of society, felt as Richard Baxter, who confessed that he 'was not judicious enough in Politicks and Law to decide this Controversie which so many Lawyers and Wise men differed in'. But Baxter knew what reforms he wanted to see in the church, and that the only hope of achieving such reforms was through parliament; so when he became convinced that the king intended to crush the parliament by force, he could not but agree that the 'religious men' must take up arms to defend the parliament.

Groups of puritans in London and the provinces had placed their hopes for reformation in the parliament and hence their cause was bound up with the success or failure of the parliament. [. . .]

When the king and the two Houses of Parliament appealed to arms against each other, the 'godly people' did not automatically flock as a body to the defence of the latter. Like most people in 1642, they hesitated, uncertain at first what course to take. John Hutchinson, although he 'was clearly swayed by his own judgment and reason to the parliament', hung back from declaring himself and 'contented himself with praying for peace', 'thinking he had no warrantable call at that time, to do anything more'. Eventually he did take up arms for parliament and became a leading parliamentarian in Nottinghamshire; but his prolonged hesitation was significant because, although judging parliament to be in the right on legal and constitutional grounds, he did not immediately identify the cause of parliament with the cause of religion. [. . .]

Why did 'the main body' of puritans support the parliament? It seems likely that the average puritan was influenced by the example of ministers and laymen who were noted for godliness. Adam Martindale, son of a Lancashire yeoman, was drawn into the parliamentarian party because 'all the ministers in our neighbourhood, to a man, except only two tippling boon companions, and all serious Christians generally declared themselves satisfied for the cause of that party among whom I sheltered myself, whose opinion and practice all those that think I should have sleighted them, must grant to be a strong temptation'. Similarly, Baxter confessed that the very fact that godly people declared for parliament led him to do the same, and 'the Consideration of the Quality of the Parties that sided for each Cause, in the Countries, did greatly work with me, and more than it should have done'. 'The devout people' of Nottingham adhered to parliament, and 'the ordinary civil sort of people' followed them. 'Upon my knowledge', wrote Baxter, 'many that were not wise enough to understand the Truth about the Cause of the King and Parliament, did yet run into the Parliament's Armies, or take their part . . .' only because they saw other religious people do so, 'as Sheep go together for Company . . .' It was not just the lead given by some puritan preachers, for Baxter emphasized the role of puritan laymen, saying that since a great number of those persons that were accounted most religious fell in with parliament, 'the generality of the stricter diligent sort of Preachers joyned with them . . .', and indeed were acting under pressure from 'the younger unexperienced sort of religious People. . . .'

Besides, the royalist party seemed to be the party of the ungodly: '. . . the Gentry that were not so precise and strict against an Oath, or Gaming, or Plays, or Drinking, nor troubled themselves so much about the Matters of God and the World to come, and the Ministers and People that were for the King's Book, for Dancing and Recreations on the Lord's Days; and those that made not so great a matter of every Sin, but went to Church and heard Common Prayer, and were glad to hear a

Sermon which lasht the Puritans, and which ordinarily spoke against this strictness and preciseness in Religion, and this strict Observation of the Lord's Day, and following Sermons, and praying Extempore, and talking so much of Scripture and the Matters of Salvation, and those that hated and derided them that take these Courses, the main body of these were against the Parliament.' This was not just the view of a parliamentarian, for the royalist William Chillingworth reproached his own party with 'profaneness', want of piety and lack of zeal for reformation, and Clarendon criticized 'the license, disorder, and impiety' of the king's soldiers. If this were true, it must have confirmed religious people in thinking that the parliamentarian party was the party of religion and reformation. 'An abundance of the ignorant sort of the Country, who were Civil, did flock in to the Parliament, and filled up their Armies afterward, merely because they heard Men swear for the Common Prayer and Bishops, and heard others pray that were against them; and because they heard the King's Soldiers with horrid Oaths abuse the name of God, and saw them live in Debauchery, and the Parliament's Soldiers flock to Sermons, and talking of Religion, and praying and singing Psalms together on their Guards.'

If the example of a few 'godly' preachers and laymen was one factor in bringing the general body of puritans into the parliamentarian party, persecution by the anti-puritan royalists was another, and perhaps more important factor in forcing the mass of puritans into the parliamentarian armies and garrisons. Probably nothing did more to convert puritans into parliamentarians than the assumption of the king's supporters that all puritans were the king's enemies. Puritans, as the label was applied in the seventeenth century, were an obtrusive and identifiable minority, because of their appetite for sermons, their refusal to take part in sports and traditional pastimes on Sundays, their reading the bible and praying with their families, and more especially because of the peculiarities of their manners and appearance: 'When puritanism grew into a faction,' wrote a puritan lady, 'the zealots distinguished themselves, both men and women, by several affect-ations of habit, looks, and words. . . . Among other affected habits, few of the puritans, what degree soever they were of, wore their hair long enough to cover their ears, and the ministers and many others cut it close round their heads, with so many little peaks, as was something ridiculous to behold.' This invited attack.

During the summer of 1642 in Hereford puritan preachers were shouted down as 'Roundheads' and threatened with physical violence. At Ludlow puritans were called 'Roundheads' and encountered so much hostility 'that they durst not leave their homes to come to the fast'. 'There is such an antipathy in the generality of the poor and gentry here, against any one that seems but religious...', it was reported from York, that such as 'prayed and read the Scriptures, morning and evening' were denounced as 'Puritans and Roundheads'. 'Insomuch that if a Stranger past in many places that had short Hair and a Civil Habit, the Rabble presently cried, "Down with the Roundheads"; and some they knockt down in the open Streets,' wrote Baxter: 'In this Fury of the Rabble I was advised to withdraw a while from home; whereupon I went to Gloucester: As I past through a corner of the Suburbs of Worcester, they that knew me not, cried, "Down with the Round-heads", and I was glad to spur on and be gone.' After a month he returned to Kidderminster but still 'found the beggarly drunken Rout in a very tumultuating Disposition, and the Superiors that were for the King did animate them, and the People of the Place who were accounted Religious were called Round-heads, and openly reviled, and threatened as the King's Enemies (who had never medled in any Cause against the King). Every drunken Sot that met any of them in the Streets, would tell them, "we shall take order with the Puritans ere long".'

As soon as the King's army was set on foot his soldiers took all puritans for their enemies without the need for any other evidence than their puritanism. In Shropshire Baxter's father 'and all his Neighbours that were noted for praying and hearing Sermons, were plundered by the King's Soldiers, so that some of them had almost nothing but Lumber left in their Houses: though my Father was so far from medling on either side, that he knew not what they were doing, but followed his own business. . . .' When the king came to Nottingham to raise his standard in August 1642 his troops ranged over the country: '. . . a troop of cavaliers, under the command of Sir Lewis Dives, came to Stanton, near Owthorpe, and searched Mr Needham's house, who was a noted puritan in those days . . . they found not him, for he hid himself in the gorse, and so escaped them. His house being lightly plundered, they went to Hickling, and plundered another Puritan house there, and were coming to Owthorpe, of which Mr Hutchinson having notice, went away to Leicestershire; but they, though they had orders to seize Mr Hutchinson, came not at that time because the night grew on. But some days after he was gone, another company came and searched for him and for arms and plate, of which finding none, they took nothing else.' He took refuge in Northamptonshire, in 'the house of a substantial honest yeoman', and 'this man and his wife, being godly, gave Mr Hutchinson very kind entertainment. . . .' The 'godly people' of Nottinghamshire were plundered and driven from their homes 'by the rudeness of the King's army' merely 'on account of their godliness'. Henry Ireton, who belonged to the minor gentry and 'had an education in the strictest way of godliness' and was 'a very grave, serious, religious person', formed some of these refugees into a troop of horse which he led into the Earl of Essex's army. But, when the king's army marched out of Nottinghamshire, most of the refugees, including John Hutchinson, returned to their homes, 'desirous to live in peace. . .'. They found 'by experience', however, that 'they could not do so, unless the parliament interest was maintained'; and so they met in Nottingham and consulted 'how to raise some recruits for the Earl of Essex, to assist in which, Mr Hutchinson had provided his plate and horses ready to send in'. Puritans found that their only security against being beaten and plundered by the king's soldiers was to join the parliament's army or to take refuge in one of the parliament's garrisons. 'The debauched Rabble through the Land, emboldened by his Gentry, and seconded by the Common Soldiers of his Army, took all that were Puritans for their Enemies: And though some of the King's Gentry and Superiour Officers were so civil that they would do no such thing, yet that was no Security to the Country, while the multitude did what they list.So that if any one was noted for a strict and famous Preacher, or for a Man of a precise and pious Life, he was either plundered, or abused, and in danger of his Life: So that if a Man did but pray in his Family, or were heard to repeat a Sermon, or sing a Psalm, they presently Cried out, "Rebels, Roundheads", and all their Money and Goods that were portable proved guilty, how innocent soever they were themselves . . . But upon my certain knowledge this was it that filled the Armies and Garrisons of the Parliament with sober, pious Men. Thousands had no mind to meddle with the Wars, but greatly desired to live peaceably at home, when the Rage of Soldiers and Drunkards would not suffer them: some stayed till they had been imprisoned; some till they had been plundered, perhaps twice or thrice over, and nothing left them; some were quite tired out with the abuse of all comers that quartered on them; and some by the insolency of their Neighbours; but most were afraid of their Lives; and so they sought refuge in the Parliament's Garrisons.' Goodwin's warning to 'godly people' of the fate they would suffer at the hands of 'Cavaliers, Papists, and Athiests, that have taken the field against you', seemed amply justified. [. . .]

It was a general assumption among puritans that the religious people were to be found chiefly in the middle ranks of the population. 'Freeholders and Tradesmen are the Strength of Religion and Civility in the Land: and Gentlemen and Beggers, and Servile Tenants, are the Strength of Iniquity; (Though among these sorts there are some also that are good and just, as among the other there are many bad).' The rich were subject to too many temptations and to 'the three or four Sins of Sodom, Pride, Fulness of Bread, and Abundance of Idleness, and not considering the Poor and Needy. And their Fulness and Idleness tempt them to further Voluptuousness and Sensuality, to Filthiness, or to Time-wasting needless kinds of Sports.' The rich were worldly, valuing 'Riches and Honours in the World', and wanted a religion 'Consistent with a Worldly Mind; which Outside-formality, Lip-service and Hypo-crisie is; but Seriousness, Sincerity and Spirituality is not'. And, most important of all, the nobility and gentry resisted a godly discipline. A godly discipline, which was to be exercised by a minister and lay elders elected by the congregation, was the main aim of the puritans, whether it was to be within the frame-work of a reformed episcopacy, or of presbyterianism, or of congregational Independency. But the nobility and gentry did not relish being subjected to constant surveillance, and liability to public rebuke, by elders who would be likely to be their social inferiors, '. . . exposing us eternal apprentices to the Arbitrary Jurisdiction of a new Corporation of Apron Elders, Mechanical Artisans. . .', protested Sir Thomas Aston. Henry Oxinden of Barham in Kent believed that 'the multitude' aimed at such a government in the church 'wherein themselves . . . may be able to tyrannize over their betters, whom naturally they have ever hated and in their hearts despised'. 'I think it therefore high time for all gentlemen to cast about with themselves, and endeavour rather to maintain episcopal government in its former state, with some diminution in temporalities, than to introduce I know not what presbyterial government; which will upon the matter equalize men of mean condition with the gentry. . . .'

The poor, on the other hand, did not have either the leisure or the education to form their own opinions on religious questions. '. . . Plowmen, and many others, are so wearied or continually employed, either in the Labours or the Cares of their Callings, that it is a great Impediment to their Salvation . . .': the poorer peasants were ignorant and 'like Bruits'. The poor tenant-farmer was servile and took his religion from his landlord: 'his religion is a part of his copyhold, which he takes from his landlord and refers it wholly to his discretion'. 'The needy multitude' was opposed to the puritan discipline because of 'their naturall hatred of good order': they resented the efforts of the puritans to suppress their traditional sports, recreations and customs. The anti-puritan mobs at Kidderminster were composed of 'poor Journey-men and Servants' and ignorant 'Beggers at the Townsends'. They resisted the yoke of the godly middle sort of people. 'The vulgar Rabble of the carnal and prophane, the Fornicators, Drunkards, Swearers, Etc. did every where hate them that reproved their Sin, and condemned them by a holy life. This Difference was universal, and their Enmity implacable . . . So that every where serious, godly People . . . were spoken against and derided by the Name of Precisians, Zealots, Over-Strict, the holy Brethren, and other Terms of Scorn.' In places where the puritan 'middle sort of people' already had some influence and power before the civil war, the outbreak of that conflict provided the opportunity for the poor – the servants, journeymen, labourers and paupers – to free themselves from the surveillance and oppression of the godly, and 'they were like tyed Mastiffs newly loosed, and fled in the Face of all that was religious, yea, or Civil, which came in their way.'

'The freeholders', however, 'were not enslaved to their Landlords as the Tenants are', and 'the Tradesmen have a Correspondency with London, and so are grown to be a far more Intelligent sort of Men than ignorant Peasants . . .', 'their constant Converse and Traffick with London', promoting 'Civility and Piety' among them. Richard Heywood of Bolton was a yeoman by rank and a clothier by trade, and he went once or twice a year to London, where he went to hear sermons by the chief puritan preachers, such as Edmund Calamy and Thomas Case, and bought 'the best books, the most plain, practical experimental treatises in divinity such as Calvin, Luther in English, Mr Perkins, Dr Preston, Dr Sibbs, wherein he took much pleasure in reading'. The strength of puritanism at Kidderminster lay in the master weavers, who dominated the town before the civil war. They were not rich – 'three or four of the

Richest thriving Masters of the Trade, got but about £500 or £600 in twenty years, and it may be lose £100 of it at once by an ill Debtor'; and even 'the magistrates of the Town were few of them worth £40 per. An. and most not half so much'. 'The generality of the Master Workmen' got not much more than their 'Food and Raiment' and 'lived but a little better than their Journey-men, (from hand to mouth) but only that they laboured not altogether so hard'. They had some leisure and some education and 'were of such a Trade as allowed them time enough to read or talk of holy Things: . . . and as they stand in their loom they can set a Book before them, or edifie one another . . .'.

The concept of 'godliness' helped to create a selfconscious middle sort of people, for it distinguished them from the 'profane and ignorant rabble' on the one hand, and from the 'worldly and debauched nobility and gentry' on the other; and provided them with a standard other than a material one by which they could feel superior both to those not much poorer than themselves and to those very much richer than themselves. Francis Cheynell complained that in every parish there was 'a prophane and ignorant multitude who are borne with a Pope in their belly, and are not yet redeemed from that grosse superstition and vaine Conversation which they received by Tradition from their Fathers. . .'. They loved their Whitsun-ales and Lords-day sports, and they would 'stand up and make much adoe' to defend the 'ancient Ceremonies, beloved Customes and Traditions of our Fathers. . .'. 'Oh Beloved,' cried Stephen Marshall, 'the generality of the people of England, is extremely wicked. . . .' 'The bulk of our people are wicked, and their hearts are not as yet prepared to the yoke of the Lord,' lamented Edmund Calamy: 'They are unreformed themselves; and it is no wonder they are so opposite to a thorough reformation. . . .' 'The maine bent and stream of nations runnes downward to vice and profanenesse: the generall desires and endeavours of men are tending to loosenesse: nor unstained worship in the Church, nor impartial justice in common-wealth, would they have. . . .' [. . .]

The middle sort of people, being the yeomen and better-off peasant farmers, the master craftsmen and small traders, were characterized by an independence of thought and opinion, which was rooted in their economic independence. They owned their own land, or had sufficient land on a long lease to be independent of landlords; or they had their own businesses, and they were employers of labour. They were the independent small producers and in this period production in both agriculture and industry was largely under their control. They were a distinct economic class: above them stood the class of rentiers (the landlords who lived chiefly off rents) and financiers (the merchants who lived chiefly by the manipulation of money and credit), and below them lay the class of wage-earners (the servants and labourers who lived off wages in money or kind). Suppression of the peasantry and reduction of the independence of the towns were the conditions for the development of monarchical absolutism on the continent of Europe, and prevented the growth of a middle class. But in England the rise of a significant

154

middle class was the main obstacle to the development of monarchical absolutism. Godliness encouraged the middle sort of people to assert their independence and to oppose any trends towards absolutism. According to [John] Corbet it made them 'more knowing' than the rest of the common people and so more 'apt to contradict and question' and not so easily 'brought to the bent'; and it enabled them to form their own opinions on 'such things as concern the life of a morall man'. The puritan was responsible for his own salvation: he had to be sure in his own mind and conscience that he was following the truth, for he would not be able to excuse himself from error by saying that he merely took his opinions from another man, nor excuse himself from sin by saying that he merely followed the lead of another man. He had 'a knowledge of things pertaining to divine worship according to the maine principles of the Christian profession. Which religion is not according to the will of man, but grounded upon an unchangeable and eternall truth . . . and it hath . . . in its nature an irreconcileable enmity against arbitrary government . . .' The bible was god's word, and it contained the law by which human beings were to conduct themselves in all their affairs, ecclesiastical and secular: this law was true and just, unchanging and unchangeable, and to put human will above it, or to put human invention in place of it, was to usurp god's authority. Man was a sinner, his will was self-seeking and a law made by a man would be for his own rather than the general good, and to extend his own power. Slavery lay in obedience to man and his law, liberty lay in obedience to god and his law. A tyrannical and arbitrary ruler was one who obeyed only laws that he made himself, or who put his sinful and self-seeking will above the law and claimed to be able to make or change the law merely at his own discretion. The fundamental laws of the constitution, and the laws which were made by the whole community, which could not be changed at the whim of the ruler or any one individual, were laws which sought the good of all and not just one. Puritans believed in the rule of law in both religion and politics, and that in obedience of both rulers and ruled to the law lay both religious and political liberty. It is not necessary to suppose that they transferred their concept of liberty from religion to politics, for this concept included both church and state in its inception.

The middle sort of people had secular as well as religious grievances against the government of Charles I. The king and some of the nobility and gentry had tried to cash in on the profits of industry by means of royal monopolies and projects, such as the Westminster Soap Company, through which it was alleged 'that many Citizens of London were put out of an old Trade, in which they had beene bred all their time, and which was their onely lively-hood, by Knights, Esquires, and Gentlemen, never bred up to the Trade . . .' This was also resented by many of the nobility and gentry, but in their case because they were excluded from a share in monopolies and projects. The nobility and gentry generally were opposed to shipmoney and so were the middle sort of people, but not on the same grounds. In a tract, written in 1637 but not published until 1641, William Prynne noted that the 'middle rank of the people' objected to shipmoney because of 'the inequalitie of taxing of it': '... Ordinary Merchants charged, to pay, ten, twelve, fifteene, yea, twenty five pound, or more; when as diverse of your great Officers, Earles, and Lords, who had fortie times greater Estates and Annuall revenewes, payd but two, three, foure, or five pounds at the most'; in cities and corporations 'the middle and poore sort of people, payd more than the richest; and in the Countrey ... some Farmers pay more than the richest Knights and Gentlemen...' In 1638 a group of yeomen led the opposition to shipmoney in the parish of Enfield in Middlesex, and their complaint was that the sheriff had altered their assessments 'so as to ease the burden on the wealthy landholders in the county, forcing it to fall more heavily on the yeomen and farmers'. Thus the middle sort of people had grievances not only against the government of Charles I, but also against the nobility and gentry and the rich in general. Though resentment against shipmoney united different social groups in opposition to the Personal Government of Charles I in the 1630s, it also sharpened the antagonism between 'the middle and poore sort of people' and the rich and powerful.

The complaint against shipmoney was part of a general grievance of the middle sort of people against the system of taxation, whether imposed 'unconstitutionally' by the royal prerogative or 'constitutionally' with the consent of parliament, and that was that it fell disproportionately upon them. 'There is reason to believe that in the century after 1523 there was a steady shift of the burden from the larger to the smaller taxpayers right down the social scale.' The nobility and gentry and the richer classes were not paying their fair share of taxation: they were increasingly successful in passing on the burden to the rest of the population, which meant the middle sort of people, for the poor had nothing with which to pay. Indeed it was one of the aims of shipmoney to reverse this process and to make the rich pay more. Such success as it had in doing this – though Prynne claimed that it had none –was ended when it was abolished by the Long Parliament, and the middle sort of people were left entirely at the mercy of the taxes voted by parliament, which had for a long time fallen more heavily on them than on the rich. This grievance of the middle sort of people found expression in a pamphlet of 1641 which urged on parliament 'the inequality, and unconscionable disproportion of rating of the subsidies ...' 'The poorer sort cannot pay the King: the greater sort, as having the law in their own hands, will pay but what they please, but the middle sort, they must and shall pay; and in such a disproportion as is insufferable...' A yeoman of £100 a year was rated at £5, but a landowner of £1,000 a year was rated at only £20, a mere four times as much though his income was ten times greater; and a landowner of £10,000 a year was rated at only £100, a mere twenty times as much though his income was a hundred times greater. This reduced the king's revenue and 'must necessarily begger most of the poore inferiour Yeomandry of the Kingdome' and ruin 'poore Renters and Farmers'.

So the pamphlet demanded: '... let every mans estate ... bee made liable to pay proportionally. And as your ... middle sort of people, are usually rated by the Justices or their appointment, then shall you doe right, both to the King and the middle sort of subjects. Wherefore you can never doe your selves more right, then to redresse this abuse ...' The gentry, who dominated the House of Commons, were aware that the subsidies fell more heavily on the middle sort of subjects than on the rich, but a parliament of landowners was not ready to reform a system from which they benefited, and the grievance of the middle rank of the people remained and was taken up again after the civil war by the Levellers.

As in the state so in the church taxation fell more heavily on the middle and poorer sort of people, and though townsmen generally tended to get off lightly, the burden of tithes fell disproportionately on yeomen and farmers. Furthermore, since many tithes went into the pockets of lay landowners who had impropriated them, this amounted to a tax for support of the nobility and gentry. So there were grounds for the warning in 1641 that freedom from tithes 'is the secret thing which our common Freeholders and Grand-Jury-Men [usually yeomen] doe so much ayme at, if Bishops and their Courts were over-throwne'.

From the 1590s to the 1630s the middle rank of people in the towns – 'the small tradesmen and the better-off craftsmen' – was engaged in a struggle to secure or recover a voice and a share in the government of the towns from the oligarchies of wealthy merchants and richer townsmen who monopolized the government and commerce of the towns. They also demanded a vote in the elections to parliament and a voice in the affairs of their local church, especially in relation to the choice of ministers and the establishment of a godly discipline within their own congregation. But the middle rank of people in the country-side – the yeomen and the better-off farmers – had a better established status and a more secure place in the community than the middle rank of the people in the towns: they had a share in the running of their own village, they sat on juries and had a voice in the government of their country, and they usually had a vote in parliamentary elections. This tended to make them less radical than their social counterparts in the towns, though they did want a part in the government of their parish church. The parish church, however, was subject not only to the central control of the bishop and his officials but also to the local control of the nobility and gentry, who appointed the ministers of most churches and provided a considerable proportion of the income of many churches. In order to increase their part in the running of their parish church, men of the middle rank had thus to challenge not only the bishops but the nobility and gentry, and seek to transfer the control of the local church to elders elected by the congregation, who would often be men of the middle rank, especially since they would have to be men of approved godliness. It is this that lies behind the warning that Viscount Conway received from his chaplain in October 1641, that in Somerset '... our chiefest farmers have their loins girt with a divinity surcingle, and begin to bristle up for a lay eldership'.

For the middle rank of the people the civil war came at the climax of a struggle for a greater measure of democracy in local affairs, parliamentary elections and ecclesiastical government – a democracy not extending so far as to include the mass of the poor (servants, labourers, paupers), but confined to the better-off farmers and craftsmen. [. . .] The tradition of democracy was very much alive in 1642 among the middle rank of the people, who tended to believe that ancient rights had been filched from them by the richer people and must be recovered by a struggle. Their views were expressed by a pamphlet of 1642 which justified the Militia Ordinance of the two Houses of Parliament by claiming that according to 'the most ancient practice and custome of this Kingdoms . . . the Lieutenants and supream Commanders of the Militia in every County, were elected . . . by the Common-counsell . . . through every Province, Countrey and County, in a full Folkmoth or County Court by the Freeholders of the County': '. . . The Freeholders in ancient times did thus in every County elect their Lieutenants and Captains of their Militia, to Train and Order them; yea, and the high Sheriffs too, who had the command of the whole power of the County, whom they then likewise elected . . .'

The democratic movement of the middle sort of people involved both church and state, but it tended from 1640 onwards to find a focus in the campaign for a change in the government of the church, which could not be without the abolition of episcopacy. William Lilly observed that the Londoners who went to Westminster to demonstrate against the bishops 'were most of them men of mean or a middle quality themselves, no aldermen, merchants or common-council men, but set on by some of better quality; and yet most of them were either such as had public spirits, or lived a more religious life than the vulgar, and were usually called Puritans, and had suffered under the tyranny of the Bishops; in the general they were very honest men and well-meaning . . . as men in whose breasts the spirit of liberty had some place; and they were even glad to vent out their sighs and sufferings in this rather tumultuous than civil manner; being assured if ever this Parliament had been dissolved, they must have been wrackt, whipt and stript by the snotty clergy and other extravagant courses . . .' 'The Bishops and their Courts' had oppressed 'the meaner sort of tradesmen and artificers', impoverishing 'many thousands' of them and forcing 'great numbers' of them to flee during the 1630s, 'some into New England and other parts of America, others into Holland'. The hostility of the middle sort of people to the bishops was not just the result of a difference of view about ecclesiastical government, for it was compounded in large measure of anti-clericalism. This had its roots in resentment against clerical taxes and exactions, dislike of clerical interference in lay affairs, and the feeling of the godly people that they were as competent as the clergy, indeed more competent than most of the clergy to decide theological and moral questions, to live religious lives and to teach the people. But the nobility and gentry were not much less obstacles to the reform of the church than the bishops, and although the middle rank of the people rallied to parliament when they feared that the king intended to dissolve it by force, they did so because without parliament there would be little hope for reform of the church at all. Their support did not spring from any sense of identity of interests with the nobility and gentry, more often the reverse, and was conditional upon parliament carrying out the reform of the church.

The parliamentarians made a deliberate effort to win the support of 'the yeomanry' and the middle rank of the people. Henry Parker, the foremost apologist for parliament's stand against the king, claimed 'that most of the faulty, and decayed Nobility, and Gentry, are of the King's party, and so are the Lees of the people; but almost all of the Yeomanry (which is the most considerable ranke of any Nation) and a very choyse part both of Nobility and Gentry at this time side against the King and the Papists'. Corbet said that the nobles and gentlemen who sided with the king did so from 'a desire of vast dominion, dignity, revenge, or rapine' and out of 'an hatred of the commons, and a strong disposition to the ends of tyranny', caring not 'to render themselves the slaves of princes, that they also might rule over their neighbours as vassals'. [Edmund] Ludlow held that 'many of the nobility and gentry were contented to serve' the king's 'arbitrary designs, if they might have leave to insult over such as were of a lower order . . .' In a sermon Jeremiah Burroughes explained 'why so many of the Gentry in most Counties throughout the Kingdome' supported the king: because '. . . many of them had rather inslave themselves and their posterities to those above them, then not to have their wils upon those that are under them: they would faine bring it to be with us as it is in France, that the Gentry should be under the Nobility and Courtiers, and all the country people, the peasants, bee under them as slaves, they live in miserable bondage under the Gentry there, who generally are Cavaliers. There is no Countrey in the world, where countrey men, such as we call the yeomandry, yea, and their Farmers and workmen under them, doe live in that fashion and freedome as they doe in England, in all other places they are slaves in comparison, their lives are so miserable as they are not worth the enjoying, they have no influence at all into the government they are under, nothing to doe in the making of Laws, or any way consenting to them, but must receive them from others, according to their pleasure; but in England every Free-holder hath an influence into the making and consenting every Law he is under, and enjoyes his owne with as true a title as the Nobleman enjoyes whatsoever is his. This freedome many of the proud Gentry are vexed at, and hence it is their hearts rise so against those that are chosen by them, and against their Ordinances. But the Commons begin to discerne this more than they have done, and to be so wise as to hold their own faster then they have.' Another parliamentarian tract alleged that the royalists 'intend in England a government at discretion, and all made in all probability, or after the French fashion . . .'; but, the author claimed that 'the middle sort of people of England, and Yeomanry' 'will especially oppose the change as whereby they from being in the happiest condition of any of their rank perhaps in Europe, nay in the world (who here live like men, and are wont to fight, or die like men in honour or defence of their country) might well be reduced to the terms of the peasants of France, of villeinage, and slavery..'. When the Earl of Derby was repulsed from Manchester, the defenders appealed: '. . . O England's Yeomen and husbandmen look to yourselves, for if you stand not to it, as we of Manchester do, but be overcome, look for ever to be slaves . . .'.

The parliamentarians played upon the fear of the middle rank of the people that, if the royalists won the war, not only their desire for a greater share in the affairs of the community would be frustrated, but also their existing share would be taken from them. They represented the royalist cause as being directed specifically against them and exploited any evidence of royalist disregard for them. The fears of the yeomen were confirmed when in the summer of 1642 royalist gentry tried, often successfully, to exclude yeomen from the grand jury, 'the representative body of the county'; and when the king had a meeting with the gentry of Yorkshire, the freeholders of the county protested at being excluded, '. . . conceiving our selves according to the proportions of our estates, equally interested in the common good of the countie . . .'. When the king took the arms of the trained bands the two Houses of Parliament accused him of practising one of 'the most mischievous principles of tyranny . . . that ever were invented, that is to disarm the middle sort of people, who are the body of the Kingdome . . .'. A parliamentarian pamphleteer claimed this as proof that the royalists 'intend in England a government at discretion, and all made in all probability, or after the French fashion', for 'the middle sort of people of England, and Yeomanry' were the chief obstacle to such a change, and since they composed the main part of the trained bands, 'then by policy, or even plain force' the trained bands must be disarmed. The parliamentarians also played upon the fear of the middle rank of the people that their wealth which they had gained by their hard work and their status which distinguished them from the mass of the people were threatened by the royalists. The 'yeomen, farmers, petty-freeholders, and such as use manufacture that enrich the country,' wrote Corbet, were 'a generation of men truely laborious, jealous of their properties', and their enemies were 'powerfull gentry' who, 'detesting a close, hardy, and industrious way of living, doe eate their bread in the sweat of other men . . .' An effective piece of parliamentarian propaganda was based on the allegation that the royalist Lord Poulett had said 'that it was not fit for any yeoman to have allowed him from his own labours, any more than the poor mite of ten pounds a year, and withall manifested to this purpose, though not perhaps in these words, that when the power should be totally on their side, they shall be compelled to live at that low allowance, notwithstanding their estates are gotten with a great deal of labour and industry . . .'. 'Heaven grant that neither he nor his faction have either will or power to do this . . .' 'If the yeoman's estate were his offence, therefore for that crime he must be limited a petty proportion of 10 pounds a year, the tradesmen and merchants were rich, and by this consequence being guilty of the same crime receive the same punishment, and have such a limitation or less (as the Yeomen)...' The royalist leaders testified to the success of this propaganda in winning the support of the middle rank of the people for parliament.

At the outbreak of the civil war there seems to have been a great deal of support for parliament among the middle sort of people. In Yorkshire the freeholders were expected to support parliament; in Shropshire they were said to be firm to parliament; and from Warwickshire it was reported that 'the yeomen of our country stands out very well...' for parliament. 'The county of Derby, full of nobility and gentry, was much swayed, even from the beginning of these distractions, against the Parliament; for scarce did any Gentleman in all that county, but Sir John Gell, appear for it at the first. He, with his brother, and some of his kindred, by the help of those freeholders and yeomen that inclined that way, made a party to resist those great ones...' In the eastern and south-eastern counties 'the freeholders and yeomen in general adhered to the Parliament', and 'though many of the chief gentry of those counties were for paying obedience to his Majesty's Commission of Array, yet the freeholders and yeomen being generally of the other side, as oft as they attempted to show themselves, they were crushed, and their endeavours defeated'. In Nottinghamshire, related Mrs Hutchinson, '... most of the middle sort, the able substantial freeholders, and the other commons, who had not their dependence upon the malignant nobility and gentry, adhered to the parliament'. In Gloucestershire, according to Corbet, besides a few of the gentry, 'the yeomen, farmers, clothiers, and the whole middle ranke of the people were the only active' supporters of parliament. 'On the Parliament's side,' claimed Baxter, 'were... the greatest part of the Tradesmen, and Freeholders, and the middle sort of Men; especially in those Corporations and Countries which depend on Cloathing and such Manufactures'. And the royalist Clarendon agreed that 'the common people, especially in the clothing parts of Somersetshire, were generally too much inclined to' parliament, while in the West Riding of Yorkshire 'Leeds, Halifax, and Bradford, three very populous and rich towns, (which depending wholly upon clothiers naturally maligned the gentry)' were for parliament. At Bristol '... the king's cause and party were favoured by the two extreames in that city; the one the wealthy and powerfull men, the other of the basest and lowest sort, but disgusted by the middle ranke, the true and best citizens'. At Worcester the supporters of parliament 'were but of the middle rank of people and none of any great power or eminence there to take their parts...'; and from Chichester a parliamentarian reported that 'the strength of our parts consists mainly in honest tradesmen, the gentry are nought... and the country people are for the most part blinded and misled by their malevolent hedge-priests, there being not above 6 or 7 honest ministers hereabouts. . . '.

When parliament first raised its army under the command of the Earl of Essex, the citizens of London 'listed themselves plentifully for soldiers . . .', and among the first volunteers were 71 dyers, 88 butchers, 186 weavers, 157 tailors, 124 shoemakers, 88 brokers and 49 saddlers. After the first engagement of the civil war, near Worcester, Lord Falkland reported that the royalists had taken 50-60 prisoners – 'most of them were men of mean quality, and so raw soldiers that they understood not the word quarter, but cried for mercy; being demanded of what condition they were; some saith, they were Tailors, some Embroiderers and the like'. But it was the apprentices of London who were most forward in the cause of parliament and it was claimed that 8,000 of them enlisted under the Earl of Essex. By origin and vocation they belonged to the middle rank of the population. They insisted that they were not 'of the base and mechanick scum of the people' but 'have trades and callings, the most of them young men of good parentage; whose friends live honestly and thriftily in the country'; and that they 'are servants to honest and sufficient men, and by their own honest laborious endeavours can be both serviceable and profitable to their masters, and be very beneficial to them, in working at their trades'. But London, important as it is, must not be allowed to overshadow the fact that parliament necessarily recruited most of its soldiers from rural areas. The trained bands of the capital played a crucial role, but so did Oliver Cromwell's regiment, who were 'most of them freeholders and freeholders' sons'.

Parliament's support, of course, was not confined to 'the godly' nor to 'the middle rank of the people', and at the outset in some parts of the country support was very widespread, but this broad popular enthusiasm soon evaporated. At first in Gloucestershire 'the full streame of the country' ran for parliament, but after Prince Rupert took Cirencester '. . . the country-men in generall were taken off, who in their jocund beginnings still concluded on the victory, but never prepared for a blow, that the whole businesse was dashed at one clap . . .' The yeomen and farmers in the west country who in the beginning rose for parliament, faded away during the siege of Sherborne Castle: 'If a bullet come over their heads, they fall flat upon their bellies, and some 4 or 5 being slain hath made about half of them run away and we are confident half of those that are left will follow; so that of 4 and 20 hundred that came with us out of Somersetshire and 900 that came out of Dorset-shire and Devonshire, we have not 1200 left, and God knows how many may slip away this night . . . The short of all is we have no army, nor can possibly with these men do this work.' Parliamentarian supporters had expected a quick victory and underestimated the strength of the royalists, and '. . . such spirits as wanted greatnesse of minde or strong fidelity to persevere, did greedily comply' with the royalists. Unarmed and untrained masses did not make an army and parliament turned to professional soldiers and conscripts who would serve for the pay, but serving only for the pay (and plunder), and lacking belief in the righteousness of the cause, they did not have the morale to surmount defeats and win victories. Lord Brooke urged parliament to 'employ men who will fight merely for the cause sake, and bear their own charges, than those who expect rewards and salaries': 'I shall therefore freely speak my conscience, I had rather have a thousand or two thousand honest citizens that can only handle their arms, whose hearts go with their hands, than two thousand of mercenary soldiers, that boast of their foreign experience.' Cromwell told Hampden: 'You must get men of a spirit . . . of a spirit that is like to go on as far as a gentleman will go, or else I am sure you will be beaten still . . .' He found this spirit in godly freeholders. 'I have heard him oftentimes say that it must not be souldiers nor Scots that must doe this worke, but it must be the godly to this purpose . . .' He recruited his regiment from among 'freeholders and freeholders' sons, . . . who upon matter of conscience engaged in this quarrel, and under Cromwell. And thus being well armed within, by the satisfaction of their own consciences, and without, by good iron arms, they would as one man stand firmly and charge desperately.' '. . . At his first entrance into the wars, being but a captain of horse, he had a special care to get religious men into his troop. These men were of greater understanding than common soldiers, and therefore were more apprehensive of the importance and consequence of the war; and making not money but that which they took for the publick felicity to be their end, they were the more engaged to be valiant; for he that maketh money his end doth esteem his life above his pay, and therefore is like enough to save it by flight when danger comes, if possibly he can; but he that maketh the felicity of Church and State his end esteemeth it above his life, and therefore will the sooner lay down his life for it. And men of parts and understanding know how to manage their business, and know that flying is the surest way to death, and that standing to it is the likeliest way to escape, there being many usually that fall in flight for one that falls in valiant fight. These things it's probable Cromwell understood, and that none would be such engaged valiant men as the religious.' And besides, they would avoid 'those disorders, mutinies, plunderings, and grievances of the country which deboist [i.e. debauched] men in armies are commonly guilty of'. It was the godly people, mostly of the middle rank of the nation, who stood firm, while those who were not inspired by religion fell into defeatism, or neutrality, or deserted to the king.

This converted the conflict from a constitutional one into a religious one. This change was generally noted to take place during 1643. 'I must confess,' wrote John Greene in his diary at the beginning of 1643, 'I see little hopes of any accommodation, least of a final victory on either side yet . . . God grant I never see it made a war merely for religion . . .' But at the beginning of 1644 he wrote: '. . . Our trouble still menaces, the war being fiercer than ever and may probably hold a long time, for now 'tis made a war almost merely for religion, which I feared.' The assumption of the early parliamentarian pamphleteers that the issues were constitutional and political were challenged, and the ground of the quarrel was said to be not 'whether the town of Hull shall be the King's: but whether this Kingdom shall be the Lord's'. '. . . To what end should we waste time about a discourse of Hull, and the Militia? Come speak to the point. If a King of the Protestant Profession should give his strength and power to his Queene a Papist, and she give it to the Jesuits, to the Beast, it is neither Rebellion nor Treason to fight for the King, to recover his power out of the hand of the Beast; I say, *for* the King, that the power regained may be settled upon the Kings Royall person, and posterity; and then it is to be hoped that the King and they will take warning and beware how they trust out their power another time. We are engaged to fight against the Anti-Christian faction by our very Baptisme' but we must 'fight from Scripture motives, not from Politique considerations'. Puritan preachers admitted that they had been misled at first into thinking that the issue was only constitutional: '. . . at the first, the enemy did so disguise their enterprises, that nothing cleerly appeared, but only that you were compelled to take up Armes for the defence of your Liberties, and to bring Rebells and Traytors to condigne punishment, but now they have ingaged all the Antichristian world so farre, that all Christendome, except the Malignants in England, doe now see, that the question in England is, whether Christ or Antichrist shall be Lord or King. . . .'

Baxter dated the change in the character of the parliamentarian cause from the publication of a pamphlet called *Plaine English* at the beginning of 1643. Its author insisted that the only peace settlement acceptable to the supporters of parliament would be 'such an one as may extirpate Popery and superstition, lay the grounds of a pious painfull Ministry, and to that end cast out those scandalous seditious persons, who have now showed themselves as ill affected to the state as formerly to the church. . . . Such an one as may purge our doctrine, . . . reforme our Discipline and make it more conducible to the end of all Discipline, the preservation of a Church from corruption in Doctrine and manners. And let it be weighed whether that can be done without the supplanting . . . the Bishops. . . .' But the tract also linked religion and politics, saying that the issue of the war was 'liberty or tyranny, Popery or true piety', and demonstrated that the emphasis on religious issues was accompanied by a greater radicalism in politics: the tract threatened parliament that if it did not perform what the people desired, if 'the representative body cannot, or will not, discharge their trust to the satisfaction not of fancy, but of reason in the people; they may resume (if ever yet they parted with a power to their manifest undoing) and use their power so farre as conduces to their safety. . . .' Gentlemen who had supported parliament on constitutional grounds alone were alarmed by the social consequences of the abolition of episcopacy, but they were even more alarmed by the assertion that the people were the judge of whether parliament performed its trust and could revoke the mandate of their representatives. This association of religious radicalism with political radicalism was precisely what Baxter found among some of the horse regiments of the New Model Army:

'. . . they were resolved to take down, not only Bishops, and Liturgy, and Ceremonies, but all that did withstand their way. They were far from thinking of a moderate Episcopacy, or of any healing way between the Episcopal and the Presbyterians. . . .' They talked 'sometimes for State Democracy and sometimes for Church Democracy'. 'I perceived that they took the King for a Tyrant and an Enemy, and really intended absolutely to master him, or to ruine him . . . They said, What were the Lords of England but William the Conquerour's Colonels? or the Barons but his Majors? or the Knights but his Captains?' Not only religious and political radicalism but social radicalism as well: thus the change in the character of the parliamentarian cause was not just a change from a constitutional cause to a religious cause, but to a greater radicalism in politics and society as well as in religion; and this sprang from the fact that the change was caused by the growing importance in the parliamentarian party not just of the godly but of the godly middle sort of people.

There was a growing tension between the leaders of the parliamentarian party, who were drawn from the gentry, and the rank-and-file, who were drawn from the middle sort of people. Colonel Hutchinson, as governor of Nottingham, found 'the townsmen, being such as had lived free and plentifully by themselves, could not subject themselves to government; but were so saucy, so negligent, and so mutinous, that the most honourable person in the world, could expect nothing but scandal, reproach, and ingratitude, for the payment of his greatest merit. . .'. Parliamentarian soldiers would follow only officers of whom they approved, and obey only orders with which they agreed: 'Although the horse would not obey Sir Thomas Fairfax, it was not out of cowardice, for the men were very stout and cheerful in the service, but only had the general fault of all the parliament party, that they were not very obedient to commands, except they knew and approved their employment.' This sprang from puritanism, for Corbet had observed that those who had had the benefit of 'a practicall ministry' were 'apt to contradict and question, and will not easily be brought to the bent'. 'The most religious and the best people were so pragmatical,' confessed Mrs Hutchinson, herself a puritan but also a gentlewoman, 'that no act, nor scarcely word, could pass without being strictly arraigned and judged at the bar of every common soldier's discretion, and thereafter censured and exclaimed at'. Soldiers in the Earl of Essex's army objected to being commanded by 'profane wretches' and 'ungodly' officers or by a 'God-dam blade, and doubtless hatched in hell', and secured their dismissal. But this sprang not just from godliness: the fundamental source of the rank-and-file's suspicions of their leaders lay in difference of class. Robert Kyrle, a major of horse in the Earl of Essex's army, complained that parliament's soldiers 'wanted not Scripture for every mutiny, who plunder and call it God's providence, who if they cannot prove any of quality to be a Papist, yet as he is a Gentleman he shall want grace; and that is title enough to possess the estates of all that are more richer than themselves. . .'. Up to a point godliness could unite the puritan gentry and the godly middle sort of people, but it could not overcome the difference of class. The puritan Colonel Hutchinson had 'his experience not only of the ungodly and ill-affected, but even of the godly themselves, who thought it scarcely possible for any one to continue a gentleman, and firm to a godly interest, and therefore repaid all his vigilancy and labours for them with a very unjust jealousy'. This shows that what underlay the godliness of the godly middle sort of people was class feeling. They were conscious that their aims were not always the same as those of the parliamentarian nobility and gentry, and that their grievances were as often as not grievances against the nobility and the gentry and the richer sort of people as such.

POLITICAL THOUGHT
AND PHILOSOPHY

14 PEREZ ZAGORIN

The Leveller Theorists: Lilburne, Overton and Walwyn

1. JOHN LILBURNE

The greatest party leader of the Levellers was John Lilburne. It is no exaggeration to describe him as for a time the most popular man in England. He was certainly the only man of his day who seems continuously to have enjoyed the affection of large numbers of people. Cromwell's impact on contemporaries was different: he was admired, feared, held in awe towards the end of his career, and, by some of his associates, liked. Lilburne, however, with all his contentiousness, seems to have been loved. His whole adult life until his early death at the age of forty-three was given to ceaseless struggle for the principles on whose behalf he had engaged. Almost two-thirds of his mature years were spent in the prisons to which the enmity first of the bishops, then of the Long Parliament, finally of Cromwell, consigned him. He was absolutely incorruptible, and a great-hearted and fearless agitator. He was no professsional theorist, for his political ideas were evolved in the closest connection with his own experience of injustice, and were never expressed in any formal treatise. They must be sought in all his writings, where they lie embedded amidst long passages of auto-biography, self-defence, and denunciation of his political opponents. Nevertheless, in their totality, they comprise a true political theory appropriate to the left-wing democrat Lilburne became.

When he first began to write, it was before the revolution as a pious and enthusiastic separatist who held no considered political theory. He was then a London apprentice, and for disseminating seditious litera-ture against the bishops had been barbarously sentenced by the Court of Star Chamber to whipping, the pillory, and prison. At that time, he spoke exclusively as a martyr to the prelates' unchristian rage, and his political ideas were the commonplace ones of non-resistance such as were often found among Protestant communions a century before. The king's authority is from God, he said, and to disobey it is to disobey God. If the king should command anything against God's word, though he dare not obey, he will submit his body for punishment, 'for I doe hold it unlawfull for any of Gods people, in their greatest Oppression by the Majestrate, to rebell or take up any Temporall armes . . .'.

But his views on the church were pregnant with possibilities for the redefinition of the political order. The point is of some importance. In the manner of the sectarian, he emphasized the voluntary and contract-

From Perez Zagorin, *A History of Political Thought in the English Revolution* (Routledge and Kegan Paul, 1954), pp. 8–29. Footnotes have been deleted.

ual character of church government. A true church, he said, is created by the free consent of the believers 'to enter into that . . . holy State, City, or Kingdome . . . and by the power of Christ to become a constituted or Politique Body or Corporation . . . and then by virtue of their . . . uniting & joyning themselves together each to other & so unto the Lord . . . they become a true visible Church of Jesus Christ . . . & so hath power from Christ . . . to cast out offenders . . . to chuse elect & ordaine her owne officers . . . and to reprove . . . her owne Officers . . .'.

Lilburne first applied these ideas on the polity of the sect to secular subjects when he forsook his belief in non-resistance and supported Parliament in the civil war. It was not, however, until 1645 that he began to seize on their wider implications. In that year, after having risen to the rank of lieutenant-colonel in the Parliamentary army, he resigned his commission rather than take the Presbyterian-inspired Covenant which was being imposed on the officers. Retired into civilian life, he was soon stimulated by several personal encounters with oppression to give shape to his radical programme. First, there was his experience of Presbyterian efforts to suppress liberty of conscience; next, he was prevented by the monopoly of the Merchant Adventurers Company from pursuing the cloth trade in which he had been apprenticed; then, in the summer of 1645, Commons ordered him into custody on a charge of slandering its speaker, and when he refused to answer interrogatories against himself, his refusal was voted a breach of privilege and he was committed to Newgate. Treatment of this sort was exactly calculated to teach Lilburne that Parliament was spokesman for interests that could be as tyrannous as Charles I. It caused him to become a self-constituted tribune of the people and to launch the career of agitation out of which the Leveller movement grew. And it resulted in the first announcement of those perspectives of change and reform which so disquieted the Levellers' opponents.

Immediately after his detention by Commons, he denounced the House's proceedings as a violation of rights guaranteed him by Magna Carta. Already, then, it is clear, he regarded Commons 'as the supream Power of England, who have residing in them that power that is inherent in the people . . .' Yet its members, he insisted, 'are . . . not to act according to their own wils and pleasure, but according to the fundamentall constitutions and customes of the Land, which I conceive provides for the safety and preservation of the people . . .'

At last, after several failures to obtain his freedom, he published his pamphlet, *Englands Birth-Right Justified* (1645), perhaps the earliest statement of radical policy to appear in the revolution. Here, making himself spokesman for the 'poore, and men of middle quality', he not only denounced such grievances as tithes, unjust laws, monopolies, and the excise tax, but also demanded a Parliament which should be under popular control. No pretended privileges, he declared, can justify Parliament in acting against law. The people never gave it such power, and the unknown privileges it claims are as dangerous as an unlimited royal prerogative. Moreover, while men are members of Parliament, they should exercise no other functions, he said, 'for to me it is one of the most unjust things in the world, that the Law-makers should be the Law executors...' Let Parliament be dissolved and a new one summoned, he proposed, and let the people elect new members annually so that they can call unworthy representatives to account. Further, every freeman should contribute one year's service to the nation, and those elected for this purpose who lack means must have a competent allowance provided them.

These demands, innovative as they were, were still further expanded by Lilburne upon his release from prison in the autumn of 1645. Continuing his agitation, he now called for the trial of the king, who must be made, he said, to expiate with his own blood the blood shed in the war. He also proposed the complete reform of law and legal procedure, asking why Englishmen should be subject to the legal system introduced by the tyrant, William the Conqueror. Even Magna Carta, which he had appealed to only a short time before, is but little, he now pointed out. Though it is commonly thought to be the Englishman's inheritance, it falls far short of the Saxon laws, and is merely the best that could be wrung from a despot by force. As for the House of Lords, Lilburne resolved its status in the summer of 1646, when, for refusing to testify against himself at its bar, he found himself once more in prison. The peers, he straightway declared, have no right to the constitutional position which they enjoy, for they sit by the prerogative patents of kings, not by consent and election of the people. In attempting to exercise jurisdiction over him, a commoner, they have transgressed against the majesty of the House of Commons, 'the absolute supream derivative power of all the Commons of England...'. They may exercise no negative voice, because if the king's coronation oath requires him to pass such laws as the people choose – and this, Lilburne points out, is what Parliament had asserted in its declarations – then he can grant no power to the peers '(his meer creatures made by his will & pleasure) for them to oppose or to give a Law unto the people'.

With this, Lilburne's political position was essentially complete, and its outlines fixed in a clear and definite programme. By the end of 1646, he was urging that the monarchy should be dispensed with, and supremacy recognized in a free and popularly elected Commons acknowledging its subjection to law effecting broad reforms. Step by step, he had been led to the realization that the justice he sought would have to be general, and would require extensive changes in the political order and in legal and economic practices. Basic in the evolution of his ideas was, as I have already emphasized, his own personal experience of oppression. But it is doubtful that he could have come to project reforms on so large a scale had he not by this time also acquired a far-reaching theory of the nature of government. Its immediate source lay in the radical side of the Parliamentary declarations and publicists and, beyond this, in the ideas of the sect on Church-government. But what had been in the Parliamentary writings a mere suggestion Lilburne expanded to the point where his position emerged as a distinct entity in its own right, standing, because of the extensiveness of its claims, in opposition to the very thought that had helped beget it. And what in the sects had applied to a select handful of believers, he now demanded on behalf of mankind at large. No longer would he appeal to precedent as his ultimate sanction. Henceforth, he would invoke Christian right reason itself as the justification for his radical programme. At this tribunal only would he plead.

A remarkable passage written in 1646 while he was in prison illustrates these considerations so well that it is worth printing at length. God, he said, created man in His own image, which consists principally of reason and understanding, and made him lord over the earth.

> But made him not Lord . . . over the individuals of Mankind, no further then by free consent, or agreement, by giving up their power each to other, for their better being; so that originally, he gives no Lordship . . . to any of Adams Posterity, by Will and Prerogative, to rule over his Brethren-Men; but ingraved by nature in the soule of Man, this goulden and everlasting principle, to doe to another, as he would have another do to him; but man by his transgression, falling from the perfection of reason . . . became tyrannical, and beastly . . . [then] God taking mercy of Mankind . . . and not executing the fulnesse of his wrath . . . to revenge that beastlinesse . . . that, by the fall, had now entred into the Spirits of all Mankinde, institutes a perpetuall, moral . . . Law . . . That whosoever . . . would be so beastly . . . as to fall upon his neighbour, brother, or friend, and do unto him that, which he would not he should do to him, by taking away his life and blood from him; God ordaines and expresly saith he shall lose his life without mercy for so doing . . . And when the fulnesse of time was come, that Christ the Restorer and Repairer of mans losse and fall, should come and preach Righteousnesse & Justice . . . He saith, it is the Law & the Prophets, that whatsoever we would that men should do unto us, that wee should do to them. . . . So that by this, it is clearly evident, that . . . Christianity . . . doth not destroy morality, civility, justice, and right reason; but rather restores it to its first perfection, beauty, splendor, and glory . . .

These words make clear how long a journey Lilburne had come since his imprisonment as a young apprentice by the Star Chamber. Then his preoccupation had been with man as a believer. Now it was with man as a citizen. Then he had denied a right of resistance. Now he was affirming the right of all men to consent to the government under which they live. Then he had stressed man's sinfulness from which the elect were to withdraw into separate congregations. Now he was stressing man's reasonableness. Optimism breathed in all his thoughts. Despite the fall, man had not lost his native freedom. Christ had restored the pristine law of right reason as a norm for judging all the

172

powers of the world. Man, as a rational creature, could not be bound by commands emanating from a government to which he had not consented. When a government attempts to take away the people's freedom, men are absolved from obedience, for they are not obliged 'to destroy ... their Fundamentall naturall Liberties ... the injoyment of which makes them to differ from bruit and savage Beasts which were never created with reason ... that glorious Image, that God made man in ...'. Because consent alone gives scope to reason, it must follow that 'the poorest that lives, hath as true a right to give a vote ... as the richest and greatest ...' And it must follow, too, that an unrepresentative Parliament can have no standing, and that no enactment of the past can qualify as fundamental law unless it accords with reason.

These ideas lead straight on to the great conception in 1647 of an agreement of the people as the basis for a settlement of the problems raised by the revolution. By proposing the complete reform of the existing system of representation, the first Leveller *Agreement of the People* exhibited a democratic vision beyond anything yet known in English history. But even more remarkable, we shall see, was the form in which this vision was embodied. The first *Agreement* appeared in the autumn of 1647, when the army, irritated by arrears of pay and other grievances, had ceased to be controllable by Parliament, and when many regiments, under Leveller influence, had elected representatives who were voicing radical demands. Published in the name of the elected agents of five cavalry regiments, its title reads: *An Agreement Of The People For a firme and present Peace, upon grounds of common-right and freedome ... offered to the joynt concurrence of all the free Commons of England.* As a platform of settlement, it was a statement of rights and of fundamental law declaring the powers of any future government, and a mutual covenanting of the people with one another to establish the principles thus set forth as the basis for the state's subsequent functioning. Most important of all, it was to obtain its validity by the subscription of individual Englishmen, not by act of Parliament, for, as Lilburne wrote: 'An Agreement of the People is not proper to come from Parliament, because it comes from thence ... with a command ... it ought not so to do, but to be voluntary and free. Besides, that which is done by one Parliament ... may be undone by the next ... but an Agreement of the People begun and ended amongst the People, can never come justly within the Parliaments cognizance to destroy ...'

Though the conception in 1647 of such a form of settlement was, doubtless, a collective product of Leveller thinking, it would seem to owe more to Lilburne than to anyone else, and his ideas, in particular, throw light on its genesis. The *Agreement* could never have been conceived without his earlier practice in the polity of the sect and his belief in contract as the origin of government and in consent as its basis. It was these, I think, which united with his evaluation of the political situation in 1647 to be the chief factors in producing this unprecedented form of settlement.

We have seen how Lilburne's experience as a sectary had familiarized him with the covenant made between believers as the basis of the church. In 1638, it will be recalled, he described a true church, in language reminiscent of the secular order, as 'a constituted or Politique Body or Corporation' established by common consent. It was the transfer of this notion to society at large that was partly responsible for the *Agreement's* conception.

But a church in these terms may be created at any time because it is merely a grouping within society and, from the sectarian's point of view, can never be identical with society itself. How was it that in 1647, Lilburne and his friends, ignoring Parliament, proposed a covenant or agreement among all Englishmen, thus presupposing the inauguration of a new political order? The answer to this question will show that the *Agreement* goes far beyond the notion of democratic constitutionalism and the formulation of fundamental law in which its significance has commonly been discerned. The first *Agreement* was a democratic constitution, and much more. It was also the re-enactment of the great myth of the social contract, indeed, the very pact by which political society was to be created anew, and England removed from the state of nature into which Lilburne believed she had now been dissolved.

This, it is essential to realize, was literally the case in which he thought his country to be in the middle of 1647. The previous year, we recall, he had been imprisoned by the Lords. Neither his denial of their jurisdiction over him, a commoner, nor his calls for liberation to the House of Commons were of avail. In consequence, by January 1647, he was threatening an appeal from Parliament to the whole people. In February, he and Richard Overton, who was also a prisoner by decree of the peers, denied that an appeal to the people would make them enemies of all magistracy. Not themselves, they declared, but the Parliamentary tyrants 'dissolve the legall frame and constitution of the civill policy and government of the Kingdome, by suffering will and lust, but not lawe to rule and governe us, and so reduce us into the originall Law of nature, for every man to preserve and defend himselfe the best he can . . .' When those whom the people have trusted with power betray their trust, those who had trusted them may withdraw all subjection and look to their safety how they can.

This gives us the clue to a full understanding of the genesis of the *Agreement*. Lilburne maintained that his long failure to obtain justice, the oppressions to which he, a symbol of all commoners, was being subjected, and the government's refusal to redress grievances had dissolved the country into a state of nature. There was no longer a true magistracy. Beastly will held sway, not reason. Tyranny and no government were the same. Hence, he concluded that the law of nature is warrantable against Parliament, and urged the people to take up arms. He turned for support to the army, which in defiance of Parliament, had sworn its famous *Solemn Engagement* not to disband until its own and the nation's grievances were removed. Holding that the country was in a state of nature and that Parliament no longer possessed any standing, Lilburne denied that the army was subject to

Parliament or that it now existed in virtue of the powers Parliament had conferred on it. It had betaken itself to 'the prime Laws of Nature', he affirmed, and its actions were based on 'the principles of Saifety, flowing from Nature, Reason, and Justice, agreed on by common consent' of the soldiers as expressed in their *Solemn Engagement*. The only visible authority remaining was the sword, '(for it is cleerly evident, there is now no power executed in England, but a power of force, a just and morall act done by a troop of Horse, being as good law as now I can see executed by any Judge in England) . . .'

Since Lilburne was convinced that the people had been reduced to a state of nature, the problem, as he now saw it, was greater than simply formulating a fundamental law which Parliament should enact. Parliament as an authoritative body no longer existed. The task was that of reconstituting society. He made no distinction between a pact creating society and another creating government, evidently regarding them as one and the same. What was required, then, was to make the social-political contract anew.

There can be no greater evidence of the strength inherent in the contractual idea than the proposal of a settlement in the form of an agreement of the people. It showed that to Lilburne and the Levellers, the social contract was no mere hypothetical premiss of the political order, nor, if historical, an act sealed once for all in the distant past. It was a living and literal source of a common political existence. If this existence were destroyed by tyranny, the social contract alone could re-establish it.

The *Agreement*, therefore, goes beyond the analogy to a constitution and presents us with the very terms of the social contract which must be entered into if the political order is to be resurrected. Given this, it becomes fully clear why the *Agreement* needed to be ratified by every man, and not by Parliament. It was not merely that what one Parliament enacts, another can rescind. It was also because men in a state of nature retain their natural rights entire, and can give up a portion of them only by their own consent; no one can do it in their names. And so also, the future state which the *Agreement* envisages is to act exclusively in virtue of the power the subscribers have transferred to it. The reservations – the matters over which jurisdiction is reserved from the state – are only explicable as that part of the subscribers' natural rights which they have withheld and will transfer to no earthly authority. In all these respects, the *Agreement* is the social contract. At the same time, it is also, of course, the fundamental law which we associate with the notion of constitutionalism. Lilburne had wrestled with the problem of fundamental law. Though he went in search of it to the law books, he never regarded it as merely equivalent to the enactments of the past. Only that part of the law agreeable to reason and the word of God would he call fundamental. Now, however, the problem was solved at last. By laying down what the people would permit the government to do, and what not, the fundamental law was given visible and forever unmistakable definition.

Thus the Levellers' form of settlement goes to the ultimate assumptions of democratic political thought in the seventeenth century, and is one of its classic expressions: its individualism, manifest in the requirement that only the consent of the subscribing individuals can make the *Agreement* valid; its belief in the social contract, which the *Agreement* was literally intended to be; its allegiance to the principle of natural rights, the transfer of which the *Agreement* was intended to effect; and finally, its assertion of a fundamental law, the exemplification of reason, which the historic past could never quite disclose, but to which the *Agreement* at last gave palpable shape.

Lilburne had hoped that the army general council, on which the Cromwellians and the Levellers sat together in uneasy alliance, would sponsor the *Agreement of the People*. This was not to be. Cromwell and Ireton, his son-in-law, opposed the *Agreement's* resort to the law of nature, and denounced its specific proposals for reform as a menace to property. Alarmed by the implications of the Leveller position, they immobilized the general council and silenced the Leveller soldiery by force. Fearing that Cromwell was seeking to erect a military dictatorship, Lilburne again had recourse to Parliament at the beginning of 1648 as the only alternative to rule by martial law. But to whatever strategies political developments forced them, the Levellers continued to uphold an agreement of the people as the only tenable settlement. Two later versions of their *Agreement* were far more detailed than the brief one of 1647, and the elaborate list of powers and reservations in the former gives prominence to the aspect of fundamental law. The idea of social contract continued conspicuous, however, in the insistence upon individual ratification. Such a method, the Levellers asserted, was the only way to fix 'the Common-wealth upon the fairest probabilities of a lasting Peace, and contentfull establishment'.

Cromwell's purge of Parliament at the end of 1648 brought about his final breach with the Levellers. Thenceforth, Lilburne remained in opposition until his death in 1657. He condemned the illegality of putting Parliament under military force, and denied the lawfulness of the king's trial on the ground that the power that carried it out had no authority whatever. A rightly constituted republic is superior to monarchy, he told Cromwell, but '. . . to have the name of a Common-wealth imposed upon us by the Sword, wherein we are and shall be more slaves than ever we were under kingship . . . such a Common-wealth as this I abhor . . . and therefore I had rather be under a King reasonable bounded than under you, and your new Sword Tyranny called a Common-wealth'.

While in banishment in 1652 by government decree, Lilburne made acquaintance for the first time with Machiavelli and some of the classical writers. The Italian theorist, whose ideas were so often used in the seventeenth century to justify reason of state, he straightway adapted to his own philosophy. Once he had employed Machiavelli's name as a reproach. Now he praised him as 'one of the most judicious, & true lovers of his country of Italies liberties, and . . . the good of all mankind that ever I read of in my daies... who though he be commonly condemned... by all great state polititians... yet by me his books are esteemed for real usefulnesse in my streits to help me clearly to see through all the disguised deceits of my potent, politick... adversaries...' He was also deeply impressed with the classical authors, and compared England's military rulers 'with what I have read with a great deal of observation (in those most excellent and famous Roman and Greek Historians Titus Livius and Plutark) of the Triumvery of Rome' who totally subdued the people's liberties.

As an incentive to the government to allow his return from banishment, Lilburne promised to put forward proposals that he said would increase his country's population, win commercial supremacy over Holland, raise the price of land, and help the 'poor Husband-men' and the 'middle sort of people'. He seems to have had in mind the settlement of lands incapable of alienation upon the soldiery and the poor, comparable with 'the Law Agraria amongst the Romans'. He very probably conceived this scheme under the influence of Plutarch's lives of the Gracchi. Despite the fact that he never developed it, it was a sign of his mind's capacity for growth that amidst exile and other difficulties, his new reading in the classics should have suggested such schemes to him.

This was almost his last word. Upon his unauthorized return from exile, he was placed on trial for his life, and though his courageous defence won him acquittal, he was sent to the final imprisonment during which he died. His career spanned the rise and decline of the movement whose greatest leader he was. At his death in 1657, the royal restoration which doomed all hopes was near. Yet Lilburne's ideas had many a long day to live, and his objectives were espoused by a generation of radicals one hundred and fifty years later. His lode-star was the principle of popular rights and the subjection of government to reason. To the question, who shall judge of reason, he answered, '... Reason is demonstrable by its innate glory... and man being a reasonable creature, is Judge for himself...' But because a man may be partial in his own case, 'Reason tels him, Commissioners chosen out and tyed to such rational Instructions as the Chusers give them, are the most proper... judges...' Yet, he concludes, '... a Commission given unto them against the Rules of common Reason is Voyde In It Self...'

And on this last – the sovereign individual conscience judging the rationality of all commands, enfranchized to do so by the law of Christ, which is itself reason – he took his ultimate stand.

2 RICHARD OVERTON

Almost nothing is known of Richard Overton's life. From obscure antecedents, he comes before us for a few brief years during the 1640s to fade into the shadows after 1649, and into total darkness after the Restoration. This is a pity, because Overton was an exceedingly able theorist about whom we should like to know more. He began his career by publishing inferior verse satires against the bishops, but attracted attention only with the anonymous appearance in 1643 of his work, *Mans Mortallitie*, which contended that the soul is mortal and perishes with the body to rise only at the resurrection. This book has provoked some discussion centring on whether or not Overton was a materialist whose assertion of a resurrection was merely an insincere concession to contemporary prejudice. The point is of some importance, I think, as indicating the extent to which a seventeenth-century democrat united a naturalistic philosophy to his left-wing politics.

Overton's seems to have been a mind which harboured notions basically incompatible. I see no reason to doubt his belief in a resurrection. Yet he was also, it will be seen, materialistic. The coexistence of these positions, however, apparently created no serious problem for him, because from all evidences, the non-materialistic elements lacked the vitality to evoke serious tension.

The real significance of *Mans Mortallitie* lay less in its assertion that the soul perishes than in its conception of the nature of the soul. He conceived of it, it is quite clear, not as a distinct entity temporarily united with body, but as the sum total of the operation of man's faculties resting indispensably on a basis entirely physical. 'Soul' for him was, in effect, nothing but a metaphor for designating man's higher powers, without any intention of regarding them as supernatural.

After defining the soul as 'the internall and externall Faculties . . . joynly considered', he goes on to urge that as 'All the Faculties of Man . . . are all, and each of them mortall . . . and if all those, with his corpulent matter compleating Man . . . be mortall; Then the invention of the Soule upon that ground vanisheth . . .' As heat, he says, is the property of fire and 'cannot be, if fire cease: nor fire be, if it cease . . . as well may we say the heat of the fire continueth after the fire is dead out, as those Faculties when their Body is dead . . .' The soul must be matter because 'that which is not material, is nothing'. And as all matter, he continues, is compounded of the four elements, 'whole man being matter created, is elemental, finite, and mortal; and so ceaseth from the time of the grave, till the time of the Resurrection'.

Why he believed the soul was raised then we have no way of knowing. It is clear that his reasoning gave him no basis for admitting this without a miracle. Nor can we tell on what grounds he thought there were a heaven and hell after the resurrection, though he does say that such a doctrine is an aid to virtue. But it is obvious that Overton was of an empirical turn of mind. He was familiar with the work of the great physician, Ambroise Paré, and had apparently studied chemistry. Interests of this sort account for his materialistic arguments. He was, without doubt, a rationalist over whom dogma had all but lost its hold.

From the first, Overton was an enemy of religious persecution. He had attacked the intolerance of the bishops, and in 1645, following his bold excursion into philosophy, he joined the fight against Presbyterian bigotry. He held views remarkably broad for his time, and far beyond those of most men, for he would have extended liberty of conscience to Jews and Roman Catholics, and lamented the latters' persecution by

Protestants as much as the Protestants' persecution by them. But these affirmations were unaccompanied by any large formulation of his political thought. And strange to say, his tone towards Parliament in his known pamphlets was, on the whole, mild, despite Commons' treatment of John Lilburne to a term of imprisonment in the summer and fall of 1645.

Only in the next year, when Lilburne was made a prisoner by command of the peers, did Overton turn to the expression of his political ideas. First he took up his pen on Lilburne's behalf, then on his own, because in August, he was himself imprisoned by the peers for refusing to acknowledge their jurisdiction over him. Now he began to state his position in writings astonishingly bold. In plain terms, he denied the Lords any standing. They are, he wrote, 'but painted properties . . . that our superstition and ignorance, their own craft and impudence, have erected: no naturall issues of lawes, but the exuberance and mushrooms of Prerogative, the Wens of just government . . . Sons of conquest they are and usurpation, not of choice and election, intruded upon us by power, not constituted by consent, not made by the people from whom all power, place, and office that is just in this kingdome ought only to arise.'

He also laid down the essence of his political theory in a statement that presented nature as a norm and as the origin of right. Quite in accord with his rationalistic temper, he set aside all received arrangements, acquiescing in nothing but what nature itself holds forth. Overton's thought, as he here expressed it, was almost detached from the Christian context which was its ultimate source. Where Lilburne in a similar declaration had spoken of Adam, the fall, and Christ's law, Overton spoke of God and nature, and the latter as the agent of the former. His words could almost have been those of a deist.

By natural birth, he said, 'all men are equally born to like propriety, liberty and freedome, and as we are delivered of God by the hand of nature into this world, every one with a natural, innate freedome . . . even so are we to live, every one equally alike to enjoy his Birthright and priviledge; even all whereof God by nature hath made him free'. As men are born free, the only just origin of power is in a grant from every individual, '. . . and no more may be communicated then stands for [their] better being, weale, or safety . . . and this is mans prerogative . . . he that gives more, sins against his owne flesh; and he that takes more, is a Theife and Robber to his kind; Every man by nature being a King, Priest and Prophet in his own naturall circuite . . . whereof no second may partake, but by deputation, commission, and free consent from him, whose naturall right and freedome it is'.

These conceptions were linked with a definite programme in Overton's great pamphlet, *A Remonstrance Of Many Thousand Citizens . . . To their owne House of Commons* (1646), one of the most brilliant of revolutionary manifestos. The imperious tones in which this work addressed the Commons had never been equalled by any monarch, but they were only such as befitted the majesty of the people in whose name

179

Overton spoke. Ever since the Norman conquest, he said, the people have been kept bondsmen by force and craft. At last they would endure it no longer, 'and then yee,' he told the Commons, 'were chosen to work our deliverance . . . for whatever our Fore-fathers were; or whatever they did or suffered, or were enforced to yeeld unto; we are the men of the present age, and ought to be free . . .' But instead of fulfilling its proper task, the Commons still temporize with the royal tyrant and maintain his doctrines. Let the House abolish monarchial government, he demanded, along with the negative voice of the Lords, for 'Yee only are chosen by Us . . . and therefore in you onely is the Power of binding the whole Nation . . .'

The Commons have also been acting despotically in claiming unlimited privileges for their members and in aiding the Presbyterians, 'as if also ye had discovered . . . That without a . . . compulsive Presbytry in the Church, a compulsive mastership, or Aristocraticall Government over the People in the State could never long be maintained'. They permit heavy grievances to continue, and unjust laws, including Magna Carta, which is itself 'but a beggarly thing, containing many markes of intollerable bondage . . .' A change must be made, Overton declared. Let the House but trust the people, and do what is just, and 'Wee will therein assist you to the last drop of our bloods . . . Forsake . . . all craftie and subtill intentions; hide not your thoughts from Us, and give us encouragement to be open-breasted unto you'; and '. . . let the imprisoned Presse at liberty, that all mens understandings may be more conveniently informed, and convinced by the equity of your Proceedings'.

Overton's pamphlet was a demand for a democratic republic. His rationalistic philosophy would have no truck with tradition. It would brook only what reason found justifiable, and claimed for the present generation what Englishmen's forefathers had been tyrannically denied. His fearless language made perfectly clear that he and those supporting him would not be satisfied with half a loaf. But certainly no House of Commons like that he addressed would ever trust the people or carry out the programme he proposed.

Overton soon realized this. Imprisoned in August 1646, all his efforts to have the Commons liberate him failed. Together with his fellow-prisoner, Lilburne, he determined to appeal above the Commons to the sovereign people. Like Lilburne, he believed that their failure to obtain justice proved the country had relapsed into a state of nature. Why then may they not tread in Parliament's steps by appealing to the people against the Houses as the latter did against the king?

Overton's appeal came forth in July 1647 in *An Appeale From the degenerate Representative Body The Commons . . . To the Body Represented The free people in general . . . and in especiall . . . to all the Officers and Souldiers*. This is his last great pamphlet. It is nothing less than a call for a new revolution. Had its demands been carried out, the events which began in 1640 would have achieved ends which not even two hundred and fifty years of subsequent English development were able to gain fully.

Overton admits that history gives no precedent for his appeal to the people. But he is warranted, he says, by right reason which, though all forms of law and government fall, endures forever, 'the fountain of all justice and mercy to the creature . . .' Among the principles of right reason are that men should preserve themselves, that necessity is the highest law, that equity is superior to the letter of law, and that all entrusted power, if forfeited, returns to those who had entrusted it. These justify him, he insists. Henceforth, he will hold invalid any order of Parliament. By their tyranny, the Houses have lost their capacity. Their acts should be fought to the death, and the promoters of them judged and condemned as traitors to the safety of the people.

To preserve themselves, the people may exercise their inherent sovereignty and depute or create persons for the removal of tyrants. If it be objected, Overton says, that by reason of the prevailing confusions, such a deputation cannot be formally effected, 'I answer, that the Body naturall must never be without a mean to save it selfe, and therefore by the foresaid permanent unalterable rule of Necessity and safety, any person or persons . . . may warrantably rise up in the . . . behalf of the people, to preserve them from imminent ruine . . .'. It is the army, he declares, which now has this duty, for it is 'the only formall and visible Head that is left unto the people for protection and deliverance'. He summons the soldiers' elected agents 'to preserve that power and trust reposed in . . . you by the body of the Army intire and absolute and trust no man . . . how religious soever appearing, further than hee acts apparently for the good of the Army and Kingdome . . .'.

The *Appeale* closes with an appendix of proposals presented for the army's consideration. These include a free and popularly chosen Parliament with provision for the recall and punishment of unworthy members; the reform of law and the abolition of imprisonment for debt; the banning of all compulsion in religion and the removal of tithes and trade monopolies; the establishment of free schools throughout the country; organized care for the sick, poor, and aged; and the restoration of lands which lay in common for the poor's use and were wrongfully enclosed.

Such was the revolutionary programme Overton sketched out. He had appealed to the masses; he had not merely justified the right of revolution abstractly, but had urged the people and the soldiers to act outside all legal channels in defiance of every traditional authority. His appraisal of contemporary institutions had issued in demands which he believed were coined in the very mint of reason itself. And the conception of reason he employed was one almost secularized and dissociated from its roots and commitments in Christian tradition. Short of communism, Overton's was as extreme a vision as English radicalism attained to during the revolution.

3 WILLIAM WALWYN

William Walwyn was the son of a country gentleman and the grandson of a bishop. He was, in addition, a member of the Merchant Adventurers Company. It would not seem, therefore, that he was good material for the Levellers. But he was also a sceptical and questioning personality, ceaselessly seeking truth, and insisting that reason should try all things. Like his colleagues, he was first an advocate of liberty of conscience, and was drawn from the toleration controversy into the Leveller movement by his desire for social justice and for a government which would be no respecter of persons.

Walwyn's outstanding contribution to the revolution was in his writings on liberty of conscience, several of which are among the best pamphlets of the seventeenth century. Very early, he entered the toleration struggle, and in his remarkable *The Power of Love* (1643) called for the use of reason in the free examination of every religious opinion. During the course of his argument, some characteristic tendencies in the religious development of the left-democratic movement are made clear. The dogmatic element is dissolved, and with it, the claim of any persons whatever to be specially qualified interpreters of the word of God. There is nothing essential to the religious enlightenment of men, Walwyn said, which God has not made accessible to the meanest capacity. No special learning is needed, for with the Bible in English, any man may declare its true meaning. As dogma disappears, the essence of true religion is located in conduct. Only love manifested in action is true religion, Walwyn says, God is love, and only love can make men God-like. The obligation to scrutinize all religious tenets is stressed. 'Come, feare nothing', he exhorts, 'you are advised by the Apostle to try all things . . . 'tis your selfe must doe it, you are not to trust to the authority of any man . . . you will finde upon tryall that scarcely any opinion hath been reported truly to you.' Finally, there is antinomianism and the belief in universal redemption. All men are sinners, Walwyn declares, but God's love is boundless and will redeem them. Mankind is no longer under the law, but under grace.' . . . your feares, nor sinnes, nor doubtings cannot alter that condition . . . Christ hath purchased for you, for though the sting of death be sinne, & the strength of sin be the law, yet thankes be unto God, for he hath given us the victory through our Lord Iesus Christ'. Thus men are all as privileged in God's eyes as they ought to be in the state's.

In his great pamphlet, *The Vanitie of the present Churches* (1649), Walwyn, ever anti-clerical, expressed a view which justified an anonymous enemy's charge that he maintained 'the largest Independency that ever was heard of; that every man and woman shall have no dependence upon any Church . . . but be his own Minister, hearer, officer, all'. Despite the claims of Presbyterians and Independents, Walwyn said, no church has the mark of a true church. Though ministers profess to deliver God's word, their doubts and wranglings prove the uncertainty of their opinions. They make religion complicated so as to gain a maintenance and live in wealth and honour. Instead of aiding the poor and oppressed, they deliver sermons full of dubious notions. But the one necessary religious doctrine is that Jesus is the saviour whose blood takes away all sin and who died even for his enemies. Many things in Scripture may exceed understanding, Walwyn declares, but this doctrine is plain and full of comfort. The people ought therefore to break their bondage to churches. Let them study the Scriptures and perfect their knowledge in small meetings by mutual discussion, without sermons. As their knowledge grows, they will come to realize that true religion consists in doing good, and that the way to show love for mankind is to free the commonwealth from tyrants and deceivers.

Walwyn's temper was pragmatic. 'I abandon all niceties and uselesse things', he said. '. . . my manner is . . . to enquire what is the use: and if I find it not very materiall, I abandon it . . .' He was addicted to reading Plutarch, Seneca, Lucian, and especially Montaigne, and suggested that Christians should discard superfluities and realise, as even the heathen do, that 'a life according to nature' is pleasantest. According to his friend, Dr Brooke, Walwyn did not think communism evil, but held that it might only be instituted by the unanimous assent of the people.

In 1645, leaving his hitherto exclusive concern with liberty of conscience, Walwyn came to the defence of the imprisoned John Lilburne. Lilburne's claims, Walwyn said, are justified by reason itself, and do not require Magna Carta as a precedent. Besides, he told Lilburne, 'Magna Carta hath been more precious in your esteeme than it deserveth . . .' It is not the sum of English liberty, but the record of the little that has been wrung by force from tyrants who held the nation in bondage. Only mere ignorance will call the grants of conquerors the people's birthright and find in them the meaning of freedom. Rather than patch up an old charter, what is needed is to make a new and better one.

This depreciation of Magna Carta, and Walwyn's demand that a new charter should be drawn up, throw light on the attitude of the left-wing thinkers to the problem of history. That problem was defined for them by the necessity to make the past justify a programme which seemed innovative, and failing this, to find other sanction than precedent. Simultaneously, two attitudes towards history were developed, each of which was to put to use. First, the recent past with its tyrannous monarchy, its arrogant peerage, and its unjust laws was brushed aside, as innovations imposed on a free people by the Norman conquest, and appeal was made to a past more ancient, and therefore more hallowed, when men lived in a freedom the Normans destroyed. In this way, the Levellers tried to appropriate history for their own ends. Analogously to the fall of man and his restitution, they represented English history as the fall of liberty and its possible restoration in their own day. Second, because they were aware that the past could not always be used to support their demands, they appealed to reason. This is what inspires the affirmation of Overton that '. . . whatever our Fore-fathers were . . . we are the men of the present age, and ought to be free . . .' and Lilburne's refusal to accept previous legal enactments as fundamental law unless they are consonant with reason. But their appeal to reason as an ultimate basis of judgment constituted, it is evident, a rejection of history. For lacking any conception of the present, both as the past's product and its negation, they had necessarily to dismiss history as an irrational departure from the norm of justice, and to desert it for a higher principle.

It may be regarded as a general rule of the development of democratic and radical thought throughout this period and for long afterwards, that it tended to eschew history in favour of reason. A Parliamentary writer such as Henry Parker exhibited the same tendency as the Levellers when he took refuge in the rational principle of *salus populi* in defiance of all traditional arrangements. The Levellers carried this much further. Their literal acceptance of the state of nature is a remarkable illustration of this. For what did the stress on the state of nature signify, if not a reading away of all the determinate historical conditions under which men lived, with all their corporate privileges, customary rights, and traditional ties? All that remained was man as a rational creature and what he could claim in virtue of being a man – a claim more compelling than any sanctioned by immemorial custom.

The invocation of reason by the radicals left the royalists in possession of history. Reckoned by precedents, history was on their side, and most royalist writers countered the arguments of their opponents by taking their stand on the historic constitution. Even Sir Robert Filmer's patriarchal theory was, if anything, an exaltation of history, a mythical history, to be sure, but real enough to him and some of his contemporaries. By upholding father-right, and tracing the right of kings back to the first fathers, to Adam and to Noah, he was appealing to the ties of tradition and the patriarchal family organization that reinforced them.

The Levellers' appeal to reason was still, on the whole, to the right reason of the Christian tradition, synonymous with the law of Christ. Owing to this, their social criticism, despite all its sharpness, did not range with entire freedom, and left religion itself exempt from scrutiny. If Leveller rationalism was moved to denounce the churches, it did so only in the name of a higher religious principle. If it attacked the beneficed clergy, it had not yet learned to treat the promise of heaven as a calculated clerical manoeuvre by which men's attention was diverted from their earthly oppressors. If it declared dogma irrelevant to salvation, it had not yet diluted the Christian God into an impersonal but beneficent nature. Moreover, it did not yet question that salvation was achieved through the sacrifice of Jesus Christ. All the same, the Leveller notion of reason was deeply tinged with secular elements, and looked forward to the Enlightenment when Eternal Reason, autonomous and untrammeled, would hail every aspect of life to judgment at its bar and reduce to rubble the sanctuaries which the past had regarded with awe. This development is fully plotted in the ideas of Overton and Walwyn, less so in those of Lilburne; for the two former, as we have seen, were of a more sceptical turn of mind than their great colleague.

In common with the other Leveller leaders, Walwyn's aim was the supremacy of a democratic House of Commons. Under the present Commons, he pointed out, oppression is as great as it was under the king, and all the quarrel between Presbyterians and Independents 'is but this, namely, whose slaves the people shall be'. Unless the House sets a time for its dissolution, he warned, and enacts reforms, it will be repudiated by the people, for 'the just freedom and happiness of a Nation [is] above all Constitutions . . .'.

Perhaps Walwyn's profoundest political belief was in the method of discussion as the indispensable basis for free government. There is nothing, he declared, 'that maintains love unity and friendship in families: Societies, Citties, Countries, Authorities, Nations; so much as a condescension to the giving, and hearing, and debating of reason'. It is a striking tribute to the breadth of the Leveller movement that it could attract this urbane and questioning mind. And it is a greater tribute to the man himself that, though he loved nothing so much as a good book and a discoursing friend, he could yet leave the quiet of his meditations to press for the freedom in which he believed amidst the alarums and strife of political life.

15 KEITH THOMAS

The Social Origins of Hobbes's Political Thought

Ever since the Earl of Clarendon commented upon his 'extreme malignity to the nobility' it has been customary to associate Hobbes with the social and political pretensions of the English middle classes. The general neglect into which his works fell in the eighteenth century was subsequently attributed to their anti-aristocratic tone. Hobbes came to be regarded as the philosopher of the city and the market-place. 'We have heard of a village Hampden', said Sir Henry Maine, 'but a village Hobbes is inconceivable'. In due course Marxist terminology was invoked to characterise his thought, and Professor Strauss concluded in his influential study that Hobbes's 'political philosophy is directed against the aristocratic rules of life in the name of bourgeois rules of life'. For Miss Arendt, Hobbes was 'the only great philosopher to whom the bourgeoisie can rightly and exclusively lay claim', while Lucien Febvre described his thought as 'bourgeois d'essence, d'origine et d'esprit'. Most other modern commentators who have considered the problem have echoed this verdict. It is unlikely that so many authorities can have been completely mistaken in this interpretation, and there will be no endeavour here to refute it altogether. Indeed the position under review is in any case too imprecise to allow of clear refutation: *bourgeois* is not a term which can be translated into English, or easily adapted to fit any section of seventeenth-century English society. Professor Strauss's analysis was based upon Hegel's conception of the *bourgeoisie*, which derives, as his English editor remarks, from a completely different political tradition. Similarly Professor Macpherson is obviously indebted to Marx, yet attempts to fit the Marxist pattern of class structure to seventeenth-century England usually involve classifying at least some of the gentry among the *bourgeoisie*, which makes it very difficult to see where the *bourgeoisie* ends and the aristocracy begins. Nor does it help to drop the term *bourgeois* and speak simply of 'the middle-class' or 'the middle-class outlook', for the term is notoriously vague and it is far from clear that the fluid structure of seventeenth-century English society generated distinct ethical or political codes peculiar to different classes. Simple models of 'aristocratic virtue' and 'middle-class virtue' can be dismissed as grossly unhistorical, if only because the English middle classes have been notoriously imitative of their social superiors.

From *Hobbes Studies*, ed. K.C. Brown (Basil Blackwell, 1965), pp. 185–236. Foot-notes have been deleted.

Most previous commentators have, therefore, had to proceed with *a priori* models of conduct appropriate to different social classes. These models have sometimes been elaborately justified, sometimes taken for granted; in either case they have necessarily been inadequate, so long as the basic sociological analysis of seventeenth century English society remains to be carried out, and so long as the association of different ethical codes with different social classes is an unproved assumption. At the moment, therefore, any move to reconstruct the social affiliations of Hobbes's thought must necessarily be of a tentative kind. An attempt will be made here to identify some of the actual elements in seventeenth-century society from which Hobbes derived his assumptions and to which his recommendations were likely to have appealed. The results, however inconclusive, may help to prevent future commentators from automatically characterising Hobbes's thought as *bourgeois* and thereby over-simplifying what is a highly complex position.

* * *

Commentators usually begin their analysis by drawing attention not to Hobbes's recommendations but to the kind of human nature and society which is reflected in his writings. Thus it has been said that Hobbes observed not man but 'bourgeois man' or *homo oeconomicus*, and that his citizens inhabited 'a possessive market society'. One must therefore ask how far the lineaments of the society with which Hobbes thought himself concerned accord with this description.

The impression which Hobbes's writings convey is that he took for granted a relatively advanced economy, where men may sell their labour, where the market is a stimulus to the increase of manufactures, and where 'all things obey money'. Titles of honour are available to moneyed men, and riches, if not always power in themselves, are at least a sign of it. Nevertheless, there is no mention of the role of capital (although Hobbes's antipathy to direct taxation may be said to favour capital accumulation) and, as in any underdeveloped society, labour is indisputably the basic factor of production: 'plenty dependeth, next to God's favour, merely on the labour and industry of men'. Consequently, a large population is thought to be desirable, whatever the ultimate risk of over-population. As for riches, they still come not from investment, but from 'thrift', and although poverty may result from misfortune it is more likely to be caused by folly, sloth or luxury. The ultimate economic goal seems to be represented by the Dutch, who grew rich as a trading nation without any natural resources, and this reminds us that, although Hobbes considered his society to be steadily progressing, it belongs firmly to the pre-industrial era.

Nor does there seem to have been anything very new about the state of affairs he was describing. Violence in daily life still hindered commerce (when a man goes on a journey 'he arms himself, and seeks to go well accompanied'); while the distribution of property was not entirely controlled by market forces, but could be determined by the sovereign. And, as a source of power, riches had to compete with knowledge, honour, nobility, reputation, friends and even natural beauty. By comparison with so obvious a *bourgeois* theorist as Spinoza, who envisaged the total abolition of landed property so that everyone might engage in trade, Hobbes has a decidedly old-fashioned look.

In his analysis of the social hierarchy, however, Hobbes appears more radical. He is unequivocal in his view that all class differences stem from convenience and agreement, rather than from innate differences of blood, race or capacity. He does not deny that men differ in ability and that some are gifted with extraordinary natural endowments, but he regards these differences as in no sense the cause of existing social distinctions. Nor does he consider that custom justifies any form of social subordination. It has therefore been asserted that Hobbes regards men as entirely free from relationships based on status. But there are traces in his writings of a patriarchalism which he did not succeed in justifying in wholly contractual terms. His effort, for example, to base the institution of the family upon considerations of utility, by arguing that the child agrees to submit to the power which protects it, was ultimately unsuccessful; for, as Thomas Hardy observes in *Tess of the d'Urbervilles*, and as Hobbes himself concedes elsewhere, it is impossible to see how infants can consent to anything. Indeed, his views on the rights and duties of parents and children can only be fully understood as the product of a society in which patriarchal ideals were still living ones. For, although he refutes the simple patriarchal theory of government, he considers that paternal government was created by God, and that the father, who was absolute lord over his family in the state of nature, still retains in the civil state those powers over his children *and servants* which the sovereign has not specifically taken away. It is thus a law of nature to honour one's parents, who should be given 'the honour of a sovereign'. No man is obliged to accuse his parent, a son would rather die than obey a command to execute his father, and the state is to treat parricide as a greater offence than murder. Coming from a philosopher who is normally thought of as having put all human relations on to a contractual basis, such statements are a powerful reminder of the strength of the family bond in the seventeenth century. They are most probably to be explained as the product of a society where the household was still the basic unit of production, and where an ethical code based on kinship and requiring such extreme measures as the avenging of a father's murder by his sons, was only gradually decaying.

The picture of human nature which Hobbes constructs is likewise reminiscent of a feudal society, or at least of one in which status is all-important. Professor Macpherson suggests that for Hobbes the goal of individual activity is 'wealth and power'. But the obsessive passion of Hobbes's men seems to be not acquisitiveness, but pride. They inhabit a world where 'all the pleasure and jollity of the mind consists in this, even to get some, with whom comparing, it may find somewhat wherein to triumph and vaunt itself'. 'Men take it heinously to be laughed at or derided', and 'there is no greater vexation of mind' than 'scorn and contempt'; indeed 'most men would rather lose their lives . . . than suffer slander'. Some of Hobbes's contemporaries may have considered that the most frequent cause of human contention was property, but for Hobbes himself it is 'honour and dignity' for which 'men are continually in competition'; this indeed is one of the attributes which distinguish men from beasts.

These men who take insults so heinously, who so resent obligations to their equals, and who even care for their children out of a hope to receive posthumous honour from them, are not very obviously recognizable as the denizens of a commercial world. They are ready to engage in money-making, it is true, yet not from possessiveness, but vanity, 'for their treasures serve them but for a looking-glass, wherein to behold and contemplate their own wisdom'. Professor Macpherson argues that it is the growth of capitalism which, by emancipating men from their previous social bonds, makes social ambition so widespread a characteristic. But a general sensitivity to reputation seems to have been a feature of a much older form of society. Dr Ruth Benedict, for example, has portrayed the 'shame-culture' of the Kwakiutl Indians, who are obsessed with self-esteem and recognise only one emotion, 'that which swings between victory and shame'. Similarly, the literature of the medieval Teutonic world suggests that reputation there was even more important than ties of blood. Even if it were true that it is only in the higher levels of these primitive societies that so extreme a value is set upon honour, this would not distinguish them from Hobbes's world. For he does not say that every one will sacrifice his life to his reputation, but only that 'most men' will do this: and these turn out to be those who live above the subsistence level. 'All men naturally strive for honour and preferment; but chiefly they, who are least troubled with caring for necessary things', and 'who otherwise live at ease, without fear of want'. In fact, in seventeenth-century England only a minority came into this category, for between a quarter and a half of the population lived uneasily at subsistence level, while the truly prosperous were few indeed. Hobbes, who explicitly excluded the poor from this contention for honour, was by implication confining his analysis to that section of the population, 'who have most leisure to be idle'. In thus limiting a serious concern for honour and reputation to a relatively aristocratic minority he had the opinion of contemporaries on his side.

A preliminary glance at the society reflected in Hobbes's writings thus suggests that it differs in several important respects from the picture usually presented by his interpreters. In particular, the economy is somewhat less advanced than is usually suggested; the social hierarchy, although largely contractual, still retains marked traces of patriarchalism; and the concern for reputation and honour in the upper reaches of society is more marked than any desire for riches. Nevertheless, the growth of capitalism is reflected in the emancipation of individuals from many of the old customary bonds and in the obvious presence of acquisitive appetites. In fact, in Hobbes's world elements of old and new in social organisation are to be encountered side by side. It is only to be expected that his own social sympathies should reveal a similar transitional character.

* * *

Hobbes's apparent anti-aristocratic prejudices have received their fair share of attention from commentators. It has been pointed out that he explicitly denied that one man's blood was better than another's, and directly refuted the claims of the peerage to be regarded as the king's natural counsellors. 'Good counsel comes not by lot, nor by inheritance'; hence the appointment of the Earl of Arundel as the King's general against the Scots, on the grounds that one of his ancestors had distinguished himself in a similar campaign, is described in *Behemoth* as 'but a foolish superstition'. Similarly Hobbes displays great concern lest justice be perverted by the influence of the rich and powerful; and, condemning the maintenance of private armies and superfluous retainers, he inveighs against the presumption of the great that their misdemeanours should be treated more leniently than those of the vulgar. For 'the violences, oppressions, and injuries they do, are not extenuated, but aggravated by the greatness of their persons'.

Yet his hostility to the nobility should not be exaggerated. Much of what he had to say amounted to no more than a conventional attack upon the decaying relics of bastard feudalism, and was by no means out of keeping with the mood of cultivated aristocratic society either before or after the Civil Wars. The extent to which the mid-seventeenth century nobility retained vestiges of their former military power is uncertain, but it is clear enough that their estates were primarily a source of social and economic rather than military strength. The denial of their military pretensions by Hobbes was, therefore, far from equivalent to the denial of the claims of nobility altogether. Unlike Spinoza, Hobbes makes no attempt to urge that the nobility should be abolished and his attitude to the House of Lords is often more sympathetic than his reference in *Behemoth* to their 'war-like and savage natures' might suggest. Thus, one of the features of 'the excellent constitution of the courts of justice' which Hobbes commends is the privilege of the Lords to be judged by their own peers. Indeed he cites the example of the House of Lords in its judicial capacity to show that difficult cases can be satisfactorily determined by judges who are not professional lawyers. Even his remarks on counsel can be regarded as but an application of the old Renaissance principle, which had found much favour in aristocratic circles, that virtue rather than birth constituted true nobility. After all, the hollow pretensions of the Earl of Arundel had been similarly exposed by Clarendon in his *History*.

Still more striking is the series of concessions which Hobbes makes to the old aristocratic code. According to aristocratic theory, for example, it was essential that a gentleman should devote some effort to winning the esteem of his fellows. Sensitivity to reputation and a concern for posthumous fame lay at the heart of aristocratic morality, for to lose one's reputation was to lose the 'immortal part'. Hobbes was by no means unsympathetic to this preoccupation. For him indifference to reputation was impudence, that is to say shamelessness. (Hence blushing in young men was to be commended, as 'a sign of the love of good reputation'.) He was aware, moreover, that with the cult of reputation went some sort of hierarchy, since honour consists 'in comparison and precellence' and 'if all men have it no man hath it'. Not only did he countenance titles of honour; he was even prepared to elevate a man's concern for his reputation into a natural right, so that a citizen could refuse to carry out a shameful action if another could discharge the same command without incurring ignominy. Thus a son could refuse the injunction to execute his father, rather than 'live infamous and hated of all the world'. There were, thought Hobbes, 'many other cases' of this kind.

Nor does Hobbes dismiss the aristocratic concern for posthumous fame as entirely absurd. True, one could be deceived by worldly fame into making a false estimate of oneself, or pusillanimously relying on fame whether it was justified or not. 'Yet is not such fame vain; because men have a present delight therein, from the foresight of it, and of the benefit that may redound thereby to their posterity: which though they now see not, yet they imagine.' Furthermore, desire of praise and fame 'disposeth to laudable actions'. Hobbes's tributes to the fame of the Cavendish family in such works as his poem on the wonders of the Peak district are therefore not merely the conventional hypocrisy of client to patron.

In one sphere, however, the aristocratic cult of honour produced consequences of which Hobbes did disapprove. The duel was a relatively recent institution, which had only taken root in England during the later sixteenth century, but by Hobbes's day an elaborate duelling code existed; and an increasing sensitivity to insult was becoming the hall-mark of the courtly class. The tone of the duelling code was extremely aristocratic: only a gentleman's honour could be preserved in this way, tradesmen having no 'honour' to defend. It was not surprising, therefore, that, apart from the preachers and moralists, who objected to the taking of life, the main source of opposition to the duel should have been the urban middle classes, who saw in violence a threat to property, and in the code of honour an elaborate excuse for not paying debts to tradesmen. 'Men of trade and corporations', said a preacher, 'understand not the word *business* in the quarrelling dialect'. Conversely, the defenders of the law of honour regarded the duel as a buttress of the social hierarchy. 'Banish this defence of honour', wrote a subsequent advocate of duelling, 'and it will soon become a monied aristocracy'.

Yet it would be wrong to trace Hobbes's opposition to the duel to such *bourgeois* origins. It is true that the duel was partially a substitute for an inadequate law of defamation, and that Hobbes's dismissal of the need to avenge insults on the ground that 'the hurt is not corporeal, but phantastical' might appear to derive from quarters which were indifferent to injuries involving no financial consequences. But his other remarks imply that the sources of his moral attitude were quite different. For, side-by-side with the middle-class objections to the duel, there had always existed a strongly aristocratic sentiment to the effect that the truly magnanimous man should despise the practice because it was beneath him. Even Aristotle's *Ethics*, the most important sourcebook for the conception of aristocratic honour, had stressed that the magnanimous man should not be over-hasty in seeking revenge. Theorists had thus come to hold that honour was too precious to require so coarse a reinforcement, and that the truly generous man forgave his injuries rather than avenging them. Likewise he was required to reserve his courage for the wars, where the duellist so often proved a coward. The most determined opponents of duelling included aristocrats like Scipione Maffei in Italy, and the Earl of Northampton in England.

It was on such essentially aristocratic grounds that Hobbes himself rejected duelling, denouncing it as 'a custom not many years since begun' that 'a gallant man, and one that is assured of his own courage, cannot take notice of'. It was, he asserted, only those lacking sufficient faith in themselves who bridled at insults by words or gesture. Consequently, he dissociated himself from the proposal so frequently made in his own day that the state, by altering the law of slander and providing a new system of financial compensation, should offer that satisfaction which the duel had hitherto supplied. Hobbes's analysis was more acute than this. Aware of the conflict between the law of the land, which forbade duelling, and the actual tone of the administration, which required officers and soldiers to be 'men of honour', he accordingly urged governors 'not to countenance anything obliquely, which directly they forbid'. But by the time of the Latin version of the *Leviathan* he had grown more pessimistic, and although duelling was one of the few topics given more space in the new edition, he now admitted that he could not envisage the time when society would cease to regard a refusal to fight as dishonourable. His new proposal for eliminating the duel was both original and penetrating. He had already remarked that the practice would never cease 'till such time as there shall be honour ordained for them that refuse, and ignominy for them that make the challenge'. He now advised that the nobility, or those who aspired in that direction, should be compelled to take an oath not to issue or accept challenges; they would thus be obliged to desist or else, by breaking their plighted word, forfeit that claim to be men of honour which the duel was meant to demonstrate. But, although Hobbes thus attempted to eliminate the social pressures which made it difficult to refuse challenges, he still held that the braver course was to decline. For even Hector had reserved his energies for foreign enemies and did not fight his fellow-citizens.

Hobbes, therefore, was not rejecting all notions of honour and courage. On the contrary, he was prescribing a course of action which only the truly 'gallant' could follow, and inveighing only against the latest fashion, the 'fine clothes, great feathers, civility towards men that will not swallow injuries, and injury towards them that will', which constituted 'the present gallantry in love and duel'. In its place he preferred (and the aristocratic tone of his language should not go unnoticed) the gallantry of one 'that knows how to bring his business to pass (without the assistance of knavery and ignoble shifts) by the sole strength of his good contrivance'. [. . .]

By the time that Hobbes was writing [. . .] the nobility had ceased to be a military class. The peculiarly aristocratic code of honour was concerned with personal and family matters (chastity, love-affairs, sensibility to insult) rather than with warfare. The feudal magnate was giving way to the town-loving aristocrat, whose lack of military prowess was notorious. Hobbes, whose values were civilised ones ('decency . . . elegancy . . . benevolence'), saw that the notion that the only form of honour was 'virtue military' belonged to an earlier stage of historical development, and inherent in his discussion of honour is a whole theory of historical change, according to which ethical codes change to reflect the changing basis of power in society.

It can therefore be argued that, although in no way opposed to an aristocracy as such, Hobbes was concerned to eliminate all the more offensive forms of aristocratic behaviour. He certainly set a greater value on life than did many of his aristocratic contemporaries. Thus he dismissed suicide, which had been held up by many gentlemen as an honourable course and the sign of greatness of heart, as the action of one who is not *compos mentis*. His rule that a man cannot lay down the right of resisting those who come to take away his life contrasts sharply with the studied behaviour of a man like Raleigh at his execution. His view that insults were unworthy of the attention of the magnanimous removed the most frequent occasion for the gentleman to prefer death to dishonour. Similarly, his assertion that honour and honesty were the same thing at different social levels was an implicit denial of the convention that a gentleman should defend with his life what he had said, even if it happened to be untrue.

Hobbes indeed protested against most forms of upper-class arrogance: it was against the law of nature to scorn or deride other men, or to make another's weakness the occasion of one's own triumph by laughing at him. Although sumptuousness and magnificence were normally regarded as essential attributes of nobility, Hobbes disapproved of most forms of conspicuous consumption, of 'riot and vain expense', 'luxurious waste', and the prodigality which some called magnanimity. His dislike of intemperance and insobriety because of their effect upon health contrasted sharply with such characteristic aristocratic activities as feasting and health-drinking. So did his aversion to lechery and gambling.

For Hobbes was a man of humble origins: 'I am one of the common people', he said. 'Of plebian descent', he owed his rise in the world to his own abilities. Throughout his life he retained some trace of a provincial accent. As one who caught colds going 'up and downe to borrow money' for his master, 'who was a waster', he had every opportunity to see the aristocracy at its worst, and it would not have been surprising if he had ended up a fierce egalitarian and enemy of social pretension. But in fact he seems to have fitted into his new *milieu* happily enough, and to have imbibed a good number of its prejudices, just as his metaphors sometimes remind us that he was well acquainted with the usages of polite society. Hobbes stressed that there was to be nothing in his doctrine contrary to 'good manners', and he dissociated himself from any intention 'to encourage men of low degree, to a saucy behaviour towards their betters'. He was hostile to 'that liberty which the lower sort of citizens, under pretence of religion, do challenge to themselves', and misunderstood the nature of the Levellers, whom he treated as land-grabbers. In company with his Royalist contemporaries, he poured scorn upon the Barebones Parliament as composed of 'obscure persons', and denounced the Rump for glutting itself with noble blood. For him the rebels were base as well as false.

Accordingly, Hobbes shows himself ready enough to assume the role of obsequious client in his prefaces and correspondence. 'The image of your nobleness decays not in my memory', he assures Sir Gervase Clifton, while the Earl of Devonshire is praised for treating 'his inferiors familiarly; but maintaining his respectfully'. His own political works were addressed to a relatively aristocratic audience. The translation of Thucydides (commended by Hobbes for his 'honour and nobility') was intended for noblemen, while the *Elements of Law* circulated in manuscript form among the cultivated members of the Great Tew circle before the Civil War. 'Of this treatise, though not printed', remarks Hobbes, 'many gentlemen had copies'. *Leviathan* itself was specifically directed at the 'many honourable persons, that having been faithful and unblemished servants to the King, and soldiers in his army, had their estates then sequestered'. 'I believe', Hobbes proudly asserted, 'it hath framed the minds of a thousand gentlemen to a conscientious obedience to present government, which otherwise would have wavered in that point'.

Hobbes's political recommendations were common enough in the 1650s and they were calculated to appeal to men of landed property as much as to merchants. The quietism to be found in his writings, exemplified in the view that participation in politics involves unnecessary neglect of one's own affairs and in the general commendation of a retired life, has no immediately obvious social affiliation. But if it is not to be taken as the characteristic political attitude of the philosopher living quietly so as to pursue his own enquiries, then its most immediate affinities may lie with the 'garden' poetry of the 1650s, largely Royalist and aristocratic in inspiration, the product of the enforced inactivity of the defeated side. The great popularity of Walton's *Compleat Angler* (1653) testifies to the contemporary cult of the quiet country life away from the political turmoil and moral corruption of the city. This reached a peak in the 1640s and 1650s in the writings of men like Denham, Cowley, Evelyn, Fane, Vaughan and Benlowes. These authors, in Miss Rostvig's words, 'gradually came to attribute peace, innocence, and happiness to a meditative country life, while, conversely, religious disorder and civil disobedience became associated with life in towns, where the Puritans had their chief strength'. Similarly Hobbes, who had a taste for country life, and who had accompanied Bacon 'in his delicious walkes at Gorambery', complained of 'an insincereness, inconstancy, and troublesome humor of those that dwell in populous cities' and found 'a plainness, and though dull, yet a nutritive faculty in rurall people, that endures a comparison with the earth they labour'. In so far as his political thought reflects this theme of rural retirement it is profoundly out of sympathy with the more *bourgeois* trends of his age. [. . .]

Hobbes believed that opinion was the bond of government. 'The power of the mighty hath no foundation but in the opinion and belief of the people.' [. . .] Indeed he is justly remembered for his view that the people at large were capable of learning political virtue, the poor no less than the rich. For it was, he said, not want of wit which brought the nation to Civil War, and the nimblest minds were often those politically most mistaken. This was, of course, a striking position to adopt at a time when the indifference of the great mass of the people of seventeenth-century England to the political issues of the day had been remarked upon by many contemporaries, including Hobbes himself. The characteristic attitude of the advanced European thinkers of the day was to allow freedom of thought to an aristocratic minority, but to prevent its dissemination among the people at large. Thus the neo-Stoics permitted speculative activity among the *élite* only, allowing no independent moral judgment to the masses, while the French *libertins* regarded their scepticism as a luxury for gentlemen. The same attitude was shared by the indisputably *bourgeois* thinkers of the period. Louis Turquet de Mayerne despised the people; Spinoza and the Dutch republicans were notorious for their lack of faith in the multitude. Clarendon, sharing Hobbes's admiration for Sidney Godolphin, bewailed his loss in terms the philosopher of Malmesbury could never have employed: 'such inestimable treasure . . . ventur'd against dirty people of no name'.

It is true that Hobbes occasionally permitted himself an aristocratic snarl at the insolent rabble, or 'the lees of the people', or the 'credulous vulgar'. He even seems to have approved of the contemporary obscurantist doctrine that religious disputes are useful distractions 'by diverting the thoughts of the people from matters of state, and consequently from rebellion'. His disciple, Walter Charleton, specifically stated that elaborate ethical theories were not for 'the vulgar . . . and all that herd', who could never be taught to regulate their passions in accordance with reason.

Such an attitude was intelligible enough in the seventeenth century when the common people, hovering around subsistence level, and deprived of educational opportunities, led in many cases poor and brutish lives. It is all the more striking, therefore, that Hobbes should have dissociated himself from it, pointing out the evil consequences which such disdain was likely to provoke. At a time when many of the lower classes were illiterate and superstitious, capable of no greater political self-consciousness than that involved in flocking in thousands to be touched by a magical hand for the King's Evil, Hobbes propounded a system which by laying the burden of ultimate political decision upon the individual conscience 'both supposes and favours the widest diffusion of intelligence among the body of the people'. His aim was to remove that credulity which enabled 'crafty ambitious persons' to 'abuse the simple people'. If 'the poor seduced people' were ignorant, said Hobbes, that was the fault of the sovereign. [...]

* * *

What now is to be said of the role played by the middle classes or *bourgeoisie* in Hobbes's political theory? It seems obvious enough that his basic recommendation – effective government which would preserve peace and secure life – would appeal to those engaged in trade and industry. The dislike of civil war and desire for peace, manifested by a variety of sixteenth- and seventeenth-century political writers, is indisputably connected with the shift away from the society organised for war and dominated by a military class which had been characteristic of the Middle Ages. It is worth noting that Hobbes's political values are to some extent anticipated in the early fourteenth-century frescoes of Ambrogio Lorenzetti in the Palazzo Pubblico at Siena depicting Good and Bad Government. Here the ethic of the Italian city state is reflected in the emphasis upon material welfare as the outcome of peace, contrasted with the horrors of bad government, where Pride is rampant and Fear hovers over all. This reaction against the scholastic classification of virtues, according to which it had been doubtful whether peace was a virtue at all, began, predictably enough, in a commercial environment. The writings of Hobbes can be similarly interpreted as the product of a society in which war is no longer a necessary field of endeavour but an interruption of the real business of life.

The initial difficulty about such an interpretation is that Hobbes was not prepared to make the interests of trade a ground for political resistance. Only a direct threat to life itself will justify rebellion, although prosperity may well be expected to follow obedience. Hobbes thought it misleading to suggest a connection between Dutch prosperity and Dutch republicanism. Indeed he considered that its form of government was utterly irrelevant to a country's economic well-being, which depended simply upon the industry and obedience of its inhabitants. There was, therefore, no point in disputing the relative merits of monarchy, aristocracy and democracy, for 'the present ought always to be preferred'. Yet, although it might have been true enough that there was no logical link between the form of a government and its attitude to economics, there was in practice a good deal of connection. Because of the different social forces which they represented, there was a tendency for republics to foster the economic interests of their subjects and for monarchies to sabotage them. It was a contemporary platitude that banks and republics went together, and it was no accident that the Bank of England was not established until after the Revolution of 1688. Yet Hobbes criticised the English middle classes for their opposition to the Crown in the Civil War. For, had they 'understood what virtue there is to preserve their wealth in obedience to their lawful sovereign', they would never have sided with Parliament.

Hobbes's opinion that the interests of the English commercial classes in 1640 lay not with Parliament but with Charles I is difficult to reconcile with any of the conventional interpretations of the English Civil War, according to which the interests of trade and industry were more or less incompatible with those of a monarchy whose capricious incursions into the economic sphere constituted an essential cause of the conflict. On the continent the alliance between a strong monarchy and the commercial and industrial classes was familiar enough, for the help of the crown was necessary to overcome tolls, customs barriers and feudal restraints and make possible the practice of large-scale commerce. But in England, although foreign trade still required the backing of the state, a fluid class structure and a favourable domestic environment for economic growth made the economic case for absolutism a weak one. The economic results of the period 1640–1660 are still a subject of controversy, but he would be singularly perverse who maintained that the English middle classes lost more by the Great Rebellion than they gained. Hobbes therefore offers an interpretation of the Civil War which stands the conventional assessment of English economic interests upon its head.

It is not surprising that the men of trade appeared to Hobbes to dwell in a permanent state of discontent, the justification for which he was not prepared to concede. It was no wonder that he observed 'an insincereness, inconstancy, and troublesome humor' in 'those that dwell in populous cities' and regarded corporations as 'many lesser commonwealths in the bowels of a greater, like worms in the entrails of a natural man'. He saw that rebellions were associated with overgrown cities and that merchants hated paying taxes. To the historian the obvious remedy for their discontent may now seem to have been their admission to a larger share of political power, but this Hobbes will not admit. Indeed he is hostile to the tendency of assemblies to depend upon the counsel of 'those who have been versed more in the acquisition of wealth than of knowledge'.

Professor Strauss, while recognising that Hobbes criticised the policy adopted by the middle classes in the Civil War, maintains that Hobbes was sympathetic to the middle class itself. He has an ally in Professor Macpherson, who attributes to Hobbes the 'novel' *bourgeois* view that 'material appetites are boundless and that no moral restraint can or need be placed on them'. There was, however, nothing new in Hobbes's assertion that man's acquisitive tendencies are unlimited, for it was made by both Aristotle and Aquinas, although neither lived in an infinitely expanding economy. Of course, both these authors thought that limits should be placed to human desires, while Hobbes is well-known for the proposition that 'the desires, and other passions of man, are in themselves no sin'. But in practice his political and moral recommendations did involve curbing a great number of human passions. Among them was covetousness. For although Hobbes concedes that 'it be prudence . . . in private men, justly and moderately to enrich themselves', he considers that definite limits should be set to the pursuit of riches. Because infinite competition for wealth may disturb the public peace, it is against the law of nature for a man to 'strive to retain those things which to himself are superfluous, and to others necessary'. Thus to contend for 'superfluities', that is to say for more than is necessary for one's preservation, is a troublesome way of proceeding. Not only that, but endless acquisitiveness is bad in itself because it serves no useful purpose. Hobbes indeed displays signs of an older moral attitude, reminiscent of a static society, where wealth tends to be regarded as fixed in quantity rather than capable of infinite expansion. Aware that merchants make it their peculiar glory 'to grow excessively rich by the wisdom of buying and selling', he nevertheless questions the fundamentals of their existence. What, he asks, 'to one that hath sufficient' is 'that overplus of monie . . . good for?' Since his economic analysis gives no suggestion that he, any more than other contemporary economists, had any conception of an infinitely expanding market, it is not surprising that he should have believed that there are limits to the amount of money which anyone may reasonably acquire, and he could thus prescribe that the good judge should be distinguished by *contempt of unnecessary riches*. He regarded avarice, which is love of money 'si modum exedat', as one of the greatest vices, and he always employed the expression 'covetousness' pejoratively, recognising it as the root of men's estates, but laying his emphasis upon its importance as a cause of crime.

The basis of Hobbes's attitude to money-making is well expressed in the dedication of his unpublished treatise on optics. 'The desire of knowledge and desire of needlesse riches are incompatible, and destructive one of another.' Men seek riches as a prop to their vanity, and the richer they become the blinder do they grow to 'anything but their present profit'. Their avarice impedes the pursuit of any form of true knowledge, hiding the laws of nature, concealing the existence of God, and standing in the way of true political self-consciousness. For 'man is then most troublesome, when he is most at ease: for then it is that he loves to show his wisdom, and control the actions of them that govern the commonwealth'. For Hobbes the example of the Athenians showed that 'much prosperity . . . maketh men in love with themselves' and that 'men profit more by looking on adverse events, than on prosperity'. Hobbes's attitude to prosperity was thus fundamentally

198

ambivalent. He held that 'superfluous riches' were among the benefits of political society and that subjects should be enriched as much as was compatible with safety. At the same time his notion that prosperity must sooner or later prove incompatible with peace and political wisdom seems to derive from the old medieval tradition, according to which peace, plenty, pride, war, poverty and peace again succeeded each other in an endless cycle. Like most cyclical theories of history this notion may be regarded as the product of a society where genuine progress is thought to be unattainable and of an economy which is static rather than dynamic.

It is misleading, therefore, to base too optimistic an interpretation of Hobbes's attitude to wealth upon his statement that 'riches, are honourable; for they are power'. Professor Macpherson uses this text, together with its companion assertion that 'covetousness of great riches, and ambition of great honours, are honourable', to argue that Hobbes regarded unlimited accumulation as morally justified. This interpretation is very hard to accept. For when Hobbes says that something is 'honourable' he means that it is regarded as a source of power, since 'all power is honourable, and the greatest power is most honourable'. Hence when he comments upon the honourable character of riches or covetousness he is indicating no moral approval of the pursuit of wealth, but is simply making a statement about the working of a society in which possession of wealth carries with it power. Thus Hobbes, despite his passionate opposition to duelling, can remark without inconsistency that 'at this day, in this part of the world, private duels are, and always will be honourable . . . for duels also are many times effects of courage; and the ground of courage is always strength or skill, which are power'. But Hobbes did not approve of duels, neither did he approve of covetousness.

None the less, he considered that all passions were morally neutral and that it was only actions which could be praised or blamed. Accordingly he explains that *covetousness* is 'a name used always in signification of blame; because men contending for [riches], are displeased with one another attaining them', whereas properly speaking the desire for wealth should be judged only 'according to the means by which these riches are sought'. This would suggest a distinction between what Hobbes might advise a man not to do, viz. pursue riches to the exclusion of all else, and what he regarded as justifiably subject to out-and-out moral condemnation, viz. pursuing them by foul means. The striking fact, however, is that he clearly considered that foul means were those most characteristic of the manner in which wealth was pursued by the commercial community of his day. For he criticises the Presbyterian clergy, who 'did never in their sermons, or but lightly, inveigh against the lucrative vices of men of trade or handicraft; such as are feigning, lying, cozening, hypocrisy, or other uncharitableness'. Such vices he must have considered to be well-nigh universal among traders, for he observes that this omission on the part of the preachers 'was a great ease to the generality of citizens and the inhabitants of market-towns'.

Preservation apart, Hobbes's own personal goals were intellectual ones, and he shared the disdain of the scholar for the making of money. In *De homine* he came to the conclusion that riches were only an apparent good for, although great wealth might enable a man to purchase security, possessions tended to awaken envy. Provided one did not lack necessities, the better state was poverty, for then one would be free from the envious designs of others. Hobbes was well aware that this was a minority viewpoint, but he remained firm in his view that the pursuit of wealth and sensual comfort kills intellectual curiosity, while those who lack the spirit of inquiry 'pass their time in making provision onely for their ease and sensual delight'. Curiosity, however, was a stronger passion that avarice and represented a higher form of human endeavour, for it distinguished men from the beasts. A minimal standard of prosperity was necessary, of course, as a pre-condition of intellectual activity, for '*leisure* is the mother of *philosophy*' and 'the most part [of men] are too busy in getting food' to have time to spare for inquiry into the laws of nature. Hobbes reserved his scorn, however, for those men who had the leisure, but were too 'negligent' or too childish or too brutish to pursue the truth for its own sake, but merely sought profit or sensuous delight. For although Hobbes is normally associated with the 'Baconian' belief that knowledge is power and that speculation should aim at human benefit, he also shared an academic hankering after knowledge for knowledge's sake. He frequently stressed that it was the arts and sciences which distinguished his contemporaries from 'the wildest of the Indians' or 'the rude simpleness of antiquity', but he nevertheless maintained that science was not mere technology; for if inventors were to be regarded as philosophers, then 'not only apothecaries and gardeners, but many other sorts of workmen, will put in for, and get the prize'. The social overtones of the gibe are unmistakeable. It is consistent with this highly un-*bourgeois* outlook that he should have regarded the universities as a place for those who 'being free to dispose of their own time, love truth for itself', rather than for those 'sent by their parents, as to a trade to get their living by'. [...]

Although Hobbes rejected the idea of a *summum bonum* or 'utmost end', it is not hard to see where the supreme values of this most cerebral of philosophers lay. He tells us that he did little else with his long life but meditate upon free will 'and other natural questions' and that he did this for his mind's sake. He held that the delight of intellectual enquiry 'exceedeth the short vehemence of any carnal pleasure', and he was appalled by the obscurantism of the Roman Catholic Church which attained its power 'by suppression of the natural sciences, and of the morality of natural reason'. A man's private opinions are notoriously dangerous aids in the elucidation of his philosophical doctrines. But it is worth noting the psychological improbability of the view that Hobbes, who openly boasted of his contempt for riches, devoted his political philosophy to making the world safe for the acquisitive classes.

Nor did his system give the acquisitive classes the security they sought. It has sometimes been implied that Hobbes was by no means unsympathetic to the *bourgeois* conception of independent property rights. The preface to *De Cive* can be taken as an indication that the justification of property lay at the heart of Hobbes's investigation into politics. 'My first enquiry was to be, from whence it proceeded that any man should call anything rather his *own*, than *another man's*.' It is notable also that Hobbes rejected communism in favour of a system of private property, while stressing that the latter could not exist in the state of nature, where there is 'no inheritance, to transmit to the son, nor to expect from the father'. There is no doubt that for Hobbes property was 'an effect of commonwealth' and so was any subsequent inequality of riches. In many respects his state can be regarded as a bulwark of property. The sovereign levies taxes so as to maintain private men in their callings and by upholding property rights against the incursions of other subjects gives every citizen the security he requires. 'Each one securely enjoys his limited right.' Out of the commonwealth 'no man is sure of the fruit of his labours; in it, all men are'. Moreover, the men of property gain more from the state than do the other citizens, since, although everyone receives 'the enjoyment of life, which is equally dear to poor and rich', Hobbes adds the important qualification that 'the rich, who have the service of the poor, may be debtors [to the state] not only for their own persons but for many more'.

It may well be true, therefore, that, as Mr Schlatter says, Hobbes conceived of his system as affording the best possible protection for private property. There are, however, a number of important respects in which his view of property rights diverged from that held by the propertied classes of his own day. For, in the first place, there is some reason for thinking that Hobbes valued private property, not for the private satisfactions it afforded, but simply because it appeared to him the best remedy against violence. For 'from a community of goods there must needs arise contention, whose enjoyment should be greatest. And from that contention all kind of calamities must unavoidably ensue'. It was for similar reasons that he made it a law of nature '*that such things as cannot be divided, be enjoyed in common*', stressing that any division contrary to the interests of peace and security was to be reputed void.

Secondly, Hobbes was disinclined to encourage endless acquisition. His traditional views on the subject of covetousness have already been emphasized. It should, furthermore, be noted that he was unwilling to permit men the luxury of private property rights when they jeopardized the livelihood of other men. He seems, indeed, to have postulated an ultimate natural right to a subsistence existence, for he stresses that a man can never abandon the right 'of defending his life, *and means of living*'. There would be contexts where this provision might constitute a serious bar to indefinite accumulation.

Thirdly, Hobbes's views on property differed in a crucial respect from those of his property-conscious contemporaries in that he allowed no property rights against the sovereign. 'The property which a subject hath in his lands, consisteth in a right to exclude all other subjects from the use of them; and not to exclude their sovereign, be it an assembly, or a monarch.' As a consequence, the notion that private men had any absolute property rights against the state or could withhold taxation without consent was to be abhorred as a doctrine tending to the dissolution of the commonwealth. Thus, in the one issue where property rights in Hobbes's day were seriously disputed, Hobbes abandoned the interests of possessing classes altogether. It was not surprising that his contemporaries classed his views on property with those of the Royalist clergy, Sibthorp and Manwaring, who taught that all property was subject to the king. Indeed Hobbes himself told Aubrey that Manwaring 'preach'd his doctrine'. He had no sympathy with the reluctance of propertied members of Parliament to grant taxes, and openly scoffed at Hampden's case and the 'grievance' of ship-money. 'Mark the oppression; a Parliament-man of 500l. a year, land-taxed at 20s.' Like Pericles, Hobbes regarded public property as far more important than that of the private citizens, and he displayed positive malevolence to the great guardian of private rights, the common law. Ironically, it fell to the conservative Clarendon to refute Hobbes's views on property, on the characteristically *bourgeois* grounds that 'if trade be necessary to the good of a nation, it must be founded upon the known right of propriety, not as against other subjects only, but against the sovereign himself'.

It has sometimes been argued that Hobbes's views on sovereignty were fundamentally harmonious with the true interests of the pro-pertied classes of his day, in the sense that the notion of such a sovereign is logically required if independent property rights are to be conceivable and enforceable in the first place. It is obviously true that in a warlike or disturbed society the only true guarantor of property is the sovereign; and there were certainly some of Hobbes's contem-poraries who thought that an absolute monarchy was in practice a better guardian of private property than a more democratic regime. In the actual context of the reign of Charles I, however, Hobbes's political views were correctly diagnosed by contemporaries as constituting a threat to the interests of the propertied classes, and it would be impossibly over-ingenious to argue to the contrary. Arbitrary taxation, though slight by continental standards, was indisputably a threat to the interests of landowners and merchants alike, so that even Professor Macpherson has to admit that, in the context of the time, Hobbes's approach 'did not recommend his views to those who thought property the central social fact'. As Sir Matthew Hale remarked, 'If once men be under that jealousie that the laws of the landes doe not sufficiently fix their properties and liberties, mens mindes will be pendulous and unquiett and subject to feares and doubts, and thereupon industrie and paines will wither and decay, whatsoever orations men of witt and eloquence may otherwise make to secure them'.

It is difficult to avoid the conclusion that Hobbes provided no effective guarantees for private property because he was not primarily concerned to do so. For him the greatest value was not property but life, as is symbolised by his maintenance of the proposition that it is no crime to steal in order to keep alive. 'When a man is destitute of food, or other thing necessary for his life, and cannot preserve himself by any other way, but by some fact against the law; as if in a great famine he take the food by force, or stealth, which he cannot obtain for money nor charity . . . he is totally excused.' In the economic conditions of the seventeenth century this was no mere academic issue; the weavers of Hobbes's home town of Malmesbury, for example, had been reduced to pilfering as the alternative to starvation in the dearth of 1614. In condoning such desperate measures Hobbes was re-stating a traditional medieval doctrine, for the casuists of the medieval church had come to maintain that all things were common in time of necessity, so that theft was a permissible alternative to starvation. This doctrine had been given papal sanction in 1279 and had secured the support of the civil lawyers. Even the common law of medieval England had treated theft in the time of necessity as unpunishable if below the value of twelve pence. By the middle of the seventeenth century, however, a decisive change was taking place. Sir Matthew Hale pronounced authoritatively that in England, where a system of state poor relief had existed since the reign of Elizabeth, such concessions could no longer be permitted, for otherwise 'men's properties would be under a strange insecurity, being laid open to other men's necessities, whereof no man can possibly judge, but the party himself'. He further took the opportunity to observe that some 'very bad use hath been made of this concession by some of the Jesuitical casuists in France, who have thereupon advised apprentices and servants to rob their masters, when they have judged themselves in want of necessaries . . . and by this means let loose . . . all the ligaments of property and civil society'. This new and harsher interpretation carried the day, receiving ultimately the endorsement of Blackstone, who observed that 'in England, where charity is reduced to a system, and interwoven in our very constitution . . . it is impossible that the most needy stranger should ever be reduced to the necessity of thieving to support nature'. As a consequence the excuse of necessity could no longer be pleaded.

A comparable evolution can be traced in the works of the casuists. The doctrine of necessity had been upheld in the works of continental writers like Covarruvias and Grotius and was at first sympathetically received by English moralists. During the course of the seventeenth century, however, the general attitude visibly hardened and the concessions to the poor were whittled down until Richard Baxter in his *Christian Directory* (1673) could assert that '*ordinarily* it is a duty, rather to dye, than take another man's goods against his will', on the ground that 'in ordinary cases, the saving of a man's life will not do so much good as his stealing will do hurt. Because the lives of ordinary persons are of no great concernment to the common good. And the violation of the laws may encourage the poor to turn thieves, to the loss of the estates and lives of others.'

In championing the rights of the poor Hobbes was thus upholding a doctrine whose origins lay in the Middle Ages and whose foundations were coming under attack in his own day as a result of the new pressure to secure absolute rights in private property. Yet he stuck to a point of view which was being rejected by all the obviously *bourgeois* thinkers of his age. In a number of important respects his ideas on property were thus strikingly unprogressive. His assumption that rights in property were conditional upon the wishes of an arbitrary sovereign and the needs of the poor had no future. Indeed the denial of such conditions was a necessary element in the philosophical background to the Industrial Revolution.

* * *

There remains the question of Hobbes' attitude to the economic relations between men obtaining in political society. According to Professor Macpherson, Hobbes 'found no room for moral principles not deducible from market relations' and reduced 'life itself . . . to a commodity'. This interpretation would make Hobbes the arch-exponent of the moral and jurisprudential conventions of early capitalist society. It has been persuasively argued and deserves careful consideration.

It is obviously the case that Hobbes accepted 'market values' in so far as he thought there could be nothing unjust about buying and selling conducted in accordance with the rules laid down by the sovereign. This does not mean that he held there was no morality relating to commercial dealings, but simply that he considered the only morality was that enforced by the state. He had accordingly no notion of 'just price' other than market price and set no limits to legitimate private profit. 'The value of all things contracted for, is measured by the appetite of the contractors: and therefore the just value, is that which they be contented to give.' For 'though the thing bought be unequal to the price given for it; yet forasmush as both the buyer and the seller are made judges of the value, and are thereby both satisfied: there can be no injury done on either side'. Hobbes thus maintained what, at the time, was said to be a common maxim in 'the shops of trade', namely that a thing was worth whatever a man would give for it, a doctrine which Baxter was still concerned to refute years later. Hobbes was clearly a step ahead of many of his contemporaries in his readiness to treat just price as synonymous with market price. He believed in the market as a commercial institution, considering that all manufactures increased 'by being vendible' and that a man's labour was 'a commodity exchangeable for benefit, as well as any other thing'. He was even capable of employing commercial metaphors to describe political relationships.

There is also reason to think that he favoured what we should regard to-day as an extreme state of internal *laisser-faire*. Thus when observing that the liberty of the subject comprises those 'things, which in regulating their actions, the sovereign hath praetermitted' he cites as instances 'the liberty to buy, and sell, and otherwise contract with one another; to choose their own abode, their own diet, their own trade of life, and institute their children as they themselves think fit; and the like'. It is hardly necessary to emphasise that not one of these 'liberties' had been recognised by previous Tudor and Stuart governments, whose elaborate codes of social and economic regulation had extended to these and many other matters. But we have no reason for thinking that Hobbes himself intended them to stand as unassailable liberties. They are presented as hypothetical examples of freedom from control and are omitted altogether in the Latin version of *Leviathan*. Indeed they are implicitly refuted in those passages where Hobbes advocates sumptuary laws regulating the consumption of food and clothes, for these measures would presumably be incompatible with any liberty for men to 'choose their own diet'. His educational proposals would similarly conflict with men's liberty to 'institute their children as they think fit'.

None the less, it may be fairly concluded that Hobbes objected to many features of the old industrial code, notably to internal mono-polies, and considered that the state should concentrate its main attention upon the regulation of overseas trade. His attitude seems to be that the commonwealth exists to provide a framework of security in which wealth may be pursued, but not to interfere with its distribution. The only specific limit set to private acquisitive activity appears to be the requirement that it shall involve no 'danger, or hurt to the commonwealth', by which it is presumably meant that defence is to come before opulence. This reservation is an important one, for it reminds us that Hobbes put power before plenty and was envisaging no simple society of shop-keepers as the end-product. Nor is he in-different to the interests of the consumer, for it is from his point of view that he objects to monopolies. He was also prepared to countenance primogeniture, a system of inheritance which Professor Macpherson has elsewhere described as obstructive to the growth of capitalist relations. In general, however, his economic position was, in the context of his age, extremely advanced and it constitutes the most obviously *bourgeois* aspect of his thought.

His economic recommendations, however, were not an indispens-able part of his political thought, for he left to the sovereign the right to determine 'what we may contract for, and what not'. This position is as much the necessary preliminary to a programme of elaborate state interference as to one of *laisser-faire*. Hobbes's own preferences are clear enough, but his political ideas were consistent with either course.

The alternative economic policy is revealed by Hobbes's state Poor Law, which is intended not only to compel the idle to work, but to guarantee the necessities of life to those who 'by accident inevitable, become unable to maintain themselves by their labour'. In such a society, where relief is afforded the impotent poor, whose labour will never be of advantage to the state or to any private individual, it seems misleading to say with Professor Macpherson that Hobbes has reduced 'life itself . . . to a commodity'. For Hobbes presupposed that all men have a natural right to the means of livelihood, and intended that the state should secure this for them when they had become unable to do so for themselves. Similarly, it is because he recognised the plight of the poor that he held that 'to rob a poor man, is a greater crime, than to rob a rich man; because it is to the poor a more sensible damage'. In a purely market society the impotent and old would presumably be abandoned since they command no market price. In Hobbes's state they are preserved.

Professor Macpherson, however, bases his interpretation upon Hobbes's statement that 'the *value*, or WORTH of a man, is as of all other things, his price; that is to say, so much as would be given for the use of his power: and therefore is not absolute; but a thing dependent on the need and judgment of another'. He presumably takes this to support his view that there is no room in Hobbes's theory for any assessment of men in terms of their contribution or their need. Although this interpretation would probably have had the support of Marx, it would seem to be misleading. It is quite possible that, in its widest sense, Hobbes's statement is not concerned with economic transactions in early capitalist society at all, but rather with the nature of human reputation, which, in any society, is by definition 'no more than it is esteemed by others'. In the courtly literature of medieval Germany, for example, it was recognised that men are judged by repute rather than by any intrinsic value. In such a context the value of a man is his price. [. . .] This does not indicate the extent of market relationships; it simply means that reputation must necessarily depend upon the opinions of others. Accordingly Hobbes concludes 'For let a man, as most men do, rate themselves at the highest value they can; yet their true value is no more than it is esteemed by others'.

But whatever the meaning of Hobbes's statement (and it would seem too terse and too isolated to be capable of adequate clarification) it is clear that he was at pains to provide other standards by which men may be assessed. A man's *value* depends upon the opinion of others, as we have seen, but his *merit* or *desert* arises from the contractual relationships into which he has entered; while his *worthiness* stems from his capacity for well discharging some particular function. In the civil state, moreover, a man's *worth* is determined by the will of the sovereign. 'The public worth of a man, which is the value set on him by the commonwealth, is that which men commonly call DIGNITY.' Of these four criteria, *value, merit, worthiness*, and *dignity*, it is only the first two which in any sense arise from the operation of a market society. Furthermore, the function of the state is to replace the value set on a man by other men by his official value, which is determined by the sovereign, thus interrupting the market process. Hobbes has no intention of permitting the *price* of a man to supersede all other criteria. True, he restricts his use of the word *value* to those occasions when it is synonymous with price, the main purpose of this device being to inhibit judgment upon market transactions deriving from some external moral standard. Accordingly he stresses that we can *injure* no one when distributing our own, though giving 'more to a man than he merits', nor when making a contract, though selling 'dearer than we buy'. This position certainly involves the rejection of older standards of distributive and commutative justice as some of his contemporaries would have understood them. It does not, however, give us an adequate account of how Hobbes thinks that men in fact should be treated, whether by their fellows or by the state. For the laws of nature require citizens to recognise each other's claims to life, as those of their equals by nature. Men must further recognise that in civil society it is the sovereign, not the market, which determines differences of human worth. Furthermore, the state, by its protection of the poor and impotent, serves as a barrier against the unimpeded operation of the market. The sovereign in his distribution of offices and rewards will take into account the differences in human contribution; in his social policy he will be aware of differences of need. In neither case will life be treated as a commodity; nor will men be left to the mercy of the market.

Finally it must be emphasised that Hobbes did not altogether share the assumptions animating the legal code under whose protection early English capitalism first flourished. We have already noticed how his concession to the starving man of the right to steal in time of emergency conflicted with the growing desire to provide more elaborate protection for the rights of property. Like the radical law reformers of his day Hobbes held that 'there is no proportion between goods and life'. Unlike the English common lawyers he was prepared to recognise that the necessity for self-preservation was good grounds for disobeying the criminal law. It is true that he does not specifically urge the abolition of those branches of the criminal law of his day which made life the penalty for infringements of property; indeed he seems to think that capital punishment could sometimes be a useful deterrent against stealing. But in general he appears more ready to place life above the requirements of property and commerce than were his contemporaries.

It has sometimes been said that the stress on covenants which figures so largely in Hobbes's work is an echo of the preoccupations of an increasingly capitalist society, where the legal enforceability and negotiability of contracts is an essential preliminary to economic expansion. But his views on contracts are by no means those of his more *bourgeois* contemporaries. He had the law on his side when he argued that a man was bound to endeavour to perform an obligation he had undertaken, even when it subsequently turned out to be impossible. But whereas contemporary casuists maintained that a man should stick by his word even if it turned out to involve his self-destruction, Hobbes is consistent in his view that self-preservation must come first. A covenant of mutual trust in the state of nature is void 'upon any reasonable suspicion', while in civil society 'the obligation of subjects to the sovereign, is understood to last as long, and no longer, than the power lasteth, by which he is able to protect them'. To this extent, therefore, Hobbes did not believe in the absolute sanctity of contracts.

So far as can be ascertained, the law seems to have been behind Hobbes in his view that contracts could not bind to the point of self-destruction, but he parts company from it, at least in spirit, when he comes to define the other circumstances in which a contract might be set aside. In the common law courts of his day it was generally accepted that a contract made by duress or extortion – that is, by actual or threatened violence or imprisonment – could not be upheld. 'If a man makes an obligation by duress, he shall avoid it.' Hence if a thief demanded a man's money or his life and he chose to hand over his money, this would not be a free contract, but robbery. Nor is this merely a legal principle. In Hobbes's day most moralists would have agreed with Locke's subsequent assertion that promises obtained by force do not bind. As Ames put it, 'the consent which is wrested by extreme feare is not sufficient to a firme contract'.

Ever since the devastating analysis by Marx it has been generally realised that this definition of duress as consisting only of threatened violence or imprisonment is impossibly narrow. The formal freedom of the contracting parties can conceal a fundamental inequality of bargaining power, which can effectively restrict freedom of choice, even though no physical duress is employed. By concentrating solely on physical coercion the English common law courts made no allowance for the various forms of economic coercion which might lead a man 'freely' to contract to work for low wages or to pay high prices for food, when loss of life was as much the alternative as it would have been, had the agreement been made at the point of a pistol. The freedom of contract so often proclaimed as an essential liberty, and indubitably essential for the growth of capitalism, was thus freedom of the most formal and deceptive kind.

It is striking, however, that this artificial distinction between physical duress, which is good grounds for voiding a contract, and economic duress, which is not, receives no support from Hobbes, to whom the distinction is a spurious one. Instead he treats contracts as equally binding whatever their origins. 'It is', he admits, 'a usual question, whether compacts extorted from us through fear, do oblige or not. For example, if, to redeem my life from the power of a robber, I promise to pay him 100l. next day, and that I will do no act whereby to apprehend and bring him to justice: whether I am tied to keep promise or not.' To this conventional problem Hobbes gives an unconventional answer, maintaining firmly that such a promise *is* binding. 'Covenants entered into by fear, in the condition of mere nature, are obligatory.' In the civil state they still bind unless the thing promised is specifically forbidden by the sovereign. 'For whatsoever I may lawfully do without obligation, the same I may lawfully covenant to do through fear: and what I lawfully covenant, I cannot lawfully break.'

It is easy to see why Hobbes feels it necessary to maintain this paradoxical position. Since the covenant upon which his common-wealth rests is itself founded upon fear, he cannot deny the validity of such agreements. 'If it were true [that all covenants "as proceed from fear of death or violence" were void] no man, in any kind of commonwealth, could be obliged to obedience.' Hobbes's system therefore requires him to deny that there is any good distinction between contracts into which coercion has entered and those into which it has not. He is, moreover, able to reinforce his position with some curious logic. A covenant obliges if it has been undertaken voluntarily. But what makes an act voluntary? Hobbes's answer is that it is voluntary if it 'proceedeth from the *will*, and no other'; that is to say, if it is not involuntary like blinking or sleepwalking. But since will *'is the last appetite in deliberating'*, it follows 'that not only actions that have their beginning from covetousness, ambition, lust, or other appetites to the thing propounded; but also those that have their beginning from aversion, or fear of those consequences that follow the omission, are *voluntary actions'*. A covenant made at the point of a pistol is therefore as voluntary as one made out of friendship or generosity, and there are no grounds for distinguishing between the two. So, to employ Aristotle's famous example, when a man throws his goods overboard to stop the ship sinking 'there is nothing there involuntary but the hardness of the choice'.

Modern philosophers may feel that so elastic a definition of 'voluntary' raises more problems than it solves, since they have now to search for a fresh analysis of what it is we feel to be unsatisfactory about a covenant made at the point of a gun. But Hobbes has the advantage of a consistent position, which serves to remind us that, if we shift our attention from the voluntariness of the act to the appetites or aversions which prompted it, we will find no qualitative distinction between actions impelled by physical fear and those prompted by economic coercion. In sum, Hobbes, far from subscribing to one of the most fundamental jurisprudential assumptions of a laissez-faire capitalist society, has gone a long way towards removing its philosophical basis altogether. He was not alone among his contemporaries in manifesting scepticism about the distinction between bargains arrived at by physical force and those dictated by other forms of coercion, but it has seldom been emphasized just how incompatible his position on this matter was with the assumptions of what Professor Macpherson calls 'a market society'. Admittedly, Hobbes does not advocate interference with bargains made under market pressures, and his political theory is directed towards the removal of non-economic forms of coercion in daily life. But when physical force does enter into the making of a contract, he specifically rejects the common law doctrine of duress, the fundamental doctrine in a system of jurisprudence which served to protect the interests of those with superior economic power.

* * *

It seems that no simple formula is adequate to convey the peculiar flavour of Hobbes's political thought. He lived in an age of change and it is not surprising that he should have subscribed to a variety of what were to some extent contradictory social assumptions. An effort to disentangle the strands only serves to reveal how closely aristocratic, *bourgeois* and popular elements were interwoven. Some of the resulting paradoxes have emerged in this paper. It has been shown that, in his efforts to persuade the aristocracy to adapt themselves to a world where military power was ceasing to be the basis of personal influence, Hobbes went back to ethical standards deriving from the age of chivalry. It has also been seen that, although he looked forward to the time when all men would attain political self-consciousness, he nevertheless restricted many of his most important political recommendations to the gentry and the men of leisure. Finally, it has been noted that the very economic trends which his political recommendations were perhaps best calculated to advance were precisely those with which he was personally most out of sympathy. It is salutary to recall that his ultimate goals for human endeavour – peace, civilisation and intellectual progress – have a social appeal which will always be potentially universal.

16 R.H. TAWNEY

Harrington's Interpretation of his Age

[. . .] It is of the nature of political thought that much of its best work is
topical. It achieves immortality, if at all, not by shunning the limitations of period and place, but by making them its platform. We know
that the first book of Harrington had been long on the stocks; nor need
we take too literally his subsequent statement, made under examination in the Tower, that it had been completed in response to the appeal
of a group in the army who had besieged the Protector with demands
for a Commonwealth, and, when snubbed with the retort that neither
he nor they knew what, if anything, the term meant, had turned to
Harrington to provide a working model to convince him. But the story,
if overdramatized, is true in spirit. The *Oceana*, the long restatement of
its argument in *The Prerogative of Popular Government* and *The Art of
Landgiving*, and the eighteen shorter controversial pieces, which form
with them his legacy, were crowded into a space of less than four years
between September 1656 and February 1660. All, including the most
ambitious, were tracts for the times. Their target was the problems of
'Rome or London, not fool's paradise'; and, while their author believed
that he had discovered a principle of universal validity, it was the
relevance of that principle to the issues of a particular crisis which
turned him temporarily from a student into a propagandist and
pamphleteer. The most insistent of the questions of the day did not
need to be stated. It was that which had moved Cromwell, who did not
love paper constitutions, to prick up his ears when the Petition and
Advice made much of the word 'settlement', and which caused
Harrington himself to enumerate eight different essays in political
architecture in seventeen years, with the obvious expectation of seeing
several more. Constantly sought, and as constantly receding, stability,
finality, permanence, an end of 'disputes about Government, that is to
say, about notions forms and shadows', had already, when his earliest
work appeared, become an obsession, and remained a hope, though an
ever more forlorn one, when he published his last. The civic temper,
which was one of the noblest qualities of his age, burned strongly in
him. He was convinced that he had hit on a political secret of vital
importance to mankind in general and to England in particular. It was
with the object of persuading his fellow-countrymen to act on it that he
became an author. [. . .]
    Hobbes had spoken scathingly of young gentlemen persuaded that

From *History and Society: Essays by R.H. Tawney*, ed. J.M. Winter (Routledge and
Kegan Paul, 1978), pp. 67–82. Footnotes have been deleted. This essay was first
published in *Proceedings of the British Academy*, **XXIV** (1941), pp. 199–223.

they knew the meaning of liberty, because they had read in the classics of kings branded as tyrants; but the taunt that Harrington was a paper-reformer, who judged the world from his study, missed the mark. His six years on the Continent had not been the conventional scamper, but the occasion of a serious study of the history and constitutions of half a dozen states, pursued in the spirit of what to-day would be described as scientific research. Made a member, on his return, of the Privy Council Extraordinary; later in constant attendance on the King during a critical two years; related to a score of different families on both sides of the struggle; with his most intimate friend an active politician, a cousin who was a member of most of the Councils of the Commonwealth and Protectorate, and a brother in the City when the City was a power – he would have suffered from an imbecility which no critic ascribes to him if his experiences had left him a political innocent. A niche in public life was not easily found by an enemy of monarchy who was a friend of the King; a Republican who denounced the Republic as, not a commonwealth, but an oligarchy; an enthusiast for toleration to whom wars of doctrine, as he had seen them in Germany, were an abomination, and the rule of the saints a contradiction in terms; an aristocrat who, while rating high the public role of an educated gentry, epitomized the pre-war politics of most of his class as a settled determination to prevent the Crown from interfering with their hunting and the lower orders with their shooting. It is not surprising, perhaps, that Harrington should have been denounced as an atheist and a democrat, have been dogged by secret service men under Cromwell and imprisoned under Charles, and have suffered the confiscation of his papers under both. But the reasons which first isolated him from public affairs, and then drew him into contact with them, were not merely personal. The intellectual movement which accompanied the Revolution passed through two distinct stages. The first was repugnant to him. He was in sympathy with the second.

The zeal for regeneration, which found expression in the official affirmation of popular sovereignty at the birth of the Commonwealth, in the attacks launched by the democratic movement in the army and in London on a Parliament whose declarations were belied by its actions, in the programmes of law reform, land reform, ecclesiastical reform, political, economic, and social reconstruction that beat on the new régime for the better part of four years, was genuine, but short-lived. To those who had hailed the Republic as the dawn of a new era, the relapse into the light of common day was a cruel blow. Its effects can be felt in the descent from triumphant confidence to something like despair, which makes the later political writings of Milton – Parliament, Protector, and people tried in turn and found wanting – a study in disillusionment. But the reaction which shocked the idealists as the victory of Mammon had its positive side. Its counterpart was the growth of a new climate of thought, of which the progress of Natural Science and the recognition accorded it were the most important product, but which left its mark on the attitude to the world of men, as well as of nature.

Realism; objectivity; the appeal to experience; the conviction that expediency is a surer basis for government than natural right and interests than ideals; the attempt to discover, beneath the shifting sands of controversy, the operation of impersonal, constant, and, it might be, measurable, forces, which, to be controlled, must be understood – such were the notes of the new temper. In spite of his irreverent jest, made not without provocation, at Dr Wilkins and his disciples, with 'their excellent faculty of magnifying a Louse and diminishing a Commonwealth'; in spite, also, of the fanciful form in which he cast his speculations, Harrington found in that increasingly naturalistic outlook some affinities with his own. The fragment, *The Mechanics of Nature*, written during his last illness, does not deserve Toland's eulogy; but the standpoint from which he wished his work to be judged was shown by his description of it as 'political anatomy', and by his comparison of himself with Harvey. His circle included half-a-dozen future members of the Royal Society, in addition to his brother. His central conception, that institutions are not accidental, or arbitrary, or susceptible of change at will, but are the necessary consequence of causes to be discovered by patient analysis, was all in the spirit of the New Learning of the day. One attempt to introduce that spirit into a field hardly yet touched by it was made by the rising school of Political Arithmeticians, with their deliberate application to economic phenomena of the quantitative methods of Natural Science. Harrington made another. 'No man', he wrote, 'can be a politician' – by which he meant a student of politics – 'except he be first a historian or a traveller'. The path which he chose was comparative history. [. . .]

If, however, Harrington's method is historical, his history has a purpose. With not only the English Civil War but the Thirty Years War beneath his eyes, he is convinced that in Europe as a whole, as well as in England, the world is out of joint. The key which he applies to the disorders of both – at once a generalization from experience, a principle of interpretation, and a programme of reform – is contained in his famous formula, the Balance of Dominion or Balance of Property, which, since property confers power, are, on a long view, two terms for one fact. Societies, he argues, may be classified in different ways; but, as far as their internal well-being is concerned, one division of them is fundamental. Given that they are crossed – a point which, like most of his contemporaries, he assumes as self-evident – by sharp lines of class stratification, the crucial question is the relations, particularly in respect of property, between the successive stories of the pyramid. Different property systems have different types of government as their necessary consequence. Great demesnes in the hands of a prince become the foundation of an absolute monarchy; mixed monarchy arises when the estates of the nobility overshadow those of the rest of the nation and enable them to deal on equal terms with the ruler; a wide distribution of land among the mass of the population produces the popular sovereignty properly known by the

213

term 'Commonwealth'. But the distribution of property is subject to change. There are longer or shorter periods, therefore, in which political systems and economic facts drift apart. When the Crown, for example, sheds its estates, but continues to claim the power which formerly it owed to them; or when the nobility is bought out by a rising middle class, but will not abdicate its privileges; or when the un-privileged masses lose their hold on the land, but cling, nevertheless, to rights which they can no longer enforce, the result – whether tyranny, as in the first case, or oligarchy, as in the second, or anarchy, as in the third – is an interlude of dislocation. The only possible remedy for the resulting disorders is the reconstruction of political institutions in accordance with the requirements of the changed social structure.

Such a crisis, Harrington thinks, has now overtaken both the Continent and England. The Roman world, though it crumbled from within, through the curse of *latifundia*, before shattered from without, had known how to maintain a political system in which private were subordinated to public interests, and the principle of which was 'the rule of laws not of men'. The feudal societies which rose on its ruins, with the organized inequality which he calls 'the Gothic Balance', and their dispersion of sovereignty in private hands, had as their character-istic the rule of men, not of laws, in the sense that the idea of the common good was submerged beneath a welter of particular and incompatible ambitions. Their equilibrium, when they succeeded in establishing one, had been of its essence unstable. Their much-vaunted representative institutions had been, at best, a long wrestling-match between king, nobility, and people with different victors in different countries, and, at worst, as destructive as gunpowder. They had prepared an explosion, and the explosion had at last occurred.

> What is become of the Princes . . . in Germany? Blown up. Where are the Estates, or the power of the people in France? Blown up. Where is that of the people of Aragon and the rest of the Spanish kingdoms? Blown up. On the other side, where is the King of Spain's power in Holland? Blown up. Where is that of the Austrian Princes in Switz? Blown up. . . . Nor shall any man show a reason that will be holding in prudence why the people of Oceana have blown up their king, but that their kings did not first blow up them.

For England, though a particular case of a general rule, is a highly peculiar one. Her political destiny, like that of other countries, has been determined by her social history; but her social history has flowed in a channel of its own. Partly for economic reasons; partly through the policy of a dynasty uncertain of its title, conscious that the great houses, which had brought it in, could also throw it out, and bent, therefore, on ensuring its future by the creation of a counterpoise, the successor of feudalism in England had been neither the absolutism of France nor the commercial republicanism of the Netherlands, but a society in which property in land, while remaining the basis of political power, had floated from its moorings, and had given birth, as it shifted and disintegrated, to a new type of State. Encouraged by the growth of an active land-market to turn estates into cash; stripped of their military force by the dissolution of their private armies, and of their hold on their tenants by the protection given tenant-right; over-shadowed by new families founded on ecclesiastical wealth, the petty sovereigns of the past had become the courtiers, the *entrepreneurs*, or the bankrupts of the future. But, if the nobility had been the first victims of the rise of a *bourgeois* society, they were not the last. In deliberately depressing them, the monarchy exorcized one danger but created another. Haunted by the fear of feudal revolts, which remained to the end the Tudor nightmare, it had courted the middle classes in country and town, without reflecting on the possibility that its allies might one day aspire to be its masters. Now, deprived by its own action of the buttress which only a powerful aristocracy could offer it, it found itself face to face with a new force 'so high and formidable unto their princes that they [have since] looked pale' on it – the rising power of the House of Commons. As a result of the new wealth of the gentry and yeomanry, the shadow of the approaching revolution could already be discerned in the later years of Elizabeth. Her successors lacked the arts by which she had beguiled the monster, and, in attempting to arrest its encroachments, only taught it its strength. Thus the fall of the monarchy was hastened by the measures taken by the Tudors to preserve it. Its collapse was not a matter for surprise, but as natural and inevitable as the death of an individual. It was not the Civil War which had destroyed the old régime, but the dissolution of the social foundations of the old régime which had caused the Civil War.

The same forces, Harrington argues, as acted then, have acted since, and are acting as he writes, with the result that whereas, under Henry VII, the nobility and clergy together may have owned three-quarters of the land of the nation, to-day some nine-tenths of it is in the hands of other classes. As a consequence, popular sovereignty is not a theory or an aspiration; it is already a reality in all but name. Under the influence of classical studies, the examples of the Netherlands and Venice, and an unshakeable assurance of the political virtues of the mass of his fellow-countrymen, he had fallen in love with the Republican ideal. Now hard facts, it seems, confirm his preferences, for they prove that a Republic is not only the best form of government, but the only form possible in the England of his day.

> The course of England into a Commonwealth is both certain and natural. The ways of nature require peace; the ways of peace require obedience to the laws; laws in England cannot be made but by parliament; parliaments in England are come to be mere popular assemblies; the laws made by popular assemblies . . . must be popular laws; and the sum of popular laws must amount unto a Commonwealth.

In such circumstances, the question whether there is a Restoration or not is of minor importance. What matters is not words, but facts. Though the king may return, the monarchy of the past will not return with him, for his friends will be as determined as his enemies to draw its teeth and cut its claws. The business of the statesman, therefore, is not to perpetuate civil strife by attempting the impossible task of making history run backwards. It is to accept the results of developments which he is powerless to reverse, to stabilize by legislation the social situation created by them, and to adjust the political system to the conditions which it imposes.

> That empire follows the balance of property [wrote the earliest editor of Harrington's complete works] is a noble discovery, where-of the honour belongs solely to him, as much as those of the circulation of the blood, of printing ... or of optic glasses to the several authors. It is incredible to think what gross and numberless errors were committed by all who wrote before him ... for want of understanding this plain truth, which is the foundation of all politics.

The first reaction of the modern reader is apt to be less favourable. Wearied by the pertinacity with which Harrington harps on a few darling themes, he is tempted to dismiss them as the extravagances of a doctrinaire unable to escape from the charmed circle of his own paradoxes. There is something in the criticism; but phrases whose remorseless reiteration arouses suspicion ought not to prejudice the verdict on Harrington's thought. The truth is that his terminology, if not actually common form, was at any rate in the fashion. [...]

Few rulers have acted more remorselessly than the early Tudors on the maxim that the foundations of power are economic. They had made the augmentation of the royal demesne, and the protection of the peasant cultivator, two of the keystones of the New Monarchy. By the later years of Elizabeth, the former policy was crumbling badly, and the latter, always unpopular with the larger landowners, was encountering an ever more tenacious opposition. As a result partly of the new strains encountered by both, but still more of changes in the economic environment, opinion became conscious of a shift in the balance of social forces. A discussion began which continued for the greater part of a century, and in which Harrington's work is one landmark, but no more. The decline in the position of the nobility through personal extravagance and political ineptitude; the readjustment of rents in favour of landlords as long leases fell in; the continued plunder of ecclesiastical property; the impoverishment of the Crown as royal estates melted; the rise in the income of a gentry in process of conversion to up-to-date methods of land management, and quick to seize the opportunity of rising on the ruins of ancient fortunes – such were the common themes. Bacon, Raleigh, Goodman, Selden, the Venetian Embassy in London in the instructive reports which it wrote for its Government, select for special emphasis different passages in the story, but point to identical conclusions. A precocious statistician who wrote with the aid of official sources, Thomas Wilson the younger, the nephew of Elizabeth's Secretary of State, attempted to express in figures the result of the change in the distribution of wealth which, in common with them, he held to have been taking place. In a book composed in 1601, when the most sensational changes were still in the future, he estimated that the aggregate income of some 16,000 families of gentry was approximately three times that of the peerage, bishops and deans and chapters, and richer yeomen combined. It is not surprising that a quarter of a century later, in 1628, it should have been said that the House of Commons could 'buy the Upper House thrice over'.

To examine at length the forces which were changing the structure of English society would take us too far afield; but it may be noted that the picture drawn by political theorists and men of letters is confirmed by recent work on the economic history of the period. Behind the complexities of detail which at first confuse the eye we can discern a three-fold process of decay, growth, and stabilization, which profoundly modified the contours of the social landscape. In a period of sensational monetary depreciation, the economy of many noble landowners was an obsolete anachronism. With heavy overheads in the shape of great establishments, troops of servants and retainers, cumbrous administrative machines, their expenses steadily rise. Managing their properties on conservative lines, drawing part of their revenue from majestic, but unremunerative, franchises, with interests of a dozen different kinds scattered over a dozen different counties, they find their real incomes not less steadily diminishing. Given such conditions, a crisis is hardly to be avoided; and, in the difficult years between the accession of Elizabeth and the meeting of the Long Parliament, the number of such families which encounter one is not small. Some weather the storm, ruthlessly curtailing their expenditure and rationalizing their estate-management, amid cries of lamentation from dismissed serving-men and rack-rented tenants. Many of them are too wedded to routine, too immersed in amusements or politics, not infrequently too impoverished or easy-going, to be capable of effecting it. The game, they say to themselves, is almost up; but the world may change again, and, at worst, the old ways will last their time. So they plunge into debt, at first borrowing small sums from friends or tradesmen, then mortgaging their estates wholesale to *nouveaux riches* in the City. Ultimately, unless they retrieve their fortunes by marrying money, they sell.

They have no difficulty in finding buyers. For the new economic climate, which struck one type of landowner with paralysis, was to another a forcing-house. Professor Pirenne, in a well-known essay, has argued that the capitalists of each successive era are normally recruited, not from those of the preceding one, but from individuals of humble origin, who fight their way upwards; form in time a new plutocracy; relapse, having done so, into dignified torpor, and in their turn are superseded. There are periods when somewhat the same alternation of progression and stagnation can be observed in the history of the landed classes. The three generations before Harrington wrote were one of them. The progress of internal unification; the growing population of the larger towns such as Bristol, Norwich, and, above all, London; the progressive permeation of rural districts by the decentralized industry of the day, with the result of creating deficiency areas which could be fed only from the surplus of other regions – all provided an expanding market which the business farmer could exploit. The long upward movement in prices, which hit the landed *rentier*, meant a rising income for the agricultural *entrepreneur* who managed his demesnes, not to meet domestic needs, but to produce wool and grain in bulk. The great redistributions of property by acts of authority, which were character- istic of an age when the financial system of the past was crumbling, worked in the same direction. They at once accelerated the rise of new wealth and stabilized it, when achieved.

They had taken place at intervals on an impressive scale – first with the confiscation of monastic lands yielding a net income put by Dr Savine at approximately £110,000; then with sales of Crown property at the three crises of Elizabeth's reign, realizing in all some £807,000; then with further sales to the value of nearly twice that figure, roughly a million and a half (£1,425,000), under her two successors. On the precise effect of these grandiose transactions much detailed work still remains to be done, and we must speak with due reserve. Such knowledge, however, as we possess suggests that it was neither the leviathans nor the minnows, neither the owners of great estates nor the peasant cultivators, but the intermediate stratum of country gentry and their connexions, who were their principal beneficiaries. It is the latter, for example, who in the few counties for which figures have been put together, acquire between two-thirds and three-quarters of the monastic manors confiscated at the Dissolution, and who – a fact even more significant, since it shows their superior staying-power – have absorbed nine-tenths of them by the beginning of the next century. It is they who appear – though here our evidence is scantier – to take much of the land off the hands of the financial syndicates employed to underwrite sales of Crown property under James I. It is they, again, who purchase some two-thirds of the estates sold by the Commissioners who handled the same business under his son. The last, and not the least sensational, chapter in the story was still to come. In spite of previous alienations, the land still remaining to the Crown in 1640 was no trifle, and when, at the crisis of the Civil War, Parliament threw it on the market, the sum realized was in the region of £2,000,000. The transaction was followed by the sale of the estates of the bishops and of deans and chapters; and, that, again, by the confiscation of some properties of malignants, and the forced sale of others by their owners to pay fines and taxation. Dr Tatham has shown that half the purchases of episcopal property were made by gentry in the provinces or the capital, just under a third by London tradesmen and merchants, and rather less than one-tenth by yeomen and husbandmen. No equally full analysis has been made of the buyers of Crown estates at the same period; but such sample figures as we owe to Dr Madge suggest somewhat the same story. The land settlement of 1660 was based on the principle that confiscated lands should return to their former owners, so that, in theory, the Crown and the Church recovered what they had lost. In practice the difficulties of complete restoration appear to have been almost insuperable; while, in the case of lands sold, even though sold under duress, restoration was not attempted. The general results, therefore, of the extensive redistribution of property which had taken place during the interlude of revolution were qualified, but not reversed, by the limited measures of resumption which closed it.

It was movements of that order, denounced by some as fostering the evil known as 'a parity', and applauded by others as a symptom of prosperity more widely diffused, which were the background of Harrington's thought and the premise of his proposals. Burke compared him with Siéyès; but the ingenuities of his political mechanism are less significant than the analysis which impelled him to construct one; and, if later analogies are to be sought, his affinities are less with the architects of constitutions than with the thinkers who have attempted to depict their conception of the society of the future as a necessary deduction from the facts of social history. His interpretation of his age has the weakness of all theories which rely on one key. The range of his vision is not equal to its acuteness. He simplifies the springs of political action to fit his formula for manipulating them; has an unshakeable confidence in the magic of institutions; and, while propounding a scheme for a national Church, with tolerance for Dissenters, which resembles in principle that accepted in the future, habitually under-estimates the dynamic power of religious conviction.

Within his own limits, however, he stands on firm ground. The modern criticism that he ignores the revolutionary effects of the expansion of trade was rarely heard in his own day. Contemporaries were aware that the sharp division between the landed and commercial classes which obtained in most parts of the Continent had no parallel in England. Accustomed to a society in which substantial landowners were not a parasitic *noblesse*, but what a French admirer of their business activities applauded as *bons bourgeois*, and in which most successful business men were themselves substantial landowners, they saw nothing paradoxical in doctrines which found the clue to the transference of political power in changes in the distribution of real property intimately affecting both. In reality, Harrington's analysis found favour in quarters where his practical proposals were regarded with repugnance, for common experience appeared to confirm it. It was natural enough, no doubt, that officers floated upwards by the acquisition of Crown estates should protest against the establishment of a hereditary second chamber on the ground that 'the gentry . . . now have all the lands'; that, in the year of anarchy which followed Cromwell's death, Harrington's proposals should have been pressed on Parliament as one port in the storm; and that, after his death, his most intimate friend,

Henry Neville, should have restated the argument of the *Oceana* in the light of the political experience of the quarter of a century since its publication. That personalities so different in political sympathies as Sir Edward Walker, a theologian like Thorndike, and Whigs such as Algernon Sidney and Burnet – to mention no others – should have agreed in endorsing the view that the political crisis of their age had social roots offers more significant evidence that men not predisposed to welcome Harrington's theories were none the less impressed by the facts which suggested them.

If, however, within a generation of his death, his main thesis was on the way to become a commonplace, it was a commonplace from which different conclusions were drawn than those which it had first been formulated to support. He had foretold that, were the monarchy restored, England would be governed, nevertheless, not by a king but by her landowners, and in substance, if not in form, that prophecy was fulfilled; but the effects of its fulfilment did not correspond with his hopes. The latest study of the land-system in the two generations following 1688 has suggested an explanation which, though partial, is of a kind which would have appealed to the author of the *Oceana*.

The economic tide, which for more than a century had favoured the disintegration of great estates, now, it appears, turned and ran the other way. Hard hit by war taxation, the smaller squires and country gentry, whose advance had been the theme of earlier writers, were selling out. Large properties, which could stand the strain better, instead of dissolving, were coalescing into larger, which, once formed, were stabilized by the extension of entails and the more favourable attitude to the practice shown by the judiciary. The general tendency, Mr Habakkuk argues, was to strengthen 'the stable and conservative elements in society' through an increase in 'the number of great proprietors and the area of land owned by them'. If that view is correct, Harrington's political ideals received their *coup de grâce* from forces of the kind once invoked as their ally. At the moment when his theory that property does rule was at once confirmed and superseded by Locke's demonstration that property ought to rule, the practical significance of both doctrines was transformed by a shift in the centre of social gravity – a shift which Harrington would have deplored, and Locke, perhaps, welcomed, but which neither could foresee.

17 PEREZ ZAGORIN

The Royalists and Sir Robert Filmer

Although much has been written about the importance in the seventeenth century of the theory of the divine right of kings, I cannot find that it played a conspicuous role in the doctrines advanced by English royalist writers either before or during the revolutionary decades. According to Dr Figgis, the divine-right theory of royal power meant not only that monarchy is ordained by God, that its hereditary right is indefeasible, and that, by the law of God, it may not be resisted; entailed as well was the view that kings are legally unlimited and that positive law is solely the product of their will. Now this last article was upheld by scarcely any royalist theorist. Before 1640, we may find much fulsome rhetoric in adulation of kingship, and much talk of nonresistance: the well-known sermons of Roger Manwaring are an example. But James I seems to have been the only writer to state unequivocally that the king alone, and without the consent of Parliament, can make law. This claim, however, was advanced by James in a purely speculative manner, and he never urged it, and even repudiated it, in his dealings with his Parliaments. After 1640, the same position was maintained by but a single royalist thinker, Sir Robert Filmer. In doing so, moreover, Filmer placed himself well outside the main body of royalist publicists. For the latter, while they certainly agreed that the king was, in some sense, above positive law, were also clear that he could not make law without the concurrence of his Parliament. Indeed, it was just this which appeared to some of them the chief advantage and special glory of the English monarchy.

If the majority of royalist writers had asserted that the king could make law of his sole will, or that the privileges of Parliament were merely a concession which the king could at any time revoke, they would have been unequivocally adopting the doctrine of sovereignty. But they made no such assertion, and we must be careful to read them accurately on this point. They may say that there must be some power above law in every government and that, in a monarchy, such a supremacy is the king's. They may even characterize the king as absolute. But almost always they go on to explain that in England, the king's supremacy or his absoluteness does not exclude the right of Parliament to share in the making of law. On this subject, the statement drawn up by Charles I's advisers in reply to Parliament's Nineteen Propositions (1642), is characteristic. 'Nothing . . . is more (indeed) proper for the High Court of Parliament,' wrote Culpepper

From Perez Zagorin, *A History of Political Thought in the English Revolution* (Routledge and Kegan Paul, 1954), pp. 189–192, 196–202. Footnotes have been deleted.

and Falkland, 'than the making of Laws, which not only ought there to be transacted, but can be transacted nowhere else . . .'

In thus denying that the royalists were claiming for the king a power to make law, I do not mean to overlook the aggressive measures taken by Charles I and his ministers before 1640. It is necessary, however, to understand clearly what these measures amounted to. No doubt, the Laudian attempt to suppress Puritanism and impose a strict religious uniformity was disturbing to Commons. No doubt, too, the king's endeavour after 1629 to rule without summoning Parliament, and his exaction of forced loans and ship-money, aroused justifiable anxiety. But these, and much else which Charles undertook to do, had their basis in the legal position of the crown and were no more than his Tudor predecessors had done before him. Supremacy over the Church had been vested in the crown ever since the Reformation. It had always lain with the king whether or not to summon Parliament. Moreover, the ship-money case is significant as showing that the judges were not upholding an unlimited power on the king's part to impose what taxes he pleased without Parliamentary consent. Such a power was expressly denied. What was held lawful was the king's power to exact an extraordinary tax for purposes of national defence when, in his judgement, the kingdom was in danger. The obvious reply, of course, is that the kingdom was not in danger. But this, as we shall see, was a question which, under the king's prerogative, he alone had, legally, power to decide.

Was there, then, no real danger of a royal despotism in the decade before the Long Parliament met? The answer, I think, is that there was. But such a danger lay in prospect not because the crown was claiming new powers, but because the existing constitution had ceased to correspond to reality. After its long apprenticeship during the sixteenth and early seventeenth centuries, Parliament, and Commons especially, had achieved maturity, and could no longer be expected to remain in its traditional subordination to the king. It was absurd that the royal prerogative should enable the king to disregard Parliament's will, exclude the Houses from considering crucial questions of policy, and carry out measures which they opposed. Despite all the limitations which that age placed upon the franchise, Commons was representative in a sense that the crown was not. Together with the Lords, it spoke for the bulk of the economically dominant class in the country. That the king should act against Parliament's wishes, that he should summon and dismiss Parliament as he willed – this was despotic. Inevitably, Charles's effort to rule without Parliament and to raise extra-Parliamentary forms of revenue called forth alarm and opposition. It seems probable that the king's continued enforcement of policies which Parliament condemned would only have led to further repression and, eventually, even to the virtual nullification of those rights and privileges which Parliament had come to possess.

In 1640, however, matters had not gone nearly so far as this, and the issue was not the survival of Parliament. Nor was it a theory of monarchy which ascribed legally unlimited power to the king. It was whether supremacy in the determination of public policy should remain where, legally and traditionally, it had always been, in the king. Already before 1640, by its encroachments on the king's powers, Parliament had been threatening this supremacy. Now the effect of the Long Parliament's demands was to deprive the king of it altogether. Nothing less than a declaration of Parliamentary sovereignty is embodied in the resolution which the Houses passed in March 1642, 'That when the Lords and Commons in Parliament . . . shall declare what the Law of the Land is, to have this not only questioned and controverted, but contradicted, and a Command that it should not be obeyed, is a high Breach of the Privilege of Parliament'. And in this same month, by their ordinance on the militia, the Houses did actually and unconstitutionally assume legislative power to themselves.

Under these circumstances, the standpoint which the royalist writers took up was a defensive one. Not by the utterance of new claims, but by the reaffirmation of the king's legal position in England – this was how they met the innovative measures of the Long Parliament. There is, accordingly, little that is new in royalist doctrine after 1640. Right through the previous decades, in reply to the growing attempts at resistance of the exercise of the king's supremacy, the details of the royalist position had been elaborated. Now these were marshalled and restated to comprise the royalist argument in the controversy that broke forth after the Long Parliament's assembling. There were a few able writers who performed this task, notably Dudley Digges and Henry Ferne. But neither of these, even, was of much significance, and the only thinker of real importance to appear on the royalist side was Sir Robert Filmer. [. . .]

For purposes of analysis, Filmer's ideas fall rather easily into three categories: first, his conception of the king's position; second, his criticism of the doctrine of popular sovereignty; third, his patriarchal theory of the state. We may proceed with these in order.

On the matter of the king's position, Filmer was unequivocal. He accepted as axiomatic the theory which defines law as a command of the sovereign power. Law is will, he pointed out, and signified his agreement with Hobbes's version of the attributes which pertain to sovereignty. It followed, therefore, that in a government which is properly called monarchy, the will of the king alone makes law. Filmer was at great pains to emphasize this point. Against both his fellow-royalist, Henry Ferne, and the Parliamentarian writer, Philip Hunton, he denied that there could be any such thing as a limited monarchy. If the king is really supreme, he asked, how can he be limited by law? It is a mere contradiction to speak of a supremacy which is limited. Either the king possesses legislative power or he is no king at all.

All this might serve well as a commentary on the meaning of political supremacy; it did not, however, throw much light on the actual position of the king of England. Did the king of England, in fact, make law? This, the location of legislative power, Filmer saw, was really the constitutional issue which was at stake in the revolution. His answer was in the affirmative, and, by citing precedents, he sought to prove this in *The Freeholder's Grand Inquest* (1648), his sole writing devoted exclusively to the English constitution. He was not, I think, very happy in this enterprise, for his contention that the king legislated without consent of the estates of the realm ran counter to history. Perhaps he had been misled by Bodin's view of the English monarchy. He would have been on firmer ground if, like Hobbes, he had spoken of what the king (and in Hobbes's opinion, any sovereign power) ought logically to have the right to do, rather than of what the king had, in fact, done. As proof of his belief that the English king made law, Filmer pointed out that statutes were cast in the form of royal commands. But in explaining statutes, he expressed their character by the formula, 'the King ordains, the Lords advise, the Commons consent'. What did he think this consent signified? This is a question which he ignored, though it is the crux of the whole subject. Yet if the consent of the Commons was really required, then it is impossible to understand how the king could ordain without it.

When we turn to Filmer's criticism of the doctrine of popular sovereignty, we see him at his keenest. Like almost every other political thinker of the time, he was much concerned to provide government with some durable moral foundation, and it seemed to him that no such foundation could possibly exist were the belief, so widespread in the later 1640s, really true that men are born free and that a lawful government is one only to which they voluntarily consent to subject themselves. Against this belief Filmer directed a variety of arguments which enabled him to show quite easily that it was open to every sort of objection. He pointed out that there is no proof that all the people of the world had ever assembled at some time in the past in order to consent to government. Nor is there proof that a majority had ever done so. If a majority had thus assembled, it could not have consented for those who were absent without robbing the latter of their natural freedom. Indeed, majority-rule and representative government at any time are nothing but thin legal fictions which absolutely contradict the supposition of a natural freedom in every man. On such a supposition there can be no rightful subjection at all. Parents would have no right to command their children nor masters their servants. The various kingdoms and other political divisions in the world would be illicit, for they do not exist by nature and they were certainly not created by popular consent. Moreover, men could withdraw obedience whenever they pleased, any petty company, any family, might establish its own kingdom, and no generation would be bound by the political order under which its predecessors lived. Let it but be imagined, Filmer said, 'that the people were ever but once free from subjection by nature, and it will prove a mere impossibility ever lawfully to introduce any kind of government whatsoever, without apparent wrong to a multitude of people'.

As far as they went, these criticisms were unanswerable. The social contract was a myth: the contract had never been made; it never could have been made. There never was a government in the world that rested on the universal consent of its subjects; to say so was a clear distortion of the facts. But these and Filmer's other arguments really miss the point of the doctrine of popular sovereignty. For the latter's significance, as we can see in retrospect, did not lie in its unhistorical notions concerning the origin of government. In reality, the doctrine was not a rendering of the past at all; it was a call for the reshaping of the future. By invoking a natural and pristine freedom, it was enabled to cast aside all the accretions of history, all inherited ranks and chartered privileges, all thrones and altars, and to appeal to a higher standard than these: the appeal was now to man and to what man could claim in virtue of his mere humanity. If the existing order could not provide the measure of freedom which man, simply as man, had the right to demand, then a new order must be created to do so. Thus the myth of a natural freedom propelled society forward, opening the way to the more democratic polities which resulted from the European revolutions of the seventeenth and eighteenth centuries.

Filmer, of course, could not have known anything of this, and to him popular sovereignty was only a principle of anarchy destructively at work in social life. The political order, he held, needed a firmer basis upon which to rest than the fancy of a subjection which might be withdrawn whenever men had a mind to do so. It required a doctrine of obligation which would be both morally irreproachable and historically in accord with the facts. As fulfilling these qualifications, he advanced his patriarchal theory of the state, the idea by which he is best known and which we must note as the final aspect of his political thought.

The patriarchal theory represented Filmer's effort to derive all political obligation from the obedience which children owe their parents and, ultimately, from the obedience which the descendants of Adam owed the latter as their father and first ancestor. Like the doctrine of popular sovereignty, the patriarchal theory also sought to gain the sanction of nature for its assertions. In this effort, however, it had a decided advantage over its rival, for to the seventeenth-century mind, nothing could seem more natural than the extensive control which the father exercised, both by law and custom, over his wife and children and over his household of dependants and servants. Paternal authority being the natural thing, how, in the face of this fact, could it be said that men are born free? The truth is just the reverse: men are born in subjection to their fathers.

This was the circumstance to which Filmer could point and which he insisted had always been the case. For proof, he referred his readers to Scripture, which was not only the most sacred of books, but also, as he was at pains to emphasize, the most ancient. It is, he declared, because people foolishly take their information from the heathen Greek and Roman writers rather than from Scripture, that they have succumbed to the error that men are born free. Scripture, however, tells a different story. It tells how God created Adam as the first man and gave him entire dominion over all creatures. Adam, therefore, was a monarch, and the first government in the world was monarchical. The whole basis of obedience to superiors is contained, accordingly, in God's commandment, 'Honour thy father'. Thus from the very beginning, men have been tied in subjection to their fathers, and monarchy, as the specific form of paternal power ordained by God, alone possesses divine right.

With these conceptions as premisses, Filmer went on to contend that the right of Adam, the first king and father, can only be exercised by kings, and that all monarchs are to be regarded either as heirs of Adam or as usurpers of such heirs, but, in any case, as exercising the paternal power originally established by God. His reasoning was fanciful, and his conclusions far-fetched, to say the least. It required a fine stretch of the imagination to assume a link between Adam I and Charles I. All the same, with this argument, Filmer achieved his object. He vindicated monarchy and gave government a moral basis by connecting it directly with the unlimited power conferred by God upon Adam. Granted such a connection, resistance to kings must always be sin, for to resist them is to resist God's commandment of obedience to fathers.

Such, in brief, was Filmer's patriarchal theory. It was the most ambitious effort by any royalist writer in this period to evolve a theory of the state and to invest monarchy with the sanction of religion and nature alike. It was also the only royalist conception which deserves, in any strict sense, to be called a theory of the divine right of kings. As an argument against the right of the living rashly to alter the political order inherited from the dead, Filmer's patriarchalism inevitably suggests a comparison with the thought of Edmund Burke. Though Burke was far Filmer's superior as a thinker, the two men have more than a little in common. Both exalted prescription and tradition, and warned against the innovating temper which sought to disrupt historical continuity in the name of natural rights. Both emphasized the importance of unreasoning sentiment and natural loyalty as the chief ties keeping men in obedience to superiors and the social order together. Filmer's *Patriarcha* and Burke's *Reflections on the Revolution in France* (1790) were, each in its own way, admonitions that the accumulated wisdom of generations is preferable to the inconsiderate counsels of one day. And finally, both Filmer and Burke, it is just to add, were decidedly obscurantist when they invoked the past as a bar against the struggle of the living to realize new possibilities latent in social life. Filmer's history, with its tale of Adam's absolute monarchy and of kings as Adam's heirs, is a piece of mystification; it is just as much of a myth as the social contract, and even more far-fetched; while Burke, with his exaltation of the state as 'the mysterious incorporation of the human race', and his celebration of 'eternal society, linking the lower with the higher natures, connecting the visible and the invisible world', only imposes an occult entity upon his readers which evokes awe at the same time as it defies analysis. The social-contract theory, at least, suffered from none of these faults. It brought the state and society into the clear light of day for study and examination; it understood, even if but dimly and in a highly simplified way, what Filmer and, with less justification, Burke did not: that society is at every point the work of man, and that institutions at any time are a human creation, existing for human purposes, and to be altered in accordance with human intention.

Important as Filmer was among royalist writers, his work attracted little attention in his own time, and he became famous only after he had been dead thirty years. With the publication of *Patriarcha* in 1680 as a royalist weapon in new controversies, he acquired a posthumous renown that grew even greater when he was singled out for attack in the first of Locke's essays on civil government. But by this time, so far as political philosophy is concerned, the royalist cause had been lost. It had been lost in the years between 1640 and 1660, and no amount of talk later could nullify this defeat. It is an interesting fact that by 1648, when Filmer's first political writings began to appear, the quantity of royalist literature had markedly decreased; in the 1650s, it was a mere trickle. This is a testimony to the weakness which overtook the royalist cause. The king had been vanquished in the civil war, and the claims made on his behalf by the royalists had become dead issues compared with the new questions that were interesting political thinkers. Alongside the important writings of the Levellers, Winstanley, Hobbes, and the republicans, royalist doctrine was trivial. By the end of the 1640s belief in non-resistance had been fatally undermined and monarchy deprived of its aura. All the doctrines which were anathema in the royalist creed had come into wide acceptance. Popular sovereignty, as Filmer himself conceded, was regarded as an axiom in politics.

Thus royalism, it seems not unfair to say, had ceased to be of much importance as a theoretical force. In 1660, the king was restored as a result of the divisions on the revolutionary side, not because of the strength of royalist beliefs. The Presbyterians, who were the most influential agents in bringing about the recall of Charles II, were themselves exponents of the very ideas attacked by the royalist writers in the early 1640s. Despite the restoration, therefore, it is not a mistake, I think, to regard the revolutionaries as the victors and the royalists as the vanquished. This is true not only because much of the important work of the Long Parliament – the abolition of the king's conciliar jurisdiction and the rest – survived, not to be undone after 1660. It is true also, and above all, because the ideas of the revolution triumphantly lived on, working with undiminished force, subverting the old order in Europe. They were the basis of English Whiggism and the revolution of 1688; transmitted to later generations, they helped to inspire the great struggles in France and other countries against the *ancien régime*; they are written imperishably into the document in which the American colonies declared their independence. They live yet, a weapon in the hands of all who strive to-day for a freedom commensurate with the promise and the possibilities of the second half of the twentieth century.

SCIENCE AND THE ROYAL SOCIETY

18 K. THEODORE HOPPEN

The Nature of the Early Royal Society

[In the article from which the following extract is taken, Dr Hoppen is arguing that behind the propagandist writings of the early defenders of the Royal Society, Thomas Sprat and Joseph Glanvill, who emphasized the 'newness' of the work of the society and claimed allegiance to what they considered to be a Baconian experimental philosophy, lay the reality of a vigorous survival of ancient Hermetic traditions of alchemy, astrology, and the study of witchcraft. Without in any way denying the existence or importance of 'rationalist' or 'mechanical' attitudes and approaches among the early Fellows, Dr Hoppen argues that it is misleading to divide up the work and concerns of the early Royal Society in terms of 'ancient' and 'modern', or 'new science' and 'old learning'. No single or unified philosophy informed the society's work, but within it were juxtaposed a rich variety of intellectual traditions.]

[. . .] One of the central concerns of Hermetic philosophy had long been the pursuit of alchemical goals, both as regards transmutation proper and the discovery of universal elixirs and solvents. Hitherto, however, little attempt has been made to draw together the individual alchemical enterprises to be found among the Royal Society's early fellowship.

It is, of course, well known that [Robert] Boyle maintained an almost embarrassingly open mind on many questions of natural philosophy and was prepared to contemplate the possibility of all sorts of phenomena as long as these could be explained along mechanical lines. Thus, despite his own failure to achieve experimental results from the use of sympathetic medicines (which supposedly operated at a distance), he published in 1663 the characteristic statement that 'I have seen sometimes something follow upon the use of the sympathetick powder, that did incline me to think, that sometimes it might work cures'. His advocacy of the use of medicinal amulets, whose operation he explained along strictly corpuscularian lines, is well known. In general, he accepted that some specific medicines (those whose operation could not be explained in terms of readjustments of the Galenical humours) probably worked. Having done this, he then produced possible explanations for their doing so by means of corpuscularian action. In principle, this analysis differed little from that adopted by the eclectic Sir Kenelm Digby, F.R.S., in his classic

From *The British Journal for the History of Science*, IX (1976), pp. 10–19. Footnotes have been deleted.

treatise on the powder of sympathy published in 1658. Digby saw the powder as strictly chemical and his explanation of its operation was a serious attempt at mechanism. Of course, he had no concrete evidence for this description of the powder's operation and was in fact confusing a seeming result with a possible explanation. But it can be seen that in this respect the interests and concerns of both Boyle and Digby were being dictated by the preoccupations of earlier philosophies, while their explanations were redolent of the new mechanism. And such Janus-like ambivalence lay at the heart of much contemporary natural philosophy.

In the late 1640s Boyle had become acquainted with [Samuel] Hartlib, then already a recognized propagandist of a reformed learning, not to say of a new Jerusalem. It was through Hartlib that Boyle began to move among an eclectic medley of chemical operators such as Robert Child, Frederick Clodius, George Starkey, and Peter Staehl. Now all of these men were actively engaged in various alchemical pursuits, and Hartlib's papers for this period 'show a . . . Boyle who entered enthusiastically into the dreams of the Hartlib circle'. Boyle and Starkey, the self-styled 'Philosopher by the Fire', collaborated about 1652 in experiments in medicinal chemistry, and in the same year Boyle claimed to have so purified quicksilver into an essential mercury that the result approached the Hermetic *prima materia*. He later published a vague description of this operation in the *Philosophical transactions* for 1676, although he kept the composition of this 'incalescent' mercury a close secret.

Already in 1666 he had written that

the artificial transmutation of bodies, being as the rarest and difficultest production, so one of the noblest and usefullest effects of humane skill and power . . . I shall venture to give you the account of some observations, and tryals, about the transmuting of water into earth.

Naturally such problems were of interest to corpuscularians, but Boyle pursued them with a more than ordinary zeal. In 1677 he became involved with a mysterious adept called Georges Pierre, and in his papers there is an item dated 25 July 1677 entitled 'Lre from George Patriarch of Antioch, to some Body to see Mr Boyle, & to acquaint him with some processes touching ye Philosophical stone', which is clearly in Pierre's hand. In Pierre's letters to Boyle are to be found many of the commonplaces of alchemical dialogue: codenames, veiled hints of future revelations, and mysterious societies. In the event, Boyle corresponded with Pierre for over a year. And even though he was to come to regret the business, he simultaneously published his anonymous pamphlet *Of a degradation of gold made by an anti-elixir: a strange chymical narative* (London, 1678).

This work is in the form of a dialogue and includes the archetypal story of a mysterious stranger who had met eastern chemists and from them obtained a red powder with which one of the speakers named Pyrophilus 'degrades' gold into silver. Although its precise significance is difficult to judge, it certainly provides evidence of continuing interest and of the fact that Boyle felt it necessary to present the matter in an indirect and veiled manner. In 1675-7 Boyle also became much exercised by the activities of 'the famous frier Wencel', who, it was reported,

> has several times actually made transmutations of baser metals into gold ... [which] ... supposing the truth of this ... one positive instance will better prove the reality of what they call the philosopher's stone, than all the cheats and fictions, wherewith pretending chemists have deluded the unskilful and the credulous, will prove, that there can be no such thing as the elixir, nor no such operation as they call projection.

Although it would be foolish, of course, to see Boyle as a traditional alchemist, his prolonged interest in and concern for the possibility of transmutation and the discovery of an elixir clearly demonstrates a certain ambivalence in his handling of natural philosophy. And in this sphere he also adopted a secretive and uninformative approach. Indeed, despite his proverbial loquacity, Boyle could be extremely reticent about his discoveries. Although M.B. Hall has characterized a 'distaste for secrecy' as marking Boyle out as one of the new men of science, he himself confessed that he deliberately concealed parts of his labours so as to be 'always provided with some rarity to barter with those secretists', while one of his correspondents, John Clayton, wrote to him in 1687:

> I must remind you of wt you was most obligeingly pleasd to offer, to communicate some receits & secrets wch you said you would not trust to the hazards of a letter but under a hidden character the key of wch you sd you would send me in the first place.

Among those who displayed a persistent interest in Boyle's alchemical activities, if one may so call them, was Isaac Newton. Already, after the appearance of Boyle's paper on the 'incalescent' mercury in the *Transactions*, Newton had written a tortuous letter to Oldenburg urging Boyle

> to high silence till he shall be resolved of what consequence ye thing may be either by his own experience, or yet judgmt of some other that throughly understands that he speakes about, that is of a true Hermetic Philosopher, whose judgmt (if there be any such) would be more to be regarded in this point than that of all ye world beside to ye contrary.

After Boyle's death, Newton conducted an allusive and inconclusive correspondence with one of Boyle's literary executors, John Locke (F.R.S., 1668), to whom Boyle had earlier written about his wish 'to leave a kind of Hermetic legacy to the studious disciples of that art'. Newton was clearly anxious to know more about this and about Boyle's 'red earth'. His own deep interest in alchemy was by then long established and he had already embarked upon making those many and lengthy extracts from the great Hermetic authors – Maier, Paracelsus, Ripley, Basil Valentine, Ashmole, Thomas Vaughan, Fludd, Dee, etc. – which are such a feature of his manuscript remains. He must have known that Locke would not prove entirely unresponsive to his hints and conjectures, for Locke too had for some time exhibited a real, if less intense, involvement in alchemical pursuits. As a young man (together with other future fellows of the Royal Society such as Joseph Williamson, John Wallis, Christopher Wren, Ralph Bathurst, and Richard Lower) he had, in 1659-60, attended the chemistry classes given at Oxford by the German adept, Peter Staehl, who had been brought to that city under Boyle's patronage. Staehl was also involved with Hartlib, and was reputed to know the secret way of making Basil Valentine's medicinal *calx viva*. Anthony Wood, who also attended the classes, calls him 'the noted chimist and Rosicrucian' and claims that he acted as the Royal Society's 'operator' between 1664 and 1670. By the mid-1660s Locke was hard at work studying the writings of Basil Valentine and Helmont and reading the alchemically inclined treatise on chemistry written by Nicolas Le Fèvre, the royal physician and an original fellow of the Royal Society. Indeed his own library included over sixty alchemical books, among them the works of Becher, F.M. van Helmont, Basil Valentine, Maier, Lull, Kelley, and others.

The intensity of Newton's alchemical studies was largely the outcome of his belief in the existence of an ancient wisdom or *prisca sapientia*, which had been lost and which he was in the process of rediscovering. This was, of course, one of the characteristic tenets of Renaissance neoplatonism, and was, in one way or another, quite widely held in late seventeenth-century England. Thus Newton was able to provide a historical paternity for his own ideas as well as for those of other sixteenth- and seventeenth-century natural philosophers. The ancient Egyptians, he believed, had taught the Copernican system; the ancients had had a knowledge of the atomic structure of matter and its moving by gravity through void space – a comprehension he traced back to Moschus the Phoenician; Pythagoras had discovered experimentally an inverse-square relation in the vibration of strings and had extended it to weights and the distances of the planets from the sun. Part and parcel of such a view was the belief that this *prisca sapientia* known in ancient times had been expressed by its proponents in obscure symbolical language to protect it from the attention of the vulgar. Just therefore as with alchemy, which for Newton was probably part of this wisdom, it was open only to the initiate to penetrate the mysteries of this *prisca sapientia*. It was this approach which informed much of Newton's philosophical research and it is wrong either to deny the reality of his esoteric interests or to separate them entirely from his 'official' scientific studies. As P.M. Rattansi has written,

> Newton's assumptions . . . imply some sort of dialectic between new inductively- and experimentally-based scientific knowledge and the ancient texts: the rise of the mechanical philosophy made a deeper penetration into the meaning of those texts possible, but did not invalidate the truths they embodied.

If Newton's persistence and intensity in the matter were unusual, the approach he adopted was more widely acknowledged and its pursuit could and did lead other men along a variety of intellectual paths. The mathematician and original F.R.S., John Wallis, believed in the existence of a *prisca theologia* and in the Hebraic origin of Greek learning without being led into the ways of Hermeticism or alchemy. Boyle too saw the 'holy Seth' as one of the 'inventors of astronomy', and held it to be 'an almost uncontroll'd tradition that the Patriarch [Abraham] . . . was the first teacher of astronomy and philosophy to the Egyptians, from whom long afterwards, the Graecians learn'd them'.

It was, of course, the Cambridge Platonists who most enthusiastically, publicly, and respectably espoused this belief in a *prisca sapientia*. Ralph Cudworth, briefly a member of the Royal Society before it obtained its first charter, consciously looked back to the writings of Hermes Trismegistus, and even though he accepted much of Isaac Causabon's critique of their authenticity, still clung to the notion that some of them 'do contain Hermaical or Egyptian doctrines'. His Cambridge colleague, Henry More, was elected F.R.S. in 1664 and proved a more ardent and active (if less profound) propagandist of neoplatonic principles. Early in 1685 he and Newton tried to establish a Philosophical Society at Cambridge, presumably along the lines of that founded at Oxford two years earlier by Robert Plot, but, as Newton remarked, 'that which chiefly dasht the business was the want of persons willing to try experiments'. Earlier in the 1650s More had, with greater enthusiasm than understanding, espoused Cartesianism; had corresponded with Descartes himself and been attracted by what he regarded as the transcendent nature of Cartesianism because it seemed to provide a modern guarantee for the existence and activity of the 'spirit of nature' which he and other Cambridge Platonists saw as mediating between God the ever-active and the purely mechanical universe. Although in his youth he had been attracted by such Renaissance concepts as that which stressed the connecting link between the microcosm and the macrocosm, and indeed in 1647 had written of man as 'a microcosm, or compendium of the whole world', under the influence of Cartesianism he moved towards an outright condemnation of Paracelsian hermeticism. But he saw Cartesianism as he did Platonism as 'part of the ancient Judaical Cabbala, it being part of Pythagoras his philosophy which he had (as is abundantly testified

out of ancient writers) from the Jews'. In *The immortality of the soul* (1659)
More accepted that at least part of the Corpus Hermeticum contained
ancient 'Egyptian wisdom'. He combined the result of Cabbalistic
commentary on the Old Testament and Pythagorean number mystic-
ism, and then wove them into the teachings of Plato and the neo-
platonists, to produce his own analysis of the operation of the divine in
the universe, a practice which followed a by then well-worn Renaissance tradition.

Although More was not particularly active within the Royal Society,
he did identify himself with what he believed to be its aims, especially
after his break with Cartesianism (which by 1665 he saw as too
'mechanical' a 'way . . . [to] hold in all phenomena'). When that fierce
critic of the society, Henry Stubbe, suggested in 1670 that More had
resigned from the society, the latter immediately replied in print to the
effect that he was wholly at one with the 'experimental philosophy'
which he saw as providing the greatest possible help in proving the
existence of immaterial things. Indeed, this preoccupation lay at the
centre of More's affection for the society, for he saw its experiments
and observations as providing more and more proof for the reality of
that 'spirit of nature' so dear to the Cambridge Platonists. More viewed
the Royal Society as providing a steadily increasing number of tangible
instances tending to prove the existence of his imperceptible spirit. He
produced long lists of sympathetic cures, the scalding of men's entrails
at a distance by the burning of their excrements, pregnant women
producing monsters under the forceful impress of imagination, of
'speakings, knockings, opening of doores when they were fast shut,
sudden lights in the midst of a room floating in the aire'. He adopted a
full belief in occultism, spiritualism, and witchcraft, for, as he succinctly
put it, 'No Spirit, no God'.

More's view of the mechanical philosophy exercised a pervasive
influence on Newton's early work published as 'De gravitatione' and
his notion of 'forces', far from 'carrying the embarrassing animistic
associations it had for the first generation of mechanical philosophers,
served Newton as a manifestation of the divine in the sensible world'.
Again, More's interest in the occult and especially in witchcraft
brought him into association with one of the Royal Society's most
active defenders and propagandists, Joseph Glanvill, elected F.R.S. in
1664. Glanvill contributed three papers to the *Transactions* on mining
and mineral waters, but is best known for his ringing enunciation of the
society's public aims in such works as *Plus ultra: or, the progress and
advancement of knowledge since the days of Aristotle* (London, 1668). Glanvill
saw himself as the epitome of the 'modern' philosopher and the design
of the society as extending 'to all the varieties of the great world', and
aiming 'at the benefit of universal mankind'. Like More, Glanvill
regarded the world of the spirits as a proper sphere for scientific
research. It was, he asserted, 'a kinde of America, and not well
discover'd region', and he urged the society to investigate it 'for we
know not anything in the world we live in, but by experiments and the

236

phaenomena'. Nor did he see himself as in any way credulous, and in fact was prepared to grasp at the mechanical philosophy in order to give his projects the benefit of science. Thus he explained the functioning of some spiritual phenomena in mechanical terms, for "'tis now past question, that nature for the most part, acts by subtile streams and Apphoraea's of minute particles, which pass from one body to another'.

This approach was of the same order as that adopted by Boyle, when, in his *Some physico-theological considerations about the possibility of the resurrection* (1675) he suggested that chemical transformations might provide some intimation of the possibility of the Resurrection. In fact, Boyle was himself interested in occult phenomena and hastened to reassure Glanvill in 1678 that there was no truth in the rumour that he no longer believed in the reality of the accounts of the famous French 'demon of Mascon'. This rumour had been put about in the recently published *Displaying of supposed witchcraft* (London, 1677) by the Puritan chemical philosopher, John Webster, whose book is perhaps the most noteworthy contemporary critique of belief in witchcraft. More than twenty years earlier Webster had written his attack on the learning of English universities in *Academiarum examen* (London, 1654), in which he had married the outlooks of Bacon and Fludd to produce a synthesis sympathetic to the reformed chemistry of the day. Webster, who never became a member of the Royal Society, but whose attack on witchcraft received (much to Glanvill's annoyance) the imprimatur of Jonas Moore, vice-president of the society in 1676, accused those who believed in witchcraft of, in effect, minimizing the role of scientific explanation. In other words, Webster used his conception of what the Royal Society was doing to fashion a stick with which to beat the society's propagandist and champion, Glanvill. 'There is nothing', he wrote,

> that doth more clearly manifest our scanted knowledge in the secret operations of nature, and the effects that she produceth, than the late discoveries of the workings of nature, both in the vegetable, animal and mineral kingdoms, brought dayly to light by the pains and labours of industrious persons: As is most evident in those many elucubrations and continued discoveries of those learned and indefatigable persons that are of the Royal Society, which do plainly evince that hitherto we have been ignorant of almost all the true causes of things, and therefore through blindness have usually attributed those things to the operation of cacodemons that were truely wrought by nature and thereby not smally augmented and advanced this gross and absurd opinion of the power of witches.

But while on witchcraft it is Webster who adopts what would generally be regarded as the 'modern' position, on other matters the situation is reversed. In Glanvill's eyes one of the society's greatest achievements was its success in making chemistry 'honest, sober, and intelligible . . . for they have laid aside the chrysopoietick, the delusory designs and vain transmutations, the Rosie-Crucian vapours, magical charms, and superstitious suggestions'. Here he was expressing his scepticism of the grandiose claims of the Hermeticists to have discovered the philosopher's stone by the practice of manual arts and trials, claims which Webster endorsed when he defended the 'performance' of transmutation by 'Paracelsus, Lullius, Sendivogius and others' from imputation of involvement with the actions of the devil. The manuscript of Webster's book had been presented by Oldenburg to the Royal Society on 4 March 1674–5, and a group of three, which included William Petty and John Pell, was appointed 'to peruse it, and report their opinion'. Although no record of this survives, it is reasonable to believe, in the light of its subsequent imprimatur, that their judgement was not unfavourable. Webster, in fact, belonged to a line of thinkers who had made a combination of commitment to Hermeticism and scepticism about witchcraft an important theme since the sixteenth century. Indeed, scepticism about witchcraft comes, on the one hand, from 'purer' Aristotelians like Pomponazzi, and on the other, from those influenced by Hermeticism, such as Weir and Scot.

Glanvill, of course, could not allow Webster's attack on witchcraft to pass unremarked, and in his response joined hands with More in what was to be an unanswerable affirmation of their views. More contributed a long 'letter' to this work, the *Saducismus triumphatus* (London, 1681), in which, with a wealth of references to the Bible and Cabbalistic interpretation, he exposed 'the marvellous weakness and gullerie of Mr Webster's *Display*'. He also supplied a vast collection of instances of demonic action which chimed in well with Glanvill's earlier assertion to the effect that 'the more absurd and unaccountable these actions seem, the greater confirmations are they to me of the truth of those relations'.

Glanvill and More were by no means the only fellows of the society to be much exercised by the activities of witches and demons. For example, John Beaumont, the Somerset geologist and surgeon who was elected F.R.S. in 1685, wrote a compendious *Historical, physiological and theological treatise of spirits, apparitions, witchcrafts, and other magical practices* (London, 1705) which he had collected over the years and in which he pressed to his aid an eclectic bevy of supporting authors including Locke, Cudworth, Aubrey, Lilly the astrologer, Cotton Mather, and the great Hermeticist Athanasius Kircher. Beaumont was a friend of Robert Hooke and a supporter of Hooke's by no means widely accepted insistence on the animal origin of fossil remains. Many letters on geological subjects from Beaumont were read at the society's meetings, and five contributions from him, most of them careful accounts of fossils and other geological matters, appeared in the *Philosophical transactions* or in Hooke's *Philosophical collections*. When in London, Beaumont was often in Hooke's company and was regularly to be found at the coffee-houses frequented by fellows of the society. Indeed, Hooke records conversing with him at Jonathan's coffee-house about 'occult astrology'.

The friendship of Robert Hooke marks a connecting thread between Beaumont and that better-known student of unusual natural phenomena, John Aubrey. Among Aubrey's early friends were William Petty and John Pell, and he was well acquainted with those reformers of society and learning who had gathered around Samuel Hartlib. Aubrey is usually depicted as an over-credulous lover of antiquarianism and undiscriminating magpie of the bizarre. His achievement is in fact more complex than such hasty judgement allows. A strong, and at least partially convincing, case has been made out by his latest editor that 'so far from being backward-looking, he belonged to the intellectual *avant-garde* of his age and that his writings (including his antiquarian studies) were directly inspired by the methods and spirit of enquiry liberated by this great scientific revolution'. In the 1640s and 1650s he had been involved with the activities of the groups of natural philosophers meeting at Oxford and London from which the Royal Society was later to spring. He himself had undertaken experiments and had been greatly exercised by what he had seen as the Baconian task of useful discovery. His election as an original fellow of the society reflected his acceptance of many of the commonplaces its propagandists were to make popular: the pursuit of utility, the collection of natural histories, the avoidance of hasty hypotheses. Thus he was anxious to see the fellows of the society apply their techniques of analysis to the widest possible range of phenomena. As he wrote in the preface to his *Miscellanies*, 'natural philosophy hath been exceedingly advanced within fifty years last past; but methinks, 'tis strange that Hermetick Philosophy hath lain so long untoucht. It is a subject worthy of serious consideration'.

Aubrey, like so many others, hovered between different worlds. He was by no means uncritical, and although naturally inclined to a belief in the occult, he openly questioned, for example, some of the material produced by Glanvill, whom he gently chided as perhaps 'a little too credulous'. He was critical of the efficacy of touching for the king's evil and sceptical about his colleague in the Royal Society, Walter Charleton's, theories of the Danish origin of Stonehenge. In his 'Natural history of Wiltshire' he showed 'a firm grasp of the main trends in English stratigraphy and of . . . soil patterns' and was 'one of the first to describe the regional response to soil conditions'. And John Ray thought highly of the work he had collected under the title 'Adversaria physica'. What is known of the contents of Aubrey's library reflects the catholic nature of his outlook and sources of inspiration. He owned a copy of Newton's *Principia*, works by Willis, Malpighi (presented by the author), Ray, Lister, Charleton, Graunt, Petty, Hobbes, Digby, Bacon, and Seth Ward, while the astrologer John Gadbury had presented him with several of his predictive writings. Aubrey himself was a firm believer in judicial astrology, but this did not in any way bar him either from belonging to the Royal Society or from making a number of contributions to its proceedings on subjects ranging from discussions of 'spontaneous plants' to blood transfusions and medicinal springs. Of the thirteen of his closest friends – the so-called 'Amici' – still alive in the early 1660s, no less than eight were fellows of the society. And these included men of widely varying talents and outlooks, such as Robert Hooke, Seth Ward, William Petty, Sir John Hoskins (president 1682–3), and the Revd Francis Potter famous for his publication on *An interpretation of the number 666* (Oxford, 1642), in which he had connected the 'appropinque' square of 666, namely 25, with various Papist institutions.

It will be seen that the society in its early days found a place for a wide variety of outlooks and talents. Any institution that is acting as a filter through which great conceptual changes are being absorbed into the general world of intelligent men is, given its situation in an environment of conflicting opinions and philosophies, bound to reflect the intellectual contradictions (or what seem to us contradictions) and distinctions of its time. Although it may no doubt be interesting to develop a retrospective definition of what was and what was not 'scientific' in late-seventeenth-century England, it is also important to reach some understanding of the nature of the contemporary self-image of natural philosophy. And here the complexity of figures such as Newton, the ambiguity of men like More and Glanvill, is of the essence of the matter. Already we have noted that the early Royal Society was no strictly exclusive club, that it admitted men like Beaumont, Aubrey, and Potter, and allowed them to take part in its deliberations, as much as it did men such as Hooke and Halley. Indeed, in its early days the society comprehended a number of members whose attitude to natural phenomena, as evidenced by their interests and associations, was dictated by catholic and eclectic, rather than rigidly exclusive, intellectual traditions. [. . .]

19 J.R. Jacob

Restoration, Reformation and the Origins of the Royal Society

Previous scholars have overlooked the social, political and economic commitment of those who took part in the founding of the Royal Society at the Restoration. Thomas Sprat and John Wallis, the earliest chroniclers of the Society and its immediate antecedents, emphasized the studious disengagement from political and religious controversy of those who participated in the Society and in the movements in London and Oxford during the 1640s and 1650s that led to its founding after the Restoration. Subsequent scholars have either accepted Wallis and Sprat on this point and maintained without further inquiry that the early Royal Society strove to keep religion and politics out of its proceedings, or have gone on to argue that the initial religious and political stance of the Society was latitudinarian and emerged from a generalized desire on the part of its membership for religious moderation, ecclesiastical comprehension and civil order. While recognizing that there is some validity to both claims, I intend to argue here that these readings of Sprat and Wallis are misleading because they do not tell the whole story. The Royal Society in the first decade of its existence did not cut itself off from church, polity and economy, as the first reading might suggest. To be sure, it invited men of diverse political and religious backgrounds to membership and attempted to temper its discussions by the exercise of courtesy, forbearance and mutual respect. But these practices, which on the surface seem to be aimed at preventing the Society from becoming involved in politics and religion, were in fact designed to help the Society accomplish its political and religious mission. Nor did its social concerns derive from an undifferentiated, latitudinarian desire for order and harmony and nothing more, as the other reading of Wallis and Sprat insists. Rather, the leading Fellows who preached a social message in the Society's name did so with a view to building a particular kind of kingdom that would serve particular ends. Order and harmony were among these ends, but they were not undifferentiated: their accomplishment would eventuate in the establishment of a certain kind of order and harmony. The prescription for obtaining them was such that some groups in the realm stood to gain more than others. The social blueprints, moreover, were comprehensive; their implementation would affect the whole society. They were also carefully articulated: the goals were inter-

From *History of Science*, XIII (1975), pp. 155–163, 169–171. Footnotes have been deleted.

dependent – the attainment of one would promote the attainment of others – and the same mechanisms worked to accomplish more than one end at the same time. The social visionaries among the Fellows who drew up these plans looked forward to the emergence of a society integrated in specific ways calculated to serve specific interests. What were these interests and how were they to be served? To answer these questions we shall first examine the social ideas of Robert Boyle, a principal founder of the Royal Society, as these were elaborated at the Restoration, and then suggest that these ideas constituted the core of the social message preached by the Society itself.

We are beginning to recognize that Boyle was more than a brilliant natural philosopher who developed an extremely sophisticated empiricism and gave chemistry a theoretical foundation by assimilating it to the new experimental and mechanical philosophy. He was also an important social, political, and religious thinker whose views carried the more weight with his contemporaries because they had the authority of his natural philosophy behind them. It is this aspect of his thought, as it evolved in the period just before and just after the Restoration, that we wish to explore here.

At the Restoration one of Boyle's central concerns, as always, was the settlement of religion. Even more than usual was this the case because for the moment in 1660 the fall of the Protectorate and the return of the monarchy left the religious question hanging – or so it seemed. Hindsight makes it seem that the defeat of all attempts at toleration and comprehension and the creation and implementation of the so-called Clarendon code were almost inevitable. But this is not the view that many, Boyle included, held at the time. After all, the king himself had declared in April 1660 at Breda for limited toleration as one of the main building blocks of his restoration. In this atmosphere of uncertainty in 1660 Boyle and his Oxford associate Peter Pett hoped for a limited toleration but feared 'that the restored clergy might be tempted by their late sufferings to such a vindictive retaliation, as would be contrary to the true measures of Christianity and politics . . . '. To help prevent this the two of them decided that each would write and publish a piece explaining the advantages of an ecclesiastical settlement based not on 'retaliation' but on 'liberty of conscience'. Pett was to show the political advantages and Boyle the advantages accruing to foreign states where liberty of conscience was already operative. As it turned out, Boyle decided that his friend John Dury could do this better than he, rewarded him when he had finished, and sent the tract to Pett

who published it at the end of his own in 1660, (though the booksellers, according to their custom, antedated in the title page 1661) and inscribed both . . . treatises with the last letters only of the writers' names,

as one did not express openly views such as they held without risking the suspicious attention of the authorities. Boyle also asked Thomas

Barlow, who was Pett's friend too, to contribute a piece dealing with 'the theological part of the question' to the joint enterprise. Barlow complied but chose not to publish it for fear 'of losing . . . his station in the university . . . , and all hopes of future preferment'. It was finally published posthumously in 1692 by the then Sir Peter Pett.

By far the most revealing of these tracts is the one written by Pett entitled *Liberty of conscience*. Boyle seems to have read it before its publication, as Pett made this a condition of his writing it. Even if Boyle did not keep his promise in this regard, we may safely assume that Pett's tract expressed Boyle's views too because the whole project of writing and publishing was conceived and carried out as a collaborative undertaking. What then does Pett say and what does this tell us about Boyle's religious views at the time? In particular, how did he think the church should be settled and why?

Pett's position, and hence Boyle's, is chiefly characterized by a prudentialism in matters of religion. This is expressed in a number of ways in Pett's *Discourse concerning liberty of conscience* and is the basis of his and Boyle's view of church settlement. Religious toleration is mainly a matter for rational calculation. A number of factors enter into the calculus. It is better for non-conformists to be allowed to worship openly than to be persecuted, because the latter policy will drive them to secret conspiracy, whereas the former will make their activities public and hence capable of being kept in check. This proposition assumes of course that there are too many sectaries for them to be stamped out by a policy of persecution. This is one of the main considerations for Pett and Barlow alike. Indeed Barlow goes so far as to say that in the context of the Restoration to adopt a policy of toleration is merely to make a virtue of necessity; that is to say, there are too many non-conformists for persecution to work, and toleration at least wins the authorities some modest measure of good-will from them. For neither Pett nor Barlow should toleration be unlimited; indeed they would set more or less the same conditions. On this point Barlow is the more explicit. Those are not to be tolerated who claim allegiance to a higher authority than the state. This would include papists and sectaries who claim to be in touch with the spirit world. He adds that those such as Quakers and Adamites should be excluded because they endanger true religion, the latter by their nudism and the former by their social insubordination. Pett, however, is more prudential as regards the Quakers. There are so many that their persecution would alarm smaller sects and so they should be tolerated unless it is clearly determined that they constitute a menace. Just as his prudential calculus would make him lax about the Quakers in this particular, it would make him rather more severe on the sects as a whole in another regard: he would force them to work. This would prevent them from wandering and so stop the spread of their dangerous views. Not only must they work; they should be made to wear themselves out with work. They would then be too weary to study heresy or, as he says, to read Jacob Boehme, who was one of the chief progenitors of that rage among sectaries for inner light or immediate illumination. Finally, Pett saw that the multiplicity of sects was itself an inducement to toleration: there were so many different ones and there was such disunity among them that the effect of toleration would be for them to cancel one another out and hence for balance or stasis to be achieved. For Pett this situation was by contrast to one in which there were only two religions in a state vying for popular loyalty. Here prudence would not dictate toleration. This *aperçu* into the dynamics of religious pluralism was perhaps the masterstroke of Pett's and Boyle's prudentialism.

Pett's tract dealt with .more than the question of tolerating dissenters. *Liberty of conscience*, the title of Pett's discourse, referred not only to that which should be granted to non-conformists but also to that which those who stayed within the church should enjoy. Pett was devoted to a church settlement that would maximize this latter kind of liberty. In order to understand him we must find out what such liberty meant, what sort of church would best promote it and why it should do so.

Liberty in this second sense was freedom from the oppressions of religious authorities or, to put it positively, the freedom to pursue one's interests unimpeded by these authorities. The question then becomes: for whom did he presume to speak and why? He claimed to speak for gentry, merchants and a majority of the clergy, and he did so because he identified the interests of these groups with the national interest and the Protestant cause. The problem of ecclesiastical settlement, as he saw it, was to find a church that would further this interest. In other words, the church should not only serve a spiritual end but should be subordinate and expedient to various mundane interests. Thus, according to Pett, no form of church government is by divine right. Rather, that church is right which best serves the nation's good. A settlement cannot be grounded on supernatural authority but only on prudential considerations. The church to Pett's mind, and presumably Boyle's as well, had become another factor in that rational calculus by which the national good is pursued.

What are the interests of merchants, gentry and clergy which define this good and to which established religion must be made to conduce? The clergy's interest is to participate in the governing of a church which in structure and personnel commands the respect of the laity, especially the gentry. The gentry's interest is in church governors, king and bishops, who do not claim to be so by divine right. Episcopacy by divine right might disenable the king from nominating bishops and entail a system of church courts from which there would be no appeal 'to the King in Chancery' by the gentry whom Pett sees as being the group that would suffer most from a separate legal jurisdiction in the hands of the clerical hierarchy. The bishops would be a law unto themselves in religious matters, removed from responsibility to king, lower clergy, and the gentry themselves in and out of parliament. Pett obviously assumes that a system of checks on the power of bishops works to the advantage of the gentry. Nor for the same reason should the king be made all-powerful in the religious sphere. If either authority, royal or episcopal, were to be so, the gentry would lose their liberty both in and out of parliament, and should this happen, the chief bulwark in the state against ignorance, superstition, error and tyranny, according to Pett, would have been destroyed. Just as the gentry must be protected by a proper church settlement in their main interest, which is their political independence and freedom from religious domination, so the merchants must be protected in theirs, which is trade. Religion must be made to serve commerce and industry as well as clergy and gentry. These three interests are seen to overlap. For instance, what serves the gentry serves the clergy and *vice versa*: or conversely, what injures trade damages the other two. Taken together, the interests of clergy, gentry and merchants constitute the national good. So a religious formula must be found that will benefit all three because they are so much of a piece. What then is the magic word?

The answer lies in Archbishop James Usher's model or what was known as moderate episcopacy. This had been bruited about throughout the period 1640–60 as a workable means of settling the church and particularly after Usher's plan was first published in 1656. Those who favoured it did so because it represented a compromise between episcopacy and presbyterianism and so would stand a better chance than either of gaining the widest possible support. Under the scheme the office of bishop would be preserved but its powers would be pruned away. The bishops would no longer act on their own authority in the most important matters but only with the consent of the presbytery. The episcopal function would be more administrative than decision-making. Although this model was obviously calculated to alienate neither episcopalians nor presbyterians, this is not the ground on which Pett pitches his case. Rather he favours it for the service it renders to the national good, the inter-connected interests of merchants, gentry and clergy. To the lower clergy it gives a greater part in running the church because in each diocese power is diffused and shared between bishop and presbytery which would consist in large part of parish clergy. There would be an incentive in this scheme of power-sharing for the clergy to become better educated and to devote themselves more to their tasks: 'those men that could offer the best reasons for things, and shew the greatest strength of parts, would be most swaying in Ecclesiastical Conventions'. And a more effective clergy would build a stronger church. What worked to the advantage of the vast majority of clergymen would also serve the gentry. They would be more trusting and respectful of the clergy – the latter because their industry and education would command such respect and more trusting because power in the church would have been transferred from the diocesan to the parochial level where the gentry could exercise greater influence. Moderate episcopacy, moreover, would be justified on the grounds not of divine right but of the nation's good, and so the danger latent in the argument from divine right of upsetting the delicate constitutional balance between bishops, king and parliament upon which the proper governing of the church depended would be averted. Indeed, to Pett's mind, moderate episcopacy would strengthen that balance by providing a religion that would serve the allied interests of gentry, merchants and lower clergy while lessening the power of bishops. Finally, what tied the interests of merchants to church and gentry, and how would these mercantile interests also be served by moderate episcopacy? The common factor uniting church, gentry and merchants was trade. The very 'genius' of northern Protestant states like England lay in commercial undertakings and empire. Trading for Pett was virtually synonymous with the national good. In overseas trade, for instance, lay the chief defence for England and hence for the Reformation against Catholic Europe: a flourishing shipping industry gives command of the sea. In this connection, trade and navigation help to propagate the faith and to increase useful knowledge, both of which were seen to serve the cause of reformation, the latter by enhancing national power and prosperity and the former by extending the true faith at the expense of the false, whether Catholic or pagan. Trade also puts the populace on useful work and so prevents idleness and its fruit which is vice. Not only does this serve the gentry by promoting civil peace and political stability, but the church is served as well because idleness is the seedbed of heresy. How in particular does a moderate episcopal settlement such as Boyle and Pett are advocating encourage mercantile interests and hence the national good? Here there are three points to be made. First the preaching of those who favour moderate episcopacy is suited to the mercantile genius of the nation. Their sermon style is not elaborate like that of high churchmen, nor is it coarse like that of the sectarian preachers. As a result it is more persuasive than either. This factor of. style is important to the mercantile interest not by itself but when taken together with the message preached: the emphasis is on inculcating in workers morals like industry and honesty conducive to the owners' profit. Secondly, for moderate episcopalians preaching is more important than monies, and this preference also serves mercantile interests, ceremonies being regarded as a waste of both time and money. Liberty of conscience such as moderate episcopacy allows gives yet a third fillip to trade. A policy of toleration would make England a haven for mild dissent both of those who would otherwise emigrate to freer lands and of those who are persecuted abroad. The nation would thus gain in population, and a growing population would have multiple salutary effects on trade both foreign and domestic. It cheapens wages and raises prices at home and increases exports while cheapening imports, the precise mechanism for producing these last two effects being left largely unexplained.

These tracts by Pett and Barlow, and sponsored by Boyle, reveal his programme for church settlement at the Restoration. But in doing so they also reveal his social vision, because the assumption in them is that the church serves a higher end not defined exclusively by its spiritual mission of saving souls but rather largely by the mundane interests of gentry, merchants and clergy which together make up the national good. Pett's tract is almost an abstract of this vision. The rest of this paper will be devoted first to discovering its origins and secondly to showing the several ways in which Boyle translates it into thought and action in the first decade of the Restoration.

Concerning the origins of this vision Pett himself has something to say. He writes: 'The great alteration in the body of the people since these last twenty years, requires that our old ends of promoting the welfare of the Church of *England*, should be attain'd by the conduct of new means'. He is of course referring to the period 1640–60. He does not explain 'the great alteration' he sees to have occurred, but the 'new means' by which the church is to be settled is the subject of his tract – namely, liberty of conscience. As we have seen, this means both toleration of dissenters and, more importantly, the establishment of a state church that will not only allow but enable gentry, merchants and clergy to pursue their worldly interests. Knowing this, we can glimpse what he considers 'the great alteration' to be. First and most obviously, a part of it is that the civil wars and interregnum spawned a dissenting element too strong, lively and divergent to be absorbed into a national church and that the only thing for it is the provision of limited toleration combined with a heavy dose of the discipline of the work ethic. Secondly, even those who come into the state church will do so only on condition that their material interests are served by the settlement provided. This new motivation presumably is also a part of that 'great alteration', though Pett does not explain how this change came about. Whatever he thinks produced it, he is willing to base the restored church upon it, and in doing so to come dangerously close to making the church merely expedient to private gain. What saves him from this is the identity he establishes between the private interests of those groups whom he hopes to see served by the settlement, and the nation's good, which itself is identified with the cause of reformation, and so can be claimed to transcend the interests of particular individuals or groups. This identification is at the base of Boyle's social vision too, and we are not limited for evidence to support this claim to his sponsorship of Pett's *Discourse*. Boyle wrote enough of his own expressive of this view. Indeed much of his social thought before the Restoration is to this point. Both 'The Aretology' and 'Part I' of *Some considerations touching the usefulness of experimental natural philosophy*, which was not yet published in 1660, stress that private interests, pursued according to the dictates of Boyle's ethic, make for the public good. About 1658 Boyle went on to elaborate this theme chiefly in what was published as 'Part II' of *The usefulness* in 1671. In the process he anticipated and developed many of the points in Pett's *Liberty of conscience*.

The second section of 'Part II' of *The usefulness* takes up once more the question of God's purposes in the creation. In the first essays of 'Part I' Boyle reconciled to his own apparent satisfaction the purpose of God's glory to that of man's benefit. That out of the way, he turns in 'Part II' to the means by which man can fulfil the latter purpose, that is to say, how man can derive benefit from his 'Empire . . . over inferior Creatures'. His view of the means available to man is co-ordinate, as one would expect, with his notion of what constitutes human benefit in the first place. In the early 1650s when Boyle wrote the first five essays of 'Part I', he saw man in rather Hobbesian terms as insatiably covetous. But this did not lead Boyle down the path to Hobbes's Leviathan. Boyle's prescription was quite different. Man's greed, instead of making for anarchy and hence calling for the extreme remedy of Hobbes's sovereign, was a part of God's plan and thus a source of hope. This covetousness sent men out into the world for means to satisfy or at least to appease it. Hence came labour and its fruits in trade and manufacture – and best of all, the discovery of nature. In all of this, God could be glorified through the creatures, at the same time that man was being served by them. When Boyle in 'Part II' of *The usefulness* set about specifying the means by which men could obtain their own benefit, it was within the framework partially established in 'Part I' in which benefit was largely defined in terms of the satisfaction of human appetites. In 'Part II' Boyle makes it clear that this benefit will come *via* production and exchange under market conditions. The market situation in which human benefit is chiefly realized is made explicit in 'The preamble' to 'Part II'. There Boyle distinguishes between 'art' and 'craft'. 'Art' is the skill involved in producing goods; 'craft' the skill involved in buying and selling them, that is to say, knowledge of market conditions. 'And by the latter', Boyle says,

> I mean the result of those informations . . . by which the artificer learns to make the utmost profit, that he can, of the productions of his art. And this oeconomical prudence is a thing very distinct from the art itself, and yet is often the most beneficial thing to the artificer, informing him how to choose his materials, and estimate their goodness and worth; in what places, and at what times, the best and cheapest are to be had; where, and when, and to what persons the thing may be most profitably vended.

Within this framework then, the means of fulfilling God's purpose for man and benefiting human life must work. What are these means and what can they do in this context? They are those already set forth in 'Part I', namely the knowledge the naturalist gains by careful study of the physical order. Such knowledge can work in various ways to stimulate production and exchange, trade and industry. Knowledge is useful to capitalist enterprise; in fact the usefulness of knowledge is defined in essentially capitalist terms. Within these terms then God's purpose can be achieved, man can gain the benefit of his 'Empire . . . over inferior Creatures', and 'Experimental Philosophy may become useful to human life'. What is more, the interaction between knowledge and trade is circular: the naturalist can go to the tradesman for insight into his 'art' which may improve the naturalist's knowledge of the physical order, and then he can turn around, 'as well by the skill thus obtained, as by the other parts of his knowledge', and 'improve trades'. The engine in this process is private interest. Men driven on by what Boyle calls 'craft' will exploit science for the opportunities it offers for improving their 'art' and thus increasing profits, and once more this pursuit of private interest is said to make for the general good. Boyle's own statements dating from about 1658 are thus at one with the views Pett expressed and Boyle encouraged in 1661.

Nor was the alliance between merchants and gentlemen, naturalists and tradesmen, in the pursuit of useful and profitable knowledge to be exhausted on what each could teach the other about domestic production. The alliance was also meant to operate overseas wherever Englishmen went or planted themselves. The wealth of England was not limited to 'Homebred Riches'. 'Their number' could be increased 'by transferring thither those of others', and in this enterprise the naturalist would also play a leading part, collaborating this time with colonial agents, governors, natives and administrators as well as traders. So the alliance by which private interest is made to conduce to public good is not between science and trade alone but between science, trade and empire. Here again Boyle is in perfect agreement with Pett's position in *Liberty of conscience*. In Boyle's mind then, as in the minds of many of his contemporaries, the purposes of religion and empire had come to be wedded – and wedded as well to those of science and trade. It was these joint purposes that Boyle saw himself as serving from at least the late 1650s on. [. . .]

[In the passage omitted here, Professor Jacob goes on to discuss some of Boyle's activities as a member of the Council for Foreign Plantations, and as Governor of the Company for the Propagation of the Gospel in New England. He points to the close connections between the purposes of these bodies and those of the Royal Society, as set forth in its official manifesto, Thomas Sprat's *History of the Royal Society*, published in 1667.]

Sprat argues that the science of the Royal Society is a chief instrument of the Reformation. This forestalled those who said at the time that science is injurious to religion. But, more interesting from our point of view, it gives science an ideological edge. According to Sprat and Wilkins, the cause of reformation is served by religious moderation, ecclesiastical comprehension, civil obedience, private enterprise and profit. The prescription for the achievement of these mutually beneficial goals is experimental science. Its discipline tempers religious passion and helps men avoid two enemies of true religion, the enthusiasm of the sects and the wholesale submission of Catholics to papal authority and ecclesiastical tradition. If this is not sufficient incentive, there are the material advantages of science. Men will bury their religious differences in favour of the opportunities for profit that science creates. And with business investment comes employment for those who might otherwise make trouble for church and state. Science serves men's private interests and as such makes for the public good in the form of religious peace, civil order and economic prosperity. With these as its foundations the Reformation can spread abroad and ultimately defeat Catholicism. Indeed the new political economy which science can establish at home and abroad – a Protestant empire in place of the defeated Catholic ones of the past – is tantamount to a fulfilment of the Reformation. To confirm this one need only read the Bible. True religion is scripture-based, and the scriptures reveal a religion whose aims are exactly those of the Royal Society. The Society itself is a model for the nation as a whole: it invites men of various religious persuasions, talents and social backgrounds – lords, gentlemen merchants, tradesmen and mechanics – to member-ship, and submerges their religious differences, while drawing upon the variety of their skills, in the pursuit of experimental science for the common good as the Society defines it. Boyle himself provides an example of Sprat's point here. In 1665 Boyle helped Ralph Austen reissue his *Treatise of fruit-trees*. Austen was a sectary, and in 1653, when his book was first published, his observations on fruit trees were interspersed with sectarian comments. But a condition of Boyle's patronage was the removal of the offending passages. The Royal Society might serve then as the basis of ecclesiastical comprehension, advantaging the material interests of all who subscribed to its ideology while ignoring, or as in Austen's case quietly suppressing, points of doctrinal conflict among them.

There is no evidence that Boyle was one of Sprat's advisers in the preparation of his *History* or that he read and approved the finished product before it was published. Indeed the evidence suggests the reverse. But this is not to say that he would have objected or been indifferent to its content. To the contrary, it is obvious that Boyle's views expressed by Pett and in his own *Usefulness* and *Style*, as we have set them out, were close and sometimes identical to those expressed by Wilkins and Sprat in the *History*. For all three there is a harmony between scriptural and natural truths – the Bible and the natural order – that in turn serves as a foundation for a philosophy of self-interest. God's word and his work properly studied authorize an ideology of work and acquisitiveness.

After the Restoration, Christopher Wren, an Original Fellow and leading participant in the early Royal Society, wrote a 'Preamble of a charter to incorporate the Royal Society'. The 'Preamble' was never used for this purpose but it encapsulates the ideology we have been tracing and in particular the view that the science of the Royal Society is the foundation of order, prosperity and empire. Wren justifies the royal incorporation of the Society in these terms:

> ... that obedience may be manifestly not only the publick but the private felicity of every subject. . . . The way to so happy a govern-

ment... is in no manner more facilitated, than by promoting of useful arts and sciences, which, upon mature inspection, are found to be the basis of civil communities and free governments, and which gather multitudes by an Orphean charm into cities, and connect them in companies; that so, by laying in a stock as it were of several arts and methods of industry, the whole body may be supplied by a mutual commerce of each other's peculiar faculties, and, consequently, that the various miseries and toils of this frail life, may be, by as many various expedients ready at hand, remedied, or alleviated, and wealth and plenty diffused in just proportion to everyone's industry, that is, to everyone's deserts.

Science is the key to building the economy and ordering the polity and achieves both aims at the same time. It promotes industry, and uses everyone's skills to best effect; from such efficient enterprise comes wealth, distributed 'in just proportion to' contribution. Science thus creates economic opportunity which in turn drives men to greater effort. The outcome is maximal 'private felicity', conducing to public order and harmony. Wren's assumption of course is that the profit motive operates for the common good, that an invisible hand forges an identity between private and public interests – and this more than a century before Adam Smith. Nor was Wren alone in making this assumption. It shaped the social thought contained in Pett's *Discourse*, Sprat's *History* and Boyle's own writings as well as his decisions as Governor of the New England Company and member of the Council for Foreign Plantations. On the basis of such evidence it seems fair to say that the leadership of the Royal Society shared Boyle's social vision in which science, trade and empire were seen to work together to produce the Reformation.

If such is the case, we cannot accept either of the views of the Society derived from the accounts of its origins by Wallis and Sprat. We can no longer take at face value their comments that it divorced itself from religion and politics. Nor can we agree that its social message came from an undifferentiated, latitudinarian desire for religious moderation and ecclesiastical comprehension *tout court*. The leadership of the Society may have forsworn conventional theology and politics – and this may have been Sprat's and Wallis's meaning – but their own ideology of science, as we have seen, was neither apolitical nor unrelated to religion. Instead, it was an aggressive, acquisitive, mercantilistic ideology justified in the name of both Restoration and Reformation. This is not to say that those who put it forward were insincere about religion, or that even if they were sincere, theirs was a religion solely of greed and self-aggrandizement. Given the circumstances of the Restoration, it seemed the best alternative. England was divided by deep religious and political cleavages and challenged by Catholic Europe. The ideology of the Royal Society would compose internal differences by committing every group and individual in the nation to experimental science and its material fruits. Both internal order and the pursuit of science, trade, and empire, would make England strong enough to face and ultimately overcome the external threat posed by her Catholic enemies. The ideology of the Royal Society sprang then from a mixture of challenge and opportunity. It was the way to wealth and power. It was also a way of solving urgent domestic and international problems. Happily to its sponsors, the pursuit of all of these aims was synonymous with planting God's kingdom.

LITERATURE AND THE ARTS

20 T.S. ELIOT

The Metaphysical Poets

By collecting these poems from the work of a generation more often named than read, and more often read than profitably studied, Professor Grierson has rendered a service of some importance. Certainly the reader will meet with many poems already preserved in other anthologies, at the same time that he discovers poems such as those of Aurelian Townshend or Lord Herbert of Cherbury here included. But the function of such an anthology as this is neither that of Professor Saintsbury's admirable edition of Caroline poets nor that of the *Oxford Book of English Verse*. Mr Grierson's book is in itself a piece of criticism, and a provocation of criticism; and we think that he was right in including so many poems of Donne, elsewhere (though not in many editions) accessible, as documents in the case of 'metaphysical poetry'. The phrase has long done duty as a term of abuse, or as the label of a quaint and pleasant taste. The question is to what extent the so-called metaphysicals formed a school (in our own time we should say a 'movement'), and how far this so-called school or movement is a digression from the main current.

Not only is it extremely difficult to define metaphysical poetry, but difficult to decide what poets practise it and in which of their verses. The poetry of Donne (to whom Marvell and Bishop King are sometimes nearer than any of the other authors) is late Elizabethan, its feeling often very close to that of Chapman. The 'courtly' poetry is derivative from Jonson, who borrowed liberally from the Latin; it expires in the next century with the sentiment and witticism of Prior. There is finally the devotional verse of Herbert, Vaughan, and Crashaw (echoed long after by Christina Rossetti and Francis Thompson); Crashaw, sometimes more profound and less sectarian than the others, has a quality which returns through the Elizabethan period to the early Italians. It is difficult to find any precise use of metaphor, simile, or other conceit, which is common to all the poets and at the same time important enough as an element of style to isolate these poets as a group. Donne, and often Cowley, employ a device which is sometimes considered characteristically 'metaphysical'; the elaboration (contrasted with the condensation) of a figure of speech to the furthest stage to which ingenuity can carry it. Thus Cowley develops the commonplace comparison of the world to a chess-board through long stanzas (*To Destiny*), and Donne, with more grace, in *A Valediction*, the

---

From T.S. Eliot, *Selected Essays* (Faber and Faber, 3rd, edn., 1951), pp. 281–291. This article first appeared in *Times Literary Supplement*,1921, as a review of Sir Herbert Grierson (ed.), *Metaphysical Lyrics and Poems of the Seventeenth Century* (Oxford, 1921).

comparison of two lovers to a pair of compasses. But elsewhere we find, instead of the mere explication of the content of a comparison, a development by rapid association of thought which requires considerable agility on the part of the reader.

> On a round ball
> A workeman that hath copies by, can lay
> An Europe, Afrique, and an Asia,
> And quickly make that, which was nothing, All,
> > So doth each teare,
> > Which thee doth weare,
> A globe, yea world by that impression grow,
> Till thy tears mixt with mine doe overflow
> This world, by waters sent from thee, my heaven dissolved so.

Here we find at least two connexions which are not implicit in the first figure, but are forced upon it by the poet: from the geographer's globe to the tear, and the tear to the deluge. On the other hand, some of Donne's most successful and characteristic effects are secured by brief words and sudden contrasts:

> A bracelet of bright hair about the bone,

where the most powerful effect is produced by the sudden contrast of associations of 'bright hair' and of 'bone'. This telescoping of images and multiplied associations is characteristic of the phrase of some of the dramatists of the period which Donne knew: not to mention Shakespeare, it is frequent in Middleton, Webster, and Tourneur, and is one of the sources of the vitality of their language.

Johnson, who employed the term 'metaphysical poets', apparently having Donne, Cleveland, and Cowley chiefly in mind, remarks of them that 'the most heterogeneous ideas are yoked by violence together'. The force of this impeachment lies in the failure of the conjunction, the fact that often the ideas are yoked but not united; and if we are to judge of styles of poetry by their abuse, enough examples may be found in Cleveland to justify Johnson's condemnation. But a degree of heterogeneity of material compelled into unity by the operation of the poet's mind is omnipresent in poetry. We need not select for illustration such a line as:

> Notre âme est un trois-mâts cherchant son Icarie;

we may find it in some of the best lines of Johnson himself (*The Vanity of Human Wishes*):

> His fate was destined to a barren strand,
> A petty fortress, and a dubious hand;
> He left a name at which the world grew pale,

To point a moral, or adorn a tale.

where the effect is due to a contrast of ideas, different in degree but the
same in principle, as that which Johnson mildly reprehended. And in
one of the finest poems of the age (a poem which could not have been
written in any other age), the *Exequy* of Bishop King, the extended
comparison is used with perfect success: the idea and the simile become
one, in the passage in which the Bishop illustrates his impatience to see
his dead wife, under the figure of a journey:

> Stay for me there; I will not faile
> To meet thee in that hollow Vale.
> And think not much of my delay;
> I am already on the way,
> And follow thee with all the speed
> Desire can make, or sorrows breed.
> Each minute is a short degree,
> And ev'ry houre a step towards thee.
> At night when I betake to rest,
> Next morn I rise nearer my West
> Of life, almost by eight houres sail,
> Than when sleep breath'd his drowsy gale . . .
> But heark! My Pulse, like a soft Drum
> Beats my approach, tells *Thee* I come;
> And slow howere my marches be,
> I shall at last sit down by *Thee*.

(In the last few lines there is that effect of terror which is several times
attained by one of Bishop King's admirers, Edgar Poe.) Again, we may
justly take these quatrains from Lord Herbert's Ode, stanzas which
would, we think, be immediately pronounced to be of the metaphysical
school:

> So when from hence we shall be gone,
> And be no more, nor you, nor I,
> As one another's mystery,
> Each shall be both, yet both but one.
>
> This said, in her up-lifted face,
> Her eyes, which did that beauty crown,
> Were like two starrs, that having faln down,
> Look up again to find their place:
>
> While such a moveless silent peace
> Did seize on their becalmed sense,
> One would have thought some influence
> Their ravished spirits did possess.

There is nothing in these lines (with the possible exception of the stars, a simile not at once grasped, but lovely and justified) which fits Johnson's general observations on the metaphysical poets in his essay on Cowley. A good deal resides in the richness of association which is at the same time borrowed from and given to the word 'becalmed'; but the meaning is clear, the language simple and elegant. It is to be observed that the language of these poets is as a rule simple and pure; in the verse of George Herbert this simplicity is carried as far as it can go – a simplicity emulated without success by numerous modern poets. The *structure* of the sentences, on the other hand, is sometimes far from simple, but this is not a vice; it is a fidelity to thought and feeling. The effect, at its best, is far less artificial than that of an ode by Gray. And as this fidelity induces variety of thought and feeling, so it induces variety of music. We doubt whether, in the eighteenth century, could be found two poems in nominally the same metre, so dissimilar as Marvell's *Coy Mistress* and Crashaw's *Saint Teresa*; the one producing an effect of great speed by the use of short syllables, and the other an ecclesiastical solemnity by the use of long ones:

> Love, thou art absolute sole lord
> Of life and death.

If so shrewd and sensitive (though so limited) a critic as Johnson failed to define metaphysical poetry by its faults, it is worth while to inquire whether we may not have more success by adopting the opposite method: by assuming that the poets of the seventeenth century (up to the Revolution) were the direct and normal development of the precedent age; and, without prejudicing their case by the adjective 'metaphysical', consider whether their virtue was not something permanently valuable, which subsequently disappeared, but ought not to have disappeared. Johnson has hit, perhaps by accident, on one of their peculiarities, when he observes that 'their attempts were always analytic'; he would not agree that, after the dissociation, they put the material together again in a new unity.

It is certain that the dramatic verse of the later Elizabethan and early Jacobean poets expresses a degree of development of sensibility which is not found in any of the prose, good as it often is. If we except Marlowe, a man of prodigious intelligence, these dramatists were directly or indirectly (it is at least a tenable theory) affected by Montaigne. Even if we except also Jonson and Chapman, these two were notably erudite, and were notably men who incorporated their erudition into their sensibility: their mode of feeling was directly and freshly altered by their reading and thought. In Chapman especially there is a direct sensuous apprehension of thought, or a recreation of thought into feeling, which is exactly what we find in Donne:

> in this one thing, all the discipline
> Of manners and of manhood is contained;
> A man to join himself with th' Universe

In his main sway, and make in all things fit
One with that All, and go on, round as it;
Not plucking from the whole his wretched part,
And into straits, or into nought revert,
Wishing the complete Universe might be
Subject to such a rag of it as he;
But to consider great Necessity.

We compare this with some modern passage:

No, when the fight begins within himself,
A man's worth something. God stoops o'er his head,
Satan looks up between his feet – both tug –
He's left, himself, i' the middle; the soul wakes
And grows. Prolong that battle through his life!

It is perhaps somewhat less fair, though very tempting (as both poets
are concerned with the perpetuation of love by offspring), to compare
with the stanzas already quoted from Lord Herbert's Ode the following
from Tennyson:

One walked between his wife and child,
With measured footfall firm and mild,
And now and then he gravely smiled.
    The prudent partner of his blood
    Leaned on him, faithful, gentle, good,
    Wearing the rose of womanhood.
And in their double love secure,
The little maiden walked demure,
Pacing with downward eyelids pure.
    These three made unity so sweet,
    My frozen heart began to beat,
    Remembering its ancient heat.

The difference is not a simple difference of degree between poets. It is
something which had happened to the mind of England between the
time of Donne or Lord Herbert of Cherbury and the time of Tennyson
and Browning; it is the difference between the intellectual poet and the
reflective poet. Tennyson and Browning are poets, and they think; but
they do not feel their thought as immediately as the odour of a rose. A
thought to Donne was an experience; it modified his sensibility. When
a poet's mind is perfectly equipped for its work, it is constantly
amalgamating disparate experience; the ordinary man's experience is
chaotic, irregular, fragmentary. The latter falls in love, or reads
Spinoza, and these two experiences have nothing to do with each other,
or with the noise of the typewriter or the smell of cooking; in the mind
of the poet these experiences are always forming new wholes.
    We may express the difference by the following theory: The poets of

259

the seventeenth century, the successors of the dramatists of the sixteenth, possessed a mechanism of sensibility which could devour any kind of experience. They are simple, artificial, difficult, or fantastic, as their predecessors were; no less nor more than Dante, Guido Cavalcanti, Guinicelli, or Cino. In the seventeenth century a dissociation of sensibility set in, from which we have never recovered; and this dissociation, as is natural, was aggravated by the influence of the two most powerful poets of the century, Milton and Dryden. Each of these men performed certain poetic functions so magnificently well that the magnitude of the effect concealed the absence of others. The language went on and in some respects improved; the best verse of Collins, Gray, Johnson, and even Goldsmith satisfies some of our fastidious demands better than that of Donne or Marvell or King. But while the language became more refined, the feeling became more crude. The feeling, the sensibility, expressed in the *Country Churchyard* (to say nothing of Tennyson and Browning) is cruder than that in the *Coy Mistress*.

The second effect of the influence of Milton and Dryden followed from the first, and was therefore slow in manifestation. The sentimental age began early in the eighteenth century, and continued. The poets revolted against the ratiocinative, the descriptive; they thought and felt by fits, unbalanced; they reflected. In one or two passages of Shelley's *Triumph of Life*, in the second *Hyperion*, there are traces of a struggle toward unification of sensibility. But Keats and Shelley died, and Tennyson and Browning ruminated.

After this brief exposition of a theory – too brief, perhaps, to carry conviction – we may ask, what would have been the fate of the 'metaphysical' had the current of poetry descended in a direct line from them, as it descended in a direct line to them? They would not, certainly, be classified as metaphysical. The possible interests of a poet are unlimited; the more intelligent he is the better; the more intelligent he is the more likely that he will have interests: our only condition is that he turn them into poetry, and not merely meditate on them poetically. A philosophical theory which has entered into poetry is established, for its truth or falsity in one sense ceases to matter, and its truth in another sense is proved. The poets in question have, like other poets, various faults. But they were, at best, engaged in the task of trying to find the verbal equivalent for states of mind and feeling. And this means both that they are more mature, and that they wear better, than later poets of certainly not less literary ability.

It is not a permanent necessity that poets should be interested in philosophy, or in any other subject. We can only say that it appears likely that poets in our civilization, as it exists at present, must be *difficult*. Our civilization comprehends great variety and complexity, and this variety and complexity, playing upon a refined sensibility, must produce various and complex results. The poet must become more and more comprehensive, more allusive, more indirect, in order to force, to dislocate if necessary, language into his meaning. (A brilliant and extreme statement of this view, with which it is not requisite to associate oneself, is that of M. Jean Epstien, *La Poésie d'aujourd-hui*.) Hence we get something which looks very much like the conceit – we get, in fact, a method curiously similar to that of the 'metaphysical poets', similar also in its use of obscure words and of simple phrasing.

> O géraniums diaphanes, guerroyeurs sortilèges,
> Sacrilèges monomanes!
> Emballages, dévergondages, douches! O pressoirs
> Des vendanges des grands soirs!
> Layettes aux abois,
> Thyrses au fond des bois!
> Transfusions, représailles,
> Relevailles, compresses et l'éternal potion,
> Angélus! n'en pouvoir plus
> De débâcles nuptiales! de débâcles nuptiales!

The same poet could write also simply:

> Elle est bien loin, elle pleure,
> Le grand vent se lamente aussi . . .

Jules Laforgue, and Tristan Corbière in many of his poems, are nearer to the 'school of Donne' than any modern English poet. But poets more classical than they have the same essential quality of transmuting ideas into sensations, of transforming an observation into a state of mind.

> Pour l'enfant, amoureux de cartes et d'estampes,
> L'univers est égal à son vaste appétit.
> Ah, que le monde est grand à la clarté des lampes!
> Aux yeux du souvenir que le monde est petit!

In French literature the great master of the seventeenth century – Racine – and the great master of the nineteenth – Baudelaire – are in some ways more like each other than they are like anyone else. The greatest two masters of diction are also the greatest two psychologists, the most curious explorers of the soul. It is interesting to speculate whether it is not a misfortune that two of the greatest masters of diction in our language, Milton and Dryden, triumph with a dazzling disregard of the soul. If we continued to produce Miltons and Drydens it might not so much matter, but as things are it is a pity that English poetry has remained so incomplete. Those who object to the 'artificiality' of Milton or Dryden sometimes tell us to 'look into our hearts and write'. But that is not looking deep enough; Racine or Donne looked into a good deal more than the heart. One must look into the cerebral cortex, the nervous system, and the digestive tracts.

May we not conclude, then, that Donne, Crashaw, Vaughan, Herbert and Lord Herbert, Marvell, King, Cowley at his best, are in the direct current of English poetry, and that their faults should be reprimanded by this standard rather than coddled by antiquarian affection? They have been enough praised in terms which are implicit limitations because they are 'metaphysical' or 'witty', 'quaint' or 'obscure', though at their best they have not these attributes more than other serious poets. On the other hand, we must not reject the criticism of Johnson (a dangerous person to disagree with) without having mastered it, without having assimilated the Johnsonian canons of taste. In reading the celebrated passage in his essay on Cowley we must remember that by wit he clearly means something more serious than we usually mean to-day; in his criticism of their versification we must remember in what a narrow discipline he was trained, but also how well trained; we must remember that Johnson tortures chiefly the chief offenders, Cowley and Cleveland. It would be a fruitful work, and one requiring a substantial book, to break up the classification of Johnson (for there has been none since) and exhibit these poets in all their difference of kind and of degree, from the massive music of Donne to the faint, pleasing tinkle of Aurelian Townshend – whose *Dialogue between a Pilgrim and Time* is one of the few regrettable omissions from the excellent anthology of Professor Grierson.

21 P.W. THOMAS

Two Cultures?
Court and Country under Charles I

I

'And never Rebel was to Arts a friend', John Dryden pronounced with great finality in *Absalom and Achitophel* in 1679. Faced with the threat of Monmouth's reckless yielding to the temptation of Shaftesbury's eloquent, Satanic prompting, he could not refrain from recalling the great upheaval of English society in the middle of the seventeenth century. The Great Rebellion, for Tories of his generation, was a reminder of the madness that insurrection and innovation, challenging established values, might yet at any moment conjure up. They cherished the memory of a divided, deluded society as a cautionary tale apt for their own crises.

Their habit of equating 'Wit' and 'Fool' with Tory and Whig belongs to the cooler world (wary of holy enthusiasms, rhapsodical fanaticism, and all the paraphernalia of 'godly thorough Reformation') that bantering scepticism and common sense had helped to create: it is not remote from our sort of party politics. Yet plainly it was also a legacy of the not far distant conflagration when King and Parliament, Orthodoxy and Dissent (in its many forms) contended so fiercely. Their language reverberated still with meanings and associations that we may not at first hearing catch.

Dryden, in his Preface of 1682 to *Religio Laici* deliberately carried the quarrel back beyond the Revolution:

> *Martin Mar-Prelate* (the Marvel of those times) was the first Presbyterian Scribbler, who sanctified Libels and Scurrility to the use of the Good Old Cause . . .; to their ignorance all things are Wit, which are abusive; . . . Thus Sectaries, we may see, were born with teeth, foul-mouth'd and scurrilous from their Infancy . . .

That touches deep convictions about politics and literature which we must investigate.

From *The Origins of the English Civil War*, ed. Conrad Russell (Macmillan, 1973), pp. 168–193. Footnotes have been deleted.

II

Looking back we still sometimes imagine we see a Parliament of prudes in 1642 sanctimoniously bolting and barring the theatres; statues and stained glass falling before the Apostolic blows and knocks; the royal patron decapitated and his great collection of art treasures put up to auction; we behold the Universities, those 'old standing judges of good Poetry' as Humphrey Moseley the publisher called them in 1651, ignominiously purged; and men of letters scurrying for cover in the provinces or abroad. The picture is one of rampant, insane utilitarianism putting the Muses to flight as it overturns the Court, despoils the Church, and tramples through the groves of Academe. There stands the great Leviathan of the Republic, presiding grim and godly over a wasteland.

Of course, that is all rather one-sided. We may set against it the memory of Andrew Marvell, richly gifted, moderate, discreet, serving the Protectorate and writing one of the most civilised odes in the language to celebrate Cromwell's return from Ireland; or Milton, whose learning and brilliance were a byword in Europe, composing his great epic of English humanism.

We may even, on closer examination, perceive ways in which Puritanism transcended the boundaries of sect and party; asceticism was not the monopoly of nonconformity, and we confidently talk today of Anglican Puritans, citing the affinities between the fine spirituality of Richard Baxter and Jeremy Taylor, or reflecting that Laud's 'Diary' is a thoroughly Puritan document. At the same time we observe that Presbyterians and Independents – often lumped together in propaganda – were frequently at each other's throats. Prynne, Burton, and Lilburne were all Puritans but they represented in the end quite different points of view. Their careers, as Presbyterian, Independent, and Leveller respectively, display the essential diversity of nonconformity and its rooted principle of divergence. In them we trace how Puritanism grew beyond its concern with ceremonies and the sins of the flesh – for assuredly it had deep convictions about these matters – to demand root and branch political and legal reform.

Yet the simplifications of caricature were even at the time more graspable than the very complicated 'facts'; and in the event they become a sort of fact and had a real impact on events. Prynne, a moral Puritan who insisted that he was conformable to Church and Crown, became perforce a political Puritan, and so a godly hero or a deluded meddler, depending on your point of view. In his writing and in his 'martyrdom' a quarrel was polarised. We shall not be able to dispense after all with the term 'Puritan' nor with the prejudices that were attributed to it. But we may hope to come to understand them and their role more fully.

Ben Jonson unforgettably established the type on stage: his caricature of Puritanism in *Bartholomew Fair*, acted in 1614 and printed in 1631, displays the features which Cavalier propaganda so lovingly dwelt on. Zeal-of-the-Land-Busy, originally a lowborn tradesman, has risen by exercising his gift of prophetic utterance to heights of hypocrisy and indulgence: denouncing the 'vanity of the eye', 'the lust of the palate', and all 'carnal provocations' he stops his ears and averts his gaze in the Fair, but smells his way to the food instead. Ale is Satan's drink, though he imbibes it liberally; and as for 'long hair, it is an Ensign of pride, a banner'. He spouts the cant of Revelation, seeing 'the broken belly of the Beast' in a drum and an 'Idolatrous Grove of Images' in the hobbyhorse seller's stock-in-trade of musical instruments, toys, and gingerbread. With a visionary eye on the millennium he bursts in during the puppet show inveighing against 'Stage-players, Rhymers, and Morris dancers, who have walked hand-in-hand, in contempt of the Brethren, and the Cause'. He abominates the dressing up of male as female, and vice versa, on the stage; and in a scene of high farce the puppet is assailed because it has 'no Calling', no vocation – 'your old stale argument against the Players', as the puppet retorts! Unrepentant even in the stocks Busy rejoices in his affliction and foretells the destruction of 'Fairs and May-games, Wakes, and Whitsun-ales', sighing and groaning and gaping in due form for the reformation of these abuses. For prophecy is *his* calling; and he recognises no 'other Learning, than Inspiration'. Like Dryden's MacFlecknoe fifty years later, he is 'a fellow of a most arrogant, and invincible dulness', kept ever in 'seditious motion' by the conviction (which Shakespeare's Malvolio, 'a kind of Puritan', shares) that the future will be his.

Jonson expresses the growing anxiety of the early seventeenth century over militant nonconformism. To see how his caricature took shape we must carry the story a little further back to the challenge of Elizabethan Puritanism, which was contained, and in particular to the controversies of the 1580s. All the differences which in the decades prior to Civil War hardened into faction are there expressed. But the Elizabethan settlement, punitive to extremists, was sufficiently tolerant of the broad middle range of dissent. That accommodation made national unity possible, and is reflected in some of the major literary achievements of the period. Spenser could speak from reasonably close to the centres of power and, with the support of influential patrons, in tones distinctly Calvinist at times. At the same time his is a truly national ideal that embraces all the aspirations of Renaissance courtly man. His *Faerie Queene* (1596), written 'to fashion a gentleman or noble person in virtuous and gentle discipline', celebrates that unity of Church and State, of Court with Country, of 'grace' with 'policy', that the Queen's Council embodied. It concludes with a prayer breathing a millenarian faith, 'O that great Sabbath God, grant me that Sabbaths sight'. Little wonder that many Puritans in the Interregnum recalled this as a golden era. But Spenser does not need to look yet to revolutionary politics to achieve his vision. He found, as did his patron Sir Philip Sidney and Sidney's editor and friend the Chancellor of the Exchequer Fulke Greville, that his aspirations as man and artist were at least acceptable to the State.

Nor did they affront the prevailing spirit of Calvinism as it was formulated by its most notable English champion William Perkins (1558–1602). The current of reform and asceticism which spread its ripples through Europe from the source in Calvin's Geneva was in him calmly and painstakingly assimilated into English Protestant nationalism. It was his achievement to establish over the whole range of human life a scrupulously detailed, practical code of conduct. He is critical therefore not merely of Romish ritual in church but of all ostentation and ceremony. Mixed dancing, those 'frisks of lightness and vanity', cosmetics which make women 'seem what they are not', long hair in man ('a foreign trick'), any dress which does not suit a man's vocation, and especially the 'new fangled attire' that makes women 'like to an image in a frame, set bolt upright' – all are condemned in terms that shrewdly imply the idolatry of *haute couture* and the vanity of trying to appear what one is not. Carnal distractions from one's calling must be removed; and into his net Perkins swept 'vain love songs, ballads, interludes, and amorous books'. Yet as always he was discriminating and uninflammatory: 'This is the thing we are carefully to shun in the reading of Poets, yet so, as mariners do in navigation, who forsake not the sea, but decline and fly from the rocks'.

In practice Spenser showed that even the erotic impulse and the language of love songs could serve a holy ideal. His celebration of matrimony in *Epithalamion* (1595) is a major achievement of Puritan Platonism in which the senses, human feeling, and spiritual fervour triumph together. The problem which he solved there was not new: mistrust of passions and affective language was routine in Renaissance thinking. But Calvinism undoubtedly fortified that suspicion of outward show and merely carnal pleasures which is a major preoccupation of *The Faerie Queene*. This is not to say that the poem merely versifies Calvinist dogma, though the destruction of the Bower of Bliss has been interpreted as an act of iconoclasm. In fact Spenser is making a very important distinction between false beauty, which is just carnal, and true beauty which involves spirituality also. For the new poetry which Spenser and Sidney launched was sensitive to the need to establish the moral value of art and to justify poetry as a fit Christian vocation. The Calvinist Fulke Greville, editing Sidney's pastoral romance *Arcadia* (1590), defended the book's good doctrine, albeit somewhat uneasy over its fictitious garb; it afforded 'not vanishing pleasure alone, but moral Images, and Examples . . . to guide every man through the confused Labyrinth of his own desires and life'. Greville was perhaps the most distrustful of all the Calvinist poets, and elsewhere, in stricter ideological mood, he denounced all human Arts as 'beams of folly'. Yet he proceeded even then to defend their practical utility with equal conviction. Fundamentally his position is much like Bacon's: he was alert to the ways in which 'feigned history' and the 'craft of words' could seduce, and wary of affections that might colour and confound true understanding: but he argued pragmatically that poetry, properly disciplined, could perform public service by furnishing images of magnanimity, morality, and delectation.

The Puritans were heirs to the humanist position, in fact. But the poets especially seized on the ancient notion that poetry had something of divinity in it too. Here conventions of artistic inspiration might be reconciled with the Calvinist idea of being called, with the belief that God could speak through man. Christian poets, with discipline and grace, might serve the revelation of truth. Aesthetic pleasure could be a fit vehicle for moral illumination. Thus far Puritanism and Art did not conflict.

One point on which Perkins had touched was proving, nevertheless, uncomfortably divisive. He mistrusted stage plays above all as 'most commonly dangerous representations of vices and misdemeanours' which ought not to be spoken of. Spenser's jibe at 'painted faces' and 'the courting masker' in *The Ruines of Time* (1591) suggests how widespread this sort of anxiety was becoming. Sidney in his *Apologie for Poetry* (1595) was forced to admit that there were unworthy poets, and 'naughty Play-makers and Stage-keepers'. Unlike Perkins, and for that matter Greville, he did not however eschew drama. Properly purified, even it could be a worthy instrument.

Sidney's antagonist Stephen Gosson had no time for such nice points. He devoted *The School of Abuse* (1579) and the even more strident *Plays Confuted* (1582) to a doctrinaire onslaught on the whole business. 'Garish apparel masks . . ., Dancing of jigs, galliards, morrises, hobby horses'; 'amorous Poets', and all such 'peevish cattle', but above all 'Stage Plays', were nothing but the 'doctrine and invention of the Devil' to lure the carnally minded. He had read his Lactantius and trotted out all his objections: the eye, that susceptible organ, is beguiled by spectacle while the 'sweet numbers of Poetry flowing in verse do wonderfully tickle the hearers ears'. Such a combined assault on the senses was scarce to be resisted. Puritans of his temper might allow music of the right sort (since it afforded abstract images only); they could accept paintings if they were not lascivious; they could accommodate poetry; theoretically they might even accept drama. But in practice – and the spirit of pragmatism was strong – the dangers were so great that it seemed better to avoid temptation.

Gosson was in no doubt that such 'Italian devices' (he was thinking chiefly of masques) had 'poisoned the old manners of our Country with foreign delights'. To 'the hazard of their souls' and in a 'riot of their expenses', men had deserted 'the old discipline of England'. As a display of chauvinism, bourgeois thrift, prudence and fundamentalism, it is remarkable. The objections to display, to acting as a sort of lying, to the imitation of vice are conventional enough: but Gosson – though he at one point mentions 'good plays and sweet plays', his own among them – makes of the drama a matter almost of political offence by denouncing it as the 'Ratsbane to the government of commonweals'. His prayer, that 'some Hercules in the Court' might cleanse the land as the 'godly preachers' of London had urged, sounds ominously like a reproach to a negligent administration.

With varying degrees of vehemence and skill this Puritan assault on the theatre (usually combined with attacks on extravagance and idolatry, especially of the Romish sort) was maintained through the last decades of the sixteenth century. The case for the defence was basically Sidney's argument that it was foolish to equate fiction with falsehood and that plays could both teach and delight. Thomas Lodge and Thomas Heywood among others conducted the defence; but it was necessarily less emotive than the prosecution – at least for the time being.

We stand however on the threshold of a changing world; ahead lies a complicated shift of temper at the centre, which was to affect the whole range of life. As long as the Court tolerated a variety of manners in worship and doctrine, as long as the Crown was not exclusively identified with the vices of plays and players and extravagant indulgence in the pleasures of carnal arts, the broad Calvinist hostility to ritual and ceremony was not seditious. In the 1580s, despite Gosson's hint, the Court could not be made the scapegoat. Nor, for that matter, was criticism of the theatre ever exclusively Puritan or 'extra-mural'. Among the orthodox clergy, too, many were uneasy: they knew that the Church Fathers and Christian tradition were on the side of the 'godly'. Laud would go no further than arguing rather halfheartedly against Prynne that plays were not necessarily evil. There was a surprising amount of agreement between Puritan and Anglican in this matter. But in practice and in time the Puritans' habit of associating criticism of the stage with ecclesiastical and other grievances was to strike most woundingly. It was as a subversive challenge that, some fifty years after Gosson, William Prynne's *Histriomastix* would be received when it revived the issue in the most inflammatory way.

The explanation of this lies not just in Prynne's contentious stubbornness nor in some monstrous, unslakeable thirst after righteousness. It involves a decline in the public theatre and an increasing inclination at Court to patronise an art remote from the sort of concerns that the Spenserian-Jonsonian consensus insisted on. Of course, this did not happen overnight. Spenser and Sidney were dead, and their loss (in terms of enlightened patronage and the justification of poetry and drama in a Christian society) was important. But Jonson flourished, upholding neo-classical didacticism in his brilliant comedies for the public stage. Shakespeare too survived into the reign of King James, subtly adapting his drama to the changing audience, and the great Folio edition (1623) of his works belongs here. We might interpret this as some indication of a continuing vitality, perhaps even of a thriving drama. Yet the inclination of many Jacobean playwrights to pile on the melancholy, bawdiness and horror suggests jaded palates. There was plenty for Puritans to object to. Ben Jonson himself rounded on popular plays for their 'ribaldry, profanation, all licence of offence to God, and man', to say nothing of absurd plots and trivial themes. He shared the view that drama had failed to uphold unequivocally 'the doctrine which is the principal end of poesy, to inform men, in the best reason of living'. For all his mockery of ranting Puritans Jonson believed that art must rest on an unequivocal moral commitment.

Courtly taste also reacted against the coarseness of popular drama; but only to demand of art (as Jonson in the fullness of time discovered) a sort of conformity and propriety that was doubly irksome. The carnal pleasures proffered in the fashionable private theatre for the delectation of noble sophisticates and aspiring worldlings became more exquisite and ambiguous; and they framed political and social assumptions that were increasingly exclusive. This art was dutifully doctrinal but for many in the country it offered the wrong doctrine. All this, with a mounting exravagance, in the end aroused even moderate men of middle station.

Puritans meanwhile cannot have failed to take note of Jonson's caricature of their hopes, mocking them in the sight of the ungodly vulgar. His being drawn further into the orbit of the Court where he hoped for a more discriminating audience is unlikely to have eased their antipathy. Even the mounting pressure of censorship on the theatre (and only the King's Players were strong enough to survive the plague and close-down of 1625) did not help, since the Court was more than ever bent on cultivating its own entertainments in private. And if Puritans studied the offerings of those darlings of Jacobean and Caroline intellectuals, Beaumont and Fletcher, they found plays which, as Coleridge observed, carried 'even *jure divino* principles . . . to excess'. They were to become to the Cavaliers an epitome of the noblest artistic and political ideals; while Dryden, though looking back with profoundest wonder on Shakespeare's genius, significantly applauded them for bringing the conversation of gentlemen on to the stage. Such fashionable art confirmed the *élitist* tendencies of Stuart rule.

Militant Puritanism was not, in our sense, a popular mass movement: men like Prynne probably shared the genteel objection that Shakespeare had too much respected the mob; but their alternative was not a more refined drama. To the zealous, their eyes on the dawning millennium, it was all (from Shakespeare to Davenant) a dark distraction. Their objections in the end articulated what many dimly felt about the growing isolation, exclusiveness and repression of the Court. Even men of unstrict temper could reflect on the difference between a literature that had been the authentic voice of patriotic high seriousness and Protestant nationalism, and one that, however refined, seemed to speak for narrow snobbery and an effete indulgence. For too many the art the Stuarts encouraged mirrored the moral, social, and political defects of its philosophy.

III

With the advantage of hindsight we can relate that decline to a change for the worse in Church and State which eventually made containment and reconciliation impossible. The reasonableness and integrity of Perkins's case for Calvinism had been met with the answerable magnanimity and flexibility of Hooker's *Ecclesiastical Polity*. Now the enlightened moderation of Bacon, who envisaged a broad church unity encompassing divers forms and ceremonies, was brushed aside. Country and City, the old aristocracy, the property owners, the magnates, merchants and industrialists did not care to pay taxes to subsidise the salaries and pleasures of court parasites. Almost inevitably they leaned towards Puritanism.

The early Stuarts for their part, failed fully to understand the nation they had come down to rule – witness James's constant toying with the grandiose dream of reconciling Protestant to Catholic in Europe through the magic of dynastic marriages. The public rejoicing when Prince Charles and Buckingham returned empty-handed (save for some paintings) from their theatrical excursion in false beards in pursuit of a Spanish wife should have enlightened them. Yet Charles I, stubbornly devoted to the silliest aspects of his father's policies, was to take a French Catholic wife. She proved a liability.

Popery, painting and playacting – could anything be more calculated to stir the anxieties and resentments we have been discussing? The new Court espoused them all.

Charles's household was more gentlemanly: James's robust humour, to which the Jonsonian anti-masque paid tribute, and his bad manners were replaced by more cultivated behaviour. The new King was a connoisseur: his collection of paintings took Rubens's breath away when he came here in 1629 expecting to find a culture as barbarous as the climate. Such sophistication, such aesthetic sensitivity amazed him. But Charles was prepared to take a deal of trouble and spend a lot of money on these treasures. Men like Buckingham's protégé, the diplomat-adventurer Balthazar Gerbier, were equally eager to conduct tortuous negotiations to acquire art works. In 1628 Charles outbid Richelieu, lifting the Mantuan Collection from under his nose. Van Dyck, whose elegance and ostentation perfectly matched the king's, was ensconced in grand style at Blackfriars to paint his flattering dream of a wise, sensitive, dignified monarchy. Rubens himself, the most expensive painter in Europe, was engaged. His ceiling at Whitehall is beautiful; and the sensuous allegory of the 'Blessings of Peace' richly proclaims a pious aspiration. We may however wonder at the wisdom of patronising the great propagandist of the Counter-Reformation, or of doing deals with Cardinal Barberini who helped Charles import treasures from Italy, hopeful of winning a proselyte.

The king's military expeditions into Europe were even less propitious. Perhaps the fact that Gerbier, who made machines for masques, was employed to devise mines to blow up the dyke at La Rochelle sufficiently characterises that episode. It was little better than a charade. This and the earlier Cadiz adventure were felt, outside the Court at any rate, as betrayals of national pride and pious duty. The King, however, rested on the lesser Europeanism of international art dealing.

In 1637 he did make a gesture to the popular desire for England to assume her old role: he launched the *Sovereign of the Seas*. The ship's decoration was aptly assigned to the dramatist Thomas Heywood (one of those who had defended the stage against Puritan criticism). He published a careful explanation of the allegorical significance of his designs, to the satisfaction, no doubt, of a Monarch who to the last had an eye for the theatrical.

Fittingly it is in the fantastic and elaborate court masques of his reign that the King most lived up to Jonson's rather unfortunate advice that a prince should be 'studious of riches and magnificence in the outward celebration or show'. Out of the combined arts of poet, painter, musician, choreographer and architect, the masque fashioned a mirror in which the Court most loved to behold itself.

The pieces were essentially ephemeral, commonly performed but once; and the audience was small and select. But the cost of costumes, scenery and the wonderful machines was prodigious. Even under James the effects were astonishing: '[The curtain] falling, an artificial sea was seen to shoot forth, as if it flowed to the land, raised with waves, which seemed to move, and in some places the billow to break ... The *Masquers* were placed in a great concave shell, like mother of pearl, curiously made to move on those waters and rise with the billow.' Thus, Sir Dudley Carleton in 1605. Bacon, twenty years later, very sensibly dismissed such affairs as 'but Toys'. But what expensive toys!

Jonson, the greatest writer of masques, later regretted the 'jewels, stuffs, the pains, the wit' wasted on 'the short bravery of the night'. He strove for twenty years to make the masque moral and doctrinal as well as pleasurable: he dared in his robust honest man's way to lecture the Court, even to remind it of the realities of people's dissatisfaction. If the masque commands respect as a literary form, this is, *Comus* apart, Jonson's achievement. His fate is significant, however: the court of Charles would not tolerate his reminders of actualities; it wanted something more decorous, polite, Italianate than he would give; it wanted, above all, something spectacular but reassuring. In a word, the courtiers desired pageantry. Inigo Jones, with whom Jonson had long but uneasily collaborated, was their man. He did not think masques were anything more than 'pictures with Light and Motion'. He could and would devise the magnificence they desired, build scenes and devices to the measure of their dreams.

Tamer collaborators, like Aurelian Townshend, William Davenant and James Shirley, were enlisted to aid him. Jonson was left to condemn, in his *Expostulation with Inigo Jones*, the shallow profligacy of it all:

Painting and Carpentry are the Soul of Masque!
Pack with your peddling Poetry to the Stage
This is the money-get, Mechanic-Age. [. . . .]

Frank and pusillanimous hedonism reached a new height in Thomas Carew's lines of 1632. Demurring at the chance to write an elegy for Gustavus Adolphus, great hero of international Protestantism and revered by the surviving Elizabethans on the Council, he urged

> But let us that in myrtle bowers sit
> Under secure shades, use the benefit
> Of peace and plenty, which the blessed hand
> Of our good King gives this obdurate Land.
> Let us of Revels sing, and let their breath gently inspire

> Thy past'rall pipe.
> Tourneys, Masques, Theaters better become
> Our Halcyon days; what though the Genevan Drum
> Bellow for freedom and revenge, the noise
> Concerns not us, nor should divert our joys.

Two years later in his masque *Coelum Britannicum* he went further: the existence of 'obdurate' folk is not even hinted at as the three nations bend the willing knee in 'cheerful loyal reverence'.

It was into this dream world that William Prynne, defying censorship, came crashing with his immense, unignorable encyclopaedia of complaint. His *Histriomastix the Players Scourge or Actors Tragedie*, of 1632–3 voluminously annotated the Puritan code of secular and religious conduct. Its one thousand pages comprise the most exhaustive statement of Puritan asceticism. Such an exclamatory attack on idolatry and ritual in all its guises could not but set the Court by the ears. 'This man', sneered Lord Dorset, the most vindictive of Prynne's judges, 'will be frighted at a three-cornered cap, sweat at a surplice, sigh to hear music, swound to the sign of the cross . . . ' Indignation knew no bounds, nor in this case did obsequiousness: his lordship capped his observations with a nice compliment to the Queen 'in whose praise it is impossible for a poet to feign, or orator to flatter'. That was well the wrong side idolatry. It could only confirm fears that in its life and letters the Court had dispensed with all Christian restraint. The full weight of traditional opposition to the cult of personal beauty and seductive pleasure was behind Prynne's scourging assault – for it was too late for the calm tone of a Perkins. He runs through the gamut of vanity: 'long false curled hair and lovelocks' are a 'vile and abominable abuse . . . much now used in this our Realm'; they are 'an effeminate unnatural amorous practice, an incitation of lust, an occasion of Sodomy': 'coranto frisking gallants' and 'lewd lascivious dancings' indulge the most 'beastly' pleasures and draw young men from study and young women from their household duties when they should be 'keepers at home, not gadders abroad'; and the whole apparatus of 'comedies, tragedies, Arcadias, amorous histories, poems, and other profane discourses' are so many scandals in the face of God. Prynne did not reject poetry as such: he allowed that one of the Fathers could pen 'a poem of Christ's passion only to be read, which to act were most profane'; he himself composed six lines attacking Laud and praising God when he returned from his ordeal in the pillory in 1637. But he would not countenance the sort of love lyric courtiers addressed to their mistresses.

Above all, of course, he objects to plays and masques: they portray vice, they dress men as women and vice versa, they display 'lustful gestures, compliments, kisses, dalliances, or embracements', and their scenes and costumes are nothing but an 'overcostly gaudiness, amorousness, fantastiqueness, and disguisedness'. The campaign against women actors had been launched from middle ground by Sir Benjamin Rudyerd and the third Earl of Pembroke. Boldly Prynne pressed home the attack: his reflections on the acting of a play at Blackfriars in 1629 by 'some French women, or monsters rather' and his terse index entry 'Women actors, notorious whores' were taken as a frightful insult to Henrietta Maria. The king himself, in earlier days, had starchily reproached the Queen's frolicsome gambolling as 'degrading ceremonies'. Her love of dancing and dressing up had however survived his disapproval; and a public attack was different from a private rebuke.

It was commonly believed that Prynne had in mind her acting in the long pastoral drama, *Shepherd's Paradise*, written by a Catholic, Walter Montague, and played at Court in January 1633. She delighted in the sports and merry games, the fresh fair maids and wanton shepherds common in the mode; and Montague's piece began a court craze. In January 1634, for example, Fletcher's *The Faithful Shepherdess*, which had failed in the public theatre in 1609, was revived with the help of scenery by Inigo Jones and costumes by Henrietta Maria. It went down well and was subsequently acted with applause in the Blackfriars private theatre.

Unmistakably, and with fanatical courage, Prynne had flung all the age-old accusations about the idolatry of drama and Popish ceremonial in the face of King, Queen and Bishops. Never had the Court been so vulnerable, with its worship dictated by a High Church martinet and its pleasures presided over by a French consort, indulged in her extravagance and her Catholicism. Prynne did not omit to note that many of the players were Papists.

He had other cavils too. Shakespeare's plays were printed on better paper than Bibles; and playbooks, pouring from the presses in torrents, found 'better vent than sermons'. When preachers were harried and free use of the press denied the devout, such licence was intolerable. Prynne counted, despite 'late penurious times', no fewer than five 'devil's chapels' in London with a sixth theatre under construction. Such 'over prodigal disbursements' were more than enough to have financed that holy war that Protestant honour demanded. They were 'intolerable in a Christian frugal State'.

Little wonder Prynne was charged with trying 'to withdraw the peoples affections from the King and Governments'. If men believed his jeremiad, as one of his judges pointed out, with what heart would they pay subsidies and duties in future? That was a key question and exposes the root of the matter. Prynne had contrived to focus in his attack on the theatre the growing opposition to the Court's foreign policies, its ecclesiastical exactions, and its financial methods. He drew together all the practical and spiritual objections of bourgeois thrift and Puritan asceticism. *Histriomastix* was not a manual of piety but a political indictment of the Crown.

Collision with Laudian bureaucracy, equally disinclined to turn a blind eye to anything, was inevitable. If Prynne was no Perkins, Laud was certainly no Hooker. His reaction was swift and ruthless: William Cartwright and Jasper Mayne (two young sprigs of Laudian academicism) with Peter Heylin, historian and divine, were set to hound the troublesome meddler; and to exact poetic justice in full measure. James Shirley was commissioned to write a masque, *The Triumph of Peace*, for Prynne's own Inns of Court to produce at prodigious expense. The Court needed soothing: Carew's sycophantic *Coelum Britannicum* followed; and in 1638, just to show a lofty contempt, Davenant's *Britannia Triumphans* was acted on the Sabbath. [. . .]

The Laudians still did not care for a missionary European role; and when at last Charles took up arms it was in a parochial cause and against the Calvinists in the North. The first expedition ended in humiliating truce at Berwick in 1639; but the Monarch, optimism buoyed by the enchantment of a Twelfth Night masque by Davenant, prepared to march again in 1640. His half-hearted army was easily defeated at Newburn. Perhaps the contribution of Sir John Suckling best characterises the whole feckless enterprise. Suckling, gambler, rakehell and writer of licentious verse, patron saint of the Roaring Boys and 'greatest gallant of his time', raised a troop of horse for the First Bishops' War. At a cost of some £3,000 he decked them out in white doublets, scarlet breeches and scarlet coats, hats and feathers – the costumes were no less gorgeous than those used in his play *Aglaura* in 1638. So caparisoned he led them into battle. Suckling was no coward; but his band was surely more for show than for fighting. This piece of theatre and the incompetent execution of the whole royal manoeuvre suggest how far the acting out of fantasies had become a function of Personal Rule. For poor Suckling, forced into exile after the final fiasco of the Army Plot in 1641, all the gallantry and glamour ended in suicide in Paris.

All too plainly royal patronage had failed to sustain at the centre a culture (using the word in its proper, widest sense to embrace social and political *mores* as well as those of art) of unequivocal moral and intellectual vigour. It mistook flexibility for weakness and a governing clique for the nation; it confused true and spurious eloquence, so that men of real ability like Falkland and Clarendon did not have the King's ear; it cultivated an attentuated self-regarding sort of high seriousness that was in the end no match for the tough dedication of its opponents. It managed to construct a mythology of itself that was deeply divisive.

In the Root and Branch Petition of 11 December 1641 this was finally challenged on all fronts and decisively identified as the work of Antichrist. All that tolerating of sports on Sunday and that dressing up in Popish vestments, all that bowing to Popish images and ceremonies was positively heathen. So was 'the swarming of lascivious, idle, and unprofitable Books and Pamphlets, Play-books, and Ballads, as namely

Ovids fits of love, ... to the increase of all vices, and withdrawing of people from reading, studying, and hearing the Word of God, and other Books'. The petitioners saw a New Jerusalem just ahead and nothing was too great or too small for their attention. These men, no less than Laud, knew what was good for the people.

It seems indeed as if a militant radical culture was bent on sweeping away all trace of the Court, down to its very last poem or play. That was how Royalists interpreted the Ordinance of 1642 which closed the theatres and crowned the long campaign to stop that subversion of godliness. John Cleveland jested from Oxford a few years later that 'the only playhouse is at Westminster'; and *Mercurius Anti-Britanicus* about the same time joked that the stage would return to its proper home at Blackfriars only when the citizens went back to their 'old harmless profession of killing Men in Tragedies without Manslaughter'. Samuel Butler in *Mercurius Mennippeus* spelled out the lesson:

> We perceive, at last why plays went down; to wit, that murders might be acted in earnest. Stages must submit to scaffolds, and personated tragedies to real ones ... No need of heightening revels; these Herods can behead without the allurements of a dance. These tragedians have outvied invention.

In their zeal to cast out fiction and falsehood, he implies, the rebels had committed the worst confusion of all and unmasked themselves as of the Devil's party. This was twisting the old objections to plays with a vengeance. From the other side things looked different: in the Cavalier raking in 'the dunghill of ruined stages' the journalist Marchamont Nedham detected the corrupted airs of Inigo Jones and the masquers, and the noxious features of 'his grandfather Ben Jonson, and his Uncle *Shakespear* ... and his cousin-germain *Fletcher*, and *Beaumont*, and nose-less Davenant, and Friar *Shirley* the Poets'. There could scarcely be a blunter polarisation of views about literature and politics. Even in the matter of hair, which can as we know inflame passions, the opposition appears. The jeers at Cavalier lovelocks were not allowed to go unanswered: never trust a man if you can see his ears, was the advice of one Anglican divine to his fellow. Short hair became, in propaganda, the badge of the Puritan: witness Cleveland's Sir John Presbyter 'With Hair in Character and Lugs in Text', or Butler's 'long-ear'd Rout', or even Dryden's finally polished cut at the Presbyter who 'pricks up his predestinating Ears'. Powerful prejudices accumulate around seeming trivialities.

We know of course that Milton, though cropped at the insistence of a strict tutor when he was ten, wore his hair long in maturity, as did Cromwell. But in the embittered climate of the late 1630s and 1640s nice distinctions were easily disregarded. Henry Parker had good cause to protest, in his *Discourse Concerning Puritans* of 1641, that the name was being used to discredit 'men of strict life and precise opinions, which cannot be hated for any thing but their singularity in zeal and piety'.

'Scarce any civil honest Protestant' could avoid the slur. Milton in his *Reason of Church Government* (1642) and Sir Benjamin Rudyerd on the day, in November 1640, that the Long Parliament assembled, made the same point. Moderate Anglicans might equally protest that all orthodox churches, all bishops, ritual and ceremony were being tarred with the brush of Popery. In vain they proposed in 1641 the sort of reform that Bacon advocated in 1604. It was too late. Propaganda with its cries of 'Popish Arminian fry' or 'Anabaptist, Brownist scum' was in the saddle. Hooker's faith in 'visible solemnity' and Bastwick's objection to 'the bondage of the figure and shadow' could no longer coexist, even uneasily. Idolater confronted Iconoclast.

There were it seems two warring cultures. But it is more accurate to talk of a breakdown of the national culture, an erosion through the 1630s of a middle ground that men of moderation and good will had once occupied. Fulke Greville's heir, who largely shared his views, was perforce a leading revolutionary. The case of Anne Bradstreet, the Puritan poet who fled from Laudian tyranny to America in the 1630s, is similarly instructive. The 'heroes' of her Pantheon were that 'fleshly Deity' Queen Elizabeth, the poets Du Bartas, Spenser and Sidney. At the same time, in *A Dialogue between Old England and New* written in 1642, New England rejoices in the spirit of root and branch:

> Let's bring Baals vestments forth to make a fire,
> Their Mitres, Surplices, and all their Tire,
> Copes, Rochets, Crosiers, and such empty trash.

The lesson is clear: Puritanism, except in cases of extreme fanaticism, did not demand that the slate be wiped clean of everything upon it. Their objection was not to literature, not necessarily even to plays of the right sort, but to what they felt was the pollution of the high seriousness and moral earnestness of the mainstream of English humanism.

The Court behaved as though the Golden Age had arrived through the miraculous intercession of the divine Stuart. To the godly it looked a thoroughly carnal kingdom, more like Babylon than the New Jerusalem. The future demanded that it, and all its idolatrous bric-à-brac, be brushed aside.

IV

The picture of a decadent Court, its art an index to a deep malaise, is not just hindsight. Many saw the issue so at the time; and Milton confirms the diagnosis. In his life's work, as poet and pamphleteer, he endeavoured (as did others) to recover the strenuousness and dedication of the earlier phase of the English Renaissance. Could we follow him closely through the years of retreat at Horton in the late 1630s and on his journey to Rome and Geneva, we would see growing his realisation that poetry's true theme was Christian revelation. 'Church-outed' by the Laudian prelatical bureaucracy, he found his calling as a Christian and a writer to be the same. Returning to England he proclaimed his programme to use letters to 'inbreed and cherish in a great people the seeds of virtue, and public civility to allay the perturbations of the mind, and set the affections in right tune, to celebrate in glorious and lofty Hymns the throne and equipage of God's Almightiness and what he works'. Some thirty years later, when so much had changed, he still endeavoured to reveal 'What makes a Nation happy, and keeps it so', though by then it was a theme for epic tragedy.

Not only the Restoration, but a secularisation that set in well before that, overtook the Millennium. Puritanism had always appealed strongly to bourgeois fanaticism and in the end it produced a remarkable laicisation of life. When the vision of a New Jerusalem was hi-jacked by extremists and made a creed for cranks, even Milton's sort of vocation came to look a bit old-fashioned. All inspirations and enthusiasms were suspect. The poet himself in *Paradise Lost* (1667) seemed aware that it was late in the day for his sort of flight. In Book IX he invokes his

> ... Celestial Patroness, who deigns
> Her nightly visitation unimplor'd,
> And dictates to me slumbring, or inspires
> Easy my unpremeditated Verse:

He is sure of his mission, less so of the time:

> ... higher Argument
> Remains, sufficient of it self to raise
> That name, unless an age too late, or cold
> Climate, or Years damp my intended wing
> Deprest, and much they may, if all be mine
> Not Hers who brings it nightly to my Ear.

He had, as we shall see, come to share some of the prevalent concern for everyday practicalities, without surrendering the prophetic role. Like Hobbes, whose very different apocalypse had terrified the time, Milton lived on into a serene old age when he would be, as John Aubrey put it, 'cheerful even in his gout fits and sing'. Still believing in inspired inner witness, he sat quietly at home receiving the homage of men who came from far and wide to see the blind poet, the apologist who had bested the great Salmasius. Wryly he gave young Dryden permission to 'tag' his lines, to fit them to the new fashion of couplets prevailing in the smart world of professional letters. He had his own ideas about poetry.

All this is illuminated by Milton's response to the tragic events of 1649. Though at first the 'rebels' did not aim at the king, it came to that at last. The Royalists found the one martyr they needed, and proceeded to enshrine in *Eikon Basilike* the memory of his taste, grace and sanctity. Such an opposite and widely cherished image of what had been expunged could not go unanswered. Milton's crushing reply *Eikono-*

klastes sums up so much of the tension over *mores* we have been looking at that it compels attention.

Here, at first sight, the greatest Puritan poet displays the Prynne-like antipathies we might expect of one who (in *Of Reformation*, 1641) had flayed the luxury and waste of ceremonial episcopacy. He berates the vanity and theatricality of courtly taste: regrettably, Charles found Shakespeare a fit companion for his hours of imprisonment; shockingly, on the very scaffold he was so foolish as to pop a prayer from *Arcadia* into Juxon's hand. Milton was never contemptuous of Shakespeare – indeed his own poetry suggests that he was more at ease with him than many of the Cavalier *literati* and than Dryden himself. He called *Arcadia* a 'vain amatorious poem' finding it 'a book in that kind full of worth and wit, but among religious thoughts and duties not worthy to be named, nor to be read at any time without good caution'. Events between Greville's time and his had deepened suspicion but not to the point of outright rejection. Milton's concern was, like Anne Bradstreet's, that *Arcadia* might 'infatuate fools'. In the king's case it confirmed dilettantism. What appalled was Charles's lack of proper seriousness: 'It can hardly be thought upon without some laughter that he who had acted over us so stately and so tragically should leave the world at last with such a ridiculous exit...' The frontispiece to *Eikon Basilike* spoke volumes: William Marshall's engraving of the martyr king is a 'conceited portraiture... drawn out to the full measure of a masking scene, and set there to catch fools and silly gazers'. These 'quaint emblems and devices, begged from the old pageantry of some Twelfth-Night's Entertainment at Whitehall will do but little to make a saint or martyr'.

This 'idolised Book, and the whole rosary of his Prayers', the final gesture of a King and his 'deifying friends', expressed everything the Puritans objected to as fictitious and fabricated. Marvell's *Horatian Ode* admiringly draws out the 'memorable scene': the 'armed Bands' surround the 'Tragic Scaffold' clapping their 'bloody hands' at the exquisite, self-possessed performance of 'the Royal Actor'. It is a subtle, ironic reply to those Cavalier allegations about acting murders in earnest to imply that the King's addiction to artifice and gesture has brought him here. More solidly real, to the poet, is the sight of Cromwell's 'acting', inspired not by a fiction but real knowledge – he has the capacity 'to act and know'. This man, reserved, austere, reluctantly emerged from his rural retreat to answer his true calling, which was to labour with 'industrious valour' and 'wiser Art' than the Stuarts had for the living God. To his natural 'Arts' without which a nation, 'A *Pow'r*', cannot subsist, Marvell knows his own art must be answerable. It is a realistic and mature comment on the relationship between life and letters. One is reminded of Milton's recognition in 1640 that his own literary ambitions must wait upon the completion of more pressing practical tasks. That too was no denial of art but a recognition of priorities, of a man's responsibility to the whole of life.

The writer must convey to us 'things useful to be known'. This Baconian conviction, noted in Milton's *Commonplace Book*, lies behind the constant emphasis of Puritan letters on solid knowledge and plain expression. It was, we see from the eloquence and wit of *An Horatian Ode*, the reverse of crudifying. Milton in Book IV of *Paradise Regained* makes the crucial distinctions between the Ancients' purely carnal wisdom (amounting to 'dreams', 'fancies', 'fabling', 'smooth conceits') and the 'plain sense' of Christian revelation. Manifestly he did not despise the Ancients but poetry must put Christianity first and last. Truth is not, it teaches us, a matter of fine style, of 'swelling Epithets' merely: it belongs to 'songs' expressing 'moral virtue', and 'The solid rules of Civil Government' in 'majestic unaffected style'.

In them is plainest taught, and easiest learnt
What makes a Nation happy, and keeps it so.

Eikonoklastes' tart remarks about 'a masking scene' must however take us back to the 1630s. Surely Milton had not forgotten his own masque, *Comus*, that 'high ritual in Arcadia, with Plato and Spenser as priests and all mythology in attendance' as his biographer W.R. Parker describes it? Milton did not openly acknowledge *Comus* when it was published in 1637, and it may have met his father's disapproval. Possibly it was written partly in protest against *Histriomastix*: Milton was still young and destined for a Church career; and, as the early projections of *Paradise Lost* in dramatic form and *Samson Agonistes* prove, he never rejected drama. In the *Reason of Church Government*, in fact, he argued against purists that the State should sponsor the theatre. *Samson* was the sort of play he had in mind. Carefully he states that it is a tragic poem meant only for reading, which would have pleased Prynne; but he is prepared to challenge comparison with classical and modern Italian plays. It is ironic that this unmistakably Puritan piece (if it does not predict a nation's Sabbath, it proposes an ideal of personal integrity and witness that distinguishes God's people) seems now a more illuminating, serious drama, profounder in its political realism and psychological insights than anything Dryden was able to write for his fashionable live audience.

But *Comus* too was no ordinary composition; this Masque was written for the provincial aristocratic household of the Earl of Bridgewater at Ludlow, where spectacle was impossible. The Earl's family were devout and of a Calvinist inclination. So Milton wrote something very different from Carew's *Coelum Britannicum* in which the two Egerton boys had actually appeared at Court. That was no place to commend virginity in; but Ludlow was different, and *Comus* celebrates the virtue of chastity. It is a drama of the will, teaching the distinction between aestheticism and morality, but delightfully, as 'sage and serious' Spenser would have wished.

The villain, Comus, embodies the grossest enchantments of sensuality – for Milton was not one to follow Perkins's inclination to bury such things. Comus's eloquence is 'glosing courtesy' like Satan's in *Paradise Lost*: his words flow, to borrow a phrase from the *Reason of Church*

279

Government, 'at waste from the pen of some vulgar amorist or the trencher fury of a rhyming parasite'. True poetry, in this masque, is spoken by others. There is no essential contradiction between *Comus* and *Eikonoklastes*. Even the reproach that Charles had written of his wife 'in strains that come almost to sonneting' does not prove a desire to emasculate poetry. Far from suppressing the sensual and sentimental element in sexual relationships, English Puritanism exposed it to the full force of its habit of scrupulous analysis. The practical insight, refinement of feeling, and sophisticated psychology that was achieved is shown by Daniel Rogers's *Matrimonial Honour* (1642). The conviction that marriage should be a mutual joy, a sharing of physical and spiritual experience, goes back to Perkins. It was a positive ideal of family life as the ground on which worldly and religious duties met.

Hence the objections to the amorous effusions of 'libidinous and ignorant Poetasters'. An ethic which deeply respected women and the family could hardly applaud the erotic fantasies or the idealisation of extra-marital love in the writings of a Suckling or a Waller. Though some have been tempted to talk of the life-affirming hedonism of Cavaliers faced with Puritan prudery, the facts are against them. The Platonism cultivated at Court too easily declined into a mere gallantry in which a contempt for women was (as so commonly happens) disguised by an extreme outward courtesy towards them. Cavalier romanticism came, irresponsibly, to think of affection chiefly in the narrow context of wooing or seducing. It trickled down into the frivolous cynicism with which too much Restoration Comedy and hordes of blades treated marriage; until it was finally degraded in the condescending well-bred brutality (against which another great humanist, Pope, protested) of things like Halifax's *Advice to a Daughter*, which flippantly asserts that husbands and infidelities are mere *bagatelles*. The actuality of the domestic tenderness of Milton, of Colonel Hutchinson, of Richard Baxter, of Bunyan or of Cromwell puts all that to shame.

Jonson had found that the ideals of domesticity and hospitality which he celebrated in *To Penshurst* prevailed little at the centre. In Puritan literature they were reasserted; and their greatest monument is not in the works of the sons of Ben but in *Paradise Lost*. The picture of Adam and Eve's relationship breathes the spirit of Puritan marriage: here is the shared work of 'joint hands', the hospitality, the unaffected domesticity of household tasks, the family prayer at morning and evening; here too, in the frank eroticism of some of the descriptions of the naked Eve, is the ready recognition of physical joy as part of a spiritual and intellectual sharing. The hymn 'Hail wedded love' in Book IV of the epic is wholly Puritan and wholly of Renaissance humanism too. One is forced to admit that beside this the charming Cavalier love lyrics of a Richard Lovelace are as a tinkling cymbal.

Milton was not the only Puritan poet who could acknowledge sexuality. Anne Bradstreet's humble muse voices a tender desire for her absent husband in 'As loving hind that (Hartless) wants her Deer'.

Of course Puritanism did not monopolise this sort of experience; but in those successful Puritan marriages and in the literary evidence is warrant for describing the ideal in life and letters as, characteristically, an achievement of seventeenth-century Puritanism.

It marks a recovery of Spenser's vision of human love and perfectibility. Here again, however, some change is apparent: we find it in turning from his elusive allegory to the more exact definitions of *Paradise Lost*. Milton's epic has clarity and toughness, distinctness of purpose and execution. He had lived to see the dawning millennium fade; and Adam and Eve's marriage is tested by mutual betrayal. Their love-making after the Fall is degraded to a barbarous mutual rape: it is a wholly unceremonious, unlovely lust. The shattered ideal is not however the end of things: the great epic which ranges freely through all the perspectives of time and space closes on the image of a man and woman, thrust from Paradise, going forward hand in hand to work out their salvation in the world together.

This proposes (dare one say it?) a more homely, practical image than high seriousness could have achieved before the Revolution. The grand struggles of good and evil, God and Satan, finally concern Milton at that point where they touch a human couple. So, too, Christ, at the very end of *Paradise Regained* (1671) 'Sung Victor', returns quietly 'unobserv'd' home to his Mother's house. It is a simple, deeply moving action. Poetry here achieves that modest, passionate, unostentatious expression that was a goal of Renaissance critical theory.

The note recurs in Marvell's fine observations of Cromwell's qualities– 'That port which so Majestic was and strong', that 'piercing sweetness' in the gaze, and 'the wondrous softness of his Heart'. This man embodies Milton's literary ideal of a 'majestic, unaffected style'. At one time the Protector looked like the promised leader – 'If these be the Times then this must be the Man' was Marvell's typically circumspect reaction. But he was never idolised by these poets. Marvell's *A Poem upon the Death of O.C.* (1658) describes the corpse:

I saw him dead, a leaden slumber lies,
And mortal sleep over those wakeful eyes:
All wither'd, all discolour'd, pale and wan,
How much another thing, no more that man?

He launches into a significantly Spenserian lament:

Oh human glory vain, Oh death, oh wings,
Oh worthless world of transitory things!

But that is not the end of it:

Yet dwelt that greatness in his shape decay'd
That still though dead, greater than death he lay'd:
And in his alter'd face you something feign,

That threatens death, he yet will live again.

It is the portrait of mortal, redeemed man: eloquent, admiring, affectionate, it has no false glamour, no sentimental idolatry. This, to adopt a phrase of Milton's, is neither fustian nor flattery.

The man of God at the centre, who had his portrait painted 'warts and all', and the able scrupulous men who rallied to his service had displaced the false allurements of dilettantism and extravagance.

V

Far from leaving a wasteland as Restoration propaganda alleged, the Interregnum left behind it achievements too numerous to describe in painting, engraving, miniatures, architecture, music, biography and autobiography, journalism, devotional literature, education, science, and all the Baconian useful arts – for Bacon, whose influence before 1640 was negligible, became a major inspiration of the period. The Protector was not a patron in Charles's way; but he employed able lieutenants, had an eye for men of progressive views, and attracted talented writers to his government. John Hall of Durham, Marchamont Nedham, George Wither, Pepys, Dryden, Marvell, Milton – it is a formidable civil service. Cromwell's was a more enlightened, tolerant, intellectually adventurous and less monolithic regime than may popularly be imagined. It genuinely endeavoured, in its political and intellectual concerns, the recovery of England's European and overseas role, to restore, in fact, what it regarded as the best features of the Elizabethan settlement: in their different ways Milton's writing and Cromwell's policies were both shaped to that end.

Their dreams were frustrated. The Protectorate foundered when the essential divisiveness of sectarianism was exposed by Cromwell's death. Sadly it bequeathed no lasting civil or ecclesiastical institutions permanently embodying its ideals. Yet the Puritanism which for a while triumphed had (though not single-handed and not always wittingly) affected a great shift in the national temper. The Court, last of the great Renaissance princedoms against which root and branch had reared itself in 1640, went for ever; and that can be a matter for regret on aesthetic grounds only if we think of art as a commodity, something glamorous to be bought and sold, not as an expression of the condition of a whole society. The world that emerged from the long crisis was remarkably changed. The Merry Monarch, versed in the arts of survival, was not tempted to indulge his father's magnificent presumptions or his lavish patronage: equally he looked for no pious martyrdom; no apocalyptic gleam lit his eye. His new Court was neither the eldorado many an old Cavalier deliriously greeted in 1660, nor the promised land the godly generation had once envisaged.

The King, mindful of his past and of Parliament at his elbow, was ready to smile on worldly, circumspect, businesslike, urbane men and women of all persuasions, and of none. Significantly in 1663 a war-weary generation, and the young bucks to whom ancient dogmatism and high-flying rhetoric were anathema, acclaimed Samuel Butler's burlesque poem *Hudibras*. Pouring cold water on all those holy enthusiasms that had heated the nation to a blaze, Butler brilliantly caught the mood of the new era. In these years, with all their faults, a sort of middle ground was recovered, where men of wit and common sense, fearful of extremes, might meet.

Dryden's cool indictment of Rebellion as antipathetic to art with which this essay began, expressed, like his unruffled replies to Jeremy Collier's attacks on the stage, something of that new and necessary temper. Yet from our safer distance we may venture against it a very different speculation. Perhaps the Millenarian era in some ways fostered a climate sympathetic to poetry. Its conviction of the inter-penetration of present and eternal, visible and invisible, helped sustain the role of the imagination: the promptings of the Holy Ghost joined with Platonic ideals of poetic insight. It was at best a spiritualising, invigorating force. One is certainly aware that, in the cooler rational-istic air of the post-Restoration period, poetry was frequently hard put to it to justify its essential reliance on intuitive powers, on the 'gift' of genius which, as Dryden argued, was born not made. Be that as it may, in the Interregnum and its aftermath English life and letters (and the Cavaliers too were braced by the impact of Revolution) recovered some sense of shared purposes and commitment to centrally important problems that a self-indulgent patronage had vitiated. Assuredly, the Civil War was not fought over poems, plays, romances, masques and ballads, any more than it was just about economics; but in the concern with these things a sense of a deep and complicated crisis was expressed.

To portray the 'Great Rebellion' as an assault by a counter-culture is, as we see, too simple. Yet in one respect Dryden's remark was right: art and politics, literature and history do not exist in separate compart-ments of the mind. The Civil War was about the whole condition of a society threatened by a failure of the ruling caste both to uphold traditional national aims and values, and to adapt itself to a rapidly changing world.

22 F.R. LEAVIS

Milton's Verse

[This article, together with the one following, forms an important part of a wide debate among literary critics about Milton's poetry. The 'Milton Controversy', as it is often called, began in the 1930s with the publication of F.R. Leavis's essay, and one by T.S. Eliot in which he enlarged on some of his earlier comments on Milton's poetry. Eliot allowed that Milton was a 'very great poet indeed', but admitted that he found Milton, the man, antipathetic, and argued that Milton's poetry was characterized by a dominance of sound, and a rhetorical style the influence of which on later English poetry had been wholly damaging. A defence of Milton in the face of these criticisms was offered by C.S. Lewis, but his *Preface to Paradise Lost* (1942) concentrated mainly on explaining the literary form of epic poems, and failed to meet Leavis and Eliot on the crucial question of the quality of Milton's verse; indeed Lewis considered Dr Leavis to have described the properties of Miltonic verse 'very accurately'.

There were other contributions to the debate, but in 1947 Eliot published a second lecture on Milton in which he withdrew his earlier remarks on the pernicious influence of Milton's poetic style, recognizing that, even if true, this was no just ground for censuring Milton. He went on, however, to praise Milton's poetry in terms such as the following: 'The emphasis is on the sound, not the vision, upon the word, not the idea; and in the end it is the unique versification that is the most certain sign of Milton's intellectual mastership'. This drew from Dr Leavis another essay on 'Mr Eliot and Milton', in which he took issue with Eliot's apparent praise of Milton and reiterated his own earlier criticisms. Response to the 'sound' of the Miltonic music as Eliot had described it appeared to Leavis to involve 'a relaxation of attentiveness to sense', while 'our sense of words as words, things for the mouth and ear, is not transcended in any vision – or (to avoid the visualist fallacy) any *realization* they convey'.

It was in an attempt specifically to refute these detractions of Milton's poetic achievement in *Paradise Lost* that Professor Ricks published *Milton's Grand Style*, and our extracts here represent part of his argument. Although controversy over Milton and his poetry has

From F.R. Leavis, *Revaluation: Tradition and Development in English Poetry* (Chatto and Windus, 1936), pp. 42–64. Footnotes have been deleted, and Note 2 has been omitted. This essay was first published in *Scrutiny*, 1933.

since moved in other directions, most admirers of Milton would agree that the modern debate sparked off by Eliot and Leavis, and represented by the articles reprinted here, has been entirely beneficial to the criticism of Milton's poetry.]

Milton's dislodgement, in the past decade, after his two centuries of predominance, was effected with remarkably little fuss. The irresistible argument was, of course, Mr Eliot's creative achievement; it gave his few critical asides – potent, it is true, by context – their finality, and made it unnecessary to elaborate a case. Mr Middleton Murry also, it should be remembered, came out against Milton at much the same time. His *Problem of Style* contains an acute page or two comparing Milton with Shakespeare, and there was a review of Bridges' *Milton's Prosody* in *The Athenaeum* that one would like to see reprinted along with a good deal more of Mr Murry's weekly journalism of that time. But the case remained unelaborated, and now that Mr Eliot has become academically respectable those who refer to it show commonly that they cannot understand it. And when a writer of Mr Allen Tate's repute as critic, poet, and intellectual leader, telling us that Milton should be 'made' to 'influence poetry once more,' shows that he too doesn't understand, then one may overcome, perhaps, one's shyness of saying the obvious.

Mr Tate thinks that if we don't like Milton it is because of a prejudice against myth and fable and a preference for the fragmentary: 'When we read poetry we bring to it the pseudo-scientific habit of mind; we are used to joining things up in vague disconnected processes in terms that are abstract and thin, and so our sensuous enjoyment is confined to the immediate field of sensation. We are bewildered, helpless, confronted with one of those immensely remote, highly sensuous, and perfectly make-believe worlds that rise above our scattered notions of process.'

Not every one will find this impressive. If we are affected by the pseudo-scientific habit of mind to that degree, some would suggest, we probably cannot read poetry at all. But if we can and do read poetry, then our objection to Milton it must be insisted, is that we dislike his verse and believe that in such verse no 'highly sensuous and perfectly make-believe world' could be evoked. Even in the first two books of *Paradise Lost*, where the myth has vigorous life and one can admire the magnificent invention that Milton's verse is, we feel, after a few hundred lines, our sense of dissatisfaction growing into something stronger. In the end we find ourselves protesting – protesting against the routine gesture, the heavy fall, of the verse, flinching from the foreseen thud that comes so inevitably, and, at last, irresistibly: for reading *Paradise Lost* is a matter of resisting, of standing up against, the verse-movement, of subduing it into something tolerably like sensitiveness, and in the end our resistance is worn down; we surrender at last to the inescapable monotony of the ritual. Monotony: the variety attributed to Milton's Grand Style in the orthodox account can be discoursed on and illustrated at great length, but the stress could be left on 'variety', after an honest interrogation of experience, only by the classically trained.

Here, if this were a lecture, would come illustrative reading-out – say of the famous opening to Book III. As it is, the point seems best enforcible (though it should be obvious at once to any one capable of being convinced at all) by turning to one of the exceptionally good passages – for every one will agree at any rate that there are places where the verse glows with an unusual life. One of these, it will again be agreed, is the Mulciber passage at the end of Book I:

> The hasty multitude
> Admiring enter'd, and the work some praise
> And some the Architect: his hand was known
> In Heav'n by many a Towred structure high,
> Where Scepter'd Angels held thir residence,
> And sat as Princes, whom the supreme King
> Exalted to such power, and gave to rule,
> Each in his Hierarchie, the Orders bright.
> Nor was his name unheard or unador'd
> In ancient Greece; and in Ausonian land
> Men called him Mulciber; and how he fell
> From Heav'n, they fabl'd, thrown by angry Jove
> Sheer o're the Chrystal Battlements: from Morn
> To Noon he fell, from Noon to dewy Eve,
> A Summers day; and with the setting Sun
> Dropt from the Zenith like a falling Star,
> On Lemnos th' Aegaean Ile: thus they relate,
> Erring . . .

The opening exhibits the usual heavy rhythmic pattern, the hieratic stylization, the swaying ritual movement back and forth, the steep cadences. Italics will serve to suggest how, when the reader's resistance has weakened, he is brought inevitably down with the foreseen thud in the foreseen place:

> The hasty multitude
> Ad*mir*ing enter'd, and the wórk some praise
> And *some* the Architect: his hánd was known
> In Héav'n by many a Tówred structure high,
> Where Scépter'd Angels held thir résidence,
> And *sat* as Princes . . .

But from 'Nor was his name unheard' onwards the effect changes. One no longer feels oneself carried along, resigned or protesting, by an automatic ritual, responding automatically with bodily gestures – swayed head and lifted shoulders – to the commanding emphasis: the verse seems suddenly to have come to life. Yet the pattern remains the same; there are the same heavy stresses, the same rhythmic gestures, and the same cadences, and if one thought a graph of the verse-movement worth drawing it would not show the difference. The change of feeling cannot at first be related to any point of form; it comes in with 'ancient Greece' and 'Ausonian land', and seems to be immediately due to the evocation of that serene, clear, ideally remote classical world so potent upon Milton's sensibility. [See Note 1.] But what is most important to note is that the heavy stresses, the characteristic cadences, turns, and returns of the verse, have here a peculiar expressive felicity. What would elsewhere have been the routine thump of 'Sheer' and 'Dropt' is here, in either case, obviously functional, and the other rhythmic features of the verse are correspondingly appropriate. The stress given by the end-position to the first 'fell', with the accompanying pause, in what looks like a common, limply pompous Miltonicism –

> and how he fell
> From Heav'n, they fabl'd, thrown . . .

– is here uncommonly right; the heavy 'thrown' is right, and so are the following rise and fall, the slopes and curves, of the verse.

There is no need to particularize further. This much room has been given to the fairly obvious merely by way of insisting that the usual pattern of Milton's verse has here an unusual expressive function – becomes, indeed, something else. If anyone should question the unusualness, the doubt would be soon settled by a little exploration. And to admit the unusualness is to admit that commonly the pattern, the stylized gesture, and movement, has no particular expressive work to do, but functions by rote, of its own momentum, in the manner of a ritual.

Milton has difficult places to cross, runs the orthodox eulogy, but his style always carries him through. The sense that Milton's style is of that kind, the dissatisfied sense of a certain hollowness, would by most readers who share it be first of all referred to a characteristic not yet specified – that which evoked from Mr Eliot the damaging word 'magniloquence'. To say that Milton's verse is magniloquent is to say that it is not doing as much as its impressive pomp and volume seem to be asserting; that mere orotundity is a disproportionate part of the whole effect; and that it demands more deference than it merits. It is to call attention to a lack of something in the stuff of the verse, to a certain sensuous poverty.

This poverty is best established by contrast, and tactical considerations suggest taking the example from Milton himself:

> Wherefore did Nature powre her bounties forth,
> With such a full and unwithdrawing hand,
> Covering the earth with odours, fruits, and flocks,
> Thronging the Seas with spawn innumerable,

287

But all to please, and sate the curious taste?
And set to work millions of spinning Worms,
That in their green shops weave the smooth-hair'd silk
To deck her Sons, and that no corner might
Be vacant of her plenty, in her own loyns
She hutch't th' all-worshipt ore, and precious gems
To store her children with; if all the world
Should in a pet of temperance feed on Pulse,
Drink the clear stream, and nothing wear but Frieze
Th' all-giver would be unthank't, would be unprais'd,
Not half his riches known, and yet despis'd,
And we should serve him as a grudging master,
As a Penurious niggard of his wealth,
And live like Natures bastards, not her sons,
Who would be quite surcharged with her own weight,
And strangl'd with her waste fertility:
Th' earth cumber'd, and the wing'd air dark't with plumes,
The herds would over-multitude their Lords,
The Sea o'refraught would swell, and th' unsought diamonds
Would so emblaze the forhead of the Deep,
And so bestudd with Stars, that they below
Would grow inur'd to light, and com at last
To gaze upon the Sun with shameless brows.

This is very unlike anything in *Paradise Lost* (indeed, it is not very like most of *Comus*). If one could forget where one had read it, and were faced with assigning it to its author, one would not soon fix with conviction on any dramatist. And yet it is too like dramatic verse to suggest Milton. It shows, in fact, the momentary predominance in Milton of Shakespeare. It may look less mature, less developed, than the verse of *Paradise Lost*; it is, as a matter of fact, richer, subtler, and more sensitive than anything in *Paradise Lost*, *Paradise Regained*, or *Samson Agonistes*.

Its comparative sensuous richness, which is pervasive, lends itself fairly readily to analysis at various points; for instance:

And set to work millions of spinning Worms,
That in their green shops weave the smooth-hair'd silk . . .

The Shakesperian life of this is to be explained largely by the swift diversity of associations that are run together. The impression of the swarming worms is telescoped with that of the ordered industry of the workshop, and a further vividness results from the contrasting 'green', with its suggestion of leafy tranquillity. 'Smooth-hair'd' plays off against the energy of the verse the tactual luxury of stroking human hair or the living coat of an animal. The texture of actual sounds, the run of vowels and consonants, with the variety of action and effort, rich in subtle analogical suggestion, demanded in pronouncing them, plays an essential part, though this is not to be analysed in abstraction from the meaning. The total effect is as if words as words withdrew themselves from the focus of our attention and we were directly aware of a tissue of feelings and perceptions.

No such effect is possible in the verse of *Paradise Lost*, where the use of the medium, the poet's relation to his words, is completely different. This, for instance, is from the description, in Book IV, of the Garden of Eden, which, most admirers of Milton will agree, exemplifies sensuous richness if that is to be found in *Paradise Lost*:

> And now divided into four main Streams,
> Runs divers, wandering many a famous Realme
> And Country whereof here needs no account,
> But rather to tell how, if Art could tell,
> How from that Sapphire Fount the crisped Brooks,
> Rowling on Orient Pearl and sands of Gold,
> With mazie error under pendant shades
> Ran Nectar, visiting each plant, and fed
> Flours worthy of Paradise which not nice Art
> In Beds and curious Knots, but Nature boon
> Powrd forth profuse on Hill and Dale and Plaine,
> Both where the morning Sun first warmly smote
> The open field, and where the unpierc't shade
> Imbround the noontide Bowrs: Thus was this place,
> A happy rural seat of various view:
> Groves whose rich Trees wept odorous Gumms and Balme,
> Others whose fruit burnisht with Golden Rinde
> Hung amiable, Hesperian Fables true,
> If true, here onely, and of delicious taste ...

It should be plain at once that the difference was not exaggerated. As the laboured, pedantic artifice of the diction suggests, Milton seems here to be focusing rather upon words than upon perceptions, sensations, or things. 'Sapphire', 'Orient Pearl', 'sands of Gold', 'odorous Gumms and Balme', and so on, convey no doubt a vague sense of opulence, but this is not what we mean by 'sensuous richness'. The loose judgement that it is a verbal opulence has a plain enough meaning if we look for contrast at the 'bestudd with Stars' of Comus's speech; there we feel (the alliteration is of a different kind from that of the Grand Style) the solid lumps of light studding the 'forhead of the Deep'. In the description of Eden, a little before the passage quoted, we have:

> And all amid them stood the Tree of Life,
> High eminent, blooming Ambrosial Fruit
> Of vegetable Gold ...

It would be of no use to try and argue with anyone who contended that 'vegetable Gold' exemplified the same kind of fusion as 'green shops'.

It needs no unusual sensitiveness of language to perceive that, in this Grand Style, the medium calls pervasively for a kind of attention, compels an attitude towards itself, that is incompatible with sharp, concrete realization; just as it would seem to be, in the mind of the poet, incompatible with an interest in sensuous particularity. He exhibits a feeling *for* words rather than a capacity for feeling *through* words; we are often, in reading him, moved to comment that he is 'external' or that he 'works from the outside'. The Grand Style, at its best, compels us to recognize it as an impressive stylization, but it functions very readily, and even impressively, at low tension, and its tendency is betrayed, even in a show piece like the description of Eden, by such offences as:

> Thus was this place,
> A happy rural seat of various view:
> Groves whose rich Trees wept odorous Gumms and Balme,
> Others whose fruit burnisht with Golden Rinde
> Hung amiable, Hesperian Fables true,
> If true, here onely, and of delicious taste . . .

– If the Eighteenth Century thought that poetry was something that could be applied from the outside, it found the precedent as well as the apparatus in Milton.

The extreme and consistent remoteness of Milton's medium from any English that was ever spoken is an immediately relevant consideration. It became, of course, habitual to him; but habituation could not sensitize a medium so cut off from speech – speech that belongs to the emotional and sensory texture of actual living and is in resonance with the nervous system; it could only confirm an impoverishment of sensibility. In any case, the Grand Style barred Milton from essential expressive resources of English that he had once commanded. Comus, in the passage quoted, imagining the consequences of the Lady's doctrine, says that Nature

> . would be quite surcharged with her own weight,
> And strangl'd with her waste fertility;
> Th' earth cumber'd, and the wing'd air dark't with plumes,
> The herds would over-multitude their Lords,
> The Sea o'refraught would swell . . .

To cut the passage short here is to lame it, for the effect of Nature's being strangled with her waste fertility is partly conveyed by the ejaculatory piling-up of clauses, as the reader, by turning back, can verify. But one way in which the verse acts the meaning – not merely says but does – is fairly represented in the line,

> Th'earth cumber'd, and the wing'd air dark't with plumes

where the crowding of stressed words, the consonantal clusters, and the clogged movement have a function that needs no analysis. This kind of action in the verse, together with the attendant effects of movement and intonation in the whole passage, would be quite impossible in the Grand Style: the tyrannical stylization forbids. But then, the mind that invented Milton's Grand Style had renounced the English language, and with that, inevitably, Milton being an Englishman, a great deal else.

'Milton wrote Latin as readily as he did English.' And: 'Critics sometimes forget that before the *Nativity Ode* Milton wrote more Latin than English, and one may suggest that the best of the Latin is at least as good as the best of the English.' At any rate, one can believe that, after a decade of Latin polemic, Latin idiom came very naturally to him, and was associated with some of his strongest, if not necessarily most interesting, habits of feeling. But however admirable his Latin may be judged to be, to latinize in English is quite another matter, and it is a testimony to the effect of the 'fortifying curriculum' that the price of Milton's latinizing should have been so little recognized.

'This charm of the exceptional and the irregular in diction,' writes Mr Logan Pearsall Smith in his extremely valuable essay on English idioms (*Words and Idioms*, p.267), 'accounts for the fact that we can enjoy the use of idiom even in a dead language which we do not know very well; it also explains the subtlety of effect which Milton achieved by transfusing Greek or Latin constructions into his English verse'. But Milton's transfusing is regular and unremitting, and involves, not pleasant occasional surprises, but a consistent rejection of English idiom, as the passage quoted from Book IV sufficiently shows. So complete, and so mechanically habitual, is Milton's departure from the English order, structure, and accentuation that he often produces passages that have to be read through several times before one can see how they go, though the Miltonic mind has nothing to offer that could justify obscurity – no obscurity was intended: it is merely that Milton has forgotten the English language. There is, however, a much more important point to be made: it is that, cultivating so complete and systematic a callousness to the intrinsic nature of English, Milton forfeits all possibility of subtle or delicate life in his verse.

It should be plain, for instance, that subtlety of movement in English verse depends upon the play of the natural sense movement and intonation against the verse structure, and that 'natural' here, involves a reference, more or less direct, to idiomatic speech. The development in Shakespeare can be studied as a more and more complex and subtle play of speech movement and intonation against the verse. There is growing complexity of imagery and thought too, of course, but it is not to this mainly that one could refer in analysing the difference between a characteristic passage of *Othello* and Romeo's dying lament: the difference is very largely a matter of subtle tensions within, pressures upon, the still smooth curves of the still 'regular' verse of *Othello*. No such play is possible in a medium in which the life of idiom, the pressure of speech, is as completely absent as in Milton's Grand Style. That is why even in the most lively books of *Paradise Lost* the verse, brilliant as it is, has to the ear that appreciates Shakespeare a wearying deadness about it. That skill we are told of, the skill with which Milton varies the beat without losing touch with the underlying norm, slides the caesura backwards and forwards, and so on, is certainly there. But the kind of appreciation this skill demands is that which one gives – if one is a classic – to a piece of Latin (we find writers on Milton 'appreciating' his Latin verse in the same tone and spirit as they do his English).

'An appreciation of Milton is the last reward of consummated scholarship.' Qualified as Mark Pattison prescribes, one may, with Raleigh, find that Milton's style is 'all substance and weight', that he is almost too packed to be read aloud, and go on to acclaim the 'top of his skill' in the choruses of *Samson Agonistes*. But the ear trained on Shakespeare will believe that it would lose little at the first hearing of a moderately well-declaimed passage, and that *Samson Agonistes* read aloud would be hardly tolerable, because of its desolating exposure of utter loss – loss in the poet of all feeling for his native English. The rhythmic deadness, the mechanical externality with which the movement is varied, is the more pitifully evident because of the personal urgency of the theme and the austerity: there is no magniloquence here. To arrive here, of course, took genius, and the consummation can be analytically admired. But then, there have been critics who found rhythmic subtlety in *Phoebus with Admetus* and *Love in the Valley*.

Up to this point the stress has fallen upon Milton's latinizing. To leave it there would be to suggest an inadequate view of his significance. His influence is seen in Tennyson as well as in Thomson, and to say that he groups with Tennyson and Spenser in contrast to Shakespeare and Donne is to say something more important about him than that he latinized. The force of associating him with Spenser is not that he was himself 'sage and serious'; and in contrasting him with Donne one is not, as seems also commonly to be thought, lamenting that he chose not to become a Metaphysical. The qualities of Donne that invite the opposition are what is shown in this:

> On a huge hill,
> Cragged and steep, Truth stands, and hee that will
> Reach her, about must, and about must goe;
> And what the hills suddenness resists, winne so;
> Yet strive so, that before age, deaths twilight,
> Thy Soule rest, for none can worke in that night.

This is the Shakespearian use of English; one might say that it is the English use – the use, in the essential spirit of the language, of its characteristic resources. The words seem to do what they say; a very obvious example of what, in more or less subtle forms, is pervasive being given in the image of reaching that the reader has to enact when he passes from the second to the third line. But a comparison will save analysis:

For so to interpose a little ease,
Let our frail thoughts dally with false surmise.
Ay me! Whilst thee the shores, and sounding Seas
Wash far away, where ere thy bones are hurld,
Whether beyond the stormy Hebrides,
Where thou perhaps under the whelming tide
Visit'st the bottom of the monstrous world;
Or whether thou to our moist vows denied,
Sleep'st by the fable of Bellerus old,
Where the great vision of the guarded Mount
Looks toward Namancos and Bayona's hold . . .

The contrast is sharp; the use of the medium, the attitude towards it in both writer and reader, is as different as possible. Though the words are doing so much less work than in Donne, they seem to value themselves more highly – they seem, comparatively, to be occupied with valuing themselves rather than with doing anything. This last clause would have to be saved for Tennyson if it were a question of distinguishing fairly between Milton and him, but, faced with the passage from Donne, Milton and Tennyson go together. Tennyson descends from Spenser by way of Milton and Keats, and it was not for nothing that Milton, to the puzzlement of some critics, named Spenser as his 'original': the mention of Tennyson gives the statement (however intended) an obvious significance.

The consummate art of *Lycidas*, personal as it is, exhibits a use of language in the spirit of Spenser – incantatory, remote from speech. Certain feelings are expressed, but there is no pressure behind the words; what predominates in the handling of them is not the tension of something precise to be defined and fixed, but a concern for mellifluousness – for liquid sequences and a pleasing opening and closing of the vowels. This is the bent revealed in the early work; the Shakespearian passage in *Comus* is exceptional. Milton, that is, someone will observe of the comparison, is trying to do something quite other than Donne; his bent is quite different. Exactly: the point is to be clear which way it tends.

The most admired things in *Comus* – it is significant – are the songs.

Sweet Echo, sweetest Nymph that liv'st unseen
    Within thy airy shell
   By slow Meander's margent green,
  And in the violet imbroider'd vale
    Where the love-lorn Nightingale
Nightly to thee her sad Song mourneth well . . .

Quite plainly, the intention here is not merely to flatter the singing voice and suit the air, but to produce in words effects analogous to those of music, and the exquisite achievement has been sufficiently praised. The undertaking was congenial to Milton. Already he had

293

shown his capacity for a weightier kind of music, a more impressive and less delicate instrument:

> Blest pair of Sirens, pledges of Heav'ns joy,
> Sphear-born harmonious Sisters, Voice, and Vers,
> Wed your divine sounds, and mixt power employ
> Dead things with inbreath'd sense able to pierce,
> And . . .

We remember the Tennysonian felicity: 'God-gifted organ voice'. *At a Solemn Musick*, though coming from not long after 1630, anticipates unmistakably the 'melodious noise' of *Paradise Lost*, and suggests a further account of that sustained impressiveness, that booming swell which becomes so intolerable.

This, then, and not any incapacity to be interested in myth, is why we find Milton unexhilarating. The myth of *Paradise Lost*, indeed, suffers from deficiencies related to those of the verse. 'Milton's celestial and infernal regions are large but insufficiently furnished apartments filled by heavy conversation,' remarks Mr Eliot, and suggests that the divorce from Rome, following the earlier breach with the Teutonic past, may have something to do with this mythological thinness. But it is enough to point to the limitations in range and depth of Milton's interests, their patent inadequacy to inform a 'sense of myth, of fable, of ordered wholes in experience'. His strength is of the kind that we indicate when, distinguishing between intelligence and character, we lay the stress on the latter; it is a strength, that is, involving sad disabilities. He has 'character', moral grandeur, moral force; but he is, for the purposes of his undertaking, disastrously single-minded and simple-minded. He reveals everywhere a dominating sense of righteousness and a complete incapacity to question or explore its significance and conditions. This defect of intelligence is a defect of imagination. He offers as ultimate for our worship mere brute assertive will, though he condemns it unwittingly by his argument and by glimpses of his own finer human standard. His volume of moral passion owes its strength too much to innocence – a guileless unawareness of the subtleties of egotism – to be an apt agent for projecting an 'ordered whole of experience'. It involves, too, a great poverty of interest. After the first two books, magnificent in their simple force (party politics in the Grand Style Milton can compass), *Paradise Lost*, though there are intervals of relief, becomes dull and empty: 'all,' as Raleigh says, 'is power, vagueness, and grandeur'. Milton's inadequacy to myth, in fact, is so inescapable, and so much is conceded in sanctioned comment, that the routine eulogy of his 'architectonic' power is plainly a matter of mere inert convention.

But even if the realized effect were much less remote than it actually is from the abstract design, even if the life and interest were much better distributed, the orthodox praise of Milton's architectonics would still be questionable in its implications. It would still be most commonly found to harbour the incomprehensions betrayed by the critic cited in the opening of this chapter.

In his time (as in ours) there was a good deal to be said for the Spenserian school against the technical breakdown to which the Jacobean dramatists had ridden English verse. Webster is a great moment in English style, but the drama was falling off, and blank verse had to survive in a non-dramatic form, which required a more rigid treatment than the stage could offer it. In substance, it needed stiffer and less sensitive perceptions, a more artificial grasp of sensation, to offset the supersensitive awareness of the school of Shakespeare, a versification less imitative of the flow of sensation and more architectural. What poetry needed, Milton was able to give. It was Arnold who, in the 1853 preface to his own poems, remarked that the sensational imagery of the Shakespearian tradition had not been without its baleful effect on poetry down to Keats: one may imitate a passage in Shakespeare without penetrating to the mind that wrote it, but to imitate Milton one must be Milton; one must have all of Milton's resources in myth behind the impulse: it is the myth, ingrained in his very being, that makes the style.

If that is so, the style, as we have seen, condemns the myth. Behind the whole muddled passage, of course, and not far behind, is the old distinction (see, for instance, Raleigh) between the 'Classical style' and the 'Romantic' – the 'Romantic' including Shelley (and, one presumes, Swinburne) along with Shakespeare. It is enough here to say that the inability to read Shakespeare (or the remoteness from the reading of him) revealed in such a passage and such a distinction throws the most damaging suspicion upon the term 'architectural'. The critic clearly implies that because Shakespeare exhibits 'more sensitive perceptions', and offers a 'versification more imitative of the flow of sensation', he is therefore indifferent to total effect and dissipates the attention by focusing, and asking us to focus, on the immediate at the expense of the whole. As a matter of fact, any one of the great tragedies is an incomparably better whole than *Paradise Lost*; so finely and subtly organized that architectural analogies seem inappropriate (a good deal of *Paradise Lost* strikes one as being almost as mechanical as bricklaying). The analysis of a Shakespeare passage showing that 'supersensitive awareness' leads one into the essential structure of the whole organism: Shakespeare's marvellous faculty of intense local realization is a faculty of realizing the whole locally.

A Shakespeare play, says Professor Wilson Knight, may be considered as 'an extended metaphor', and the phrase suggests with great felicity this almost inconceivably close and delicate organic wholeness. The belief that 'architectural' qualities like Milton's represent a higher kind of unity goes with the kind of intellectual bent that produces Humanism – that takes satisfaction in inertly orthodox generalities, and is impressed by invocations of Order from minds that have no

295

glimmer of intelligence about contemporary literature and could not safely risk even elementary particular appreciation.

NOTE I. Proserpin Gath'ring Flow'rs

Another of the finest of those passages (it is rightly one of the most current pieces of Milton) in which life suddenly flows is that with which the description of the Garden of Eden closes (Bk IV, l. 268). To bring out the contrast with the stylized literary opulence of what goes before (see p. 289 above) quotation had better start a dozen lines earlier – I use the Grierson text:

> Another side, umbrageous Grots and Caves
> Of cool recess, o'er which the mantling Vine
> Lays forth her purple Grape, and gently creeps
> Luxuriant; meanwhile murmuring waters fall
> Down the slope, hills, disperst, or in a Lake,
> That to the fringed Bank with Myrtle crown'd,
> Her chrystal mirror holds, unite thir streams.
> The Birds thir quire apply; airs, vernal airs,
> Breathing the smell of field and grove, attune
> The trembling leaves, while Universal Pan
> Knit with the Graces and the Hours in dance
> Led on th' Eternal Spring. Not that fair field
> Of Enna, where Proserpin gath'ring flow'rs
> Herself a fairer Flow'r, by gloomy Dis
> Was gather'd, which cost Ceres all that pain
> To seek her through the world; not that sweet Grove
> Of Daphne by Orontes, and th' inspir'd
> Castalian Spring might with this Paradise
> Of Eden strive; nor that Nyseian Isle
> Girt with the River Triton, where old Cham,
> Whom Gentiles Ammon call and Lybian Jove,
> Hid Amalthea and her Florid Son
> Young Bacchus from his Stepdame Rhea's eye;
> Nor where Abassin Kings thir issue Guard,
> Mount Amara, though by this some suppos'd
> True Paradise under the Ethiop Line
> By Nilus head, enclos'd with shining Rock,
> A whole day's journey high, but wide remote
> From this Assyrian Garden . . .

The effect, when we come to the Proserpin passage, is like a change from artificial flowers and elaborated decoration to something alive with sap that flows from below.

> Not that fair field
> Of Enna, where Proserpin gath'ring flow'rs
> Herself a fairer Flow'r, by gloomy Dis

Was gather'd . . .

– that might, in its simple, inevitable rightness and its fresh bloom, have come from Shakespeare, the Shakespeare of the pastoral scene in *The Winter's Tale*. It is in the repeated verb that the realizing imagination is irresistibly manifested; it is the final 'gathered' that gives concrete life to a conventional phrase and makes Proserpin herself a flower. And to make her a flower is to establish the difference between the two gatherings: the design – the gathered gatherer – is subtle in its simplicity. The movement of the verse seems to be the life of the design, performing, in fact, in its suggestive appropriateness, something of the function of imagery. The phrasing – e.g.,

> which cost Ceres all that pain
> To seek her through the world

– has a direct and sensitive naturalness.

It is notable that inspiration here is of the same kind as in the Mulciber passage – 'the freshness of the early world', the 'wonder and bloom' of the legendary classical morning. In the lines that follow, about Abassin Kings and Mount Amara – lines so curiously echoed in *Kubla Khan* – the delighted romantic wonder is plain.

In contrast with this smuggled-in (for such it is with reference to the theme of *Paradise Lost*) piece of imaginative indulgence, the famous description of Adam and Eve –

> Two of far nobler shape, erect and tall,
> God-like erect

– that comes immediately after is, in its conscious and characteristic moral solemnity and poetic decorum, more distasteful than it might otherwise have been.

23 CHRISTOPHER RICKS

Milton's Grand Style

[. . .] To meet the anti-Miltonists' case as it should be met, it is best to take a passage where an objection by Mr Eliot was endorsed by Dr Leavis. In the council in Hell, Moloch advocates open war:

> My sentence is for open Warr: Of Wiles,
> More unexpert, I boast not: them let those
> Contrive who need, or when they need, not now.
> For while they sit contriving, shall the rest,
> Millions that stand in Arms, and longing wait
> The Signal to ascend, sit lingring here
> Heav'ns fugitives . . . (II. 51–57)

Mr Eliot murmured that 'it might, of course, be objected that "millions that *stand* in arms" could not at the same time "*sit* lingring" '. And Dr Leavis seized on this example to insist that 'there is no sharp challenge to a critical or realizing awareness – there is the relaxation of the demand for consistency characteristic of rhetoric'.

It is easy enough to guess two of the traditionalist defences that might be put forward. First, that stand in arms does not mean *stand* but merely *be* in arms – whereupon the use of stand in a Latinate way can be demonstrated elsewhere in the poem. The snag about so schoolmasterly a defence would be that, in clearing Milton of the charge of inconsistency, it immediately lays him open to a far worse one: that of being so insensitive to words that he uses *sit* in one line, *stand* in the next, and *sit* in the third, and apparently doesn't realize that the two *sit*'s will exert a pressure on the word 'stand', making us want to take it literally. The schoolmaster plays straight into Dr Leavis's hands.

So does another conceivable academic defence: that to complain about such an inconsistency is merely to niggle, that we are swept along by the grand majestic flow, the Miltonic music, the epic style. Exactly, would retort the anti-Miltonists, when you stop and look at it, it's muddled. Its effect depends on a confidence trick, on what Milton himself deplored as 'the plausibility of large and indefinite words'.

But is it possible to accept the demand for consistency and still defend Milton here? Of course. Mr Eliot's slip (and Dr Leavis's) is in objecting that 'millions that stand in arms could not *at the same time* sit lingring'. They could not, but Milton doesn't say they could. He has a future and a present tense:

From Christopher Ricks, *Milton's Grand Style* (Oxford University Press, 1963), pp. 10–21, 27–31, 75–77. Footnotes have been deleted.

> *shall* the rest,
> Millions that stand in Arms, and longing wait
> The Signal to ascend, sit lingring here . . .

There is no inconsistency here, there is a deliberate clash. Moloch begins (without any 'Ladies and Gentlemen', or the 'O Peers' of Belial) with a bluntly *open* and straightforward voice: 'My sentence is for open Warr'. We can see how fatal any suggestion of indirection would be here when Dryden, in *The State of Innocence*, rewrites the line as 'My sentence is for War; that open too'.

Moloch's syntax then becomes circuitous, not because Milton is trying to elevate his native tongue, or because he has a habit of Latinizing, but because the circuitousness is to ridicule the devious people who hold a different point of view from fiercely direct Moloch:

> Of Wiles,
> More unexpert, I boast not: them let those
> Contrive who need, or when they need, not now.

The openness of open war is clashed against the roundabout wiles of military planners; and the manipulation of ordinary syntax brings *Wiles* hard up against its alliterating monosyllable *Warr*, so that the manly fortitude of the one blasts the procrastination of the other. 'I boast not' is a boast; as who should say 'Of course I don't know anything about manoeuvres, I've only been in the front line for the last eighteen months'. It is just this traditional antagonism which Moloch plays on.

Planners need to *contrive*; and Moloch toys with the word again contemptuously, tossing in the equally contemptuous *sit*: 'For while they sit contriving, shall the rest . . .'. At which, he brilliantly numbers those that are of his way of thinking (and acting), and contrasts their military stance with the sitting-about of the non-numbered 'they':

> shall the rest,
> Millions that stand in Arms, and longing wait
> The Signal to ascend . . .

And at that dramatic point, the superb upward thrust of *sit*, *stand*, *ascend* is razed by the deliberate bathos of *sit* again:

> Millions that stand in Arms, and longing wait
> The Signal to ascend, sit lingring here . . .

The contrivers (the Belials) want to turn standers into sitters. And with fighting skill, Moloch answers the participle in 'sit contriving' with the same construction in 'sit lingring'. Men who stand will be made to sit. Men who long will be made to linger, as the echo from the previous line (longing/lingring) reminds us.

'Does this make sense?' asked Milton's judges, but did not stay for an answer. Yet without their question, it may be that we would not have noticed exactly what was being said. And when the crank Charles Eyre rewrote the lines in 1852, his version brought out just how powerful were the words he omitted – *contrive*, for one, but above all the placing of *stand* and *sit*:

> My sentence is for open war; of wiles
> More inexpert I boast not; them let those
> Invent who need – and when there's need – not now.
> For while they sit contriving, shall the rest,
> Millions in arms, who with impatience wait
> The signal to ascend, here lingering stand,
> Heaven's fugitives . . .

This particular example, though, can make two points. One, that the anti-Miltonists haven't always been careful enough. The other, that the eighteenth-century editors are still in many ways the best guide to Milton. In fact, the whole argument had been thrashed out two hundred years before Mr Eliot and Dr Leavis. Bentley in 1732 had growled: 'Observe the Inconsistence, *Stand* in Arms *sit* ling'ring. No doubt therefore he gave it, STAY *ling'ring here.*' Pearce in 1733 took refuge in the schoolmasterly: '*stand* does not always signify the posture . . . *stand in Arms*, signifies *are in Arms*'. And he was supported by Jonathan Richardson in 1734: '*Stand and Sit* are Metaphorical, and no Contradiction therefore; Stand, as being Prepar'd, and Sit, as Idly Lingering'. But what is surely the true meaning was seen in 1749 by Thomas Newton, who made his point with admirable brevity: '*Sit ling'ring* to answer *sit contriving* before. While they sit contriving, shall the rest sit ling'ring?'

The eighteenth-century arguments about Milton are in many ways a mirror of the modern one. Bentley, like the anti-Miltonists, had a great gift for getting hold of the right thing – by the wrong end. Again and again he sees exactly what is happening in a passage of Milton. He then deplores it, but we need not do so, and can be grateful for his insight. He may be wrong-headed, but at least he is headed.

He is particularly quick to spot the kind of clash which Milton is so fond of and which is not carelessness.

> Uplifted imminent one stroke they aim'd. (VI. 317)

'*Uplifted* and *Imminent* contradict each other: for *Uplifted* has a Motion upwards, and *Imminent* a tendence downwards.' Bentley is right about how the style works here, but wrong about its value, as Pearce insisted: '*Uplifted* is what has *had* a Motion upwards, but has that Motion no longer, when it is already *uplifted*: and *imminent* is what hovers and is ready to fall, but has not as yet in the least begun to do so. In these two Senses the two words may meet very lovingly together.' Yet, as Miss

Darbishire remarked, 'Such interrogations not only stamp Bentley's failure in poetic imagination, they also awaken us to a boldness, a violence, a tendency to paradox in Milton's imaginative phrasing which the splendour and sustained majesty of his style in *Paradise Lost* tend to mask'.

Similarly Bentley notices the contradictions in the presentation of the fallen angels, but fails to see how they are part of Milton's purpose. Moloch remembers

> With what compulsion and laborious flight
> We sunk thus low ... (II. 80–81)

'The Ideas of *Flight* and of *Sinking* do not agree well together.' Indeed they don't – that is just the point. Any more than the words *fallen* and *angel* agree well together. But it was for De Quincey to explain the principles involved:

> Each image, from reciprocal contradiction, brightens and vivifies the other. The two images act, and react, by strong repulsion and antagonism. ... Out of this one principle of subtle and lurking antagonism, may be explained everything which has been denounced under the idea of pedantry in Milton. ... For instance, this is the key to that image in the 'Paradise Regained', where Satan, on first emerging into sight, is compared to an old man gathering sticks, 'to warm him on a winter's day'. This image, at first sight, seems little in harmony with the wild and awful character of the supreme fiend. No; it is *not in* harmony, nor is it meant to be in harmony. On the contrary, it is meant to be in antagonism and intense repulsion. The household image of old age, of human infirmity, and of domestic hearths, are all meant as a machinery for provoking and soliciting the fearful idea to which they are placed in collision, and as so many repelling poles.

With his usual mistaken acuteness, Bentley brings out the superbly contemptuous pun when the devils shrink:

> Thus incorporeal Spirits to smallest forms
> Reduc'd thir shapes immense, and were at large ... (I. 789–90)

'By being *at large*, the Author means, *being not crouded*. ... But here it's shocking at first Reading: contracting their Shapes to the *smallest* Size, and yet being *at large*.' Certainly it's shocking, but it's meant to be. Nothing could more effectively belittle the devils.

Bentley seems to me to be helpful, too, when he objects to the leviathan 'slumbring on the Norway foam' (I. 203). 'We allow *Foam* to be sometimes put for Sea or *Water* by our best Poets. ... But here it comes unhappily; for it must be very solid Foam, that can support a sleeping Whale.' This to me brings out how unobtrusively important is the word *foam*. There *is* something sinister and mysterious, something of black magic, about Satan the leviathan. Once we notice the word *foam*, we see that the effect is very like that other moment of horror twenty lines later, when Satan is

> Aloft, incumbent on the dusky Air
> That felt unusual weight. (I. 226–7)

And it is not just the similarity of the idea that links the two passages together (and in so doing explains the poetic power of *foam*) – the phrases are linked too by their exactly parallel syntax. 'Slumbring on the Norway foam': 'Incumbent on the dusky Air.' Adjective . . . on the . . . adjective . . . noun (in each case, one of the elements). Perhaps even the echoing in *slumbring/incumbent* does something to tie the two phrases together. But in any case the parallelism of idea seems to me enough to yoke the phrases. In which case, it is not irresponsible to apply the words 'that felt unusual weight' not only to the air but also to the foam. Bentley in a way was right to remark that 'it must be very solid Foam, that can support a sleeping Whale'. But as is often the case with an anti-Miltonist, we can disagree with him and find the phrase moving and relevant in its sinister mystery.

There would be little point in trying to defend all the passages which the modern anti-Miltonists have attacked. When Mr Eliot faintly praised the leviathan simile, he was endorsed by Dr Leavis: 'Miltonic similes don't focus one's perception of the relevant, or sharpen definition in any way'. Likewise with the *sit/stand* inconsistency. It would be foolish to claim that all the disputed passages are of this fairly straightforward kind, a kind where it can plausibly be suggested that there has been a misreading. But it is as well to remember that there are such things as simple misreadings.

The charges against Milton, then, can be simply classified. First, there are misreadings. Second, there are convincing accounts either of general faults in the Miltonic style, or of particular moments when the poet's mind was not fully on what he was doing. Third, there are the large-scale accusations of imprecision and insensitivity.

But before I try to defend the style against these last accusations, I must first concede that it cannot always be defended. There are moments when the language seems to be manipulated more from habit than from inner necessity. There are aridities, such as the digestion of the angels (V. 433–43). There is the 'untransmuted lump of futurity' at the end: 'and what makes it worse is that the actual writing in this passage is curiously bad' (C.S. Lewis). Dr Broadbent says trenchantly that ' "*Egypt*, divided by the River *Nile*" is one of the worst lines of verse in English and demeans every previous reference in the poem to Pharaoh, the Nile, the Red Sea, Moses'.

But the occasions when the verse falters seem most often to be those that are also open to general complaint. 'He does even to a *Miracle* suit his *Speech* to his *Subject*' (1694) – so when the subject is hollow, the speech is too. The verse (honourably, in a way) fails to keep up the pretence that all is well.

Let me take one passage to illustrate an important (though infrequent) failing of the style, its insensitive overemphasis. Milton has recourse to such overemphasis when he is trapped by some difficulty or other. For example, the narrative inconsistencies into which he is forced are nowhere clearer than in the War in Heaven. Voltaire in 1727 protested at 'the visible Contradiction which reigns in that Episode', since God commands his troops to *drive them out*: 'How does it come to pass, after such a positive Order, that the Battle hangs doubtful? And why did God the Father command *Gabriel* and *Raphael*, to do what he executes afterwards by his Son only.' And Mr Peter has skilfully and wittily analysed this muddle.

In God's speech to the Messiah, the painful hesitation that comes over the verse is made the clearer by the magnificent lines which begin and end the speech – lines which are not uneasy because they depend not upon the story but upon an intuition. But the speech itself is most disappointing:

> two dayes are past,
> Two dayes, as we compute the dayes of Heav'n,
> Since Michael and his Powers went forth to tame
> These disobedient; sore hath been thir fight,
> As likeliest was, when two such Foes met arm'd;
> For to themselves I left them, and thou knowst,
> Equal in their Creation they were form'd,
> Save what sin hath impaird, which yet hath wrought
> Insensibly, for I suspend thir doom;
> Whence in perpetual fight they needs must last
> Endless, and no solution will be found:
> Warr wearied hath perform'd what Warr can do,
> And to disorder'd rage let loose the reines,
> With Mountains as with Weapons arm'd, which makes
> Wild work in Heav'n, and dangerous to the maine.
> Two dayes are therefore past, the third is thine;
> For thee I have ordain'd it, and thus farr
> Have suffered, that the Glorie may be thine
> Of ending this great Warr, since none but Thou
> Can end it... (VI. 684–703)

As Mr Empson has said, 'The recent objections to the style of *Paradise Lost* seem to me wrong-headed when Milton is using it to say something real, but they do apply to the Sixth Book'.

First, Milton mistakenly tries to make the argument run smoothly (a thing it could never do) by greasing it with asides. But all they do is emphasize the staginess by which one member of the Trinity speaks to another. 'Two dayes, *as we compute the dayes of Heav'n*': not only is this a flabby footnote, but it is one that is utterly inappropriate as spoken to the Messiah, who hardly needs to be told it. There is the same weakness in 'as likeliest was' (all too likely, might murmur Voltaire), or in 'and thou knowst'. Such phrases in another context might have helped to give the impression that the argument was unfolding in easy stages. But here they are made absurd by the Messiah's omniscience – it is pointless to say 'and thou knowst' to someone who is omniscient. The phrase rings as falsely as the famous interchange from *The Critic*, which also fastens on the characteristic pedantry about the passing of time:

> *Sir Walter* You know, my friend, scarce two revolving suns,
>   And three revolving moons, have closed their course,
>   Since haughty Philip, in despight of peace,
>   With hostile hand hath struck at England's trade,
> *Sir Christopher* – I know it well.
> *Sir Walter* Philip you know is proud Iberia's king!
> *Sir Christopher* He is.
>
>   (Act II, scene ii)

The whole of God's speech is betrayed by this narrative difficulty into a wordiness that is meant to disguise the muddle. 'Equal in their Creation they were form'd': this merely duplicates 'They were formed equal' and 'They were equal in their creation'. A 'perpetual fight' is sure to be 'endless'. The difference between 'perform' and 'do' is merely metrical when we hear that 'Warr wearied hath perform'd what Warr can do'. Similarly in such a context 'arm'd' already means 'with Weapons', so those words are hardly needed.

And there are other weaknesses. There is the inept introduction of the effects of sin – immediately cancelled in an afterthought. There is the bathos of 'and no solution will be found', and the rather empty use of 'let loose the reines', which would in this context have come fully alive with the help of a word or two. And there is the dangerous ambiguity of *suffered*: 'and thus far have sufferd'.

As Bagehot saw, 'by a curiously fatal error, Milton has selected for delineation exactly that part of the Divine nature which is most beyond the reach of the human faculties, and which is also, when we try to describe our fancy of it, the least effective to our minds. He has made God *argue*.'

It is at such moments that something goes wrong with Milton's style.

> But all conventions have their pomp
>   And all styles can come down to noise.

Yet it is very seldom that the style of *Paradise Lost* comes down to noise, and (having made a few concessions) I shall now turn to the positive qualities of the Grand Style. But I must first say something briefly about the question of 'reading things into' a poet.

Plainly there is no theory or dial which will tell whether or not a particular critical insight is true. We cannot expect *proof*; but we have a right to some degree of substantiation – an insight must be plausible. Naturally there are moments when critics may seem to be proclaiming 'the more the merrier' – the more suggestions, or ambiguities, or paradoxes, the better the poem. But one's objections may not be to their creed, but to the particular moments when their creed does not fit the evidence, when it demands that we reject the different kinds of substantiation to which one may appeal: the aptness of the insight itself, both locally and in the poem as a whole; the practice of the poet elsewhere; the practice of his contemporaries; the observations of his critics, especially the earliest ones; and so on. In each case there will be a unique balance of evidence. My own *general* position is very like Mr Empson's [in *Milton's God* (1961)]:

> If one view makes a bit of poetry very good, and another makes it very bad, the author's intention is inherently likely to be the one that makes it good; especially if we know that he writes well sometimes. . . . To try to make a printed page mean something good is only fair. There is a question for a critic at what point this generous and agreeable effort of mind ought to stop, and with an old text (the *Hamlet* of Shakespeare for example) it is no use to impute a meaning which the intended readers or audience could not have had in mind, either consciously or unconsciously.

Yet, naturally enough, I do not agree with all Mr Empson's particular insights; some of them – and each would have to be argued separately – seem to me improbable. He is, I think, in danger of giving a false primacy to the fact that the insight makes the poetry better. There is something risky in a formulation like 'Such a critic will often impute to an author a meaning too nasty-minded for the author to have intended . . .'. After all, some authors are very nasty-minded. The beauty of an insight is certainly one piece of evidence about it – but no single such point can claim an absolute majority over the other kinds of substantiation. Though the following pages owe everything to Empsonian criticism, they try to slow down the process which in Mr Empson is so agonizingly nimble. They try to offer, wherever possible, some kind of substantiation. That is why I have made so much use of Milton's earliest commentators. And if I too am sometimes anxious about the 'more the merrier' critics (and about my own leaning), the school seems to me preferable to the one whose dusty answer seems to be 'the *less* the merrier', and which takes a lugubrious relish in trying to scotch any close criticism which might suggest that a poet's use of words is subtle, delicate, ingenious, or new. [. . .]

One of Dr Johnson's most famous criticisms of Milton was prophetic of much of the twentieth-century dissatisfaction:

> The truth is, that both in prose and verse, he had formed his style by a perverse and pedantick principle. He was desirous to use English

words with a foreign idiom. This in all his prose is discovered and condemned, for there judgement operates freely, neither softened by the beauty nor awed by the dignity of his thoughts; but such is the power of his poetry that his call is obeyed without resistance, the reader feels himself in captivity to a higher and a nobler mind, and criticism sinks in admiration. . . . Of him, at last, may be said what Jonson says of Spenser, that 'he wrote no language', but has formed what Butler calls 'a Babylonish Dialect', in itself harsh and barbarous, but made by exalted genius and extensive learning the vehicle of so much instruction and so much pleasure that, like other lovers, we find grace in its deformity.

This is not quite to say, with the sturdy frankness of Dr Leavis, 'we dislike his verse'. But it is clear that, for Johnson, Milton's verse was good in spite of his deviation from normal English, not because of it. The reader willingly puts up with the deformity, but there is no doubt about its being a deformity.

Plainly there are times when Milton deviates from the usual word-order for the bad reason that he is in the habit of it. And there are times when he does so for the inadequate and well-known reason that the result sounds more magniloquent, or – in Addison's phrase – 'to give his Verse the greater Sound, and throw it out of Prose'. Yet it is interesting that Addison went on to say, 'I must confess, that I think his Stile, tho' admirable in general, is in some Places too much stiffened and obscured by the frequent Use of those Methods, which *Aristotle* has prescribed for the raising of it'. But this, as he saw, does not apply to the usual run of the verse, in which the syntax is meaningfully controlled with great success.

Its first success is obvious enough: his natural port was gigantic loftiness. Milton achieves this loftiness as much by word-order as by the sonority, dignity or weight of the words themselves. Mr Eliot has put the positive side excellently:

It is only in the period that the wave-length of Milton's verse is to be found: it is his ability to give a perfect and unique pattern to every paragraph, such that the full beauty of the line is found in its context, and his ability to work in larger musical units than any other poet – that is to me the most conclusive evidence of Milton's supreme mastery. The peculiar feeling, almost a physical sensation of a breathless leap, communicated by Milton's long periods, and by his alone, is impossible to procure from rhymed verse.

The power and sublimity of a 'breathless leap' are there in the opening lines of the poem:

Of Mans First Disobedience, and the Fruit
Of that Forbidden Tree, whose mortal tast
Brought Death into the World, and all our woe,

With loss of Eden, till one greater Man
Restore us, and regain the blissful Seat,
Sing Heav'nly Muse . . .

Matthew Arnold acutely commented: 'So chary of a sentence is he, so resolute not to let it escape him till he has crowded into it all he can, that it is not till the thirty-ninth word in the sentence that he will give us the key to it, the word of action, the verb.'

But such withholding of the verb 'sing' (*Of Mans First Disobedience . . . Sing*) might be no more than perverse. Its justification is in the heroic way that it states the magnitude of the poem's subject and so the magnitude of its task

(*Disobedience . . . Death . . . woe . . . loss of Eden . . . one greater Man*),

while still insisting that this vastness is within the poet's compass. The word-order quite literally encompasses the huge themes. 'Where couldst thou words of such a compass find?' asked Marvell, wondering at Milton's achievement of his *vast Design*: 'a Work so infinite he spann'd'.

A poet is always insisting, as if by magic, that his control of words is a control of experience; and here we are given a 'breathless' sense of Milton's *adventrous Song* with at the same time a reassuring sense of how firmly it is within his control. The curve of the sentence is not discursive – however wide the gyre, this falcon hears its falconer.

The verb is, as Arnold saw, the 'key' to the sentence – in the sense that it embodies Milton's power to open the subjects of his poem. Yet we would not be very interested in, or impressed by, a key unless we had first been given some idea of what riches we will be shown.

'So *resolute* not to let it escape him . . .' said Arnold, and the word may be used as a transition to a fine comment by Mr Empson. He quotes Valdes's lines to Faustus, lines which deliberately hold back until the end the ominous condition *If learned Faustus will be resolute*:

> Faustus,
> These books, thy wit, and our experience,
> Shall make all nations to canonise us.
> As Indian moors obey their Spanish lords
> So shall the spirits of every element
> Be always serviceable to us three;
> Like lions shall they guard us when we please,
> Like Almain rutters, with their horsemen's staves,
> Or Lapland giants, trotting by our sides,
> Sometimes like women, or unwedded maids
> Shadowing more beauty in their airy brows
> Than have the white breasts of the queen of love:
> From Venice shall they drag huge argosies,
> And from America the golden fleece

That yearly stuffs old Philip's treasury;
If learned Faustus will be resolute.

'That a conditional clause should have been held back through all these successive lightnings of poetry, that after their achievement it should still be present with the same conviction and *resolution*, is itself a statement of heroic character.' That is nobly said, and such heroism is one of Milton's glories too. He is even able to sustain such effects over vaster distances. Though his single lines may not be mightier than Marlowe's, his sentences often are.

Take Belial's reply to Moloch during the council in Hell. Moloch has asked rhetorically 'what can be worse than to dwell here,' and Belial seizes the phrase and holds it aloft:

What can we suffer worse? is this then worst,
Thus sitting, thus consulting, thus in Arms?

And at once he launches his argument, wheeling through six lines with a hawk's-eye view of their past torments, and plunging home with *that sure was worse*. But that telling reminder offers no pause, and Belial circles again, this time above their future torments. He drives relentlessly through 'what if . . . or . . . what if . . .' and then sweeps to his annihilating climax, foreseen and deliberately held back:

What if the breath that kindl'd those grim fires
Awak'd should blow them into sevenfold rage
And plunge us in the Flames? or from above
Should intermitted vengeance Arme again
His red right hand to plague us? what if all
Her stores were op'n'd, and this Firmament
Of Hell should spout her Cataracts of Fire,
Impendent horrors, threatning hideous fall
One day upon our heads; while we perhaps
Designing or exhorting glorious Warr,
Caught in a fierie Tempest shall be hurl'd
Each on his rock transfixt, the sport and prey
Of racking whirlwinds, or for ever sunk
Under yon boyling Ocean, wrapt in Chains;
There to converse with everlasting groans,
Unrespited, unpitied, unrepreevd,
Ages of hopeless end; this would be worse.   (II. 170–86)

When a sentence surges forward like that, the end of it seems less a destination than a destiny.

It is this ability to harness the thrust of his syntax which sustains Milton's great argument – even the smallest passages have a dynamic force of the astonishing kind which one finds almost everywhere in Dickens. And lines which one has long admired for their brilliant succinctness, lines like 'Better to reign in Hell, then serve in Heav'n' which from one point of view have the free-standing strength of proverbs – even such lines take on greater force when they come as the clinching of a surge of feeling:

> What matter where, if I be still the same,
> And what I should be, all but less then hee
> Whom Thunder hath made greater? Here at least
> We shall be free; th' Almighty hath not built
> Here for his envy, will not drive us hence:
> Here we may reign secure, and in my choyce
> To reign is worth ambition though in Hell:
> Better to reign in Hell, then serve in Heav'n. (I.256–63)

It is easy to see how much the power of the last line is created by its context if we remember Dryden's setting in *The State of Innocence*. In Dryden the line is witty:

> Chang'd as we are, we'er yet from Homage free;
> We have, by Hell, at least, gain'd liberty:
> That's worth our fall; thus low tho' we are driven,
> Better to Rule in Hell, than serve in Heaven. (Act I)

Yet in Milton the line was not the less witty for being heroic. [. . .]

There is always the danger in discussing Milton's Grand Style of assuming that it is merely grand, of conceding too much, of leaning over backwards not to make claims. Professor Kenneth Muir, for instance, is unnecessarily magnanimous on Milton's behalf when he says that 'it is futile to expect the nervous energy, the subtle involutions of style, the tentacular imagery, the linguistic daring and the colloquial ease of Shakespeare's best verse'. This is true, if it means no more than that Shakespeare's best verse is better than anybody else's. But beyond that – no, Milton's style *does* command nervous energy, subtle involutions, tentacular imagery, and linguistic daring – though these often take unShakespearian forms. (Colloquial ease we may dispense with, as an extraordinary critical shibboleth.)

Yet Milton's grandeur and his subtlety often co-exist in the very same lines, which makes it particularly important not to cordon off the poem from meddling practical critics. The following lines would generally be agreed to belong to Milton's sterner style, but their bareness is combined with local subtlety to produce an effect of astonishing breadth and power:

> So glister'd the dire Snake, and into fraud
> Led Eve our credulous Mother, to the Tree
> Of prohibition, root of all our woe. (IX.643–5)

These lines stamp themselves at once as in the Grand Style. What is remarkable, though, is that they are verbally subtle and active without any fussiness or any blurring of the grand austerity. I am thinking not only of the sombre gleam in the pun on *root*; but also of subtler effects: the playing of the bright *glister'd* against the dark *dire*, for instance. Or the superb use of the curt 'snake'. (Milton calls it the serpent fifteen times in Book IX; but the snake only three times: once literally, before Satan enters it; and twice with calculated brutality: 'So talk'd the spirited sly Snake', and here.)

There is the superbly suggestive diction: 'our credulous Mother', which must be one of the finest, most delicate, and most moving of all the oxymorons in the poem. A mother ought to be everything that is reliable and wise – here she is credulous. And *our* clinches the effect; *credulous* is pinioned on each side ('our . . . Mother'), and the full tragic pathos of the oxymoron is released. Sylvester's Du Bartas has two unusually good lines using 'credulous', but in the end how much smaller they are:

> poor Woman, wavering, weak, unwise,
> Light, credulous, news-lover, giv'n to lies.

There is the majesty of 'the Tree of prohibition' – no mere stilted Latinism, since it is literally true: the Tree is not just 'the prohibited Tree', but the Tree of *all* prohibition. And there is at this fatal moment the ringing echo of the opening lines of the poem in 'all our woe'. But perhaps the most irresistible of all the effects here is syntactical. 'Into fraud led Eve . . .' overlaps magnificently with '. . . led Eve to the Tree', so that what begins as a moving and ancient moral metaphor (lead us not into temptation) crystallizes with terrifying literalness. There is a touching change of focus, superbly compressed and yet without a shock or a jerk.

But the astonishing thing is not that these excellent explicable subtleties are there, but that they do not at all disturb the lines' serene, almost Dantesque, austerity. Milton, as so often, combines what are apparently incompatible greatnesses. Hazlitt remarked that 'the fervour of his imagination melts down and renders malleable, as in a furnace, the most contradictory materials'.

Clearly even those passages which are most in the Grand Style may also contain riches of a different kind. Macaulay was right to insist on how many and varied are the excellences of Milton's style, 'that style, which no rival has been able to equal, and no parodist to degrade, which displays in their highest perfection the idiomatic powers of the English tongue, and to which every ancient and every modern language has contributed something of grace, of energy, or of music'.

24 D.W. JEFFERSON

Milton's Austerity and Moral Disdain

The following paragraph from the survey of the false gods in Book I of
Paradise Lost is a splendid example of a special kind of virtuosity that
distinguishes Milton:

> For those the Race of *Israel* oft forsook
> Their living strength, and unfrequented left
> His righteous Altar, bowing lowly down
> To bestial Gods; for which their heads as low
> Bow'd down in Battel, sunk before the Spear
> Of despicable foes. With these in troop
> Came *Astoreth*, whom the *Phoenicians* call'd
> *Astarte*, Queen of Heav'n, with crescent Horns;
> To whose bright image nightly by the Moon
> *Sidonian* Virgins paid their Vows and Songs,
> In *Sion* also not unsung, where stood
> Her Temple on th'offensive Mountain, built
> By that uxorious King, whose heart though large,
> Beguil'd by fair Idolatresses, fell
> To Idols foul. *Thammuz* came next behind,
> Whose annual wound in *Lebanon* allur'd
> The *Syrian* Damsels to lament his fate
> In amorous dittyes all a Summers day,
> While smooth *Adonis* from his native Rock
> Ran purple to the Sea, suppos'd with blood
> Of *Thammuz* yearly wounded: the Love-tale
> Infected *Sion's* daughters with like heat,
> Whose wanton passions in the sacred Porch
> *Ezekiel* saw, when by the Vision led
> His eye survay'd the dark Idolatries
> Of alienated Judah. (I. 432-57)

The sombre and condemnatory parts of the passage are so satisfying
rhetorically and sensuously, that it is as if righteousness and purity of
life were demonstrating their superiority by the beauty of the words

From *The Morality of Art: Essays Presented to G. Wilson Knight by his Colleagues and
Friends*, ed. D.W. Jefferson (Routledge and Kegan Paul, 1969), pp. 156–64. Slightly
revised for the present volume by the author. Footnotes have been deleted.

alone. All Milton's humanistic equipment is present in this statement of what we should otherwise refer to, in commonplace terms, as 'Old Testament severity' or 'puritanical rigour'. The poetry compels us to seek different terms, if we are to do justice to our pleasure in the extraordinary refinement that he gives to these attitudes. For example, in the lines about the 'uxorious King', the verbal effect of the stages of descent from 'heart though large' through 'fair Idolatresses' down to 'Idols foul', aided by piquant alliterations and vowel sequences, is most felicitous; and the closing cadence of the passage conveys impressively the fine denunciatory gaze of the prophet. If austerity delights us here more than sexuality this does not mean that the poet has no awareness of the wanton appeal of the pagan rites. There is no lack of sexual suggestion in the lines about the wound and the blood. The story excites real lust in 'Sion's daughters' and, superbly distant though the poet's moral position is from all this infamy, the words convey the atmosphere of voluptuousness. 'In amorous dittyes all a Summers day', the one lightweight line in the whole passage, has the effect of bringing into contempt, through its very thinness as poetry (though it would pass muster elsewhere) and through its presence in such a context, a convention of erotic lyricism in which such slightness is the norm. Milton in this passage establishes an ascendency, moral and poetic, of the most august order; and a reader not of his party can submit to it wholly. The ascendancy is personal. Though not one of the personal passages of *Paradise Lost*, it has a tone in keeping with them.

A somewhat hostile view of Milton as a man has been widely accepted in our century. T.S. Eliot said that he is 'antipathetic', that 'judged by the ordinary standards of likeableness in human beings, Milton is unsatisfactory'. A full discussion of such statements would involve a good deal of weighing up of what we know about his life, and it may be questioned whether the evidence assembled, for example, in the *Early Lives of Milton* edited by Helen Darbishire, warrants anything like so much animus. Some of it points to a much more sympathetic view. But we are concerned here with the Milton whose attitudes and emotions reach us through the poetry, and with the aspect of himself that he so feelingly presents here. And when we try to describe the great personal passages of *Paradise Lost* we realize that they cannot be discussed in terms of personal qualities such as would be made manifest in relationships with the man himself. The voice in these passages is not that of a man speaking to men about himself. The epic medium – and this is sacred epic – permits him to project a lofty fiction, to represent himself in relation to a uniquely exalted function rhetorically conceived. This places him beyond the accusation of ordinary spiritual pride or egoism. Any attack would have to be against the fiction itself and its treatment, and the uniquely elevated quality of the poetry forestalls this. Milton is equal to the representation of himself in this sublime role. But, paradoxically, his achievement has immense *personal* appeal; with the authority of his art Milton imposes himself supremely.

His manner of introducing himself into the epic situation has an audacity which succeeds by not being noticed as such. It was surely an extraordinary audacity to halt the action of the poem at heaven's threshold (Book III) to dwell at length on himself, his blindness and his sublime confidence in the divine inspirer of his colossal undertaking. To use the theme of Light to bring this about was resourceful: he did not live in an age of poetic ingenuity for nothing. The transition from the poet in his august function as epic narrator ('Thee I revisit now with bolder wing...') to the poet as a man, addressing light from the standpoint of his loss ('but thou Revisit'st not these eyes...') is masterly. When Milton dwells upon his personal situation in the passage that comes after, it is in language of the greatest poignancy. The perfection of the note of religious and poetic vocation already established gives a special beauty and pathos to the lines where the thoughts relate to self, albeit a self in harmony with the vocation:

> ... nor sometimes forget
> Those other two equal'd with me in Fate,
> So were I equal'd with them in renown,
> Blind *Thamyris* and blind Maeonides ...

and

> ... Thus with the year
> Seasons return, but not to me returns
> Day, or the sweet approach of Ev'n or Morn.

Perfect as the tone is we are still left with the fact that Milton has been able to divert his epic for so long a space into a personal channel, an exquisite indulgence.

This personal poetry belongs to his greatest period. The moral and spiritual idealism of his earlier years does not find expression in anything so satisfying. The work especially devoted to the theme of chastity, the Ludlow *Mask*, lacks an appropriate moral focus, in spite of the fine eloquence of its key speeches. To quote the Lady's own words, Comus uses 'lickerish baits fit to ensnare a brute'. The tempter, with his 'rabble' and the 'oughly-headed monsters', and the form of the temptation (the cup), have nothing that could possibly appeal to her. Spenser's exponent of chastity, Britomart, confronts situations involving love and passion. It is in the previous book of the *Faerie Queene* that the hero, Guyon, represents the plodding virtue of mere abstinence; and this would seem to be the theme of Milton's little drama, though A.S.P. Woodhouse, by very careful scanning of parts of the text not obviously relevant to the central debate, found much more. There have been many conflicting interpretations of the *Mask* in recent years, some so elaborately abstract as to deflect attention almost entirely from what, to an uninstructed reader, looks like a very straight scene of attempted seduction. It has been argued, reasonably, that the work was intended primarily as an entertainment, an occasion for spectacle, with

actors not only young but also the offspring of the noble house that
commissioned it, and that moral tension should not be too much
stressed. Virtue undismayed and nobly eloquent, scorning vice with its
fine speeches: this, in all its simplicity, one might claim, is as much as we
should look for. Certainly we need something to mitigate the effect of
the Lady's robust invulnerability:

> Foole do not boast
> Thou canst not touch the freedom of my minde . . .

If these approaches do not come to our aid we are liable to find Milton
tactless in exposing the Lady to such crude allurements.

C.L. Barber, in an essay on the *Mask*, describes chastity in beautiful
terms: 'For preserving chastity involves keeping a relation with what is
not present: the chaste person is internally related to what is to be
loved, even in its absence'. But in spite of his reference to the Epilogue
('The end of Chastity is love fulfilled, "Two blissful twins . . . Youth and
Joy" ') the implication that Milton's *Mask* is about any such thing seems
to be contrary to its tone and atmosphere. It announces only a simple
moral disdain of sensuality (seen in brutish and degrading terms) and a
chastity characterized by little more than conscious dignity and pride in
its power to resist. And this attitude, with all its limitations as an
attitude, does not come to us, through the poetry of the *Mask*, with
sufficient human impact. If we cannot quite believe in the Lady's
predicament, it does not help very much if we treat the affirmation as
relating to Milton himself.

A much more personal note is present in a moving passage of *Lycidas*
('Alas! What boots it with incessant care . . .'), where thoughts of an
early death and of the strain and deprivation in a life of chastity and
disciplined effort produce a crisis of emotion. 'To sport with Amaryllis
in the shade' is not nothing; and the 'blind Fury with th'abhorred
shears' conveys a real terror. The word of reassurance comes to
'trembling ears'.

One of the advantages of Milton's mature style, and, in particular, of
the exalted role that he succeeds in filling as the poet of *Paradise Lost*, is
(as we have already noted) that ordinary human qualities which in
themselves might be jarring become transformed into something of
rare purity and power, so that ordinary moral criticism does not touch
them. The language of the *Mask* contains elements, here and there,
uncomfortably suggestive of a haughty, rather unlovely antipathy to
sexual pleasures. The dreadful word 'priggish' could almost be used for
these touches of harshness in the feeling. But the moral elevation of the
personal passages of *Paradise Lost* is something to which we might
respond as we would to Michelangelo's face of the prophet Daniel in
the Sistine Chapel.

As for the fine disdain in the passage quoted on the first page the
question of what place moral disdain has or should have in our outlook
need not arise, or not directly. The Milton of *Paradise Lost*, whatever

conjectures we may hazard about the man, is a figure who impresses us and moves us by qualities that seem not those of common clay. In this age not to seem to be of common clay may be no recommendation; but to the reader who can respond to Milton there is a special joy in the encounter with a mind and spirit so superior. (One regrets that the word 'superior' has now become impossible.) The superiority may express itself in great tenderness and refinement of sensibility – for example, in the treatment of Eden and of Eve – or it can make itself felt in an incredible strength, buoyancy and control in passages like the following:

> . . . through many a dark and drearie Vaile
> They pass'd, and many a Region dolorous,
> O'er many a Frozen, many a Fierie Alpe,
> Rocks, Caves, Lakes, Fens, Bogs, Dens and shades of death,
> A Universe of death, which God by curse
> Created evil, for evil only good,
> Where all life dies, death lives, and nature breeds,
> Perverse, all monstrous, all prodigious things,
> Abominable, inutterable, and worse
> Then Fables yet have feign'd, or fear conceiv'd,
> Gorgons and Hydras, and Chimeras dire. (II. 618-28.)

To produce the avalanche of the great monosyllabic line, and not make it the ending of the paragraph, was in itself an heroic gesture. Milton keeps up the pressure for seven more lines; and the two lines that follow the avalanche are, in their totally contrasting way, just as shattering. This kind of poetic impact is the expression of an unusually un-trammelled energy. We need not enter here into the question of the nature of Milton's Hell, of the relation between his epic fictions and whatever metaphysical coherence the description did or did not call for. The important thing about the effect is its magnitude, the sheer art with which so much force is brought to bear. Some modern critics have referred to Milton's heroic energy as a quality less valuable than other qualities in poets. But it may be noted that energy of this order does not often manifest itself in poetry.

We may refer to it as moral energy. The theme of the tremendous passage is the fact of a world under God's curse, its denizens swept across unimaginable spaces of desolation; the poetry is a statement of wrath and judgment. But it is not more moral than personal. Milton's ability to discharge this kind of epic function with the maximum effect maintains the immensity of his subject and also of his work, establishing him ever more irresistibly in his role and reducing his reader to willing subjection.

The opening of Book VII has something in common with the opening of Book III, but with significant differences. It has, in the last line, what appears to link it with our main theme: that is, a note of repudiation, in the dismissal of the pagan muse as an 'empty dream'. As in Book III an epic invocation at an important turning point in the action provides the poet with an opportunity for personal self-expression. He begins with the address to Urania, 'by that name if rightly thou art call'd'. It is 'the meaning not the Name' that he calls; and here, as in the earlier passage, we are in an atmosphere especially Miltonic: one of clear, serene religious faith that turns for inspiration to the divine source. Urania is not one of the nine muses; she is to be contrasted later with the fiction that he dismisses; but nevertheless, under cover of these opening words or in spite of them, we have been persuaded to accept a fiction. At least Urania is a 'she', and if Orpheus' feminine guardian failed him in his hour of terror this poet can turn to another feminine being for succour. In the personal part of the passage the tone at first has an elevated calm; but then, with the extraordinary account of the fate of Orpheus, he creates an image of vulnerability which, applied to himself, gives the poetry a daring and wonderful pathos:

> Standing on Earth, not rapt above the Pole,
> More safe I Sing with mortal voice, unchang'd
> To hoarce or mute, though fall'n on evil dayes,
> On evil dayes though fall'n, and evil Tongues;
> In darkness, and with dangers compast round,
> And solitude; yet not alone, while thou
> Visit'st my slumbers Nightly, or when Morn
> Purples the East: still govern thou my Song,
> *Urania*, and fit audience find, though few.
> But drive farr off the barbarous dissonance
> Of *Bacchus* and his Revellers, the Race
> Of that wilde Rout that tore the *Thracian* Bard
> In *Rhodope*, where Woods and Rocks had Eares
> To rapture, till the savage clamor dround
> Both Harp and Voice; nor could the Muse defend
> Her Son. So fail not thou, who thee implores:
> For thou art Heav'nlie, shee an empty dreame.

To come so near to the thought of horrible danger to himself might have looked like a falling off had the note of dependence not been given special appeal through the feminine character of the succourer. There is the suggestion of a need for the maternal, an indulgence of weakness. A simple invocation of the Deity would hardly have accommodated this effect. The repudiation of the 'empty dream', within the same line and a half that contains this moving appeal, completes the subterfuge. It is difficult to say briefly why this is such a master stroke. It has the partial air of restoring austerity, of cutting pathos short by the scornful dismissal of heathen delusions; but he has committed himself so deeply in the Orpheus passage that the dismissal means less than its decisive note suggests. He says that the pagan muse could not help Orpheus, that she is an empty dream; but Orpheus belongs himself to the world over which the muse presides. What has been repudiated if Milton's imagination still enjoys its freedom with the things of the classical world? The very expression 'heavenly muse' looks like a concession to this graceful tradition.

Paradise Regained contains a passage in which this repudiation of the classical world actually takes place. In this work we have a situation with limitations similar to those of the *Mask*. The tempter is as ineffective, and we are left again with the impression of calm, unshakeable virtue scorning all encroachments. But something near to a poignancy may be found in the passage in question if we see it in a certain light.

> Where on the *Aegean* shore a City stands
> Built nobly, pure the air, and light the soil,
> *Athens* the eye of Greece, Mother of Arts . . . (IV.ii.238 ff.)

Readers have remarked that Satan is liable to have the best speeches, as if this pointed to a failure on the part of the poet to control his intentions. But Milton was brought up in a period when rhetoric was valued for its own sake, and it was an educational exercise to argue effectively on a question not always of one's own choosing. This convention provides cover for the eloquence of Satan, which we need not see as evidence for a displacement of the poet's sympathies. But if we take the debate as going on within the life of Milton: if the first speaker represents the side of him that greatly loved Greek literature and could refract its beauties so exquisitely in his own poetry, and the second speaker the side of him that craved, for his declining years, a strict, unequivocal attachment to the divine message and to *'Sion's* songs, to all true tastes excelling', this section of the poem becomes moving and of great personal interest. The fact that the repudiation of Greece is harsh and uncompromising, which some readers have found so offensive, may be regarded simply as part of the price to be paid for a decisive farewell; and it helps if we can feel that the other side, after all, has been heard. If the passage as a whole were viewed in this way one could say that here two worlds are presented with a spacious fulness, two rival cultures spanned, that Milton gives epic breadth to his statement – the theme has large implications for civilization – and speaks with an authority that ranges over the whole field of reference. But as the speakers are in fact Satan and Jesus, and the context is strictly that of the Temptation, this would imply that what we are admiring is again a poetic subterfuge. But this use of the word 'subterfuge' does not mean that the poet deliberately did one thing while pretending to do something else, but rather that it is in the nature of creative genius to be infinitely resourceful, achieving fulfilment in many ways that were not necessarily part of the plan. Milton's devotion to his plan and the solemnity of his sense of vocation give a special felicity to those places where his poetry transcends the prescribed limits of the theme.

317

25 ARNOLD KETTLE

The Precursors of Defoe: Puritanism and the Rise of the Novel

The connections between the development of Puritanism in seven-teenth-century Britain and the rise of the novel are complex but interesting and seem to throw a certain amount of light on both phenomena and also the tricky but central question of the growth of 'realism'. [. . .]

The thesis of this short paper is that the development of Puritanism in the seventeenth century at first prevented but ultimately made possible the growth of the realistic novel. It is not easy for us at this distance to grasp the liberating power of Puritanism. We tend to think of the Puritan spirit in terms of restrictions: sexual prudishness, the Lord's Day Observance Society, Blake's chapel with 'Thou shalt not' writ over the door. Yet, for all its unsympathetic quality to the twentieth-century mind, Calvinistic Puritanism was able to fire the minds of aspiring people of the seventeenth century with a generous enthusiasm. This was primarily because Puritanism was a democra-tizing force which preached a conception of value and moral order entirely different from that of feudal society and the medieval church. As Professor Haller puts it in his fine book *The Rise of Puritanism*:

> Calvinism helped this movement [the democratization of English society and culture] by setting up a new criterion of aristocracy [the 'elect'] in opposition to the class distinctions of the existing system . . . It became difficult not to think that election and salvation by the grace of God were available to everyone who really desired them. Moreover, once the Calvinist preachers admitted that the only true aristocracy was spiritual and beyond human criteria, they had gone a long way toward asserting that all men in society must be treated alike because only God knows who is superior.

Calvinism, in fact, by its vivid insistence that all men were damned, had the paradoxical effect of insisting that all men were equally capable of being saved.

The seventeenth-century Puritans, everyone knows, were

From *On the Novel: A Present for Walter Allen on his sixtieth birthday*, ed. B.S. Benedikz (Dent, 1971), pp. 201–216. Footnotes have been deleted.

suspicious of fiction because it is not true. Yet two forms at least of Puritan literature undoubtedly contributed to the development of the novel: one was the allegory, of which more later; the other the spiritual autobiography. One might, indeed, go further and draw a general parallel between the development of a Puritan prose style and the growth of the sort of 'realism' which was to emerge in the style of the novelists. Just as one finds in seventeenth-century fiction and sub-fiction a distinction between the style of the courtly romance and that of plebeian realism, so is there also a distinction between the two main types of religious writing of the period. Whereas the prose of the defenders of the Anglican Church (the sermons of Donne, Andrewes and their successors) was of a style which contemporaries described as 'witty', rich in complex verbal play, learned allusion and rhetorical devices suitable to a highly educated audience, the style of the Puritan preachers had quite a different basis.

> The Puritans demanded plain sermons, addressed to the under-standing not of scholars but of ordinary men. The object of the Puritan preachers was not to impress, not to delight, but to convince . . . Both pulpit orators and political pamphleteers had to cultivate the virtues of clarity and directness, straight-forwardness and simplicity.

This type of preaching came to be described as 'spiritual' as opposed to 'witty', and it is interesting to notice how this demand for plainness links with the growing pressure of the contemporary scientists who, for their own purposes, were encouraging a more down-to-earth manner of writing. It is important to recognize that the growth of realism in almost all aspects of seventeenth-century writing was to a great extent a class matter. The demand for realism tallied with the underlying demand of the up-and-coming burghers and capitalist farmers for a sweeping away of the mystifications which they associated with attempts to perpetuate the feudal order.

The spiritual autobiographies were an important part of the literature of Puritanism and enjoyed a considerable vogue in the early seventeenth century. Many of the leading Puritan preachers wrote journals in which were expressed the private thoughts and experiences of the man seeking salvation and hoping to help others along the same road. Some were by members of the sects (Baptists, Quakers, Ranters) and it is not hard to see their links with Bunyan, for the interest of such books is not so much psychological (in the modern sense) as illus-trative: they view the individual life as a kind of parable. Others were by more conservative figures (Presbyterians and Anglicans). The interesting thing is to see how the connection between the practical and the spiritual, the realistic and the allegorical, enters into the very prose of these writers. Oliver Heywood (1630-1702) in his *Autobiography* can write that one purpose of his book is to inferre a good caution from the by-past for the remaining part of my life, that where I have seen danger of a shipwreck I may observe such rocks and quicksands and charge my owne hart with more jealousy and watchfulness, and make a covenant with my senses, members, facultys, and know satans devices, and where my strength and weakness lyes: and what a helpful improvement may former experiences prove to future closewalking.

Within such a passage the significance of a metaphor like a voyage or journey becomes very clear. For the writer there is very little distinction between the allegorical and the real.

Professor G.A. Starr has shown how the spiritual biographies tended to become more secular so that by 1708 we have *An Account of Some Remarkable Passages in the Life of a Private Gentleman; with Reflections thereon. In Three Parts, Relating to Trouble of Mind, some violent Temptations, and a Recovery; in order to awaken the Presumptuous, and encourage the Despondent*, a work which has sometimes been attributed to Defoe himself. The *Private Gentleman* clearly marks a significant stage in the transition from spiritual autobiography to fiction, and one can see how the shape of such a book – the shape of a man's life – was to determine the typical shape of the eighteenth-century novel. And, again, the contrast between allegory and realism is seen to be less decisive than we often tend to think. In the *Private Gentleman* anecdotes and experiences are given the force of 'illustrations'. Which takes one straight to Fielding and the first sentence of *Joseph Andrews*: 'It is a trite but true observation that examples work more forcibly on the mind than precepts'.

The spiritual autobiographies gave more to the novel than the idea of a man's life as a basic form of literary organization: they are brimful of a sense of life as struggle. This is one of the qualities that distinguish them from the content of the typical romance. The chivalric hero has many adventures and, often enough, battles. He may even be a kind of crusader; but his adventures are essentially straightforward. He fights the enemy a great deal but it is seldom that he has to fight himself. He may well carry his lady's favour, but he doesn't carry a burden. Whereas Puritan literature is full of a sense of struggle and conflict of the most intense kind – both physical and spiritual.

Defoe's novels – to take a somewhat formalistic view of them – link together the realistic, if episodic, tradition of the picaresque stories and the moral tensions of the literature of Puritanism. Robinson Crusoe, like Bunyan's Christian, sets out on a pilgrimage, and, though it is not an allegorical pilgrimage, it is a Puritan one. For Puritanism by the beginning of the eighteenth century has changed, or rather split. The split is indicated by the choice Defoe himself had to make as a lad at a Dissenters' Academy when he had to decide whether to become a minister or a business-man. Had he chosen the first career then he would have been faced, like Bunyan, with another choice – between giving up his faith and going to jail. Bunyan, after the Restoration, stuck to his guns and his people, the artisans and petty bourgeoisie of

Bedfordshire, who, faced with the defeat of the Puritan Left, refused to compromise, were persecuted, jailed and driven underground. A persecuted minority is very likely to express and maintain its faith in allegorical rather than realistic terms, partly for tactical reasons, but also because its *thinking* will be in those terms.

Defoe, on the other hand, when he decided not to become a dissenting minister and took to public life and business enterprise in a big way, chose the opposite path to Bunyan's – the path of that section of the Puritan middle-class who *had* got something out of the seventeenth-century Revolution and were quite prepared to accept the 1688 compromise. These were people who were indeed now in a position of considerable strength and power. Freedom for them was a very *real* thing, associated with what they could now *do* (as opposed to the sects for whom freedom meant, above all, freedom to believe, to maintain, to cling onto the truth, a truth that was always – as far as its actual manifestation was concerned – in the future). The shift within Puritanism from the allegorical to the realist tradition is bound up with the growing material success of the bourgeoisie. Because the well-to-do Puritans were now to a considerable degree in control of their situation, their interest in conscience and morality became much more practical, more bound up with action, less inward and more outward; interest in the here and now as opposed to the future; therefore, in literary terms, more realistic.

There is at least one seventeenth-century book within the Puritan tradition that illustrates this development fascinatingly. I am thinking of Governor William Bradford's *History of Plymouth Plantation (1606-1646)*. Bradford was one of the Pilgrim Fathers who crossed the Atlantic in the *Mayflower* and was chosen Governor of Plymouth, New England, in 1621, and most years from then until his death in 1657. His *History* tells the story of the Pilgrims' departure, for conscience' sake, from England to Holland, and of the years of their settlement in Leyden and their decision not to stay there. Here the description of the close, harassed, conscientious community has very much of the tone of allegory, of the early preachers and of *The Pilgrim's Progress*.

After they had lived in this citie about some 11. or 12. years, (which is the more observable being the whole time of that famose truce between that state and the Spaniards,) and sundrie of them were taken away by death, and many others begane to be well striken in years, the grave mistris Experience haveing taught them many things, those prudent governours with sundrie of the sagest members begane both deeply to apprehend their present dangers, and wisely to foresee the future, and thinke of timly remedy. In the agitation of their thoughts, and much discours of things hear aboute, at length they began to incline to this conclusion, of remoovall to some other place. Not out of any newfanglednes, or other such like giddie humor, by which men are oftentimes transported to their great hurt and danger, but for sundrie weightie reasons ... And first, they saw and found by experience the hardnes of the place and countrie to be such, as few in comparison would come to them, and fewer that would bide it out, and continew with them. For many that came to them, and many more that desired to be with them, could not endure that great labor and hard fare, with other inconveniences which they underwent and were contented with. But though they loved their persons, approved their cause, and honoured their sufferings, yet they left them as it weer weeping, as Orpah did her mother in law Naomie, or as those Romans did Cato in Utica, who desired to be excused and borne with, though they could not all be Catoes. For many, though they desired to injoye the ordinances of God in their puritie, and the libertie of the gospell with them, yet, alass, they admitted of bondage, with danger of conscience, rather than to indure these hardships; yea, some preferred and chose the prisons in England, rather then this libertie in Holland, with these afflictions.

The vocabulary here is typical of the Puritan discourse of the time and is, in an interesting way, both concrete and abstract. 'The grave mistress Experience' is invoked and the advice she offers shows her to be concerned with practical considerations, above all with the fact that life in Leyden is really too difficult to be feasible since it puts off well-disposed people who might otherwise join the community. But the practical problems Bradford is discussing, though piquant enough, are not the core of his concern. The word 'transported', half way through the passage, is used metaphorically rather than literally, the 'dangers' which beset the community are spiritual (above all the danger of a disintegration of purpose). Bradford's people look on their moves as a pilgrimage, but because they are weighed down by their situation and can find little practical to do to improve it, they tend to think all the time in terms of metaphors and analogies. Liberty and bondage, in such a situation, become qualities dependent less on the ability to do this or that than on states of mind. Prison in England seems to some less oppressive than the 'free' conditions of life in Leyden. The sense of oppression and difficulty, in fact, tends to lead to allegorical rather than practical thinking. To maintain a spiritual integrity becomes the overwhelming consideration, and the pilgrimage, though it involves physical movement, is a spiritual pilgrimage, conceived essentially in the terms of allegory. The obvious comparisons, in considering this part of Governor Bradford's *History*, are with Bunyan's allegorical city of Mansoul in *The Holy War*. It is not just a question of language but of a whole mode of experience. The pilgrims need to see themselves in the terms of allegory in order to survive.

If we now turn to an episode in the same book some twenty years later, in 1638, after the same people have settled in New England, the contrast is most illuminating:

Amongst other enormities that fell out amongst them, this year 3.

men were (after due triall) executed for robery and murder which they had committed; their names were these, Arthur Peach, Thomas Jackson, and Richard Stinnings; ther was a 4., Daniel Crose, who was also guilty, but he escaped away, and could not be found. This Arthur Peach was the cheefe of them, and the ring leader of all the rest. He was a lustie and a desperate yonge man, and had been one of the souldiers in the Pequente warr, and had done as good servise as the most ther, and one of the forwardest in any attempte. And being now out of means, and loath to worke, and falling to idle courses and company, he intended to goe to the Dutch plantation; and had alured these 3., being other mens servants and apprentices, to goe with him. But another cause there was allso of his secret going away in this manner; he was not only rune into debte, but he had gott a maid with child, (which was not known till after his death,) a mans servante in the towne, and fear of punishmente made him gett away. The other 3. complotting with him, ranne away from their maisters in the night, and could not be heard of, for they went not the ordinarie way, but shaped such a course as they thought to avoyd the pursute of any. But falling into the way that lyeth betweene the Bay of Massachusetts and the Narrigansets, and being disposed to rest themselves, struck fire, and took tobaco, a litle out of the way, by the way side. At length ther came a Narigansett Indean by, who had been in the Bay a trading, and had both cloth and beads aboute him. (They had mett him the day before, and he was now returning.) Peach called him to drinke tobaco with them, and he came and sate downe with them. Peach told the other he would kill him, and take what he had from him. But they were something afraid; but he said, Hang him, rougue, he had killed many of them. So they let him alone to doe as he would; and when he saw his time, he tooke a rapier and rane him through the body once or twise, and tooke from him 5. fathume of wampam, and 3. coats of cloath, and wente their way, leaving him for dead. But he scrabled away, when they were gone, and made shift to gett home, (but dyed within a few days after,) by which means they were discovered; and by subtilty the Indeans tooke them. For they desiring a canow to sett them over a water, (not thinking their facte had been known,) by the sachems command they were carried to Aquidnett Iland, and ther accused of the murder, and were examend and comitted upon it by the English ther . . . The Govrt in the Bay were aquented with it, but refferrd it hither, because it was done in this jurisdiction; but pressed by all means that justice might be done in it; or els the countrie must rise and see justice done, otherwise it would raise a warr. Yet some of the rude and ignorante sorte murmured that any English should be put to death for the Indeans. So at last they of the iland brought them hither, and being often examened, and the evidence prodused, they all in the end freely confessed in effect all that the Indean accused them of, and that they had done it, in the maner afforesaid; and so, upon the forementioned evidence, were cast by the jurie, and condemned, and executed for the same. And some of the Narigansett Indeans, and of the parties freinds, were presente when it was done, which gave and all the countrie good satisfaçtion. But it was a matter of much sadness to them hear, and was the 2. execution which they had since they came; being both for wilfull murder, as hath bene before related. Thus much of this matter.

The moral concern in this passage is not less than in the earlier one, the Puritan tone no less pervasive. Yet the whole effect is quite different. The morality is of a pre-eminently practical sort. All sorts of very impure but highly relevant considerations enter into the judgments made. A sense of racial superiority has already asserted itself among the colonists. Arthur Peach's attitude to the Indian he kills has a terrifyingly authentic plausibility. So does the murmuring of the rude and ignorant sort who don't like the idea of Englishmen being punished for what they have done to an Indian. The Governor himself is impelled in his thinking by other considerations besides abstract justice. Politics has entered in and the need to cope with the complexities of a colonial situation.

If the first passage reminds us of Bunyan, the second takes us nearly all the way towards Defoe. We are told all we need to know about Arthur Peach and his friends with extraordinary economy, and all the time it is the practical detail, the significant fact, the tone of voice, that makes the point. No abstract morality; simply the way people live and act and talk. Verisimilitude, achieved by factual detail in itself (the precise measurements of the stolen goods) and by the telling, 'unnecessary' detail ('they had mett him the day before, and he was now returning') which in practice adds the very necessary sense of interrelationship, continuity, life. The naming of people and things and places is 'convincing' not because it provides 'evidence' but because it reflects the actual way people do relate and establish their identities and their stories.

This second passage contains, in fact, all the essential elements of the realistic novel. The style is the style of *Moll Flanders*, right down to the final sentence, dismissing an unpleasant episode as adequately coped with, necessarily recorded and best forgotten. All the tormenting, inner strain of the Leyden days is gone, replaced by other tensions, not less exacting, but acted out in the practical pilgrimage of establishing a new society rather than in the recesses of the individual conscience. Bunyan's Christian has become Defoe's Robinson Crusoe, Puritan still, but a reasonably successful administrator of his domain. The mountain in the sunlight has become the coasts and forests of the Atlantic seaboard. Allegory has become realism, not because the new tensions are more real than the old ones, but because Puritans like Bradford and Defoe have become part of that section of humanity which is in control of things. The whole history of realism as a literary style seems to me to be bound up with this business of control and power.

324

26 CHRISTOPHER RICKS

Dryden's Absalom

The usual view of Absalom (in *Absalom and Achitophel*, 1681) is clear: that
Dryden treated him with a kind of lenience, showing him as misled by
Achitophel, and more sinned against than sinning. Obviously Achitophel is the villain, but I suggest that Absalom is culpably vulnerable,
and that a condemnation of him is required not only by the historical
situation but also by the text.

Scott rightly saw that Dryden had a delicate task because of King
Charles's mixed indignation and affection for Monmouth. But in
omitting to mention that Absalom is censured, later commentators
have contributed to the idea that Dryden was disinterestedly good-
natured: A.W. Verrall said bluntly that 'the character of Absalom is not
a satire at all'; and Professor Nichol Smith wrote that 'the line which he
took was to be kind to him and to represent him as Shaftesbury's dupe'.
Dr Ian Jack's detailed account in *Augustan Satire*, to which I shall return,
is misleading in its mention of the 'panegyric' on Monmouth. In his
edition, Mr L.I. Bredvold says that 'Dryden deftly managed the story
so as to shield the character of Absalom as much as possible'. There is a
related misunderstanding in W.J. Courthope, who said that 'Absalom –
or Monmouth – occupied a very subordinate place in Dryden's
thoughts'. All these writers seem to me to have taken insufficient
account of the irony with which Dryden treats Absalom (whom the
reader in 1681 would have expected to be censured), and so to have
accepted as charitable lenience what is instead subtle condemnation.

The political situation helps to ascertain Dryden's view of Absalom,
for that is closely bound to Charles II's view of Monmouth. Monmouth
had been sent into banishment to Holland in 1679, and he had returned
without the King's permission. Charles 'was highly displeased with his
coming and would not see him, but commanded him not to come to the
Court but to be gone beyond sea again'. Monmouth refused, and 'the
King is so angry with him and his disobedience that he has taken from
him some of his places of profit and trust' (*State Papers Domestic*, 2
Dec. 1679). Yet Monmouth did not leave the country. Instead, in 1680,
he set off on a progress through the West Country, where he was
triumphantly welcomed and became a rallying-point for dissension –
and, many thought, for civil war (that they thought rightly, was shown
in 1685). It is this triumphal progress of Monmouth that is the climax of
his career in the poem, and that is his final appearance; everything

From *Essays in Criticism*, XI (1961), pp. 273–289. Footnotes have been deleted.

works towards that scene. Moreover, it is the scene which is most in the panegyric vein. What then was Charles II's attitude to Monmouth's tour of the West? Not only did he disapprove of it, but he also wished his own supporters to disparage it. Secretary Jenkins wrote to the Bishop of Bath and Wells:

> His Majesty has commanded me to assure you and by you as many of your friends as you possibly can that he utterly dislikes the proceedings of the Duke of Monmouth; that he desires his friends not to show him any respect nor to have any commerce with him in this ramble; that the course he is now in, however the law, as it now is, lay not hold of him, is very much against common prudence and the duty he owes to his Majesty. This I have in command to tell you.
>
> (State Papers Domestic, 12 Aug. 1680)

There is the same royal disapproval on 11 September 1680: 'Such gentlemen may rest assured that he very well approves of those who did neither visit, treat or compliment the Duke . . .' In view of Charles's unequivocal condemnation of Monmouth's tour, is it likely that Dryden would have praised it? And if then the panegyric tone at the height of Monmouth's career in the poem is ironical, is it not possible that most of Dryden's presentation of Absalom is ironical?

The King's affection – and perhaps the people's – made it necessary to treat him with at least a show of sympathy. Yet Dryden could make this sympathy obvious simply because he could count on the condemnation of Absalom. The danger of Absalom was too great, and 'the memory of Civil Wars' is always present in the poem:

> The sober part of *Israel*, free from stain,
> Well knew the value of a peacefull raign:
> And, looking backward with a wise afright,
> Saw Seames of wounds, dishonest to the sight;
> In contemplation of whose ugly Scars,
> They Curst the memory of Civil Wars.
>
> (Lines 69–74. I quoted from J. Kinsley's ed., 1958)

The poem would have failed, despite magnanimity, if it had not enforced a convincing indictment of Absalom and of civil war.

That indictment is made in the poem. Dryden's protestations in the note 'To the Reader' – he protests too much – have been taken too literally at their face-value. He wishes to use a rhetorical fair-play, and it is just because the poem is not lenient to Absalom that it is necessary for Dryden to disclaim malice and to make his indictment reluctant and so authentic. The prefatory note adumbrates many themes of the poem, of which the most important is the emphatic reference to the Fall. (*Paradise Lost* is seldom far from Dryden's mind in *Absalom and Achitophel*.) It is only from the safety of a later date, without 'the memory of Civil Wars' and with the knowledge that Monmouth's rebellion will be important but not disastrous, that it is possible to imagine Dryden treating Absalom with a laxity that could not but have been dangerous.

The magnanimity does not *soften* the satire, any more than the lines, which appeared in the second London edition, on Shaftesbury's goodness as a judge *soften* the condemnation of him. On the contrary, they strengthen it by their apparent impartiality. Pope's treatment of Atticus, a more naked example, is not *softer* than that of Sporus: the skill, as Mr Eliot has said, 'depends upon the justice and reserve, the apparent determination not to exaggerate'. But in his account of Absalom, Dryden does not stop at magnanimity; he gives frequent hints at the dangers. I shall attempt a detailed study of two passages: the opening of the poem, and the account of the progress; they are the keys to Dryden's attitude.

In the opening passage, Dryden had to establish a tone which could allow the reader to be fully aware of Monmouth's illegitimacy, the fundamental point of the whole poem, without censuring Charles II. With the help of the Biblical allegory, he treats Charles with a protective irony; the appeal is to a generous and unpedantic decency. Once the tone has served its purpose, Dryden throws it aside after juggling with the term *Godlike* – at first, like Jove; finally, like Milton's God; and so by the end of the poem we confront a David of monumental gravity, echoing Milton: 'His Train their Maker in their Master hear' (938). The poem is written with great care, and that care is nowhere more evident than in the opening passage. How then does Dryden insist on Absalom's condemnation without being 'violent'?

First of all he diminishes Absalom's claims to the throne by putting him among a number of illegitimate children. The strong stress on David's fertility is not merely jovial; it is political, and it relates to Absalom before he enters the scene. Charles 'his vigorous warmth did, variously, impart': *variously* is emphasized by the alliteration and by the commas. Dryden makes the same point again in the repetitions of

> several Mothers bore
> To Godlike *David*, several Sons before.

And with the same stress yet again, Dryden introduces Absalom:

> Of all this Numerous Progeny was none
> So Beautifull, so brave as *Absolon* (8–18).

The compliments will turn out to be damaging. Absalom's beauty? In a few lines we are to be told that the beauty is a political weapon. He is brave? Part of the damage will lie in the association with war; the 'Foreign fields' soon follow, and in originating the rebellion

> *Achitophel* still wants a Chief, and none
> Was found so fit as Warlike *Absolon* (220–1).

327

The next four lines give two possible reasons for Absalom's character, and both diminish his claims; perhaps 'His Father got him with a greater Gust' (the alliteration stresses the ignoble idea):

> Or that his Conscious destiny made way,
> By manly beauty to Imperiall sway (19–22).

The heroic idiom sounds noble, but that, in this heroic satirical poem, is not proof of Dryden's praise; and the key is in 'Conscious', where Dryden takes advantage of an uncomplimentary meaning. Edward Phillips in *The New World of English Words* (1658) gave only the following meaning: 'inwardly guilty, privy to ones self of any fault or errour'. It is an important meaning, because it warns us against accepting the panegyric on Absalom. 'So Beautifull, so brave': 'By manly beauty to Imperiall sway' – within four lines it is clear that his beauty is part of his political equipment. And was he destined for empire? He himself says that he was 'made for Empire' (371), and complains that he has been 'cut off from Empire' (703); but David in his final speech is unhesitating:

> Had God ordain'd his fate for Empire born,
> He woud have given his Soul another turn (963–4).

Dryden continues his presentation of Absalom:

> Early in Foreign fields he won Renown,
> With Kings and States ally'd to *Israel*'s Crown (23–4).

The point of the first line is not merely that Monmouth had gained distinction in two campaigns; but that in his youth he did his duty and fought abroad – *now*, and the contrast is enforced by *early*, the danger is of civil war because of him. Similarly Dryden emphasises the royal rights and legitimacy of Charles by mentioning his allies and pacts: the world recognises him; it is to be one of the severest charges against Achitophel that

> the Triple Bond he broke;
> The Pillars of the publick Safety shook (175–6).

The irony against Monmouth is clear when Dryden goes on to say 'In Peace the thoughts of War he coud remove', in view of the 'thoughts of War' which Monmouth was inciting. The skill and delicacy are such that compliments about Monmouth's past furnish the satire on his present behaviour. There is the same scepticism in 'And seem'd as he were only born for love'; first, *seem'd*; and second, the puns in 'for love' (because David made love; to make love; to be loved). But it is in the four following lines that Dryden's compliments are most subtly disparaging:

Whate'er he did was done with so much ease,
In him alone, 'twas Natural to please.
His motions all accompanied with grace;
And *Paradise* was open'd in his face (25–30).

The compliment is magnificent; why should one think it anything else?
The answer is not merely that Absalom did not deserve an unqualified
panegyric; it lies partly in a satirical method which Dryden in this poem
used with great success. He chose a few key words, and he repeated
them until one aspect, generally bad, of their meaning was emphasized.
'With so much ease': Dryden knew that *ease* is often untrustworthy, as
in 'easy virtue', and his translation of Virgil provides an excellent
commentary: 'With such Deceits he gain'd their easie Hearts' (*Aeneis*,
ii.259). The reader had already been told in the prefatory note, about
Absalom, that 'since the most excellent Natures are always the most
easy; and, as being such, are the soonest perverted by ill Counsels . . .'
The Jews are 'debauch'd with ease' (47) and 'easie to Rebell' (215); and
when Absalom inflames the crowd, he 'with familiar ease repeats their
Names': 'Few Words he said; but easy those and fit' (691–6). Not every
use of such words carries condemnation; Dryden was not immaculately
consistent; but the body of them is clearly associated with the specious
rebellion.

The line 'In him alone, 'twas Natural to please' depends on our
knowing that in the Bible Absalom used his charm politically: by
flattery he 'stole the hearts of the men of Israel' (II *Sam*. xv. 1–6) – later
we see and hear Monmouth doing so. Perhaps the same goes for the
mention of his *grace*; after his insurrectionary speech, 'Youth, Beauty,
Graceful Action, seldom fail . . .' (723); and David's last speech underlines the irony with its comparison of Absalom and Achitophel (971–2):

His old Instructor, e're he lost his Place,
Was never thought indu'd with so much Grace.

Natural lends force to the passage, because it is another word which
Dryden often associates with the undesirable: 'By natural Instinct they
change their Lord' (219). Similarly, if rebellion succeeds,

Government it self at length must fall
To Natures state (793–4);

and Dryden condemns Achitophel's plea to Absalom that 'Self-defence
is Natures Eldest Law' (458). And a final example brings one back to
'Natural to please': Absalom's charm before his political speech is
described as 'form'd by Nature' (692). The mention of Paradise in the
concluding line of the compliment follows Dryden's insistence, in the
prefatory note, on the Fall, and so it too is more than a compliment.
Elsewhere Dryden shows how natural it is to think of the Fall in
mentioning Paradise: 'Whose Face is Paradise, but fenc'd from Sin'.

The Paradise of Absalom's face was not 'fenc'd from Sin'. There is a similar association in 'Had she been first, still Paradise had bin' (*Eleonora*, 172), and 'In Paradise, were curs'd' (*To John Driden*, 22).

Dryden then (in lines 31–4) switches back to David, who is to win the esteem and affection of the reader; he is indulgent, and he grants all that Absalom wishes. Dryden comments with a slyness which is intensified by the bluff parenthesis:

> What faults he had (for who from faults is free?)
> His Father coud not, or he woud not see.

By this method, the indictment of Absalom is also the praise of David; and Dryden passes at once to the 'faults' of Absalom, which are stressed by the worldly blandness of tone:

> Some warm excesses, which the Law forbore,
> Were constru'd Youth that purg'd by boyling o'r (35–8).

The image here is of the greatest importance, since it provides the only extended simile which states Dryden's views (the only other one, describing the lion, is in a speech by Achitophel, 447–54):

> For, as when raging Fevers boyl the Blood,
> The standing Lake soon floats into a Flood;
> And every hostile Humour, which before
> Slept quiet in its Channels, bubbles o'r:
> So, several Factions from this first Ferment,
> Work up to Foam, and threat the Government (136–41).

By means of the image, Absalom is clearly associated with faction; and the image recurs – Dryden ends his prefatory note with it, and he uses it with a variation in lines 809–10 and 923–6.

Then, directly after mentioning the 'warm excesses' of Absalom, Dryden produces his first shock, a condemnation of great seriousness:

> And *Amnon's* Murther, by a specious Name,
> Was call'd a Just Revenge for injur'd Fame (39–40).

Dryden is absolutely blunt; the damaging word 'specious' is out, for the first but not the last time in the poem (the *N.E.D.* gives its modern sense from the beginning of the seventeenth century); and the brave Absalom is a murderer. Yet there is apparently a difficulty. It seems agreed that this refers to the attack made on Sir John Coventry, whose nose was slit; yet he was not murdered, so the editor, G.R. Noyes, comments that 'the parallel is not accurate'. In other words, Dryden, when he might well have either not used the Biblical parallel or have substituted for 'Murther' some synonym of 'attack', has deliberately intensified the charge against Monmouth, indeed intensified it beyond the truth. The couplet shows naked the condemnation which has been underlying the portrait of Absalom, and it ends that portrait. But Dryden allows himself a final irony, by at once following the lines on Amnon's murder as if it had never been mentioned:

> Thus Prais'd, and Lov'd, the Noble Youth remain'd,
> While *David*, undisturb'd, in *Sion* raign'd (41–2).

Thus Prais'd is superb; it was indeed just thus that Absalom was praised and that Dryden was praising him. And Dryden syntactically underlines the political point of all this: Thus Absalom remained 'While *David*, undisturb'd, in *Sion* raign'd'. The praise and love for Absalom depend (*while*) on the former peace, when David (whose legitimacy is again stressed; the last words of the poem are 'their Lawfull Lord') was 'undisturb'd'. There is more than a hint that David's present disturbance is due to Absalom.

After this magnificently skilful opening, Dryden widens his scene; he describes the Jews and Jebusites; and then he presents Achitophel. Achitophel's first great speech of temptation uses many motifs which Dryden later identifies with Absalom; and it is Achitophel who speaks the panegyric on Absalom, not Dryden. Absalom's reply is introduced by an account of his fall (303–15) which is not merely polite lamentation; for example, Praise is so effective 'when Ambition Blinds'. This is direct, because ambition has both a natural and an acquired condemnation; Dryden has already described 'wilde Ambition' (198), and he is to indulge in a masterly stroke when he says in line 479 that Absalom was 'Unblam'd of Life (Ambition set aside)' – Dryden's cruellest thrusts are often casually in brackets, and this, in 1681, carries a tone as who should say 'Of course, leaving out the fact that he is prepared for his own ends to supplant his father the King, and bring back civil war . . .' It is a large setting-aside. Indeed, a pamphlet which anticipates Dryden, *Absalom's Conspiracy; or, The Tragedy of Treason* (1680), begins: 'There is nothing so dangerous either to Societies in General, or to particular Persons, as Ambition'. (This and other pamphlets *condemn* Monmouth by calling him Absalom.) So Dryden again calls him 'th' Ambitious Youth' (309); and almost the last mention of him by name in the poem, in what is a summary of the poem, baldly describes 'Absalom, ambitious of the Crown' (927). Certainly the overriding tone of this section introductory to Absalom's reply is of a useful magnanimity; but in twice stressing ambition, Dryden is an accuser, and so he is when he says that Absalom was 'too full of Angells Metal in his Frame' (310). It is yet another of the Miltonic references; some of the rebels have already been described after being thrown from court – they, 'like Feinds, were harden'd in Impenitence' (145).

Absalom's reply to Achitophel is used to fortify our feeling of David's rightness in claim and behaviour – Absalom admits it. But in his final exclamation, we see that Absalom is nearly won, especially in his insistence that he was 'made for Empire' (371). Achitophel attacks again, at the most Miltonic line of the poem: 'Him Staggering so when Hells dire Agent found . . .' (373). The attack succeeds; and Dryden deliberately plays down Absalom's character at this point. Yet there is force in the parenthetical '(Ambition set Aside)' (479); and that Absalom has not been a blessing for his country is couched as a compliment:

> His Kingly Vertues might have claim'd a Throne,
> And blest all other Countries but his own (483–4).

So Dryden concedes that ''Tis Juster to Lament him, than Accuse' – juster, and also more effective. And he passes at once into a description where the censure is scarcely veiled:

> Strong were his hopes a Rival to remove,
> With blandishments to gain the publick Love;
> To Head the Faction while their Zeal was hot,
> And Popularly prosecute the Plot (486–90).

The threat in the first line; the specious charm in the second (Dryden soon shows us the blandishments); the unmitigated stigma which *Faction, Zeal* and *Plot* – and, indeed, *hot* – carry throughout the poem: all are unequivocal. And Dryden crowns them with *Popularly*, strongly suggesting the demagogue ('studious of, or designed to gain, the favour of the common people', *N.E.D.*). Absalom had asked:

> Why then shoud I, Encouraging the Bad,
> Turn Rebell, and run Popularly mad? (335–6);

and on his next appearance he is an orator 'on each side bowing popularly low' (689).

Dryden does not slacken his vigilance during Absalom's public speech. The slyness of 'Surrounded thus with Freinds of every sort' (682 – that is, Bethel and Oates) becomes naked in the account of the performance:

> Th' admiring Croud are dazled with surprize,
> And on his goodly person feed their eyes:
> His joy conceal'd, he sets himself to show;
> On each side bowing popularly low:
> His looks, his gestures, and his words he frames,
> And with familiar ease repeats their Names.
> Thus, form'd by Nature, furnish'd out with Arts,
> He glides unfelt into their secret hearts:
> Then with a kind compassionating look,
> And sighs, bespeaking pity ere he spoak,
> Few words he said; but easy those and fit:
> More slow than Hybla drops, and far more sweet   (686–97).

It is a measure of the greatness of this poem, and of its superiority to most of Dryden, that in discussing the earlier treatment of Absalom so much has already been singled out from these lines. *Absalom and Achitophel* is brilliantly knit together, and one can study it as if it were by Pope. The focal points of censure here are clear. First, *Croud*: in this poem, Dryden condemns the *Crowd* eight times, and *Crowds* six times; the word rings through the poem, and it is damagingly associated with Absalom again in the next section. Second, the specious beauty once more, in *dazled* and the *show*, and in *goodly*, which Dryden elsewhere often dissociates from *good*. Dryden obviously disliked Shadwell and Burnet, and there is a line on Shadwell which, using *eye*, is near to that on Absalom: Shadwell's 'goodly Fabrick fills the eye'. Again, Shadwell as Og is 'Goodly and Great'; and Burnet the Buzzard (we are told he is 'goodly') bands with his accomplices to make 'a seeming, goodly Flight'. *Popularly* has been mentioned; it is intensified by the literal and figurative use of *low*. Then the orator's deceitful care, and the 'familiar ease' (and 'easy'). 'Form'd by Nature' makes its point; and 'furnish'd out with Arts' carries dispraise not merely in the ironical wording but also in the associations of Arts. For it too rings accusingly through the poem; Achitophel uses 'studied Arts' (228), talks of 'my successfull Arts' (289) and 'my Arts' (402), and stresses Absalom's deceit in saying that the Duke of York 'sees through the thin Disguises of your Arts' (443). The rebels were 'Seduc'd by Impious Arts' (498); and they will be punished 'by their own arts' (1010). In other words, 'furnish'd out with Arts' is not isolated, and so it is not mild. Absalom 'glides unfelt into their secret hearts'; *glides* is not pleasing; Satan glides, and

Into the Heart of Eve his words made way . . .
    . . . his words replete with guile
Into her heart too easie entrance won
                              (Book ix, 159, 550, 733–4).

There is irony in 'kind compassionating'; and in the next line Dryden specifically warns us against the soft view of Absalom, who uses all his arts, 'bespeaking pity'. His *Hybla drops* are merely honied words.

Absalom's public speech could hardly be misunderstood, and it does not need to be demonstrated that Dryden disapproved of it. Dr Jack describes its 'magnificent hypocrisy' (pp. 64, 66); yet in his account of the next section, which describes Monmouth's royal progress, he is misleading in not mentioning that Absalom is censured. Dr Jack says that Dryden

lavishes on Absalom some of the most brilliant lines of panegyric he ever wrote. He emphasizes his 'goodly person' (was he not the King's Son?), and describes his reception by the crowd as 'their young *Messiah*' . . . None of the members of the King's party receives such eloquent praise.

Nor would they have wanted it; since, although the idiom is heroic, the account is ironic.

The 'royal' progress of Absalom is the climax of the poem's account of Monmouth:

> The Croud (that still believe their Kings oppress)
> With lifted hands their young *Messiah* bless (727–8).

The crowd is despicable in this poem, and Dryden carefully warns us against their view of Absalom with yet another significant parenthesis, a reminder of the real political situation and of the crowd's lack of judgment. 'Their young *Messiah*'? An immediate ironical reference is to the *ending* of the heavenly war in Book VI of *Paradise Lost*, and it is stressed by 'With Chariots, Horsemen, and a numerous train' (730). Dryden's use of Milton is flexible, and to call Absalom the Messiah is an irony of the same sort as to make Achitophel describe David, rather than himself, as one who

> Like the Prince of Angels from his height,
> Comes tumbling downward with diminish'd light (273–4).

Moreover, Achitophel had praised Absalom as the future supplanter: 'Thee, *Saviour*, Thee the Nations Vows confess' (240) – it is hardly likely that Dryden should here be in polite agreement with Achitophel.

Dryden's political use of blasphemy is obvious, and in fact it received one of Johnson's strictures. The blasphemy is pervasive in the account of the progress ('Guardian God', 'Consecrates'). The progress of Monmouth was not a light matter; Scott pointed out that 'reflecting and cautious men were slow to join in what seemed to be a preliminary for civil war'; Charles II 'utterly dislikes the proceedings of the Duke of Monmouth'; and indeed Dryden is, as we shall see, blunt in his condemnation (751–2). The 'Chariots, Horsemen, and a numerous train', then, are not meant merely to augment *Messiah*; they point directly to civil war. For in the Bible the beginnings of the rebellion were seen when 'Absalom prepared him chariots and horses, and fifty men to run before him' (II *Sam*. xv.I).

Then

> From East to West his Glories he displaies:
> And, like the Sun, the promis'd land survays.

Here Monmouth is shown rebelliously acting as King, for whom the Sun was the inevitable symbol (Achitophel had, in line 268, described David to Absalom: 'Behold him setting in his Western Skies'). It is amusing that *A True Narrative of the Duke of Monmouth's Late Journey into the West* (1680) ends its defence of Monmouth with a description of the nobles 'glorious in their beams derived from the Sun of great *Britain. God bless and save the King*'. Yet in Dryden's reference to the promised land, one would expect Moses; and he is there. For Achitophel's first speech had set the tone for astronomical flattery, and ought to have made it untrustworthy:

Auspicious Prince! at whose Nativity
Some Royal Planet rul'd the Southern sky:
Thy longing Countries Darling and Desire;
Their cloudy Pillar, and their guardian Fire:
Their second *Moses*, whose extended Wand
Divides the Seas, and shews the promis'd Land . . . (230–5).

'The promis'd land', then, is one of Achitophel's arts; and our suspicion when we meet it again ought to give it some such suggestion as 'promised as spoils'. 'Fame runs before him, as the morning Star' (733) because of Lucifer – to whom Achitophel of all people had referred; the point *morning star/Lucifer* is borrowed from Milton: Satan's

Count'nance, as the Morning Starr that guides
The starrie flock, allur'd them;

then it is expanded by Nahum Tate in the *Second Part* (194–7), and it is interesting that he absorbs the present account of the progress into an inflammatory speech by Achitophel. Since Achitophel quotes and paraphrases this description, Tate can hardly have seen it as originally a panegyric. (Yet it must be admitted that the *Second Part* is not an authoritative commentary on the original poem.)

It is the more surprising that the lines on the progress have been seen as panegyric because Dryden carefully gives them a curt and bathetic worldly ending:

But hospitable treats did most Commend
Wise *Issachar*, his wealthy western friend (737–8).

Moreover, Dryden then straightforwardly explains these processions:

This moving Court, that caught the peoples Eyes,
And seem'd but Pomp, did other ends disguise (739–40).

The contemptuous pun *Court/caught* (not true Royalty, but merely a trap – Absalom 'forsakes the Court', the real one); the reminder of how the crowd were 'dazled' by Absalom; the disguise, and the 'smooth pretence of specious love' in lines 745–6 (Achitophel in line 463 had recommended to Absalom 'a fair Pretence') – all these combine into a whole-hearted condemnation:

Thus, in a Pageant Show, a Plot is made;
And Peace it self is War in Masquerade (751–2).

And yet once it could be said of Absalom, 'In Peace the thoughts of War he coud remove' (25).

The royal progress is Absalom's last appearance in the poem. Yet he is neither forgotten nor naïvely forgiven. He is baldly described as David's 'disobedient Son' (881); and the paternal feeling in David's last speech is meant to turn our sympathy to the King rather than to the supplanter. The lines which Dryden added in the second London edition, beginning 'But oh that yet he woud repent and live . . .') 957–60), hardly 'soften the satire on Monmouth' (Noyes's view); rather, they stress his father's long-suffering charity and patience, and so make the rebellion even less justifiable. David denies that Absalom was made for empire; true, he was gulled, but not in a light affair; and he became 'The Peoples Brave, the Politicians Tool' (967). *Brave*: 'a bravo, bully; a hired assassin' (*N.E.D.*) – it is not a casual charge. And in his last mention of Absalom, before he denounces the other rebels, David emphasises the danger of too much misguided sympathy for Absalom: 'My Rebel ever proves my Peoples Saint' (974). Absalom as the 'Peoples Saint': is it likely that the presentation of him as 'their young *Messiah*' was unironical? David might re-word his complaint: 'My Rebel ever proves the Critics' Saint'.

It is worth noting that Dryden's reference to Absalom in the *Second Part* is a curt and brutal allusion to his death (II *Sam.* xviii. 32):

> But of King *David's* Foes be this the Doom,
> May all be like the Young-man *Absalom* (506–7).

And the poet was accused in *Poetical Reflections on a late Poem, entituled, Absalom and Achitophel* (1681) of just the indictment which I have tried to trace: 'He calumniates the Duke of Monmouth with that height of impudence, that his Sense is far blacker than his Ink, exposing him to all the censures that a Murderer, a Traytor, or what a Subject of most ambitious evil can possibly comprehend'. Perhaps it is time to return to a view which is supported by the text as well as by historical probability, for which Narcissus Luttrell at the time provided a summary: *Absalom and Achitophel* is 'an excellent poem agt ye Duke of Monmouth, Earl of Shaftsbury & that party & in vindication of the King & his friends'.

But why does such a reading now have to be newly insisted on? One reason is perhaps that, in concentrating on the historical allusions, the main issues of the poem have been lost sight of – that the Court party, but not only they, feared civil war, a fear which was to be fully justified; and that the Biblical Absalom is a man to be condemned, as the earlier political applications of the story had made clear. A reader in 1681 would hardly have expected the Poet Laureate to condone rebellion.

A related point suggests some of the critical implications. The poem has been read too much in terms of its 'characters'; there is no 'character' of Absalom, and so despite the title, and despite history, he is less important than, say, Zimri. But the reading which I suggest is one that restores interest and force to great areas of the poem, and it would show that the poem is alert and brilliantly knit. The choice is absolutely clear: Monmouth has just carried out a tour which suggests preparations for civil war (his rebellion was in fact to begin in the West Country), and Dryden says of him, 'In Peace the thoughts of War he coud remove' (25). Dryden is either crassly insensitive, unaware and impolitic – or he is ironical. *Absalom and Achitophel* has always been recognised as a poem which gives us a generous reward if we will master some historical facts; and if we remember *attitudes* as well, the reward is even greater, and we read, not a collection of fragments, but a poem.

Index

Index by Ann Edwards